REVOLUTIONS OF THE WORD

REVOLUTIONS OF THE WORD

INTELLECTUAL CONTEXTS FOR THE STUDY OF MODERN LITERATURE

Edited by

Patricia Waugh
Professor of English Literature,
University of Durham

A member of the Hodder Headline Group
LONDON • NEW YORK • SYDNEY • AUCKLAND

First published in Great Britain in 1997 by
Arnold, a member of the Hodder Headline Group,
338 Euston Road, London NW1 3BH
175 Fifth Avenue, New York, NY 10010

Distributed exclusively in the USA by
St Martin's Press, Inc.
175 Fifth Avenue, New York, NY 10010

© 1997 Selection and editorial matter Patricia Waugh

British Library Cataloguing in Publication Data
A catalogue record for this book is available from the British Library

Library of Congress Cataloging-in-Publication Data
Revolutions of the word: intellectual contexts for the study of
modern literature/edited by Patricia Waugh.
p.   cm.
Includes bibliographical references and index.
1. Literature, Modern—History and criticism—Theory, etc.
I. Waugh, Patricia.
PN701.R48 1996
809'.03-dc20   96-18968

ISBN 0 340 64559 8 (hb)
ISBN 0 340 64560 1 (pb)

Typeset in 10/12 Palatino by J&L Composition Ltd, Filey, North Yorkshire
Printed and bound in Great Britain by J W Arrowsmith Ltd, Bristol

From time to time there occurs some revolution, or sudden mutation of form and content in literature. Then, some way of writing which has been practised for a generation or more, is found by a few people to be out of date, and no longer to respond to contemporary modes of thought, feeling and speech. A new kind of writing appears, to be greeted at first with disdain and derision; we hear that the tradition has been flouted, and that chaos has come. After a time it appears that the new way of writing is not destructive but re-creative. It is not that we have repudiated the past, as the obstinate enemies – and also the stupidest supporters – of any new movement like to believe; but that we have enlarged our conception of the past; and that in the light of what is new we see the past in a new pattern.

(T.S. Eliot, 'American Literature and American Language', 1965)

CONTENTS

ACKNOWLEDGEMENTS

The editor and publishers would like to thank the following for permission to use copyright material in this book:

Theodor Adorno: *Commitment*, by Theodor Adorno, taken from *Aesthetics and Politics*. Reprinted by permission of Verso.

A. Alvarez: Selection from *The New Poetry* (Introduction) by A. Alvarez. Copyright © 1966 by A. Alvarez. Reprinted by permission of Aitken, Stone & Wylie.

Perry Anderson: 'A Culture in Contraflow' by Perry Anderson, from *New Left Review 180*, March/April 1990. Reprinted by permission of *New Left Review*.

Georges Bataille: Selection from *Literature and Evil* by Georges Bataille. Reprinted by permission of the publishers, Marion Boyars, London – New York.

Charles Baudelaire: Selection from *The Exposition Universelle* by Charles Baudelaire, from *Art in Paris 1845–1862* by Charles Baudelaire, translated and edited by Jonathan Mayne. Copyright © by Phaidon Press Ltd. Reprinted by permission of Phaidon Press Ltd.

Simone de Beauvoir: Selection from *The Second Sex* by Simone de Beauvoir, translated by H.M. Parshley. Copyright © 1952 and copyright renewed 1980 by Alfred A. Knopf, Inc. Reprinted by permission of The Estate of Simone de Beauvoir, Jonathan Cape and Alfred A. Knopf, Inc.

Marshall Berman: Selection from *All That is Solid Melts into Air* by Marshall Berman. Reprinted by permission of Verso/New Left Books.

Edward Bond: Selection from *On Violence* (Preface) by Edward Bond. Reprinted by permission of Casarotto Ramsay Ltd.

Robert Conquest: Selection from *New Lines II* (Introduction), by Robert Conquest. Reproduced by permission of Curtis Brown Ltd, London, on behalf of Robert Conquest. © Robert Conquest.

T.S. Eliot: Excerpt from *Tradition and the Individual Talent* in *Selected Essays* by T.S. Eliot, copyright 1950 by Harcourt Brace & Company and renewed 1978 by Esme Valerie Eliot. Reprinted by permission of Harcourt Brace and Company and Faber and Faber Limited.

Paul Feyerabend: Selection from *Against Method* by Paul Feyerabend. Reprinted by permission of Verso/New Left Books.

Michel Foucault: Selection from *The Archaeology of Knowledge* by Michel Foucault, translated by A.M. Sheridan Smith. Reprinted by permission of Tavistock Publications.

Evelyn Fox Keller: Selection from *Reflections on Gender and Science* by Evelyn Fox Keller. Reprinted by permission of Yale University Press.

Francis Fukuyama: Selection from *The End of History and the Last Man* by Francis Fukuyama. Copyright © 1992, by Francis Fukuyama. Reprinted by permission of Penguin Books and The Free Press, a Division of Simon & Schuster Inc.

Paul Fussell: Selection from *The Great War and Modern Memory* by Paul Fussell. Reprinted by permission of Oxford University Press.

Anthony Giddens: Selection from *Modernity and Self-Identity* by Anthony Giddens. Reprinted by permission of Blackwell Publishers.

Erving Goffman: Selection from *The Presentation of Self in Everyday Life* by Erving Goffman. Copyright © 1959, by Erving Goffman. Reprinted by permission of Penguin Books Ltd.

Gerald Graff: Selection from *Literature Against Itself* by Gerald Graff. Reprinted by permission of The University of Chicago Press.

David Hare: Selection from 'The Play is in the Air, On Political Theatre' by David Hare. Reprinted by permission of Faber and Faber Limited.

David Harvey: Selections from *The Condition of Postmodernity* by David Harvey. Reprinted by permission of Blackwell Publishers.

Ihab Hassan: 'Toward a Concept of Postmodernism' by Ihab Hassan, from *Reader in Postmodernism* by Thomas Docherty. Reprinted by permission of Prentice Hall/Harvester Wheatsheaf.

Seamus Heaney: 'Englands of the Mind', from *Preoccupations: Selected Prose 1968–1978* by Seamus Heaney. Reprinted by permission of Faber and Faber Limited.

Martin Heidegger: Selection from *The Question Concerning Technology and Other Essays* by Martin Heidegger. English language translation copyright © 1977 by Harper & Row, Publishers, Inc. Reprinted by permission of HarperCollins Publishers, Inc.

Werner Heisenberg: 'Changes in the Foundations of Exact Science', from *Philosophic Problems of Nuclear Science* by Werner Heisenberg, translated by F.C. Hayes. Copyright © 1952 by Pantheon Books, Inc. Reprinted by permission of Pantheon Books, a division of Random House, Inc., and Faber and Faber Ltd.

Andreas Huyssen: Selection from *After the Great Divide* by Andreas Huyssen. Reprinted by permission of Macmillan Press Ltd.

Luce Irigaray: 'Sexual Difference' by Luce Irigaray, translated by Sean Hand, from *French Feminist Thought*, edited by Toril Moi. Reprinted by permission of Blackwell Publishers.

Charles Jencks: Selection from *The Language of Post-Modern Architecture* by Charles Jencks, 5th edn. Reprinted by permission of Academy Group Ltd.

C.G. Jung: 'Psychology and Literature', from *Modern Man in Search of a Soul* by C.G. Jung. Reprinted by permission of Routledge Publishers.

Julia Kristeva: 'Women's Time', from *New Maladies of the Soul* by Julia Kristeva. Copyright © 1995 by Columbia University Press. Reprinted by permission of Columbia University Press.

Thomas Kuhn: Selection from *The Structure of Scientific Revolutions*, 2nd edn by Thomas Kuhn. Reprinted by permission of the author and University of Chicago Press.

Susanne K. Langer: Selection from *Philosophy in a New Key: A Study in the Symbolism of Reason, Rite, and Art* by Susanne K. Langer, Cambridge, Mass.: Harvard University Press, copyright 1942, 1951, 1967 by the President and Fellows of Harvard College; renewed 1970, 1979 by Suzanne Knauth Langer; 1985 by Leonard C.R. Langer. Reprinted by permission of Harvard University Press.

C.S. Lewis: Selection from *An Experiment in Criticism* by C.S. Lewis. Reprinted by permission of Cambridge University Press, and Curtis Brown Group Ltd.

David Lodge: Selection from *The Novelist at the Crossroads* by David Lodge. Copyright © 1971 by David Lodge. Reprinted by permission of Curtis Brown on behalf of David Lodge and Fontana, an imprint of HarperCollins Publishers Ltd.

Jean-François Lyotard: Selection from *The Differend: Phrases in Dispute* by Jean-François Lyotard, translated by Georges Van Den Abbeele. Copyright © 1988 by the University of Minnesota. Originally published as *Le Différend*. Copyright © 1983 by Les Editions de Minuit. Reprinted by permission of the University of Minnesota Press and Manchester University Press.

Alasdair MacIntyre: Selection from *After Virtue* by Alasdair MacIntyre. Reprinted by permission of Gerald Duckworth and Company Ltd.

G.E. Moore: Selection from *Principia Ethica* by G.E. Moore. Reprinted by permission of Cambridge University Press.

Renato Poggioli: Selection from *The Theory of the Avant-Garde* by Renato Poggioli, translated by Gerald Fitzgerald, Cambridge, Mass.: The Belknap Press of Harvard University Press. Copyright © 1968 by the President and Fellows of Harvard College. Reprinted by permission of Harvard University Press.

Karl Popper: Selection from *Objective Knowledge* by Karl Popper. Reprinted by permission of Oxford University Press.

Ezra Pound: 'A Retrospect', from *Literary Essays of Ezra Pound* by Ezra Pound, edited with an introduction by T.S. Eliot. Reprinted by permission of Faber and Faber Limited.

Alain Robbe-Gillet: Selection from *Snapshots and Toward a New Novel* by Alain Robbe-Grillet, translated by Barbara Wright. Reprinted by permission of Calder Publications Ltd.

Richard Rorty: Selection from *Consequences of Pragmatism* by Richard Rorty. Reprinted by permission of Prentice Hall/Harvester Wheatsheaf, the author, and the University of Minnesota Press.

Edward Said: Selection from *Orientalism* by Edward W. Said. Copyright © 1978 by Edward W. Said. Reprinted by permission of Pantheon Books, a division of Random House, Inc. and Routledge.

George Steiner: Selection from *Language and Silence: Essays 1958–1966* by George Steiner. Copyright © 1967, by George Steiner. Reprinted by permission of Faber and Faber Limited and by Georges Borchardt, Inc. for the author.

Raymond Williams: Selection from 'Commitment' from *Politics of Modernism* by Raymond Williams. Reprinted by permission of Verso/New Left Books.

To the best of our knowledge all copyright holders of material reproduced in this book have been traced. Any rights not acknowledged here will be noted in subsequent printings if notice is given to the publisher.

PART ONE

INTRODUCTION: LOOKING BACK ON THE MODERN TRADITION

This anthology offers a collection of documents and essays which suggest ways of situating twentieth-century British writing in a variety of intellectual and aesthetic contexts. The book is organized in two parts: the first, an editorial overview of relations between modern British writing and the intellectual and aesthetic contexts of its production and reception; the second, a collection of seminal documents by writers, philosophers and scientists which allows readers to explore those relationships for themselves. Part One also examines some of the intellectual and aesthetic precursors of modern writing and considers different ways in which ideas in aesthetics, science, philosophy, anthropology and other branches of knowledge have resonated in literary cultures since the late nineteenth century. This overview is divided into three sections focusing, respectively, on aestheticism and the legacy of symbolism; on philosophy, science and the problem of knowledge; and on recent critical reconstructions of literary history.

The first section considers modern writing in the original sense of a 'revolution of the word', an idea announced by Eugen Jolas in 1929. Jolas established a modernist commitment to the notion of aesthetic autonomy or the idea of the materiality of the word: the concept is examined through a discussion of symbolist origins and subsequent postmodern critiques. The focus on autonomy highlights uncanny similarities in the aestheticist preoccupations of writers from two different *fins de siècle*. Aesthetic debates in both eras were conducted against a background characterized by varieties of cultural anxiety: about relations between art and commerce, gender and sexuality, self- and national identity; about the ethical implications of new discoveries in science and technology and the fear of social and epistemological fragmentation. Perhaps it was a sense of 'anxiety of influence' which for so long produced a denial of or indifference to the legacy of the 1890s; or perhaps the contemporary focus on issues of subjectivity, postmodernism and post-colonialism has effected a cognitive estrangement from a more familiar literary critical past and allowed us to reconnect with alternative or buried histories. Either way, it is impossible now to read our own or the writing of the earlier part of the twentieth century without acknowledging their mutual debt to ideas and assumptions which were first given life in the 1890s. This section examines the legacy of writers such as Pater, Wilde and Baudelaire, and considers the re-emergence of aestheticist preoccupations in a contemporary criticism intent on repudiating the New Critical version of modernism which is constructed in the terms of formal autonomy.

Section II of Part One focuses on the revolutions in knowledge which have occurred during the course of the twentieth century. In this section, I am particularly concerned to examine a somewhat neglected, but now newly burgeoning, area of intellectual history: the relationships between literature and science in the last hundred years. The argument of this section is that the idea of two separate cultures of science and literature is a myth constructed by commentators anxious to hold on to a nineteenth-century positivist model of knowledge which has actually been substantially challenged in modern science, philosophy and literature. This argument takes up the discussion from Section I, for the idea of autonomy is seen to be an important bridging concept – between the revolutions in knowledge led by science and philosophy, and those in language led by writers, aestheticians and critics. Intended to be a demonstration, at least in part, of some less obvious ways in which autonomy may be regarded as an important idea in modern writing, my argument also decries its over-hasty and blanket repudiation in some varieties of contemporary criticism.

In the final section of this introductory survey, a brief account is offered of some of the shifts in intellectual cultures which have produced the last revolution examined in this study: the revolution in literary criticism as a branch of knowledge. Literary criticism now exists within an intellectual culture described by postmodernists as undergoing a severe 'crisis in legitimation' and within a political and social culture which has changed the shape and feel of subjective identity. Another critic has claimed that, as a consequence, English is 'exploding'. The institution of literary criticism has certainly been revolutionized in the last thirty years and, as with all revolutions, this one too has involved extensive reconstruction of the past and realignments of power and knowledge in the present. Traditional ways of writing and conceiving of history have been challenged as much as the contents of those histories: this third section attempts to evaluate some of these shifts. The book then divides into the main anthology. Part Two consists of material drawn from a wide variety of writers, philosophers, scientists and critics, and is divided into four main sections, as follows: Manifestos and periodizations; Society and self; Art, belief and value; Theories and varieties of knowledge.

The reader may notice that, although the emphasis here is on British literature, many of the documents from science, social theory, psychoanalysis, political philosophy, literary theory and so on are drawn from American and European sources. The reasons for this are twofold. First, to demonstrate that, despite the now somewhat stale arguments about the 'insularity' of British writing and the defensive 'Englishness' of Leavisite constructions of literary tradition, British writers have shown enormous responsiveness throughout the century to intellectual currents and influences from Europe and America. Second, it is clearly the case that critical reconstructions of modernism and postmodernism have themselves drawn on a variety of international contexts of intellectual history. Cultural modernism was a movement of European origin intentionally framed by the manifestos and statements of important writer-critics such as Henry James, T.S. Eliot, Ezra Pound, Wyndham Lewis, Virginia Woolf, Gertrude Stein and others, but canonically reinterpreted for a long time after through the lenses of the American New Criticism and those of apologists for abstract expressionism such as Clement Greenberg. The vocabulary of literary critics such as Cleanth Brooks and John Crowe Ransom was assimilated into a burgeoning textbook industry in the 1950s and 1960s. This new formalism was reimported to Britain where it would provide a more rigorously technical alternative to the indigenous moral-aesthetic of F.R. Leavis and his Scrutineers. Autonomy was now to be viewed as a kind of textual or linguistic self-determination expressing an internal reconciliation of form and content, an 'equivalence' unique to literature. The literary work as 'verbal icon' required for its elucidation neither an understanding of the intentional agency of an author nor the affective response of a reader; nor, for that matter, did it require very much awareness of history. The revolution of the literary word had inadvertently provided a model for the overthrow of previous forms and practices of criticism as well as those of literature – an overthrow of the settled relations between author, text and reader which continues today.

Postmodernism is even more of a hybrid mix, originating in the 1950s American critical concern with the idea of the exhaustion of modernism, but taken up by the 1970s into the (then) largely European, post-phenomenological and post-structuralist intellectual movements which arose in the wake of the political failures of 1968. 'Post-structuralism' was then fed back into the American academy and crossed the Atlantic to Britain. Unlike modernism, however, postmodernism was always a cultural phenomenon created as much by academic categorization and intellectual reformulation as by aesthetic manifestos and the development of identifiable literary movements. Postmodernism not only requires that we situate literature in cultural and intellectual contexts, but also that we question the very categories of 'text' and 'context' previously assumed in the construction of literary traditions and canons. Postmodernists claim the exhaustion of the foundational assumptions of western traditions of art and philosophy and question the validity of the universal claims for truth and justice of the so-called Enlightenment project. These are huge assertions and their very existence might appear to contradict the fundamental postmodern tenet of the end of 'grand narratives'. They are correspondingly difficult to assess – difficult not only in and for themselves but in relation to contemporary and earlier cultural practices. This anthology attempts to respond to the postmodern challenge by offering material which encourages readers to make their own assessment of such claims in comparison with other kinds of intellectual and aesthetic argument.

For this reason, the anthology gives as much space to critical positions which attempt to articulate the notion of a 'pure' aesthetic or a 'disinterested' knowledge as to more obviously political or tendentious readings. The emphasis throughout is on *intellectual* rather than cultural history. This orientation represents a deliberate attempt to redress a contemporary critical imbalance where 'relevance' is in danger of subsuming entirely the idea of knowledge or art for its own sake. Sometimes this tendency has produced blindness to the specific practices of some writers or a skewing of their work to fit contemporary cultural or political preoccupations. This aside, more subtle and interesting political readings may be sacrificed if we fail to respond to the resonances of intellectual projects simply because they do not obviously lend themselves to politicized interpretation. In the first part of this book, for example, I have tried to show how a more subtle and complex view of Virginia Woolf's feminism may emerge if we pay attention to some of the less obvious ways in which her interests in contemporary philosophy and science are absorbed into her literary fictions. Simply to adduce from her negative portrayals of 'masculinist' science an absolute repudiation of the analytic mind *per se*, seems to be a reductive move and one which unfairly distorts both her writing and her view of the world. In attempting fully to respond to a writer's engagement with or situatedness within a variety of intellectual contexts, we may discover in his or her writing ethical and political preoccupations which resist neat packaging into our own cultural categories.

Again, because this is an anthology of intellectual contexts, the introduction and selection of materials tend to emphasize the pressure of ideas upon writers rather than determine the direct impact of historical shifts or events on those ideas. The revolutions referred to in the title are primarily represented as those occurring in the spheres of art or knowledge rather than in political history. By no means, however, is this intended to represent a denial of the importance of political and social events in the shaping of intellectual as well as literary history. A comprehensive literary history of the twentieth century would obviously require a full account of such themes as how the demise of the avant-garde in Britain was partly a direct consequence of the retreat from idealism and Continental experimentalism after the experience of the First World War; similarly, how the demise of Promethean or utopian aesthetics and politics after the 1960s followed the intellectual retreat from 'totalities' in the wake of Nazism and Stalinism; and how the subsequent ironization of myth and suspicion of collectivities was encouraged by the breakdown of social and political consensus from the 1950s. In any comprehensive historical account, literary movements and groupings such as modernism, postmodernism, Bloomsbury aesthetics and the Movement would need to be understood in relation to cultural and political history as well as to developments in science, philosophy or Continental thought.

If anthologies are maps, of a kind, perhaps we should heed Oscar Wilde's observation that there can be no true map of the world which does not contain Utopia. Our own idealisms and preoccupations are inevitably projected onto our supposedly 'representational' models: and, as in the story by Jorge Luis Borges, our discovery may be that the map itself composes no more than a sketch of the cartographer's face. Indeed, in selecting and drawing up materials for any kind of anthology, one is brought up, in miniature, against the very problems of knowledge which have so beset writers and thinkers throughout the century. What is the relationship between our models of the world and the world itself? What is the relationship between the concept and the real, between language and the world, or the word and the self? Is art a kind of knowledge suspended between myth and history, or between ideology and science, or pure reason and prejudice? Friedrich Nietzsche posited the issue in characteristically succinct terms over a hundred years ago, and in a curious way, and perhaps because of the ensuing twentieth-century experience of pogroms, revolutions and purges, of catastrophic attempts to impose concepts on the real, theorists today seem more tangled than ever in the problem which he delineated:

> Every concept arises from the equation of unequal things. Just as it is certain that one leaf is never totally the same as another, so it is certain that the concept 'leaf' is formed by arbitrarily discarding these individual differences and by forgetting the distinguishing aspects. This awakens the idea that, in addition to the leaves, there exists in nature the 'leaf': the original model according to which all the leaves were perhaps woven, sketched, measured, coloured, curled, and painted-out by incompetent hands, so that no specimen has turned out to be a correct, trustworthy and faithful likeness of the original model. . . . We obtain the concept, as we do the form, by overlooking what is individual and actual: whereas nature is acquainted with forms and no concepts, and likewise with no species, but only with an X which remains inaccessible and undefinable for us.[1]

Nietzsche's anti-Platonism suggests that 'X' is inaccessible and that authenticity lies in acknowledging, from the start, the fictitious nature of our intellectual constructs. This has been the driving force of postmodernism, given an ethical turn by writers such as Jean-François Lyotard who interpret totalitarian and fascist politics as the attempt to force onto the social, degenerate aesthetic or intellectual myths of wholeness. Hence Lyotard's famous declaration in *The Postmodern Condition* (1979):

> The nineteenth and twentieth centuries have given us as much terror as we can take. We have paid a high enough price for the nostalgia of the whole and the one, for the reconciliation of the concept and the sensible, of the transparent and the communicable experience. Under the general demand for slackening and for

appeasement, we can hear the mutterings of the desire for a return of terror, for the realisation of the fantasy to seize reality. The answer is: Let us wage a war on totality; let us be witness to the unpresentable; let us activate the differences and save the honour of the name.[2]

After Hitler and the 'Final Solution', the imposition of philosophical 'generalities' on the social is seen to be an aesthetic and intellectual act potentially diabolic in its implications. Lyotard recommends that reconciliation, particularly of 'the concept and the sensible', remain strictly the provenance of art. In effect, he recommends a return to the notion of autonomy, though for reasons quite other than those adumbrated in the original 'revolution of the word'. Outside of art, we must struggle to preserve difference, to maintain singularity. So, in the intellectual currencies of the postmodern, in the criticism of the New Historicists, for example, histories must replace History, and even to talk of modern literature and its *contexts* may be regarded as not simply an act of intellectual imperialism but one of political fascism too. New Historicism calls for a return to history, but not to historicism as the imposition of an abstract philosophical scheme which reads time in transformational and teleological terms (Marxist, Hegelian etc.). But if neither history nor religion nor metaphysics can give meaning to our lives, whence shall we derive significance? If all general categories are arbitrary or imperialistic, how shall we order our beliefs and values? Are we faced only with a choice between totalitarian order and nominalist chaos?

The essays collected in this anthology suggest alternative possibilities, but the very fact of their diversity suggests there can be no path of retreat back to the confines of an unquestioned universalism. This becomes evident if we reconsider the first of the anthologies of which this is a kind, an important document in the critical reconstruction of literary modernism, edited by Charles Fiedelson and Richard Ellmann in 1965, and entitled *The Modern Tradition*. Their anthology proceeded with its task of canonizing and codifying in a mood of the confidently self-evidential. Although they included scientific documents such as Werner Heisenberg's account of the Uncertainty Principle, the logic of Heisenberg's great assault on positivistic epistemologies was barely extended to their own critical act. Heisenberg had demonstrated that there can be no pure object of knowledge, for object and subject cannot be so radically severed. Thirty years on from this earlier anthology, we hardly need to be reminded that all categories, including those of literature, history and knowledge itself, are constructs at least in the Heisenbergian sense. In literary studies in 1965, however, it was possible to assume the existence of categories as given entities and to invoke the notion of *Zeitgeist* as a seamless and overarching historical unity binding literature to philosophy and scientific discovery in a fairly straightforward reflectionist chain. Apparently oxymoronic, the title, 'modern tradition', also implied a continuity in cultural and intellectual history which seems much more problematic when viewed from the per-spective of the dissensual and multicultural 1990s. To be 'modern' according to this earlier anthology is to recognize the universality of the symbol, the heroic necessity of art in the redemption of a fallen nature, the organicist foundation of all things, the fluidity of consciousness and the autonomy of art. This is by no means and necessarily a misrepresentation of the preoccu-pations of many writers in the first half of the century, but it is wilfully selective and curiously unselfconscious about its own New Critical project. Ellmann and Fiedelson assume there is one modern tradition: it is defined in the terms mentioned above and any text bearing such qualities is thus automatically eligible for inclusion. Since then, of course, those original terms have been challenged from a number of new perspectives which have also served to expose the self-confirmatory circularity of such argu-ments from tradition. Just as contemporary criticism seems (at times woe-fully) unable to avoid critical self-reflexivity, so it would seem we are all, if not Foucauldians now, at least marked by the impact of recent challenges to these earlier assumptions about history, tradition and authorship.

One of the virtues of looking back over the intellectual movements of the century, however, is to see that Foucault's own argument for viewing history in terms of disruption, fragmentation and differential narratives is not as new as it might seem. The position was always at least implied by the epistemological crises of the early century: in the quest for alternative and unifying forms of knowledge; the abandonment of positivism; the recognition that shifts in knowledge, particularly in the area of science, might indeed erase the past, render its certainties void and reduce its laws to subjects merely of antiquarian interest. Perhaps the obsession with tradition in Eliot, Pound, Lawrence and Leavis was always a recognition of its impossibility or provisionality. Or did we require the breakdown of the ideal of a common culture and the writings of such as Foucault before we could see this? As early as 1947, in *What is Literature?* Sartre made the point that 'never has homo faber better understood that he has made history and never has he felt so powerless before history'.[3] Since Sartre wrote this, even his sovereign subject and commitment to human agency seem to have come under the erasure of the postmodern and post-structuralist critique. Indeed, Foucault's assault on History often reads more as a pretext for his attempted demolition of the Subject. In *The Archaeology of Knowledge*, first published in French in 1969, he argued for the deconstruction of the concept of 'tradi-tion' as underpinning evolutionary and teleological notions of continuous history:

We must rid ourselves of a whole mass of notions, each of which, in its own way, diversifies the theme of continuity. . . . Take the notion of tradition: it is intended to give a special temporal status to a group of phenomena that are both successive and identical . . . it makes it possible to rethink the dispersion of history in the form of the same; it allows a reduction of difference proper to every beginning, in order to pursue without discontinuity the endless search for the origin; tradition enables us to isolate the new against a background of permanence, and to transfer its merit to originality, to genius, to the decisions proper to individuals.[4]

The terms of Foucault's argument are remarkably similar to those of T.S. Eliot in his famous essay 'Tradition and the Individual Talent' (1919). Foucault's analysis of how the new is always an effect of the construction of the same which is tradition ('a reduction of difference proper to every beginning') throws light on the binary relationship implied by Eliot's title: 'tradition' and 'individual talent' are brought into existence as effects of each other. For Foucault, tradition is the necessary correlative of the idea of a sovereign consciousness or originary subject, Eliot's 'individual talent'. Subjectivity as originality or genius is equally made possible through the concept of 'tradition'. This is indeed the ruling paradox of Eliot's essay, as he makes clear on the second page:

We dwell with satisfaction upon the poet's difference from his predecessors, especially his immediate predecessors; we endeavour to find something that can be isolated in order to be enjoyed. Whereas if we approach a poet without his prejudice we shall often find that not only the best, but the most individual parts of his work may be those in which the dead poets, his ancestors, assert their immortality most vigorously.[5]

Foucault's assault on the kind of 'tradition' assumed in Eliot's essay is, in part, a continuation of Raymond Williams' critique of its exclusive selectivity, but Foucault's argument also involves the repudiation of that democratized ideal of a common culture which Williams would recommend in place of Eliot's élitist and monumental order.[6] Although his intellectual project was more obviously concerned with the demolition of the Kantian universal subject, in some ways Foucault's assault on tradition has been rather more successful. The notion of effective subjectivity is not abolished through the deconstruction of tradition. Foucault might repudiate the idea of tradition as an insidious promise of recovered continuity, of reconciliation of past with present, as the idea of finding one's way home, but his deconstruction of such totality has actually facilitated the rediscovery or reconstruction of alternative traditions and buried histories and the energetic rewriting of so much political, cultural and literary history. In this sense, his project has also facilitated the recovery of lost subjectivities and the construction of new and unimagined future selves. Consequently, one effect of this paradoxical liberation of new subjectivities has been an intensive period of rewriting of literary history. Indeed, the map of twentieth-century literary and intellectual history begins to look more like a patchwork quilt than the seamless garment assumed by Ellmann and Fiedelson. Yet in this process of fragmentation and reconstruction, the project of reconciliation persists: difference, too, might desire to find its way home, storm the citadel and reconcile past with present. If we can no longer speak of *the* modern tradition, this does not entail abandonment of the concept of *tradition* as a still valid and desirable historical construct.

Indeed, Foucault's later idea of the *episteme* is not in contradiction with this most recent turn in the reading of twentieth-century writing. Instead of tradition, and as an alternative also to 'Spirit of the Age', *Zeitgeist* or period, Foucault would adduce the idea of the *episteme*, defined as a cluster of cultural and intellectual transformations across a period of time,

> not the sum of its knowledge, nor the general style of its research, but the deviation, distances, the oppositions, the differences, the relations of its multiple scientific discourses: the episteme is not a sort of grand underlying theory, it is a space of dispersion, it is an open field of relations and no doubt indefinitely specifiable . . . it is a complex relation of successive displacements.[7]

This particular anthology is offered in an epistemic spirit, but precisely with the accompanying belief that, as Paul de Man once said, the overriding writerly and intellectual impulse of the twentieth century has been towards reconciliation: towards that beginning and end of exploration which is the discovery of a path home.

Part One examines critically this impulse towards reconciliation as an important drive in the twentieth-century revolution of the word – first in the modernist commitment to a revolution in language articulated through the various 'autonomy' theories of art; second, in the assault on positivism and the search for alternative theories of knowledge in philosophy and science; and finally, in the construction of history itself – history as text, and history as that which, at the end of all literary and intellectual endeavour, and despite the revolt against positivism, is still, and unavoidably, that which hurts.

Notes

1 Friedrich Nietzsche, 'On Truth and Lies in a Non-moral Sense', in *Philosophy and Truth: Selections from Nietzsche's Notebooks of the Early 1870s*, tr. D. Breazeale (New Jersey, Humanities Press, 1979), p. 83.
2 Jean-François Lyotard, *The Postmodern Condition: A Report on Knowledge* (Manchester, Manchester University Press, 1985), p. 82.
3 Jean-Paul Sartre, *What is Literature?*, tr. Bernard Frechtman (London, Methuen, 1950), p. 174.
4 Michel Foucault, *The Archaeology of Knowledge*, tr. A.M. Sheridan Smith (London, Tavistock, 1972), p. 21.
5 T.S. Eliot, 'Tradition and the Individual Talent', in *The Sacred Wood* (London, Faber, 1960), p. 48.
6 Raymond Williams, *The Long Revolution* (Harmondsworth, Penguin, 1961).
7 Michel Foucault, 'Politics and the Study of Discourse', *Ideology and Consciousness*, 3 (1978), p. 10.

SECTION ONE

LANGUAGE OR THE REVOLUTION OF THE WORD

The phrase 'revolution of the word' was first used in 1929 in an essay of that name written by Eugen Jolas, editor of the avant-garde literary magazine *transition*. The magazine was publishing Joyce's *Work in Progress* (later to become *Finnegans Wake*) and the essay reappeared as 'The Revolution of Language and James Joyce' in a collection published in 1929 as an explication and defence of Joyce's work and entitled *Our Exagmination Round his Factification for Incamination of Work in Progress*. Jolas' reading of Joyce emphasized the materiality of the word as an agent of historical change and of the necessity for a new aesthetic of 'decreation' (presumably derived from Rimbaud) which might express the nature of that change: 'Modern life with its changed mythos and transmuted concepts of beauty makes it imperative that words be given new compositions and relationships.'[1] Jolas emphasized that language, like history, is in a condition of continuous flux and yet potentially expressive of a mystical or neo-Platonist realm whose modern forms have been described in psychoanalysis, myth criticism and surrealist art. This admixture of the mystical and the intellectual, of the irrational and the scientific, was derived from a number of sources: the 'magic idealism' of Novalis, the work of Jung and Freud, Bergsonian vitalism, and late nineteenth-century symbolism and the French surrealists, to name but a few. What characterizes Jolas' sense of revolution is the abandonment of ordinary waking consciousness or of everyday language, of positivism and empiricism, as instruments of knowledge. In the twentieth century, writers must explore alternative ways of knowing. They must create the means to reconcile science with mysticism, the old with the new. The essay exudes excitement: art will again become heroic, its language will open a space in which to explore the possibility of a transformed reality in which human consciousness is no longer alienated from an inert world of dead matter.

What is axiomatic in Jolas' argument, however, is that the revolution of the word is one where the new does not simply wipe out the old, but where language flows like a river, continuously overlaying one sedimented precipitation with another. History is now, in this moment, and is all time. In this great palimpsestic text, nothing is lost. Jolas' idea of the revolutionary artistic word is borrowed from the new sciences of the mind which in turn depend upon a Darwinian understanding of evolution. As he wrote two years later:

> we have learned through the discoveries of Janet, Freud, Jung, Lévy-Bruhl etc., that there are hidden forces in the subconscious which are not only the residua of our own personal lives, but are remnants of those dark ages before history began . . . we have, within ourselves, direct contact with the primitive periods of humanity, as well as with the cosmic forces. Art according to these scientists, represents in its most characteristic specimens the wisdom of the ages.[2]

In Jolas' sense, therefore, and like Eliot's before him, Revolution is less the total overthrow of one regime by another than the subsumption of an earlier into a later order. Though language must change, creative deformation facilitates the recovery of that which persists through time. So he begins the essay on the revolution of language with the assertion that:

> The real metaphysical problem is the word. The epoch when the writer photographed the life about him with the mechanics of words redolent of the daguerreotype, is happily drawing to its close. The new artist of the word has recognised the autonomy of language and, aware of the twentieth-century current towards universality, attempts to hammer out a verbal vision that destroys time and space.

Only by withdrawing from a directly reflectionist relationship to history in the immediate present and into an internalized and autonomous space may art be true to history conceived as more than a record of external moments of succession.

This annunciation of the modernist word was actually somewhat belated. Flaubert had famously declared in the nineteenth century his desire to write a 'book about nothing, a book without external attachment which would hold together by itself through the internal force of its style'.[3] Arthur Rimbaud had called for a revolutionary aesthetic which would answer to an imperative: 'Il faut être absolument moderne.' Clive Bell had placed a similar injunction upon modern art with the doctrine of Significant Form, articulated in his 1913 book *Art* in the belief that

> if a representative form has value, it is as a form, not as a representation. The representative element in a work of art may or may not be harmful; always it is irrelevant. For, to appreciate a work of art we need to bring with us nothing from life, no knowledge of its ideas and affairs, no familiarity with its emotions. Art transports us from the world of man's activity to a world of aesthetic exaltation.[4]

Jolas' version of autonomy though was specifically intended to ease into history the linguistic macaronics of Joyce's work as a monument to the new cosmos of the scientists and philosophers and the new self of psychoanalysis and anthropology. He shared the retreat from representation not as a repudiation of 'life', but in the name of a more profound connection with heretofore unimagined possibilities of its expression. Each of these disciplines had opened up worlds, vast and strange, and certainly beyond the comprehension of common sense or ordinary perception.

Jolas refers to surrealism as the first revolutionary aesthetic movement to create this sense of the new, 'destroying completely the old relationships between words and thought' and producing a 'different association of words on planes of the spirit . . . to create a universe of beauty the existence of which was never suspected before'.[5] The concept of aesthetic autonomy, viewed by Jolas as the most radical effect of the revolution of the word, would soon become virtually definitive of cultural modernism. Not surprisingly, and before the postmodern critique, therefore, the issue of autonomy became a controversial focus within Marxist aesthetics. Bertholt Brecht famously defended the formal dissolutions of modernist art in the name of a politically liberatory *Verfremdungseffekt*. But in his well-known essay 'The Ideology of Modernism', the Hungarian Marxist Georg Lukacs would seize upon the concept of autonomy as the focus for his attack on modern literature as a negation of history and withdrawal into solipsistic interiority and sterile formalism. Fredric Jameson, however, would reassess Brecht's thesis from a neo-Hegelian perspective and within the context of the later postmodern debate.[6] He would defend as laudatory the modernist attempt to achieve critical distance on the immediate impingement of history in order to preserve a sense of history as more than simply representation in a frozen present. For Jameson, neither postmodern art nor philosophy are able to achieve such critical distance: both have now been subsumed into the invincible logic of late capitalism. Art has become another throwaway product of an ever-expanding consumer culture. Cultural pessimists such as Jean Baudrillard or Daniel Bell would take this argument a stage further to suggest that art can no longer maintain its function of making strange the world in which we live precisely because that world is now commercially saturated with art and the aesthetic; reality is now indissociable from image. Daniel Bell argues that 'there is no distinction between art and life. Anything permitted in art is permitted in life as well . . . the lifestyle once practised by a small cenacle . . . is now copied by the many.' The consequence, as he sees it, is a banalizing and worrying 'conflation of self-gratification with self-realization'.[7]

Does the concept of autonomy carry the same significance within these different intellectual contexts? What exactly does Jolas mean when he talks about it as definitive of the 'revolution of the word'? The concept of autonomy is one derived from Kantian thought, and inextricably bound to a modern idea of freedom. Autonomy involves the capacity to act in accordance with self-determined principles rationally formulated and not driven by irrationalisms from within or tyrannical pressures from outside. In Kantian ethics it is associated with the idea of the 'categorical imperative': the unconditional rule which emphasizes that each individual must act in accordance with universalizable principles which respect other people as entities in themselves and not as means to one's own ends.

Transferred to the realm of the aesthetic, Kantian universalism involves the idea that art creates its own universe, one structured according to internal rules which are not subordinate to or interchangeable with the imperatives of other orders outside of the aesthetic: those of politics, morality, science or history. Reductive interpretations of aesthetic autonomy might suggest that this produces a necessary withdrawal from existential history, from ethical responsibility or political awareness. Indeed, advocates of postmodernism as the collapse of autonomy defend the turn against Kantian aesthetics as an honest recognition of the inevitable complicity of all art with the cultural assumptions of its time and they repudiate the possibility of any 'pure' position. For such commentators, the waning of autonomy represents an abandonment of the fetishization of the word and a more authentic return to history, politics and ethics. The demise of what is regarded as the cold and withdrawn pastoral of high modernist aesthetics is welcomed as a sign of the collapse of the cultural hegemony of a beleaguered leisure class.

What should emerge from a careful reading of the essays collected in this anthology, however, is that aesthetic autonomy is a highly complex concept with a fractured and contradictory history. The kind of commitment to autonomy voiced by Jolas in his famous essay was as much an attempt to expand and problematize the relations of art to history as to close them down. As the reader will see from the essays gathered here, and from the argument in the second section of this introduction, the impulse towards autonomy was not confined to art, but shared by nearly all the important branches of knowledge in the early twentieth century. What is common to science, philosophy, psychoanalysis, anthropology and art is a retreat from a common-sensical positivism, a recognition of the limits of ordinary perception, and an opening of vision to a sense of the profound strangeness of world and self discovered within these modern disciplines. The idea of autonomy is not necessarily tied to the formalism and objectivism which were drafted on to it later by movements such as the New Criticism. A more flexible approach to the concept would involve seeing it as a means to articulate the feeling that familiarity might not be the only vehicle of knowledge. Conversely, familiarity may actually pose an insuperable obstacle to some ways of knowing. After all, the idea that knowledge of the world may be dependent on detachment from, as well as immersion in, ordinary historical experience, hardly strikes one as an ethos peculiar to modernism or even to the history of western thought. The idea was revived, however, at the turn of the century, by philosophers and scientists, poets and novelists, and the subsequent revolution in knowledge was brought about by a constellation of changes across the arts and sciences. Should writers then respond to such epistemological shifts by searching for alternative continuities, or must art simply submit to an imperative to 'make it new'? Can art provide a unique way of knowing? Either way, artists felt the pressure both to explore beyond the limits of the ordinary and the common-sensical and to turn their enquiries back towards the question of the epistemological status of art itself and to ethical questions about its relation to the existentially real. Artists, scientists and philosophers share a vocabulary which is challenged and stretched in the attempt to articulate what lies outside everyday perception.

The conclusion to Bertrand Russell's *The Problems of Philosophy* (1913), for example, claims for the activity of philosophy what Jolas celebrates in modernist writing:

> The man who has no tincture of philosophy goes through life imprisoned in the prejudices derived from common sense, from the habitual beliefs of his age or his nation. . . . To such a man the world tends to become definite, finite, obvious; common objects rouse no questions, and unfamiliar possibilities are contemptuously rejected. . . . Philosophy . . . keeps alive our sense of wonder by showing familiar things in an unfamiliar aspect.[8]

What is emphasized by advocates of aesthetic autonomy is precisely this desire to recover a sense of wonder and to appreciate the strangeness of the real. This sense is echoed in Eliot's famous description of the activity of the poetic mind, and again (and we can find numerous further examples in modernist writing) this activity is contrasted with the limitations of the *ordinary* mind, of everyday habitual consciousness:

> A poet's mind . . . is constantly amalgamating experience; the ordinary man's experience is chaotic, irregular, fragmentary. The latter falls in love, or reads Spinoza, and these two experiences have nothing to do with each other, or with the smell of cooking; in the mind of the poet these experiences are always forming new wholes.[9]

Similarly, in *Swann's Way*, the first book of Proust's great *roman-à-fleuve*, the presence of art, in the shape of images on a magic lantern, releases the young Marcel from (comfortable) imprisonment in the ordinariness of his bedroom and allows the 'intrusion of mystery and beauty', so that, 'the anaesthetic effect of habit being destroyed, I would begin to think – and to feel – such melancholy things'.[10] Such statements have often been adduced by contemporary critics, particularly of a postmodernist persuasion, as evidence of the withdrawn élitism of modernist aesthetics. Yet one consequence of the relativisms and anti-foundationalisms unleashed in the acceptance of the postmodern condition has been the recourse to a neo-pragmatist invocation of common sense as the only viable alternative to philosophical nihilism. These statements from Russell, Eliot and Proust help to remind us of the limits of common sense and to remind us too why artists and thinkers earlier in the century were less happy with this kind of pragmatist compromise. To question common sense as guarantor of truth is not to repudiate history but to challenge its very construction. Doubts are inevitably raised about the epistemological reach of ordinary perception and of positivist scholarship. Autonomy theory can be seen less as a denial of history than as a means of exploring alternative kinds of knowledge, of relations between depth and surface and sensation and abstraction, in an effort to cope with the seismic disruptions occurring within the modern world. Language is no longer inert but active and heroic; words do not reflect but create the possibilities of vision. Words encourage us to see and to observe what was previously obscured or unavailable for perception. Again, to quote Proust: 'Seek? More than that: create. It is face to face with something which does not yet exist, to which it alone can give reality and substance, which it alone can bring into the light of day.'[11] This suspension of ordinary perception might facilitate the growth of a more inclusive vision. In a culture which seemed ever in crisis, politically and economically, or terminally in decline (according to the degenerationists), the idea of autonomy in art, philosophy or science might represent the existence of some more pure or more inclusive or redemptive realm of knowledge or vision outside the dictates of utilitarianism, instrumental rationality, mechanization or consumer hedonism.

What has since occurred to challenge that earliest twentieth-century revolution of the word, however, is another revolution of the text: the post-structuralist ascription of an all-pervasive textuality which invalidates not only the idea of aesthetic autonomy but also the idea of history dialectically constructed as its other. Purity now becomes suspect. A gathering anti-foundationalism has sought to root out any lingering metaphysics of presence attached to the idea of art, history or truth. Arguably, this postmodern turn is simply the extension of a logic already internal to modernity. The concept of autonomy born of modern rational scepticism was always poised to turn introspective. So, for example, Russell defends modern philosophy as a criticism of knowledge which, though unable to

> tell us with certainty what is the true answer to the doubts which it raises, is able to suggest many possibilities which enlarge our thoughts and free them from the tyranny of custom. Thus, while diminishing our feeling of certainty as to what things are, it greatly increases our knowledge as to what they may be; it removes the somewhat arrogant dogmatism of those who have never travelled into the region of liberating doubt.[12]

Those doubts were bound eventually to turn on the instruments of their own articulation and analysis, so that objects of knowledge may come to seem not so much entities on which language reflects as artefacts actually constructed through and within language. By the 1960s, in the pages of *Tel Quel* and in documents such as Derrida's 'Structure, Sign and Play', distinctions between truth and rhetoric, literature and philosophy, history and text, began to grow obscure. Colin MacCabe would then borrow the title of Jolas' essay for his own rewriting of modernist autonomy (*James Joyce and the Revolution of the Word*, 1979) in the terms of the new post-structuralist critique: 'interpretation as the search for meaning must cease when both meaning and interpreter become functions of the traverse of the material of language'.[13]

As boundaries disappear in the solvent of textuality, autonomy theory begins to seem not only suspect, but dangerous too. Purity equals violence. The sentiment is explored in Geoffrey Hill's poem, 'Annunciations', in the collection entitled *King Log* (1968). 'The Word has been abroad, is back, with a tanned look', we are informed in the typically stressed and compacted opening line. Etymological purity submits inevitably to demotic habit, for the Word is now a tourist, and apparently healthier for its cosmopolitan peregrinations. In Hill's punningly compacted articulation, however, the word has also perhaps been flogged, beaten and even discovered in its archaic sense to be a-broad (viz. old French, in error). Eliot had famously recommended that poets should purify the dialect of the tribe, but after the Stalinist purges, two world wars and the Nazi Holocaust such purification cannot itself avoid contamination. As the third line of the poem reminds us: 'Cleansing has become killing'. Hill's poem still expresses yearning for a metaphysical purity of the word, above and beyond the contingencies of history, but recognizes that the apparent autonomy of the word as Logos was only ever temporarily on loan to the aesthetic. The word in history may only be purified by acts of nationalistic or ethnic violence, mass destruction perpetrated in the name of racial preservation. Hill's poem is just one of the many recent literary testaments to the sense that not only must the word live in history, but that inevitably, therefore, and to quote Walter Benjamin's phrase, 'every document of civilisation is also a document of barbarism'. The word cannot avoid contamination and paradoxically may be the more contaminated the more it aspires to the condition of purity.

Symbolism and its legacy

The discussion of autonomy having been brought forward into its subsequent history, it would seem appropriate at this point in the argument to place the concept in relation to some of its historical antecedents. Probably the most important source of influence on the modernist aesthetic of autonomy was symbolism. Edmund Wilson argued the case powerfully in his distinguished book *Axel's Castle* (1931), and he was the first critic to attempt a systematic analysis of the connections between science and literature as they seemed to present themselves within the new paradigms of knowledge. In a chapter on Proust, for example, he argues that:

for modern physics, all our observations of what goes on in the universe are relative: they depend upon where we are standing when we make them, how fast and in what direction we are moving – and for the Symbolist, all that is perceived in any moment of human experience is relative to the person who perceives it, and to the surroundings, the moment, the mood. The world becomes thus for both four dimensional – with Time as the fourth dimension.[14]

The symbolist legacy was somewhat driven underground (though in an evasive, Bloomian anxiety-of-influence, fashion) in much of the New Critical reconstruction of modernism in the next two decades. The legacy would not be fully acknowledged again until the appearance in 1957 of three important studies: John Bayley's *The Romantic Survival*, Robert Langbaum's *The Poetry of Experience* and Frank Kermode's *The Romantic Image*. W.B. Yeats would now emerge as a key figure in the transition from Romanticism to modernism and Harold Bloom would affirm this critical reconstruction in his reading of modern literature as a form of belated Romanticism. The symbolist influences on British modernism were largely French in origin but filtered through the English lens of Arthur Symons' enormously important *The Symbolist Movement in Literature* (1899), which Eliot for one declared to be the formative text of his literary career. For Symons, however, symbolism expressed a mysterious correspondence of aesthetic form to cosmic structure rather than an absolute autonomy of the word, and was nothing if not 'the establishment of the lines which hold the world together, the affirmation of an external, minute, intricate, almost invisible life, which runs through the whole universe'.[15] Here, the symbolist poem is at least a simulacrum of universal order, and more likely integral to a vast web of correspondent forces which invisibly bind consciousness to cosmos and word to world.

Bloom's argument for the anxiety of influence helps to explain critical as well as literary acts of disavowal. Though the New Criticism articulated modernism in terms of linguistic autotelism (the verbal icon, the well-wrought urn, spatial form, the machine of words), the symbolist trace is actually never far below the surface in the interpretation of modernist writing. Rarely, however, is it acknowledged by this new and scientific and ultra-positivist critical methodology. One of the most influential of the New Critical constructions of modernism was Joseph Frank's essay 'Spatial Form in Modern Literature' (1945), which instructed an entire generation of post-war students in the 'correct way to read a modernist poem'. Frank's position was evidently indebted to symbolism despite the emphasis on the literary work as a self-contained verbal icon:

Since the primary reference of any word group is to something inside the poem itself, language in modern poetry is really reflexive . . . instead of the instinctive and immediate reference of words and word groups to the objects and events they symbolize, and the construction of meaning from the sequence of these references, modern poetry asks its readers to suspend the process of individual reference temporarily until the entire pattern of internal references can be apprehended as a unity.[16]

In the transition from symbolist correspondence to modernist autonomy, however, style no longer expresses an *analogia entis*, but a heightening of internal self-referentiality which must substitute perfect coherence for absolute correspondence. Such is the assertion, and yet, even here, a Coleridgean organicism lurks powerfully in the conception of the poem as an overarching unity which reconciles the polarities of mind and universe, particular and general, idea and sensation.

The limits of positivism: beyond Pater's subjective impressionism

Walter Pater had anticipated the modernist (and post-Kantian) move in a number of his essays and works: in *Marius the Epicurean* (1885), for example, we are told that for Marius 'it was easier to conceive of the material fabric of things as but an element in a world of thoughts – as a thought in a mind, than of mind as an element, or accident, or passing condition in a world of matter, because mind was really nearer to himself'.[17] The poet as Baudelairean interpreter of universal correspondence turns inwards to explore the relations between sensation and reflection within his own interior consciousness. Mind as a monad must now displace an earlier but thwarted dialectic of cosmos and consciousness, and style itself becomes the objective correlative for what would otherwise remain silent and invisible. The famous conclusion to the first edition of *The Renaissance* (1887) paints an even more vivid picture of that sensational bombardment which is the experience of modern life, and recommends a concomitant attitude of 'impassioned contemplation'. This response will involve the exertion of a continuous effort to arrest and reconstruct the flow as an act of self-conscious aesthetic shaping where plenitude is built upon void and a sense of the metaphysically bereft sublimated into psychological exhilaration. Of course, only a small step from this, and one arrives at the conception of the aesthetic task as purely the discovery of formal relations within language, rather than the correspondence of the word to world. So, David Lodge has argued that

> formalism is the logical aesthetic for modernist art, though not all modernist writers accepted or acknowledged this. From the position that art offered a privileged insight into reality there is a natural progression to the view that art creates its own reality and from there to the position that art is not concerned with reality at all but is an autonomous activity, a superior kind of game.[18]

Probably no more than a handful of modern writers, however, whole-heartedly subscribed to this version of aesthetic autonomy in its purest form, or arrived at Lodge's limit point of formalism. The construction of modernism in such terms was largely a retrospective critical act performed by writers such as Frank and the movement which came to be known as the New Criticism.

In fact there are very few modern writers who rest content with the idea of art as a compensatory game. Most writers exhibit at least nostalgia, if not more overt neo-symbolist yearning, for the discovery or intuition of connection between the significant forms of aesthetic language and some universal order or *Geist* to be discovered either in the world outside or, more commonly, deeper in the structures of the human mind. Often such sentiments are ironically framed, but not therefore negated. The work of Samuel Beckett is a good case in point. In the Beckettian universe, human consciousness, split off from that defective machine which is the human body, longs to retreat into a place of pure rational or aesthetic order which might subsume nature through mind into the shape of a perfect Platonic circle. Accordingly, his works are full of *a priori* games and much of the comedy is derived from the disjunction between the intensity of their pursuit and the futility of their import: the round songs, sucking of stones, permutations and combinations, hat games, endless and circular genealogies and absurd and repetitious perambulations. The fascination with enclosed systems is both recognition of the seductions of Cartesian logic and a satire on its limitations. In *The Second Meditation*, Descartes had aimed to eliminate all sensory and affective experience from his project of rational scepticism: no bodily responses, colours, smells, tastes, hopes, fears and desires. Only thus might he arrive at truth, at the absolute formalism of a realm of the purely geometric and numerical. Throughout Beckett's *œuvre*, his characters, living in shelters, huts and their own skulls, attempt to arrive at such a condition of pure Cartesian reduction. They fail, of course, because Beckett's own struggle (as he so eloquently put it) was not towards the transcendence or repudiation of contingency and sensation, but towards the discovery of a form which might *accommodate* them: a form in which to 'accommodate the mess'.[19]

Beckett's fiction was increasingly fascinated with the seduction of the closed system of pure logic (the ultimate condition of autonomy), but in order that he might expose the bleak consequences of such retreat from the messiness of contingent existence. Human life is waste in this scheme of things, not simply because his characters are tramps and outcasts, but waste as that which can never be accounted for within the terms of any intellectual or aesthetic system or logical game. As early as 1931, in a brilliant essay on Proust, Beckett began to articulate a vision which self-consciously plays off abstraction against contingency in a performance which is comically dismissive of all the great systems of western philosophy. He urges the artist to confront the difficult task of describing 'the object . . . perceived as particular and unique and not merely the member of a family . . . detached from the sanity of a cause, isolated and inexplicable in the light of ignorance, then and only then might it be a source of enchantment'.[20] His protagonists, like Murphy, who continue to try to live in philosophical systems inevitably either go mad or tragicomically fail. Neither they nor Beckett can give up their condition of yearning for correspondence between words and things, ideas and phenomena, concepts and sensations. His fiction implies that intelligibility cannot substitute for sensibility, that theories are simply games if they connect with nothing outside of themselves. It is the truth so lyrically articulated by Molloy as he lies helpless in the ditch:

> when already all was fading, waves and particules, there could be no things but nameless things, no names but thingless names. I say that now, but after all what do I know about them, now when the icy words hail down upon me, the icy meanings, all the world dies too, foully named. All I know is what the words know, and the dead things, and that makes a handsome little sum, with a beginning, a middle and an end as in the well-built phrase and the long sonata of the dead.[21]

Equally, however, such yearning is continually and ironically framed by the recognition that there may be no intrinsic and organic relationship between the form and interconnections of the language of the work of art and relations in the worlds outside it: words but no Word. The algorithmic self-reflexivity of pure autonomy might arise from the desire to withdraw art from a world in which entropy and decay seem the only truths of existence; where metaphysics is reduced to the systematic delusions of the insane – implied in Beckett's writing from *Murphy* (1938) on, and most vividly represented in the famous speech of Lucky in *Waiting for Godot* (1956); and where the evidence of the senses can provide no better guarantor of certainty. What is certain, however, is that, even in its purer forms, there is no one meaning of autonomy. Linguistic hermeticism might represent an aristocratic disdain for a vulgar and commercialized culture; a Nietzschean recommendation of aesthetic fictionality as a substitute for metaphysical presence; a means of coping with a world bereft of transcendent meaning; an exploration of the shared iconic conventionalism of art and life.

In fact all these possibilities stir embryonically in Pater's belated and frustrated attempt to rescue a discredited positivism as the basis for a theory of art. In the conclusion to *The Renaissance*, Pater is noticeably ambiguous about the desired relations between sensation and reflective analysis. Later modernists such as Pound, Hulme and Woolf would struggle to connect the contingency of sensory experience with some more granite-like substratum. In Pater, however, reflection itself is as Heraclitean in its manifestations as the stream of impressions over which it flows and into which it runs. Experience, that 'tremulous wisp', ever re-forming itself on the stream, is constantly processed by the analytic or reflexive consciousness. Experience, therefore, stands always in danger of simply disappearing into the 'narrow chamber' of the individual mind in which is kept solitary prisoner 'its own dream of a world'.[22] Analysis or reflection must be pursued with the same intensity as sensation: failure is to form habits; experience and not the fruit of experience is avowed to be the end. Philosophy too must be in the service of this passionate impressionism by continually rousing and startling the human spirit. Pater's legacy to modernism was the model of a dialectical relationship between immersion and detachment and sensation and reflection, but his subjective impressionism threatened to leave the individual mind stranded on the island (albeit a paradisial one) of its own limits. Both impression and reflection arise in and return to the same bed of subjective consciousness, each individual mind a monad or vortex into which stream the particles of a fragmented history. The continuous activity of 'impassioned contemplation' is an endlessly mobile exercise to wrest from the flux the burning, gem-like flame which might compensate or substitute for those transcendent orders of meaning that have been banished from the realm of ordinary experience. Pater's subjective impressionism is a perfect example of what Wilde would later regard as the doomed attempt to discover the soul through the senses.

Pater's attempt to rescue positivism, however, would bring him to an impasse with further epistemological implications. His phenomenological blurring of subject and object reflects a late nineteenth-century crisis in the theory of knowledge which would also produce confusion over the question of value. Does value reside in the effort of the observer to stretch out the moment of consciousness or does it reside in the object so perceived? If aesthetic value is a quality which may only be conferred upon an object by a perceiving consciousness, then does criticism itself become an aesthetic act? 'Impassioned contemplation' is incipiently aesthetic in its capacity to arrest the moment and so to redeem time. But how can we then talk about the existence of an art object outside of that act of perception? The same ambiguity would lurk in Clive Bell's concept of 'Significant Form'; it would not be thoroughly addressed until the 1970s when literary theorists such as Wolfgang Iser recovered the work of the phenomenologist Roman Ingarden and drew on his useful distinction between the 'work of art' on the page and the 'aesthetic object' in the mind. Both Pater and Bell imply that the ability to 'arrest the moment' is a gift only conferred upon the finest (artistic) minds. Again, we see how the 'ordinary' mind is seen to be incapable of offering resistance to, or transcendence of, the mundane flow of everyday experience. Yet one wonders how even the finest mind could be equal to the task of arresting the specifically modern 'flow' in all its deliquescence. By the late nineteenth century, observers are more likely to describe it as a tidal wave, and in the early years of the new century sociologists such as Georg Simmel were describing modern life as the vertiginous experience of a maelstrom: the constant battering of the nerves involved in the new metropolitan experience threatened actually to dull the senses, to paralyse response, to destroy the capacity for any kind of reflection, let alone one of continuous impassioned contemplation. Simmel views such conditions as producing a new kind of individual: one who is nervous and highly strung but incapable of spontaneous feeling; one who maintains a fragile sense of order and control through the projection of an increasingly abstract intellectualism; one who is obsessed with rationalization, quantification and measurement. What forces had combined to shape this new self? Capitalism had produced, on one hand, a sense of radical instability and uncertainty with its injunction to make it new, to constantly revolutionize production and find competitive markets. Yet, on the other hand, and in the intellectual sphere, the legacy from the mid-nineteenth century seemed to be a pervasive obsession with the certainty of decline. In physics, the second law of thermodynamics was interpreted to suggest that the universe was inexorably and mechanically winding down; and if this seemed to have the effect of dispelling freedom from space, interpreters of Darwinian evolution had performed the same operation upon time. In this context, the aesthetic, whether Paterian, Bergsonian or Baudelairean, might be the only source of redemption, the only space of individual freedom. Yet how could the fragile subjective impressionism advocated by Pater provide any kind of stay against the inexorable and universal determinism posited by science and the radical and global uncertainty which was necessary to capitalist economics?

Something more impersonal was required. If the flux was to be arrested, language must be put in the service of a constant effort of decreation and deconstruction, a making strange which might facilitate the recognition or discovery of submerged and collective forms. The shift from Paterian impressionism to modernist autonomy evolved out of a recognition of the limits of positivism and the search for alternative models of knowledge which emphasized 'depth' over 'surface'. The senses alone could not guarantee access to truth, nor redeem human experience from a degenerate temporality. But pure abstraction was not the answer either, for it condemned one to a prisonhouse of geometric perfection which seemed unable to admit 'human' experience at all. Perhaps only aesthetic language might mediate between the realms of abstraction and sensation; perhaps aesthetic language might even break the monopoly of the ordinary and bring into existence a new realm expressive of a reconciliation between these two mutually alienated orders of being. In the first book of *Remembrance of Things Past*, Proust describes Marcel as he reads, 'constantly reaching out from my inner self to the outer world, towards the discovery of Truth', and then coming to the recognition that only in the aesthetic image might these orders be conjoined:

A 'real person', profoundly as we may sympathise with him, is in a great measure perceptible only through our senses, that is to say, remains opaque, presents a dead weight which our sensibilities have not the strength to lift. If some misfortune comes to him, it is only in one small section of the complete idea we have of him that we are capable of feeling any emotion; indeed it is only in one small section of the complete idea he has of himself that he is capable of feeling any emotion either. The novelist's happy discovery was to think of substituting for those opaque sections, impenetrable to the human soul, their equivalent in immaterial sections, things, that is, which one's soul can assimilate.[23]

Repeatedly, Marcel seeks to proceed from 'these impressions of form or scent or colour – to try to perceive what lay hidden beneath them'. Proust shares the modernist preoccupation with the retreat from ordinary perception, the breaking of habit, the repudiation of common sense, as he shows the same kind of fascination with possible relations between surface and depth and contingency and abstraction. Such preoccupations were prominent not only in the writing of Eliot, Woolf, Yeats, Pound, Joyce, Richardson, Lawrence, for example, but also in the thought of Bergson, Bradley, Freud, Lévy-Bruhl, James, Russell and Moore. In the next section we will consider the impact on modern writers of the mathematical worlds of Russell's logic, the implications of Gödel's theorem, Bergson's *durée*, Jung's collective unconscious, Moore's concept of the good and Planck's understanding of the quantum. In each of these writers or thinkers there is an overriding preoccupation with the problem of connection: whether it is of form with sensation, abstraction with contingency, of id with ego, tradition with individual talent, consciousness with the unconscious (individual and collective), superficial perception with more profound intuition, with '*durée*', 'immediate feeling', vision or intuition.

Postmodernism is supposed to have banished for ever the desire for such connection and to revel in the finality of 'depthless surfaces'. In effect, postmodernism is supposed to have exiled depth. In fact, and despite the preoccupation with fictionality, self-conscious irony and pastiche, many late twentieth-century writers continue to seek in art the possibility of some transfiguration of the commonplace or some sense of innate correspondence, which serves to keep alive the symbolist legacy. The Mexican poet Octavio Paz, for example, in a recent book on our own *fin de siècle*, *The Other Voice*, argues for the continuing existence of the aesthetic as the oppositional voice of a scientistic culture. His claims for poetry, hardly modest, are couched in the organicist terms of late symbolism:

> Mirror of the fraternity of the cosmos, the poem is a model of what human society might be. In the face of the destruction of nature, it offers living proof of the brotherhood of the stars and elementary particles, of chemicals and consciousness. . . . The universe is a live tissue of affinities and apparitions, and each poem is a practical lesson in harmony and discord.[24]

Arrogating to the poet that masculinist creative power normally attributed to the Deity (for this is decidedly a fraternity), Paz late-Romantically seeks to motivate the poetic sign by finding in the organic form of the poem itself a surrogate for that harmony of the spheres radically sundered at the birth of the modern world. His redemptive neo-symbolist aesthetic enacts the paradoxical move which is a feature of most revolutionary claims for the autonomy of the word. In withdrawing from a fallen world (of commerce, scientism and over-rationalization), language in poetry ontogenetically brings forth a truer one. Moreover, he also shares with earlier formations of aesthetic autonomy a tendency towards the elision of distinctions between the idea of the poem as mirror and the poem as model. What is the fraternity of the cosmos which is mirrored in the poem? Nature reconstituted in the terms of a moral teleology? A mystical conflation of symbolist correspondence and sub-atomic valences? Is such fraternity a consequence of the equivalence of form in poetry or of some mystical or visionary correspondence between the physical cosmos and the poetic instrument which is the artist's mind? How could this provide a model of, as opposed to metaphor for, human society? Like Jolas before him, the idea of autonomy in art exists in the nexus of science and mysticism, rationalism and the irrational. It is not to be defined, simply intuited.

Paz makes Promethean claims for poetry in his conviction that the symbolist impulse is still alive – even in the postmodern condition. Postmodernists, of course, have taught us to be suspicious of mirrors and cautious about models. Neo-pragmatists such as Richard Rorty warn us to be on our guard against manifestations of the 'glassy essence': the image of mind or language as a reflection of metaphysical truth. But modernist writers too created their ironic effects out of a recognition of the gap between symbolist yearning and the acknowledgement, as Virginia Woolf put it, that 'the mirror was broken'. Contrary to the assertions of some contemporary critics, the theory of autonomy was rarely naïvely embraced. Woolf herself recognized that art can neither simply nor exclusively be mirror or model and she asks in the 'Time Passes' section of *To the Lighthouse* (1927):

> Did nature supplement what man advanced? Did she complete what he began? With equal complacence she saw his misery, condoned his meanness and acquiesced in his torture. That dream, then, of sharing, completing, finding in solitude on the beach an answer, was but a reflection in a mirror, and the mirror itself was but the surface glassiness which forms in quiescence when the nobler powers sleep beneath? . . . contemplation was unendurable; the mirror was broken.

In the next parenthetically marked breath, however, we are informed that '(Mr. Carmichael brought out a volume of poems that spring, which had an unexpected success. The war, people said, had revived their interest in poetry)'.[25] If the war shattered what science and philosophy had fractured, so that poetry might no longer even serve as bridge between consciousness and cosmos, morality and nature (let alone mirroring one in the other), then might art at least not offer the consolation of internal harmony? Could art not be valued for its own sake as an experience of the beauty of formal coherence, if not the reassurance of correspondence? Autonomy theories are thus born in the spaces left by symbolist negation and withdrawal. Woolf recognized their psychological seductiveness and admired purists of the position such as Clive Bell. Yet the satirical portrait of Augustus Carmichael, symbolist poet, is one of the many ways in which her writing exposes the limitations and contradictions of a poetics of mystical withdrawal. The character of Augustus can be read as a wryly satirical portrait of the separation between the mind which suffers and the mind which creates (Eliot's famous definition of the Impersonal Theory of Art). He is complacently and egotistically unaware of the comic disjunction between his bodily grossness and his artistic pretension. He proclaims aesthetic withdrawal while 'basking like a creature gorged with existence', feeding his body and building castles in the air while the dead are mourned, the poor starve, wars are fought and the fate of nations is signed and sealed elsewhere.[26]

Wilde, aestheticism, and psychological defences

Of course, the central paradox of modern aestheticism has always resided here: that art is valuable by being useless; withdrawal is a more profound kind of engagement; a poem cannot mean but be. In a famous letter to H.G. Wells, Henry James insisted that art makes life and there could be no substitute for the force and beauty of its process.[27] Such sentiments first walked most nakedly in the epithetical reversals of Oscar Wilde. In a utilitarian world, art exists in opposition to the useful, becomes essential only by remaining essentially useless. At the end of *The Renaissance*, Pater advised that 'art comes to you proposing frankly to give nothing but the highest quality to your moments as they pass, and simply for those moments' sake'.[28] Wilde would create not only an aesthetic but an entire lifestyle from such observations, so that Paterian aestheticism is transmuted into an existential ethics:

> as long as a thing is useful or necessary to us, or affects us in any way, either for pain or for pleasure, or appeals strongly to our sympathies, or is a vital part of the environment in which we live, it is outside the proper sphere of art. . . . It is exactly that Hecuba is nothing to us that her sorrows are such an admirable motive for tragedy.[29]

Art makes life for Wilde, as for Nietzsche, because only through iconic conventions is knowledge of the world possible, and in the absence of metaphysics (or as its last form) the aesthetic may claim to have become the ground of both knowledge and value.

All of this sounds remarkably 'postmodern'. Indeed, if my argument has suggested that the revolution of the word began rather earlier than Jolas would have it, Jonathan Dollimore has recently read Wilde as *postmodernist avant-la-lettre* in his subordination of the real to rhetoric, for his view of depth as an effect of surface, and for his refusal of essentialist subjectivity (an anti-Arnoldian and pre-Lacanian insistence on seeing the object as it is not). Here too, though, we begin to detect more of the paradoxes and contradictions of the aestheticist legacy. Postmodernists reject autonomy as a fetishization of the word in the name of a return to 'history' or 'desire', but both history and desire are now themselves treated as pure linguistic constructs which can have no unmediated existence. Any kind of fetishization of the word, of language, may represent a withdrawal from experience which is also another way of controlling experience. One could equally view Wildean aestheticism and postmodern constructivism as flights from the possibility of desire as immediate feeling. Aesthetic distance may represent a means of controlling those aspects of history (desire, passion, the irrational) which also threaten what modern art is itself supposed to oppose (scientific rationalism, bourgeois stability, utilitarian functionalism). Aesthetic distance may in some ways therefore always be complicit with the demands of industrial capitalism and its need to stabilize human desire. Postmodernism may represent a moment in its development when the dependency of consumerism on the constant but controlled stimulation of desire has produced a culture where experience has been wholly subsumed into aestheticized 'lifestyles'.

That cultivation of ironic detachment and linguistic self-consciousness which is the Wildean legacy to modernism is a very useful way of controlling threatening areas of feeling and experience and curiously complicit therefore with the so-called 'iron cage of rationality' which Weber defined as the cultural substrate of modernity. The emphasis on the creative deformation of language in all modernist aesthetics is presented as an alternative to pure symbolist negation, a distinctively modern space of freedom. Yet this freedom may be purchased at the expense of feeling or passion or even defined as their antithesis or sublimation, as in Eliot's 'Tradition and the Individual Talent' or the first chapter of Clive Bell's *Art*. Here, as in Wilde's epigrams, the notion of aesthetic detachment seems to require the repudiation of unmediated 'experience' – whether that of the world of vulgar commerce or 'ordinary perception' or the idyllic Romantic illusion of a primal Nature. Read thus, of course, autonomy comes also to represent a useful psychological defence, a way of coping with what was increasingly experienced as the panorama of futility and anarchy which is contemporary history. Perhaps this is more apparent in late nineteenth-century aestheticism. There is probably no more extreme example of it than the character of Des Esseintes in that 'dangerous book' which is imagined to prove the ruin of Dorian Grey, J.-K. Huysman's *A Rebours* (1884). Des Esseintes has withdrawn entirely from the tawdry world of history and the threatening arena of passion and into a claustrophobically elaborate world of art which is also an icon of his internal condition. He does not venture from this paradise regained, for 'travel, indeed, struck him as being a waste of time, since he believed that the imagination could provide a more than adequate substitute for the vulgar reality of actual experience'.[30] Wilde's art, too, was driven into the same kind of paradoxical relation to the world of history:

aesthetic autonomy is a means of psychological defence, not so much freedom from history as a desperate strategy for coping with history. To say as much is hardly to bring to bear on his writing some new or great psychobiographical illumination, but it does throw a rather different light on the relations between aestheticism, autonomy theory and postmodernism. Wilde, of course, knew all too well that history had staged his defeat and that art must therefore play the role of scene-shifter and wardrobe mistress in the inevitable process of his tragedy. When Henry Wotton declares in *Dorian Grey* that 'every impulse that we strive to strangle broods in the mind, and poisons us', one can see his aesthetic posturings and sublimations, like his author's, as forms of resistance to bourgeois society which are also complicit with its ethics of control. Wilde himself knew perfectly well that aesthetic 'autonomy' was never autonomous but always driven by historical and psychological structures of control and defence.

One source of contemporary critical self-congratulation seems to arise from an ability to point out such performative contradictions and, in particular, to demonstrate awareness of the dangers and moral contradictions of aestheticist autonomy. Surely though, writers such as Oscar Wilde and Henry James were perfectly cognizant of such problems as early as the 1890s and, arguably, more subtle in their analyses than much contemporary criticism. Wilde clearly recognized the contradictions of his aestheticist pose, as the painful meditations of *De Profundis* (1905) make overt, and as the evasions and Jesuitries of his last essay 'The Soul of Man under Socialism' (1891) attempt to conceal. Wilde saw why a dandyish aestheticism might be culturally compelling as a means of revolt and social opposition to late nineteenth-century bourgeois mores, at the same time that he saw its complicity with a consumer culture where artistic connoisseurship, the flamboyant cultivation of 'taste', would become important signs of bourgeois belonging. More significantly, both he and James recognized the moral dangers inherent in the cultivation of aesthetic autonomy. The portrait of Gilbert Osmond in James's *The Portrait of a Lady* (1881) is a damning indictment of the abuses of aestheticism. Osmond is the ultimate aestheticist as collector and connoisseur – of *objets d'art* which include human beings. His refusal of any ethical imperative is facilitated by an aestheticist withdrawal from the world of experience which destroys and corrupts both self and other. Yet Isabel Archer is so willing a victim because she resides almost exclusively in the idealist paradise of her own head (which is wilfully projected onto the world). Blind to Osmond's moral imperfections, she is dazzled by his aesthetic perfectionism. Because she has preferred artistic completion and the disinterested contemplation of beauty to the pragmatism, compromise and sheer monotony of living in the commercialized world of ordinary historical experience, Isabel must end her days hung with the other portraits in the Osmond museum. T.S. Eliot announced somewhat self-importantly in his essay 'Tradition and the Individual Talent' that only those who have feelings might wish to escape from them; James was implicitly rather more democratic in his apportionment of feeling. His novel suggests that in a corrupt and commercialized world, the impulse toward the kind of aestheticist autonomy which would later be incorporated into Eliot's notion of impersonality is actually a necessary psychological strategy in the construction and maintenance of the fiction of personality. Unless this impulse submits to the ethical imperative to recognize the existence of others and to discriminate between different kinds of fictionality, however, then aestheticism may threaten to shade into artistic licence of the worse sort: precisely the sort which devours other people.

Liberated from moral discrimination, aestheticism may then appear to license fascism as the imposition of an artistic vision upon an entire society. As we have seen, this has been one focus of the recent critical assaults on aesthetic autonomy. But one of the driving forces behind the modernist version of autonomy was the belief that we might come to know the world better if we look at it with the spectacles of habit removed. Even in postmodern times this is surely an indispensable activity if we are to respond adequately to the ethical imperative to recognize and acknowledge otherness and difference. Only if our world is continually made strange can we push beyond the boundaries of ego and try to imagine a world without our particular selves. Indeed, many of the currently fashionable arguments for the ethical necessity for acknowledgement of the 'other' and the avoidance of a culturally imperialistic universalism, must implicitly entail the commitment to some kind of aesthetic of decreation or aesthetic withdrawal. In the next section, I will examine this imperative in more depth and explore ways in which modern writers have incorporated this ethical imperative into their aesthetic vision.

The more recent intellectual concern with the fascistic implications of aestheticism arose in the wake of the Final Solution and the Nazi atrocities. For Walter Benjamin it was the projection of a decadent aestheticist symbolism onto the sphere of history which created the barbarous idealisms of fascist Germany. Many writers of the present generation grew up in the 1930s and 1940s and it was evident to them that the projection of a Promethean desire beyond the controlled realm of art had, as often as not, realized the hell of totalitarianism rather than a personal or social liberation from a commercialized, rationalized or authoritarian culture. W.H. Auden, who lived through some of the most barbarous episodes in history, cautioned against the impulse to extend aestheticist perfectionism in an essay entitled 'The Poet and the City' (1963). He noted here the dangerous analogy of art and life in planned mass society and observed that a society aesthetically and economically organized like a poem 'would be a nightmare of horror for, given the historical reality of actual men, such a society could only come into being through selective breeding, extermination of the physically and the mentally unfit, absolute obedience to its Director'.[31] In a technologized mass society, and once the doctrine of the purity of the word is encouraged to 'walk abroad', so that symbolist reconciliation is planted in history, then human beings begin to try to play God with other lives. The religion of art within a secularized and urbanized culture might become a blueprint for pogroms, torture and genocide.

One of the attractions of Wilde, therefore, for contemporary writers and critics, is his early recognition of the seductions and dangers of aestheticism and one of the fascinations of *Dorian Grey* is its demonstration of the lurking ethical corruption implicit in a poetics which seeks to deny ethical responsibility for its historical legacy. By the 1960s, the full account of the historical atrocities of the 1940s and 1950s, and then of the later Korean and Vietnam wars, seeped into the collective consciousness of western culture. Writers in the 1960s seemed suddenly to recognize that the ancient grand plots of literature had been dangerously appropriated by existential desires outside the traditional boundaries of art. The preoccupations of writers such as William Golding, Doris Lessing, Italo Calvino, John Fowles, Iris Murdoch, Muriel Spark and Harold Pinter, for example, and critics such as Frank Kermode, Jürgen Habermas and Jean-François Lyotard (with his postmodern slogan, 'let us wage war on totality'), reflect a growing awareness of the relations between fascism, utopianism and aestheticism and a retreat into modes of self-conscious fictionality and irony, frequently of a Wildean kind. In Jorge Luis Borges' story 'Tlön, Uqbar, Orbis Tertius', he imagines the idealist world of Tlön, a cosmos brought into existence by the conjunction of a mirror and an encyclopedia. Tlön is an aesthetic world: 'the men of this planet conceive the universe as a series of mental processes which do not develop in space but successively in time', but this Berkeleian and Bergsonian idealist cosmos gradually supplants the material universe entirely. Borges' story is actually a parable of the relations between aestheticism, idealism and totalitarianism. He makes this explicit towards the end when he observes the ease with which Tlön conquers the world and the mind:

> Almost immediately reality yielded on more than one account. The truth is that it longed to yield. Ten years ago any symmetry with a semblance of order – dialectical materialism, anti-Semitism, Nazism – was sufficient to entrance the minds of men. How could one do other than submit to Tlön, to the minute evidence of a vast and orderly planet? It is useless to answer that reality is also orderly. Perhaps it is, but in accordance with divine laws – I translate: inhuman laws – which we never quite grasp.[32]

The story was published in 1956. In much of the literature of the late 1950s and 1960s the idealism of Faustian desire is similarly contained and subverted by the ironic frames and metacommentaries of the self-conscious author. Art is used to contain rather than to exist itself as magic: artists become obsessed with the perils of enchantment and critics wage war on Prometheanism. The temper of such aesthetic self-consciousness was often deflationary, care purchased at the expense of heroism. Pessimistic commentators have regarded this as a straightforward loss of artistic grandeur, the literary effect of a cynical and fragmented culture. The literature written after 1945 is sometimes regarded as less heroic than that which was written before. A more positive response, however, might be to see writers exploring ways to retain art's magic without capitulation to a dangerous enchantment. The heroism of early aestheticism could hardly be naïvely recovered in the wake of the historical events of the twentieth century.

The upshot of the various critiques and accounts of the doctrine of aesthetic autonomy is a general feeling that the perpetration of dangerous and degenerate cultural myths may only be avoided through a continuously vigilant and self-conscious awareness of the complex and difficult relations between fictionality and history. However, if writers submit to an ethical imperative to be cautious of enchantment, does it necessarily follow that art must cease to be magical or heroic? Must all 'grand narratives' be ironized, fragmented and subjected to self-conscious deconstruction? Here is another postmodern debate with intellectual roots in the late nineteenth century: in the writings of Friedrich Nietzsche, Charles Baudelaire and Oscar Wilde (though none of these thinkers could have foreseen the realization of their fears in the political events of the next century). Michel Foucault is one postmodernist at least who has acknowledged his intellectual debt to them. In an essay entitled 'What is Enlightenment?', for example, he seized upon Baudelaire's iconization of Constantin Guys as the painter of modernity in order to demonstrate Baudelaire's own profound and prophetic grasp of how the relations between art and modern culture must be mediated through a dialectic of heroism and care.

Baudelaire read Guys as a painter whose heroism is evident in his concern to transfigure the modern world, but whose care dictates that he should achieve transfiguration without annulment. In Foucault's interpretation, this reveals to us Baudelaire's own ability to recognize the 'high value of the present' but indissociably from 'a deep eagerness to imagine it, to imagine it otherwise than it is'. His artistic endeavour is thus to 'transform it not by destroying it but by grasping it in what it is', so that the birth of aesthetic modernism in Baudelaire's hands becomes an exercise 'in which extreme attention to what is real is confronted with the practice of a liberty that simultaneously respects this reality and violates it'.[33] The dialectic of sensation and reflection, contingency and abstraction, is the means by which the reality of history may be honoured, while history is made strange in order that we see it more clearly. Art must respond to modernity defined as

the transitory, the fugitive, the contingent, the half of art, of which the other half is the eternal and the immutable. . . . As for this transitory, fleeting element whose metamorphoses are so frequent, you have no right either to scorn it or to ignore it.

By suppressing it, you are bound to fall into the emptiness of an abstract and indefinable beauty, like that of the one woman before the first sin.[34]

For the modern writer, universal form will no longer simply manifest its contours through the contingent flow of sensation, but must be imposed in a continuous shaping which both respects and violates ordinary sensory and perceptual experience.

Notes

1 Eugen Jolas, 'The Revolution of Language and James Joyce', in *Our Exagmination Round his Factification for Incamination of Work in Progress* (London, Faber, 1972), p. 80.

2 Eugen Jolas, '*transition*: An Epilogue', *American Mercury*, xxiii (1931), p. 190.

3 Quoted in Andreas Huyssen, *After the Great Divide: Modernism, Mass Culture and Postmodernism* (London, Macmillan, 1988), p. 54.

4 Clive Bell, *Art* (Oxford, Oxford University Press, 1987), p. 25.

5 Eugen Jolas, 'The Revolution of Language and James Joyce', p. 84.

6 *See* Fredric Jameson, 'Postmodernism, or the Cultural Logic of Late Capitalism', *New Left Review*, 146, pp. 53–93.

7 Daniel Bell, *The Cultural Contradictions of Capitalism* (New York, Basic Books, 1976), p. 54.

8 Bertrand Russell, *The Problems of Philosophy* (Oxford, Oxford University Press, 1959), p. 91.

9 T.S. Eliot, *Selected Prose* (Harmondsworth, Penguin, 1953), p. 117.

10 Marcel Proust, *Swann's Way*, tr. Terence Kilmartin (Harmondsworth, Penguin, 1983), p. 11.

11 Proust, *Swann's Way*, p. 49.

12 Bertrand Russell, *The Problems of Philosophy*, p. 91.

13 Colin MacCabe, *James Joyce and the Revolution of the Word* (London and Basingstoke, Macmillan, 1979), p. 2.

14 Edmund Wilson, *Axel's Castle: A Study in the Imaginative Literature of 1870–1930* (Harmondsworth, Penguin, 1993), p. 157.

15 Arthur Symons, *The Symbolist Movement in Literature*, ed. Richard Ellmann (New York, Dutton and Co., 1958), p. 95.

16 Joseph Frank, 'Spatial Form in Modern Literature', in M. Schorer, J. Miles and G. McKenzie, eds, *Criticism: The Foundations of Modern Literary Judgement* (Berkeley, Los Angeles and London, University of California Press, 1958), p. 73.

17 Walter Pater, *Marius the Epicurean* (London, Macmillan, 1910), p. 71.

18 David Lodge, *The Modes of Modern Writing* (London, Edward Arnold, 1977), p. 48.

19 *See* Samuel Beckett, *Proust and Three Dialogues with Georges Duthuit* (London, Calder, 1965).

20 Beckett, *Proust and Three Dialogues with Georges Duthuit*.

21 Samuel Beckett, Molloy in *Molloy/Malone Dies/The Unnamable* (London, Calder, 1959), p. 31.

22 Walter Pater, *The Renaissance* (London, Jonathan Cape, 1928), p. 220.

23 Proust, *Swann's Way*, p. 91.

24 Octavio Paz, *The Other Voice: Poetry and the Fin-de-Siècle* (Manchester, Manchester University Press, 1992), p. 158.

25 Virginia Woolf, *To the Lighthouse* (London, Hogarth Press, 1960), pp. 207–8.

26 Woolf, *To the Lighthouse*, p. 274.

27 *See* Henry James, *Letters*, vol. 4 of 4 vols, ed. Leon Edel (Cambridge, Mass., Harvard University Press, 1984), p. 770.

28 Pater, *The Renaissance*, p. 223.

29 Oscar Wilde, 'The Decay of Lying', in *De Profundis and Other Writings* (Harmondsworth, Penguin), p. 66.

30 J.-K. Huysman, *Against Nature*, tr. Robert Baldick (Harmondsworth, Penguin, 1959), p. 35.

31 W.H. Auden, 'The Poet and the City', *The Dyer's Hand* (London, Faber, 1963), p. 85.

32 Jorge Luis Borges, *Labyrinths*, ed. Donald A. Yates and James E. Irby (Harmondsworth, Penguin, 1970), p. 42.

33 Michel Foucault, 'What is Enlightenment?', in Paul Rabinow, ed., *The Foucault Reader* (Harmondsworth, Penguin, 1991), p. 41.

34 Charles Baudelaire, *The Painter of Modern Life and Other Essays*, tr. Jonathan Mayne (London, Phaidon, 1964), p. 13.

SECTION TWO

REVOLUTIONS OF THE WORD: KNOWLEDGE

The last section indicated some of the ways in which the desire for reconciliation has helped to shape and to sustain the idea of the aesthetic as an
autonomous and redemptive realm of experience. Such impulses, however,
are not confined simply to art and in this section I will indicate some of the
ways in which the work of scientists and philosophers reiterates or engages
issues of epistemology, value and belief which have also been central to
literature and literary criticism in this century. In his book *The Aesthetic
Dimension*, Herbert Marcuse argued that 'the truth of art lies in its power to
break the monopoly of established reality . . . to define what is real'.[1] Just as
much as poets and novelists, however, scientists and philosophers too have
broken 'the monopoly of established reality' in important and distinctive
ways since the year 1900. The theory of autonomy has sometimes been
regarded as art's revenge upon science (in the work of the New Critics, for
example). However, an equally persuasive case can be made for evidence of
its centrality in the profound conjunction of many intellectual preoccupations of scientists and philosophers as well as writers and critics in the last
100 years.

The early twentieth century is rightly regarded as a heroic age of science;
it was also one in which relations between philosophy and science were
peculiarly close, for the problem of knowledge emerged as a core preoccupation of many intellectuals and writers. In his popular book of 1933, *Where
is Science Going?*, Max Planck announced the scientific equivalent of Jolas'
aesthetic revolution of the word: 'Now the iconoclast has invaded the
temple of science. There is scarcely a scientific axiom that is not nowadays
denied by somebody.'[2] Just as Jolas accounted for the inadequacy of earlier
literary models for the representation of modern experience, so Planck
would reveal why the positivist models of nineteenth-century science
were incapable of describing the form of a reality which was stranger
than any scientist or artist had previously imagined. When Marx so
famously declared in the nineteenth century that 'all that is solid melts
into air', he could never have guessed how literally science would confirm
his observation once the physicists of the twentieth century began to over-
turn the monopoly of Newtonian mechanics as the law-giver of the cosmos.
Like the writers of the period, scientists and philosophers too would struggle

with the difficulty of reconciling the worlds of ordinary sensory experience with the strange universes of the new physics, mathematics and analytic logic. It is surprising how often writers and scientists of the period express the same kinds of frustration with the limits not simply of perception, but of expression too. Just as the ordinary perception associated with positivism seemed now to be inadequate, so too did the conventions of realism and ordinary language. Eliot uses the words 'slip, slide and perish'; Pound laments that he cannot find a language in which to make the fragments cohere; cubist artists seek to rearticulate human form through geometric decomposition; and so too, Wittgenstein would famously argue that the limits of our language provide the limits of our world. Scientists such as Werner Heisenberg would declare the impossibility of describing the new worlds of quantum physics within the conceptual spaces of available ordinary languages.

Science, literature and the two cultures

One of my aims in assembling this anthology has been to raise awareness of both the complexity and the depth of relations between literature and the wider intellectual culture. I would certainly include science within the parameters of this discussion and yet the misapprehension of their relations continues: either in the prejudicial view that the function of art in a scientistic culture must be to oppose science or in the *de facto* argument that this has actually been the case. In a recent introduction to the *Faber Book of Science*, its editor (a professor of English literature) John Carey observes that 'given the boundless implications of science, it seems strange that poets have not used it more'. A few pages later, the note of apocalypse enters:

> As science has grown, so, inevitably, has the ignorance of those who do not know about it. Within the mind of anyone educated exclusively in artistic and literary disciplines, the area of darkness has spread enormously during the later twentieth century, blotting out most of modern knowledge. A new species of educated but benighted being has come into existence – a creature unprecedented in the history of learning, where education has usually aimed to eradicate ignorance.[3]

Carey is only the most recent of a line of combatants in what C.P. Snow, in a famous lecture in Cambridge in 1959, referred to as the existence of 'Two Cultures'. Both he and Snow share an antipathy towards intellectualism (see Carey's *The Intellectuals and the Masses*, for example), a distrust of philosophy, and a decidedly positivistic interpretation of science, literature and knowledge. In his Cambridge lecture, Snow advanced a defence of the moral health of the scientific culture as opposed to the degenerate and self-indulgently tragic view of life promulgated by the literary intellectual. Modernists such as Pound and Lewis, with their 'ambiguous relations with

Fascism' and their narcissistic moral vanity, were viewed as particularly representative of twentieth-century literary trends. However, this view of the literary intellectual as a moral degenerate to be compared unfavourably with the plain-speaking philanthropic scientist, is another construction which reaches back to the late nineteenth century. Max Nordau's infamous *Degeneration* was translated into English in 1895 and advanced an image of the avant-garde artist as a decadent carrier of moral pathology, host to a morbid virus which was undermining the health of western culture and precipitating its decline. The image was reiterated either faithfully or iron-ically in a variety of contexts: in Wells' *The Time Machine* (1895), for example, where the overrefined, enervated and decadent aestheticism of the Eloi has provided perfect conditions for the proliferation of the race of worm-like but evolutionarily adapted Morlocks whose base instinctual existence will, for at least some time, inherit the earth. Even Conrad's Kurtz in *Heart of Darkness* (1899) can be regarded as the image of an over-civilized refinement: all of Europe had gone into the making of that same Kurtz who arrives as the bringer of enlightenment to the 'dark races' and ends with initiation into and control of certain unspeakable and savage rites. Conrad's novel can plausibly be read as the first fully-fledged modernist fiction: its theme of the uncertainty of knowledge is developed through a study of the interdependence of imperialism and a decadent aestheticism projected onto history.

In Nordau's book, writers and artists such as Wagner, Nietzsche, Zola, Ibsen and the French symbolists were presented as hysterical or neuras-thenic products of a negative genetic strain blossoming in the hothouse atmosphere of the new metropolitan cultures. Like Snow later, Nordau (a Lamarckian) regarded science as the means by which to control such threatening evolutionary tendencies: science, that is, conceived in the image of a robust positivism or 'method'. Only this kind of sturdy positivism might quell the rising tide of relativisms and the impending nihilism of a 'Dusk of Nations'. Oscar Wilde is here regarded as the ultimate degenerate; Dorian's 'I wish it were fin du globe' emblematic of a decadent aesthetic viewed not so much as the consequence of degeneration as its cause. In the absence of metaphysical or religious certainty, according to Nordau's reading, the aesthete cultivates an eroticized art, seeking madder music and stronger wine. Erroneously, the aesthete believes that the conversion of desire into style might provide release from a culture economically depen-dent on the cultivation of desire and a subjectivity increasingly defined in such terms. The result, for Nordau, is a morbid self-destructiveness inimical to cultural health. It is hardly surprising that Nordau turns to science as a source of social salvation. In place of the morbid, introverted and neur-asthenic artist, he upholds the salutary common sense of the scientist following the clear path set out by Newtonian mechanics, arriving at truth through careful and controlled 'Experiment and Observations, and in drawing general Conclusions from them by Induction'.[4]

Nordau's account is, of course, as simplified as Snow's. Even by the end of the nineteenth century, important shifts were occurring within science itself which were beginning to leave common sense high and dry as either guarantor or reflector of truth. Science would collapse certainty far more dramatically and effectively than Paterian aesthetics or Wildean wit. Between 1900 and 1930, in particular, the battle between idealists and realists, positivists and pragmatists, would be complicated and immensely sharpened by a series of scientific discoveries: Planck's account of the quantum in 1900, the development of the wave theory of light, the kinetic theory of gases, Bohr's theory of the atom and principle of complementarity, Einstein's papers on special and general relativity, Heisenberg's Uncertainty Principle. Similarly, in philosophy too, Russell and Moore initiated a decisive break with Bradley's Absolute Idealism with the *Principia Mathematica* and the *Principia Ethica*, and between 1910 and 1915 Russell developed his theory of knowledge and published *The Problems of Philosophy* in 1912. Wittgenstein would challenge epistemology with logic in *The Tractatus*. Each of them, and Whitehead too, wrote about and engaged with the new scientific discoveries, recognizing that philosophy itself, as a critique of knowledge, would be changed for ever by the New Science.

Why did such discoveries carry this kind of impact? Three in particular were central: Max Planck's observation that electromagnetic radiation is emitted in discrete packets or quanta introduced the notion of discontinuity, acausality and randomness into the fundamental composition of matter. Further, Heisenberg's Uncertainty Principle suggested that all physical qualities that can be observed are subject to unpredictable fluctuations – there is an inherent indeterminism in the behaviour of the fundamental particles of life, for at the quantum level no definite predictions can be made about the behaviour of any system (the founding principle for later chaos and catastrophe theories). In his book of 1930, *The Physical Principles of the Quantum Theory*, Heisenberg spelled out the implications of this insight:

> the traditional requirement of science . . . permits a division of the world into subject and object (observer and observed). . . . The assumption is not permissible in atomic physics: the interaction between observer and object causes large changes in the systems being observed, because of the discontinuous changes characteristic of the atomic processes.[5]

Heisenberg's grammar is noticeably inexact, for he wants to move beyond the division into subject and object, beyond saying that it is either matter which is discontinuous or perception which is uncertain (beyond positivism and impressionism), but language tends to reinforce the very categories which he is trying to reject. As we shall see, many of the important writers of the time and after would share his sense of the need to struggle with language in order to formulate different ways of knowing.

Niels Bohr's Principle of Complementarity (my third example) was actually taken directly into literary criticism by I.A. Richards and William Empson, as both developed concepts of irony, ambiguity and paradox which would dominate the criticism of poetry for the next fifty years. As we shall see later, the more radical implications of Uncertainty and Complementarity would also provide an epistemological justification for the abandonment of epistemology in the post-structuralist and postmodernist turn which displaced the New Critical hegemony of the 1940s and 1950s. According to Bohr's thesis, there is an ineradicable ambiguity in all quantum systems. An electron can be a wave or a particle, depending on the experimental situation, but cannot be defined exclusively as either one or the other. As in Heisenberg's theory, observation is implicated in, rather than outside of, any experiment and is crucial to the creation of form: ambiguity is an inherent feature of matter and not just an effect of perceptual limitation. Of the wave/particle thesis, Bohr claimed that its discovery necessitated the 'final renunciation of the classical ideal and a radical revision of our attitude towards the problem of physical reality'.[6] What he promised was the end of Cartesian dualism, of materialist science and the treadmill of Newtonian determinism. It appeared that consciousness might then be reconciled with matter not simply in the spaces of the organicist work of art, but as elements in the actual cosmos. If both are built out of the same fundamental particles, mutually partake of the same condition of virtuality, then the universe seems closer to a Heraclitean than a Newtonian model. Classical science is no longer 'true' but simply intelligible with reference to its own conceptual frame: what is true in the world of Newtonian mechanics cannot be true in that of quantum mechanics. Like the work of art, the quantum world is argued to be fundamentally indeterminate: the free space of the aesthetic seems now to be integral to the previously separate and deterministic world of physical science. Far from existing in relational opposition to each other then, poets and scientists appeared to be struggling with the same kinds of ontological and epistemological possibilities.

Heisenberg would come to express the problem in terms of language:

> Any concepts or words which have been formed in the past through the interplay between the world and ourselves are not really sharply defined with respect to their meaning . . . we practically never know precisely the limits of their applicability. . . . The concepts may, however, be sharply defined with regard to their connections . . . which can be expressed by a mathematical scheme. . . . But the limits of their applicability will in general not be known.[7]

Heisenberg's account of the epistemological implications of the New Science sounds uncannily like Joseph Frank's theory of the modernist text. Internal coherence rather than external correspondence may be our only source of certain meaning and, perhaps more significantly, might provide the means by which to wrest freedom from external determinisms.

Of course, not all New Physicists accepted this. Einstein continued to resist the more radical interpretations of the New Physics. He continued to believe that science must remain a realism and that matter continues to exist with well-defined properties – even when we are not there to see it. The world is stable and only apparently affected by our apprehensions. For him, quantum mechanics was incomplete and, like many another modern, he believed there must exist a deeper level of dynamic variables which bestow an apparent indeterminism at the surface level while maintaining their own core structural form. As in modernist aesthetics, we see a persisting epistemological model couched in terms of relations between abstraction and contingency, sensation and reflection.

To judge from the sales of popularized accounts of the New Science in the 1920s and 1930s, there was an intense lay interest in relativity, quantum theory and cosmology. It would be incredible if, as Snow and Carey suggest, writers and intellectuals had simply turned their backs on what must be the most significant and paradigmatic shift in knowledge since Copernicus and Newton. To suggest that literature has ignored science is like disqualifying a novelist such as E.M. Forster from being a liberal humanist simply because he fails to debate the finer points of Locke's writings on justice; or insisting that Graham Greene cannot be defined as a Catholic novelist because he chooses not to interrogate the ambiguities of scholastic philosophy or theological arguments for the existence of God. To suggest that writers have ignored science because they have not included accounts of Darwin's theory or of Einstein's papers on relativity is to be reductively literal-minded. In any case, as Harold Bloom's thesis of an 'anxiety of influence' so persuasively demonstrates, the more indirect the presentation of an influence, the more likely is that influence to have been intense and powerful. And modern science itself has taught us to beware of reductive notions of causality and determination.

Snow is surely correct though when he argues that 'it is dangerous to have two cultures which can't or don't communicate. In a time when science is determining much of our destiny, that is, whether we live or die, it is dangerous in the most practical terms.'[8] Yet if we bring imagination and flexibility to the examination of the relations between his two cultures, it should be evident that communication has been under way for most of the century. Though few writers have made positivist science their theme (excepting Wells, Huxley, Orwell, Empson and the growing numbers of contemporary writers influenced by science fiction), equally, there are few who do not in some way explore the social, moral or epistemological implications of modern scientific discovery. Neither 'science' nor 'literature' are frozen categories. One virtue of studying their relations as an aspect of intellectual history is that it encourages us to recognize the fluidity of their boundaries and relational identities. Joyce's structural play with the metaphor of relativity, Wyndham Lewis' critique of the 'time philosophy' (a curious conflation of Einstein and Bergson), Beckett's interest in mathematics, Lawrence's in eugenics and, more recently, the interest of writers such as William Golding, Italo Calvino, Jeanette Winterson, Martin Amis and Ian McEwan in physics and cosmology are obvious and evident ways in which the fascination with the epistemological and cultural implications of science has continued to engage important twentieth-century writers. My argument will be more persuasive, however, if I can demonstrate some rather less obvious and more 'fluid' ways in which such relations may be viewed.

Philosophy, science and ways of reading modern literature

In *A Room of One's Own* (1928) Virginia Woolf famously urged the woman writer in the twentieth century to 'see human beings not always in their relations to each other but in relation to reality . . . for no human being should shut out the view'.[9] What is this 'view' to which Woolf alludes? Traditionally, Woolf's concern with the 'view' has been ascribed to her commitment to a subjective impressionism partially derived from Paterian aesthetics, appropriated for a 'feminine' articulation of the world, and expressing a relational sense of personal identity. It would be fairly straightforward to make out a case for situating Woolf intellectually in relation to the various seemingly neo-Heraclitean theories of her age: to Einstein's relativity, Freud's primary processes, Bergson's *durée*, or the various indeterminacy theories in physics and mathematics. All share her concern with the rhythms of flow and randomness that seem to make up the world and the self. But if Woolf tends to be interpreted thus as a novelist of the 'rainbow', she was as much concerned with what she referred to as 'granite', and if we try to foreground the former at the expense of the latter, we will not do her justice. By concentrating on the relations between rainbow *and* granite, we begin to see a very clear example of the difficulty and complexity involved in any attempt to situate a writer in his or her intellectual culture. In Woolf's case, we may begin to discover, perhaps surprisingly, the resonance of certain themes more obviously associated with the 'hard' sciences, with mathematics and analytic philosophy, for example, as well as those from the more obvious areas of Bergsonian vitalism, Paterian aesthetics, psychoanalysis and myth. Here, our own critical vocabulary seems inadequate: 'influence' seems too strong, 'epistemic' situatedness too weak. The first implies too much intentionality, the latter perhaps not enough. Fancifully, we might imagine the writer, any creative writer, like Gulliver in Lilliput – caught and tied to the ground of culture by numerous, infinitesimal strings, finally breaking loose, and discovering how the ties that initially bind may be woven into new and more fantastic tapestries.

Setting aside for a moment, but not thereby forgetting, the more familiar 'rainbow' Woolf, we might concentrate on the less recognizable advocate of 'granite': an imagined substratum of the real which might be hard as rock or incisive as a geometric shape. The idea of granite appeared not only in Woolf's writing, but also in Worringer's notions of abstraction, in the poetics of Ezra Pound, the critical essays of T.E. Hulme, in T.S. Eliot's early 'objectivism' and in the various manifestos of Imagism. The representation of imaginary relations between granite and rainbow constituted yet another expression of the dialectic of sensation and abstraction or form and contingency. It was in *To the Lighthouse* that Woolf offered her most sustained fictional meditation on the problem. Throughout the novel, Lily Briscoe, the novelist-surrogate, struggles to come to terms with her relations with parent-surrogates Mr and Mrs Ramsay. This struggle becomes emblematic also of her attempt as a painter to find the connection between her existential investments and developing aesthetic. At the end of the novel, after Mrs Ramsay's death and as the voyage finally nears completion, James Ramsay takes up the theme of reconciliation in similar terms:

> 'It will rain,' he remembered his father saying. 'You won't be able to go to the Lighthouse.'
> The Lighthouse was then a silvery, misty-looking tower with a yellow eye that opened suddenly and softly in the evening. Now –
> James looked at the Lighthouse. He could see the white-washed rocks; the tower, stark and straight; he could see that it was barred with black and white; he could see windows in it; he could even see washing spread on the rocks to dry. So that was the Lighthouse, was it?
> No, the other was also the Lighthouse. For nothing was simply one thing. The other was the Lighthouse too. It was sometimes hardly to be seen across the bay. In the evening one looked up and saw the eye opening and shutting and the light seemed to reach them in that airy sunny garden where they sat.

Throughout her writing, Woolf expresses concern with the problem: is it all flowing (yellow eye, misty tower, rainbow, atoms, continuous halo, vision) or does it resolve into 'angular essences' (tower, stark and straight, black and white, granite, structure, underpinning iron girders). In this novel, Lily attempts reconciliation in her painting through the representation of Mrs Ramsay and child as a purple triangle: the older woman's 'essence', her 'wedge-shaped core of darkness', may only be approached through abstraction, through the kind of image discussed by Proust in the passage quoted earlier. But the abstract triangle is also a block of colour: it is both Platonic shape and sensory apprehension. For Lily, indeed, artistic seeing must involve both sensation and abstraction. Their reconciliation, the artistic problem which she has set for herself, is also the problem of knowledge as it existed for and was articulated by the thinkers of Woolf's time. Lily is thus baffled and amused by Mr Ramsay's description of his philosophic work: '"Think of a kitchen table then . . . when you're not there."'[10] Lily's mind wanders across the image of a table: her table soon dissolves into a flow of images and associations, a process rather than a form. She sees in it the texture of silvery bark, the fish-shaped leaves, even lovely evenings with flamingo-like clouds. Mr Ramsay's table, on the other hand, presents itself with a rigid and 'muscular integrity': it is form and not process. In Lily's eyes Mr Ramsay's table is faintly absurd. Tables, of course, have ever served as exempla in philosophical discussions of the problem of knowledge. Lily is not a philosopher, but neither is she a Paterian impressionist whose mind simply flows randomly and associatively over the object of perception. Hers is not quite the 'ordinary mind on an ordinary day' of Woolf's famous essay on modern fiction. To Mr Ramsay the philosopher, such impressionism, such randomness and contingency, precisely confirm the extraordinariness of women's minds, but for him it is an extraordinary *folly* which is manifested. Truth, for Mr Ramsay, has nothing to do with sensation. The beautiful evening has nothing to do with the angular essence, the granite-like substratum, of a white deal four-legged table. A parenthesized narratorial comment reminds any doubting reader that the ability to see the table in its essence 'was a mark of the finest minds' and the possessor of such a mind 'could not be judged like an ordinary person'.[11] Truth, for Lily Briscoe, however, has something to do with sensation and impression as well as form and essence. Though the 'extraordinary' analytic mind of the philosopher may arrive at granite, a world so exclusively constituted would be a grey one indeed, and in desperate need of an 'ordinary' mind to illumine it and fill it with colour.

Now it is usually assumed that Woolf is here ridiculing the reductiveness and abstractionism of the 'masculine' mind and that analytic philosophers (like Russell or Wittgenstein), as well as scientists, are her prime targets. But if we pay attention to the uses of the words 'ordinary' and 'extraordinary' in the context of an intellectual climate which was in the process of so actively questioning *ordinary* perception, consciousness and language, then we should pause before jumping to conclusions. In the essay 'Modern Fiction' we are precisely asked to imagine an ordinary mind on an ordinary day, receiving its numerous impressions (atoms) in Paterian (and positivist) fashion, but to Mr Ramsay, such associationism is, as we have seen, not 'ordinary' at all, but definitively the mark of the feminine, and 'extraordinary' in its folly. Yet we can hardly ignore the fact that so much of the satire in Woolf's novels is directed at the extraordinary folly of the masculine mind in its imposition of an abstract formalism upon this world of 'ordinary' experience: in the deathly 'proportion' of the medical men Holmes and Bradshaw in *Mrs Dalloway* (1925); in Mr Ramsay's inability to proceed beyond the letter R; in Augustus Carmichael's symbolist faith in the web of eternal correspondence evinced through the work of art; or in the male Edwardian novelist's conviction that the scientific enumeration of buttons on a waistcoat will render up some final and definitive 'truth' about the self. But we should not jump too hastily to the conclusion that Woolf simply rejects science and philosophy as evidence of the masculine over-rationalization of culture, nor that she unambiguously celebrates a feminine impressionistic fluidity or intuition as closer to the truth of things.

Writing on the problems of biography, she observed that 'if we think of truth as something of granite-like solidity and of personality as something of rainbow-like intelligibility and reflect that the aim of biography is to weld these into a seamless whole, we shall admit that the problem is a stiff one'.[12] Again, it would seem that her preoccupation is with the problem of connection: how might the world of sense or consciousness find connection with the granite-like structure which is the philosopher's 'truth'? We might note here that the new quantum sciences could have provided Woolf with one model of correspondence, but it seems that she was more attracted to the idea of arriving through analysis at some underlying structural principle which was much closer to that of the Cambridge mathematical realism of her day than that of the uncertain cosmos of the quantum physicists.

What Woolf shared with philosophers and scientists of her time, however, was a recognition of the limits of ordinary consciousness, of common sense, as a means of apprehending the increasingly apparent 'queerness' of the nature of reality. Implicitly or more overtly, this recognition was tied to an apprehension (expressed later by J. Hillis Miller) that 'nihilism is the nothingness of consciousness when consciousness becomes the foundation of everything'.[13] Consciousness might be no more than a bottomless abyss, providing only the non-foundational cosmos of intentional subjectivity as an inadequate substitute for a more impersonal or transcendent grounding of knowledge and truth. Henri Bergson's famous *Essai sur les données immédiates de la conscience* (1889) had argued that consciousness was incapable of articulating a real whose existence was a constant flux which resisted either the spatialization of grammatical tense or the ordinary logic of everyday; Freud's *The Interpretation of Dreams* (1900) represented the unconscious as a similarly underlying principle constituted through an alternative logic of the primary processes; Bradley's Absolute Idealism adduced the view that neither observation, sensation nor abstraction could arrive at the apprehension of 'immediate experience' which precedes the division of the world into subject and object; G.E. Moore's *Principia Ethica* (1902) maintained that the good must be intuited as independent of agency or intention, beyond ordinary observation, analysis or analogy. In each case, the basic model of knowledge common to all positivisms is rejected and with it the assumption that 'ordinary' consciousness might be a reliable tool of knowledge. In each case, though, the apprehension of a more profound structure of the real which was unavailable to ordinary consciousness must finally be reconciled with the realm of the 'ordinary': with the life of everyday awareness, of impressionism, of sensory experience.

This is the central problem in Roger Fry's *Vision and Design* (written for the second post-impressionism exhibition and published in 1920), and Fry's training in both science and aesthetics allowed him to provide an important and influential bridge between the worlds of art and science. *Vision and Design* presented the new post-impressionist art as an attempt to advance beyond the limitations of impressionism in its search to recover a world of underlying form and design which might then be connected to that of immediate sensory impression. Fry's 'vision' is analogous to Woolf's 'rainbow', his 'design' the equivalent to her 'granite'. Writing on Cézanne and other post-impressionists, Fry argues that

> these artists do not seek to give what can, after all, be but a pale reflex of actual appearance, but to arouse the conviction of a new and definite reality. They do not seek to imitate form, but to create form; not to imitate life, but to find an equivalent for life. By that I mean that they wish to make images which by the clearness of their logical structure, and by their closely-knit unity of texture, shall appeal to our disinterested and contemplative imagination with something of the same vividness as the things of actual life appeal to our practical activities. In fact, they aim not at illusion but at reality.[14]

What seems to emerge from this passage is a conviction that 'reality' might only be intuited through the clearness of 'logical structure', the 'disinterested' imagination and the 'closely-knit unity of texture' – a description remarkably close to what is usually regarded as the attributes of the scientific or analytic mind. This might appear to be deeply at odds with that Paterian aesthetic impressionism which demands an intense and fluid immersion in experience, a refusal of the disengagement of analysis or theory. Yet the Paterian position, searching for the means to arrest the moment, to discover in the flux some principle of form, always implied the necessity for the kind of solution which would be explored in post-impressionism as understood by Roger Fry.

In Woolf's novel, Lily Briscoe is clearly struggling to advance beyond impressionism. As she sits on the lawn attempting to complete her painting after Mrs Ramsay's death, 'visions came', but 'there was something perhaps wrong with the design'. She recognizes the need to be 'on a level with ordinary experience' but at the same time to feel 'it's a miracle'.[15] At precisely this point in her meditations, the narrative perspective shifts to the passage examined earlier which presents James' intuition of the Lighthouse as a symbol of the potential reconciliation of *vision* and *design*. As always in Woolf, however, the moment of insight is fleeting and certainly must elude those who pursue exclusively either one or other pole of this dialectic: design as nothing more than the extraordinary task of getting to the letter R in the alphabet (which is how Mr Ramsay describes his work), or vision as simply an undisciplined (ordinary) response to sensation and impression. The precise relation between granite and rainbow or vision and design defies conceptual definition and we may therefore feel that it cannot exist (the world is all that is the case). But maybe that is why art exists: as a unique way of seeing and knowing 'this other thing, this truth, this reality, which suddenly laid hands on her'.[16]

Woolf's preoccupation with the relations between these orders of experience was shared not only by those philosophers and artists traditionally acknowledged to be influences on her writing (Bergson, Freud, Fry, for example), but by the physicists mentioned earlier and the new analytic realists such as Russell and Moore. G.E. Moore is normally related to Bloomsbury writers such as Woolf and Forster through the influence of his notion of the 'good' as existing beyond analysis, but discoverable through the experience of art and human relationship. Like them and Russell too, however, he struggled with the problem of reconciling the formal and logical account of reality available in the 'bleached-out' mathematical structures of logical atomism (the extraordinary) with the world of ordinary sense-perception and experience: of colour, taste and sensation. More recently, the American philosopher Thomas Nagel has described this as the problem of knowledge recast as the problem of the 'view from nowhere': how might one 'combine the perspective of a particular person inside the world with an object view of that same world, the person and the view included? It is a problem that faces every creature with the impulse and the capacity to transcend its particular point of view and to conceive of the world as a whole.'[17] Nagel immediately recognizes the ethical implications of this epistemological issue. To some extent, literature has always performed this task, modulating the perspectives of finite human beings through a view from nowhere provided by an omniscient narrator or impersonal author. In a post-religious and post-metaphysical age, however, the question of authority becomes problematic. Does omniscience of this kind necessarily depend upon a theological postulate? If aesthetic 'impersonality' could be achieved without sacrificing personality or without the prior assumption of a divinity, then might it not serve in the absence of God as a means of resolving what James Joyce in *Ulysses* referred to as the 'incertitude of the void', the gap between consciousness and cosmos, mind and world. If the personal might be reconciled with impersonality, the situated perspective with the view from nowhere, rainbow with granite, then that dream of reconciliation which has haunted modern writing and modern thought might at last be realized.

Although Woolf is ambivalent then about scientists, she is surprisingly receptive to the possibility of finding some means to reconcile the granite-like world and analytic understanding of the scientific mind with the rainbow-like and associative vision of the artist. Moreover, Nagel's observation suggests why this might be as much an ethical as an epistemological commitment. Woolf saw in Russell's logic and Moore's ethics why it might be as important to be able to conceive of the world without a self (the novelist Bernard's preoccupation in *The Waves*), as it is to register that world through an intense Paterian subjective impressionism. In *A Room of One's Own*, she observed that 'one began to get tired of the I' and at the end of *The Years* Peggy emphatically rejects the role of mirror to male egotism characterized in Woolf's familiar image of a bird's beak: 'She had heard it all before, I, I, I, – he went on. It was like a vulture's beak pecking or a vacuum cleaner sucking, or a telephone bell ringing. I, I, I. But he can't help it, not with that nerve-drawn egotist's face, she thought, glancing at him.'[18] The dark bar of the 'I' which threatens ever to cast its shadow across the writer's page might be dispelled by a more cosmic perspective which offers release from egotism without capitulation to or sense of absorption in an indifferent nature. The wandering ego-less 'I' of 'Street Haunting' becomes the model of a cosmic and nomadic self which, like Mrs Ramsay's core of darkness, is free to roam to the limits of horizons, to escape that necessity for social articulation which either fixes the personality like a fish caught in the tides or impels it to retreat into a private space (which Elaine Showalter once described as the room of one's own which is the grave). The effort to articulate granite and rainbow involves an ethical imperative to transcend the narrow limits of egotism and to acknowledge the immense strangeness of the universe and of self and other. In this sense, and to borrow a phrase from Paul de Man, art becomes a necessary and knowing defeat of knowledge. For Woolf, Russell, Freud, Fry and the new scientists of the early twentieth century, the world was a much stranger place than common sense had supposed and the self more mysterious than the constructions of positivist observation. Conventional seeing, ordinary waking consciousness, were therefore limited in their capacity to take us into the newly discovered 'dark places' of the real.

Myth, science and tradition

Science and analytical philosophy provided alternative models of knowledge, but these were certainly not the only available systems of thought. Another literary figure trained in science, William Empson, wrote a review of Joseph Needham's *The Sceptical Biologist* in 1930 which articulated succinctly both the early twentieth-century experience of the Darwinian and Newtonian legacy and the possibility of its transcendence through the new science and philosophy: 'in the nineteenth century, one was only a pile of billiard balls, jerking about according to mathematical rules; scientific determinism spelled horror and despair'.[19] Nineteenth-century determinism had offered the image of a mathematically certain universe, but one in which the purpose, meaning or value of human existence is rendered profoundly uncertain. Within the terms of such understanding and in the absence of belief in a deity, the New Sciences of the twentieth century might offer the consolation of release from mechanistic determinism, but it was less clear how this might contribute to a sense of recovered purpose or meaning. As we shall see, that would have to await the scientists and writers of the second half of the century. For many modernists only a return to myth might ultimately offer the means to reconcile cosmic and human perspectives. But return was impossible because in the modern world, myth can no longer be mythic precisely because it is now only one among numerous models of knowledge or belief. T.S. Eliot recognized this in *The Use of Poetry and the Use of Criticism*, when he argued that 'the important moment for the appearance of criticism seems to be the time when poetry ceases to be the expression of the mind of a whole people'.[20] He sees that criticism turns scientific when art may no longer be mythic. Myth too has been laid on the chopping-block of modern scepticism, perspectivized and found to be simply one more language game in a world in which, as William James remarked with bewilderment, 'there are so many geometries, so many logics, so many physical and chemical hypotheses, so many classifications, each one of them good for so much and yet not good for everything, that the notion that even the truest formula may be a human device and not a literal transcript has dawned upon us'.[21]

For a number of writers, however, the new sciences of psychoanalysis and anthropology provided alternative models of reconciliation and knowledge which were not incompatible with some of the philosophical speculations of scientists such as Bohr and Heisenberg. We have seen earlier how Eugen Jolas sought to promote such alternative ways of seeing in the pages of *transition*, and actually combined perspectives from science, anthropology and myth in the attempt to represent new possibilities of art and knowledge. Through a creative deformation of language, art might break free of a mechanistic world and facilitate our reconciliation with a universe which would become more familiar by being made more strange. D.H. Lawrence, in particular, saw the Cartesian consciousness and Newtonian cosmos as both causes and effects of a culture of abstraction in which human beings were severed from world and body through the loss of that divine dimension of depth available to mythic cultures. Anthropologists such as Lévy-Bruhl had described this state of consciousness in primitive cultures as governed by a 'law of participation' (in *How Natives Think*), a condition of embodied thought echoed as an ideal in writers as various as Lawrence (whom Huxley would refer to as a 'mystical materialist') and the German philosopher Martin Heidegger. Huxley's description of Lawrence is interesting in the context of this discussion, for it draws attention to the similarities between the new physical sense of mind and matter as inextricably part of each other, and the pre-Socratic and particularly Heraclitean sense of a living universe misrepresented through rational dualisms. Pre-Socratic thought was important for both Heidegger and Lawrence in their different attempts to overcome the Cartesian legacy. Lawrence's refusal of a divided and reduced consciousness involved an attempt to represent mind and nature as relational manifestations of a single source. Again, we might see in this impulse the same concern to explore art as a reconciliatory form of knowledge, the same impulse to imagine a rainbow which connects the heavens to the earth in an artistic practice which neither sacrifices physical particularity or sensation nor limits its vision to the apparent certainties of positivistic observation.

For T.S. Eliot, Joyce was the writer who reinvented the mythic mode for the modern world but, as Nietzsche had already made apparent, it would necessarily be modulated through an unavoidably ironic frame. Eliot's reading (in his 1923 review of *Ulysses*) of Joyce's use of myth was another acknowledgement of the need to break with the narrative modes and structures tied to an outworn positivist model of knowledge, for they belonged, he felt, to an age 'which had not sufficiently lost all form to feel the need for something stricter'. In *Ulysses*, Joyce presents us with 'man' as conceived within scientific determinisms and suggests why even an ironic and self-consciously deployed myth might be preferable to the image of 'a conscious rational animal proceeding syllogistically from the unknown to the known and a conscious rational reagent between a micro-and a macrocosm ineluctably constructed upon the incertitude of the void'.[22] Even an ironic relation to myth allows Joyce not only to order the immense panorama and futility which is contemporary history, but to retain a sense of embeddedness in community without the sacrifice of individual vision. Ironic or otherwise, pure or combined with scientific or Einsteinian relativism, myth offers another way of knowing, another means of exploring a world with and without the self. The mythic consciousness might allow for the reconnection of fact and value sundered in the New-tonian blueprint, but its ironic and self-conscious manipulation would preserve the modern creative freedom first made possible in that act of severance. Like Eliot, Joyce explores his own version of tradition and the individual talent. For Nietzsche, heroic Greek culture was ideal precisely because it was unified by an overarching narrative which gave purpose and public cohesion. The embodied mode of the mythic allowed an imme-diacy of knowledge, and reconciliation of subject and object lost in the abstracted and fragmented world of the modern. Science is a poor sub-stitute for such nourishment, 'for what does our great historical hunger signify, our clutching about us of countless other cultures, our consuming desire for knowledge, if not the loss of myth, of a mythic home, the mythic womb?'[23] Nietzsche, however, would go on to argue that if modern culture lacked a mythic ground then a myth must be created. Yet Joyce looks forward to the postmodern relation to such claims and, through the ironic treatment of the nationalistic and fascistic citizen in *Ulysses*, for example, shows the violent dangers lurking in such a view. Even benign myths of the past may produce dangerous political futures. Throughout *Ulysses*, how-ever, Joyce himself self-consciously manipulated a diverse range of cultural myths and showed that even in a colonized culture where myth has been imposed with violence and has produced equally distorting counter-mythologies, inherent in the modern is the possibility of choice, of creative deformation, of positive reformulation of what may have previously anchored one to the world through force or oppression. The position was famously announced at the end of *A Portrait of the Artist*, with Stephen Daedalus's resolution that 'I will not serve that in which I no longer believe whether it call itself my home, my fatherland or my church; and I will try to express myself in some mode of life or art as freely as I can, using for my defence the only arms I allow myself to use – silence, exile and cunning'.[24]

At the end of that novel, Stephen attempts to reconcile a Thomist sense of the aesthetic as an autonomous laboratory of language with a symbolist theory of creative expression, and arrives at the oft-quoted assertion of aesthetic impersonality:

> the personality of the artist, at first a cry or cadence or mood and then a fluid and lambent narrative, finally refines itself out of existence, impersonalises itself so to speak. . . . The mystery of the esthetic like that of material creation is accomplished. The artist, like the God of the creation, remains within or beyond or above his handiwork, invisible, refined out of existence, indifferent, paring his fingernails.[25]

But if Joyce becomes the impersonal 'arranger' of the world of art which is the novel itself, he is Aristotelian enough to recognize that even a world of art cannot be created out of nothing. Again we see that art comes to occupy a heroic position, suspended in the void, attempting to reconcile cosmos and consciousness, to 'sublimate a disparity' in Alain Robbe-Grillet's sceptical but memorable phrase.[26]

Like Joyce, Eliot too acquired a reputation within the terms of the New Criticism for propounding an 'impersonality' theory of art. Here again we witness a struggle to find a relation to the world which is neither impersonal in the sense of being purely abstract nor reductively (or egotistically) subjective. Eliot's early 'objectivism' certainly owes something to Russell, but it is mistaken to regard this as a misplaced scientism which was later abandoned. His concern is also with the limits of consciousness, though more as the expression of an ascetic impulse toward the renunciation of ego. Self-recovery might then occur through a descent into impersonality, a negation of self as individuality and the reformulation of collective tradition through the individual talent of each particular aesthetic act. In the absence of metaphysical certainty, Eliot turns less to science (or even philosophy) than to the idea of a practical wisdom: a customary, situated and tacit knowledge that arises in the actual practices of living in a culture and provides the limits of what might be seen and the forms of its articulation. 'Impersonality' is not so much a granite-like structure (though 'monuments' are important in his earliest thoughts on tradition) as one form of a collective unconscious whose modern denial has over-inflated the rationalistic and the positivistic, the individualistic and the subjective, at the expense of other ways of knowing and seeing.

Nevertheless, Eliot is one of the few modern writers trained as a professional philosopher, completing his doctoral thesis on F.H. Bradley in 1916, having spent 1910–11 attending Henri Bergson's lectures in Paris. The enormous appeal of Bergson at this time was certainly a response to his attempt to limit the explanatory reach of mechanistic science to the realm of space and extension, and to define an interior realm of *durée* in which the mechanical laws of causality were absent and for the understanding of which reason and intellect were useless tools. T.E. Hulme had been one of the earliest proponents of Bergsonism in Britain. Reviewing his posthumous *Speculations* in 1924, Eliot saw him as decisive in the formation of English modernism, despite the brevity of his life (he was killed in 1917). Indeed, Donald Davie would go even further in his book *Articulate Energy* and argue that it was probably due to Hulme that much modern criticism is, albeit unwittingly, Bergsonian in its belief in a non-mechanistic or vitalist principle of energy. Eliot himself, however, resisted the Bergsonian influence, possibly because of its persistently dualistic understanding of the relations between objectivity and subjectivity or maybe because of its irrationalist over-privileging of an interior realm of subjectivity. Bergsonism was seductive both because of its attempt to restrict the demesne of deterministic science to space and exteriority, and because of its repudiation of abstract intellectualism as an inadequate means by which to comprehend the inner world of *durée* or radical temporality. In view of the argument developed here, though, it might be speculated that Bergson's limitation, for Eliot, Woolf, Joyce and other modern writers, was in his continuing insistence on the necessity for splitting these realms in the first place. In Bergson's philosophy, subject and object, abstraction and sensation, humanism and science, remain unalterably divided. Joyce and Beckett make comedy out of the gap, but explore ways to close it; neither Woolf nor Eliot accepts such division in the first place.

For historians such as Charles Taylor, Bergsonism, like Freudianism, represents a typical modern tendency to privilege an interior realm of subjectivity as the only potential space of freedom in a mechanistic world.[27] Yet when we examine writers as diverse as Eliot or Woolf, Fry or Lawrence, it is evident that their concern lies more with the difficulty of connection and reconciliation of internal with external: with the attempt to discover linguistic forms which pay homage to the strangeness of the universe and yet find in it some principle of order which connects with the experience of human beings. In *Time and Western Man*, Wyndham Lewis repudiated Bergsonism entirely, regarding the concept of *durée*, like that of relativity, as an erroneous attempt to organicize the mechanical which could only result in the collapse of all orders of experience into mechanized abstraction. Instead of humanizing science, he saw the effect of Bergsonism as one which threatened conversely to scientize the human.[28] Yet Lewis himself shared the impulse towards reconciliation which manifested itself in such diverse modes as Eliot's tradition and individual talent, Yeats' Hegelian concern with individuality and community, Woolf's eyeless universe with its points of subjective consciousness, Joyce's and Lawrence's interest in myth, and the interest of Eliot, Pound, Yeats and Lawrence in pre-capitalist and imaginary organic communities (which in some cases, of course, produced a commitment to or flirtation with fascism). What must be transcended in the search for such reconciliation is a reductive or exclusive 'ordinariness' which (and in the spirit of *ressentiment*, for Nietzsche) must make all things in its own image, and which cannot therefore, and unlike true art or true science, make strange.

Although Eliot abandoned Bergson, his more enduring attraction to Bradley continued the earlier preoccupation with the discovery of a realm of pure freedom beyond ordinary experience. Bradley's idea of personality as a provisional fiction constructed upon lack, a shifting and often misleading illusion, certainly helped to shape Eliot's conviction of the need to give allegiance to something outside of selfhood. His early meditation on this problem in *The Sacred Wood* shows some of the influence of Cambridge realism too: the concern with linguistic precision, the famous attack on Swinburne's verse as the 'hallucination of meaning' and the search for the poetic equivalent of a picture theory of meaning which he shared with Pound and other imagists. Later, in his poem *Four Quartets*, he would observe that 'we had the experience but missed the meaning'; and (as his erstwhile tutor Josiah Royce had taught him about his interest in Buddhism, the occult and mysticism) he came to realize that, inevitably, 'approach to the meaning restores the experience / in a different form'. We have seen how Werner Heisenberg would make the same observation about the difficulty of translating the strange worlds of quantum physics into the language of everyday physical mechanics. Science in its modern forms, mysticism in its ancient ones, seduce with the possibility of arriving at a form of knowledge which might encompass all, but neither can speak such knowledge: each requires translation into a publicly shared language. This 'intolerable wrestle with words' is seen to be our defence against the solipsistic and esoteric, but also divides us from the possibility of a more pure revelation. Moreover, Eliot's observation, though hardly postmodernist, does carry the recognition that human knowledge is always historically situated and that human interpretation is always an act which in some way actually constructs its object. His attempt to reconcile vision and design is more historicist than is sometimes allowed.

The problem of translation is a problem of historical situation. Eliot's reading in anthropology, mysticism, science and philosophy reinforced the belief that even if mathematicians, for example, are capable of defining a realm of 'universal' or abstract truth, they too must rely upon language in order to communicate their discoveries. Inevitably, therefore, meaning must be restored 'in a different form'. Indeed, from the 'Tradition' essay to the later cultural criticism, Eliot turned towards the importance of a sense of shared culture, towards the idea of knowledge as embodied in a tradition open to experience but not necessarily available through conceptual definition or conscious formulation. The aesthetic is prized as a realm of intentionally embodied knowledge, providing the means to cope with the modern proliferation of epistemologies without capitulating to an extreme historical relativism or nihilism. Art should not aspire to become philosophy, then, for it represents a different way of knowing:

I do not think you can make poetry out of ideas when they are too original or too new. . . . For the business of the poet is to express the culture in which he lives, and to which he belongs, not to express aspirations toward one which is not yet incarnate.[29]

Eliot explicitly repudiated Cartesianism in the Clarke lectures of 1926, but from the 'Tradition' essay through his fall myth of a seventeenth-century 'dissociation of sensibility' and the splitting of thought and feeling, to the idea of a poetic 'objective correlative' which overcomes the division of subject and object, and in the later writings against cultural planning, he offers the poetic as model of a more inclusive and more profound way of knowing. The theory of cultural tradition provided a recognition of the condition of situated embodiment from which arises all human activity, including art, and also offered a structured 'impersonality' which might provide discipline for the desires and promptings of the individual body. Consensus might be recovered, even if a universal foundationalism was gone for good. The poet might know this better than the philosopher.

From modernism to postmodernism and beyond

In a recent study of modernism, Christopher Butler argued that 'many of the issues which the Modernists faced are still open to debate in epistemology and moral thought; and the continuity of their aesthetic concerns is shown by the fact that our interpretation of the relationship of Modernism to Postmodernism is still a matter of dispute and probably will long continue to be so'.[30] Modernism opened up the peculiar form which these debates would take throughout the course of the twentieth century, though we have had to return to the late nineteenth century in order to understand the intellectual roots of that modernist turn. In the early part of the century, the various strands of realism, pragmatism, perspectivism, historicism, irrationalism, idealism, nihilism, anti-foundationalism, aestheticism and symbolism existed in a steady state of disequilibrium. Postmodernism has not resolved these elements into any kind of higher unity, though so much is sometimes assumed in its claims to have banished unity altogether. In some ways, the aesthetic has become even more powerful as a model for knowledge, further invading science through the influence of the various critiques of method in the 1960s and because of the increasingly difficult problem of communicating or describing the strange new worlds of physics and molecular biology. Philosophers such as Richard Rorty draw on aestheticist models to argue for a consensual definition of knowledge and value in a dissensual and multicultural society. Modernism itself has been continuously reread and reconstructed through differential contemporary cultural perspectives: New Criticism, feminism, cultural materialism, post-colonialism, postmodernism. Recent analyses, for example, have presented modernist writing as an expression of the fear of the New Woman, a version of Romanticism, a repudiation of Romanticism, an expression of the crisis in colonialism, a postmodernism *avant la lettre*, a response to the *fin de siècle*, a critique of Enlightenment, a defence of Enlightenment, a response to the dialectic of Enlightenment, and so on. We live in a very different political culture and the map of the world has changed considerably since 1900, but writers and intellectuals today are still struggling with the problems of the foundations of knowledge and value which are the legacy of the late nineteenth century.

The study of literature in relation to intellectual culture must surely convince us that reductive oppositions between modernism and postmodernism, conceived in binary terms such as depth/surface; reconciliation/fragmentation; foundationalism/anti-foundationalism, are themselves unfounded. It has become something of a commonplace, for example, that postmodernism has abandoned the utopian project of aesthetic reconciliation of subject and object, consciousness and cosmos, individual and community, which seemed definitive of the modernist project. This seems oversimplistic, and I will end this section with one more example of how a closer consideration of the relations between intellectual cultures and literature might suggest grounds for caution in responding to the fashionable assertions of epistemic rupture. Modern writers lived through a period in which certainties of faith, science and value had been overturned, and in which any remaining stability appeared only to be the effect of continued belief in or adherence to biological, physical or cultural models of determinism. Hardly surprising then that they continued often to engage with the fall myth of modernity: the idea that the birth of modern science also brought into the world its twin, a redemptive aesthetic bringing compensation for all that science would abstract from the world. In this modern myth, art or philosophy might retrieve a realm of value or freedom to set against the mechanical purposeless of the Newtonian scientific cosmos. But this overlooks the fact that many writers were also, and contradictorily, aware that science too was being revolutionized in ways which seemed to offer release from materialism, mechanism and determinism. Positivism aside, many modern writers recognized that the new worlds opened up in the latest forms of science might not be so obviously opposed to those built in the imaginations of poets and artists. Poets, philosophers and scientists might be engaged in a similar search for reconciliation and connection, working in different ways with the dialectic of abstraction and sensation, form and contingency. If we trace the continuing relations between art and science into the postmodern debate, it soon becomes apparent that reports of the death of such desire are certainly premature. The impulse towards reconciliation is as alive as ever.

Postmodernism was announced with Lyotard's 'Report on Knowledge', *The Postmodern Condition* (published in French in 1979), which continued the examination of the relations between science and the aesthetic. Lyotard here emphasized the expressive dependency of scientists on aesthetic forms and narrative modes:

> scientific knowledge cannot know and make known that it is the true knowledge without resorting to the other, narrative kind of knowledge, which from its point of view is no knowledge at all. Without such recourse it would be in a position of presupposing its own validity and would be stooping to what it condemns. . . . But does it not fall into the same trap by using narrative as its authority?[31]

Lyotard's aim was to demonstrate that the realist episteme is finally at an end and with it the rule of classical science which is now unable to provide legitimating grounds for all those 'grand narratives' of Enlightenment therefore declared to be exhausted. However, he falls into contradiction himself in seeking to validate his argument through a recourse to the vocabularies and discoveries of the New Science (dating from Einstein's work on relativity and the early twentieth-century discoveries in quantum mechanics). He uses science in order to deny the hegemony of science, and to declare the aesthetic to be the only valid model of knowledge. Paradoxically, of course, Lyotard thus constructs his own grand narrative of the contemporary condition while claiming to deny the validity of either metanarratives or foundational principles.

New science, Lyotard explains, is concerned with 'undecidables, the limits of precise control, conflicts characterised by incomplete information, fracta, catastrophes, and pragmatic paradoxes' and provides the outline of a world which, in its very essence, is uncertain: 'discontinuous, catastrophic, non-rectifiable and paradoxical'.[32] In other words, he insinuates a correspondence model of knowledge into his supposedly 'postmodern argument' – the New Science curiously shares the postmodern condition in all its details of indeterminacy and undecidability. Moreover, the New Science provides a convenient legitimation for Lyotard's construction of the postmodern, for it suggests that uncertainty is not simply a consequence of the limitations of our knowledge, but is inherent in the very structure of matter. Uncertainty is the condition of our cells and of the stars above us. Indeterminacy is all. If the Newtonian universe seemed to banish for ever the relevance of our desires and humanist values, to enact a radical split between fact and value, then we can now at last find release from this bleakest of determinisms. We can now recognize that it was only one kind of scientific language game, the working out of a particular enclosed logic, and that, within the terms of the Newest Science, the universe exists in a condition of fundamental indeterminism and Uncertainty. Within this latter paradigm, Uncertainty is a consequence of qualities inherent in a cosmos in which the material world and consciousness are once again inextricably bound together, cells and stars part of a Heraclitean-style flux which for Michel Serres, for example, signals the recovery of a reconciled universe: a curious postmodern remarriage of natural theology and natural science 'where the science of things and the science of man coincide'.[33] Whereas the modern 'incertitude of the void' called forth a painful and sceptical pre-emptive Doubt, postmodern Uncertainty reassures us that we can give up worrying: for the very cosmos is radically Uncertain. Materialism is dead. We have reached reconciliation at last, and may now renounce the painful modern condition of alienation and rejoice in our unexpected postmodern discovery.

Whether or not indeterminacy is the condition of the cosmos, it has certainly infected much contemporary criticism. Lyotard's claims are familiar in the realm of modern literary theory: that we can only talk about intelligibility or value within the rules of a given system (just as Newtonian mechanics functions only in the sphere of Newtonian science and cannot be used to make predictions in the realm of sub-atomic particles). Accordingly, in literary criticism, we can no longer criticize one language game from the position of another (the incommensurability thesis). A language game there-fore gives us more knowledge of itself than of the world or the text and cannot be open to refutation except within its own terms. If there can be no 'true' system, then there can be no belief, though a system may be 'privileged' because it produces more interesting or more coherent readings than another. If language games are radically incommensurable, we may not even recog-nize another language game from the perspective inside our own. Moreover, reason is unable to overcome such radical difference. Literary criticism, like literature itself, exists in the context of a wider intellectual culture and has been experiencing its own crisis of knowledge and value since the mid-1970s. One of the effects of the crisis in knowledge has been to question the very existence of 'literature' as anything other than an 'institutionally constructed discourse'. And when there can be no agreement about the constitution of literature, then aesthetic value must also become an arena of contestation and battle. Another consequence of the crisis in knowledge is that literary criti-cism has become intensely self-conscious about its procedures and frame-works – a process which at times seems a welcome alternative to unthinking dogmatism, but at others seems like nothing so much as a frustrated cat chasing its own tail. Ironically, that criticism most eager to repudiate aes-thetic autonomy as élitist or politically incorrect may be the very same which is caught in the prisonhouse of its own self-defeating linguistic circularity. In some ways, Decadence seems to have entered our own *fin de siècle* aesthetic as much through the activity of literary criticism as through the actual writing of literature. The descriptive tags normally attached to the writers of the 1890s seem peculiarly appropriate to some of the criticism of the 1990s: narcissistic withdrawal, obsession with desire, style as the proffered solu-tion to nihilism, linguistic onanism and dandyish theatricality. We seem unable to escape a pervasive institutional self-reflexivity, a situation of *mise-en-abîme* where the problem of knowledge becomes the problem of how we talk about the problem of knowledge. In the next section, we will conclude with an examination of what this means in relation to the construc-tion of history in general and of literary history in particular.

Notes

1 Herbert Marcuse, *The Aesthetic Dimension* (Boston, Beacon Press, 1978), p. 9.
2 Max Planck, *Where is Science Going?*, tr. James Murphy (London, George Allen & Unwin, 1933).
3 John Carey, *The Faber Book of Science* (London, Faber), pp. xix, xxv.
4 Isaac Newton, *Opticks; or, A Treatise of the Reflections, Refractions, Inflections, and Colours of Light* [1730] (New York, Dover, 1952), p. 404.
5 Werner Heisenberg, quoted by Karl Popper, *The Philosophical Principles of the Quantum Theory* (London, 1930), pp. 40–1.
6 Niels Bohr, quoted in Karl Popper, *Quantum Theory and the Schism in Physics* (London, 1982), p. 40.
7 Werner Heisenberg, *Physics and Philosophy* (Harmondsworth, Penguin, 1990), p. 80.
8 C.P. Snow, *The Two Cultures*, introd. Stefan Collini (Cambridge, Cambridge University Press, 1993), p. 98.
9 Virginia Woolf, *A Room of One's Own* (London, Hogarth Press, 1928), p. 115.
10 Woolf, *To the Lighthouse*, p. 40.
11 Woolf, *To the Lighthouse*, p. 41.
12 Virginia Woolf, *Roger Fry: A Biography* (London, Hogarth Press, 1940), p. 149.
13 J. Hillis Miller, *Poets of Reality* (Cambridge, Harvard University Press, 1965), p. 3.
14 Roger Fry, *Vision and Design* (Oxford, Oxford University Press, 1981), p. 167.
15 Woolf, *To the Lighthouse*, pp. 296–7.
16 Woolf, *To the Lighthouse*, p. 236.
17 Thomas Nagel, *The View from Nowhere* (Oxford, Oxford University Press, 1986), p. 3.
18 Virginia Woolf, *The Years* (London, Pan, 1948), pp. 272–3.
19 William Empson, *Arguifying: Essays in Literature and Culture*, ed. John Haffenden (London, 1987), p. 528.
20 T.S. Eliot, *The Use of Poetry and the Use of Criticism* (London, Faber, 1964), p. 22.
21 William James, *The Meaning of Truth* (Cambridge, Harvard University Press, 1975), p. 40.
22 James Joyce, *Ulysses*, ed. Walter Gabler (Harmondsworth, Penguin, 1986).
23 Friedrich Nietzsche, *The Birth of Tragedy and the Genealogy of Morals* (New York, Archer, 1956), p. 137.
24 James Joyce, *A Portrait of the Artist as a Young Man* (Harmondsworth, Penguin, 1960), p. 247.
25 Joyce, *A Portrait of the Artist as a Young Man*, p. 215.
26 Alain Robbe-Grillet, *Snapshots and Towards a New Novel*, tr. Barbara Wright (London, Calder of Boyars, 1965), p. 83.
27 Charles Taylor, *The Sources of the Self*, see excerpt in this anthology.
28 *See* Wyndham Lewis excerpt in this anthology.
29 T.S. Eliot, 'The Social Function of Poetry', *Adelphi*, xxi (1945), p. 145.
30 Christopher Butler, *Early Modernism: Literature, Music and Painting in Europe 1900–1916* (Oxford, Clarendon Press, 1994), p. xvii.
31 Lyotard, *The Postmodern Condition*, p. 29.
32 ibid., p. 60.
33 Michel Serres, quoted in Ilya Prigogine and Isabelle Strengers, *Order out of Chaos* (London, Flamingo, 1982), pp. 304–5.

SECTION THREE

REVOLUTIONS OF THE WORD: HISTORY

Michel Foucault indicated the direction of the most recent retreat from autonomy and formalism and the return to history in *The Archaeology of Knowledge*: 'there is no knowledge without a particular discursive practice; and any discursive practice may be defined by the knowledge that it forms'.[1] We can no longer simply return to history, because history itself is now indissociable from textuality. The circularity implied by Foucault's statement sounds, again, remarkably like a postmodern variant on Wittgenstein's idea of a language game, the anti-realist reading of Heisenberg's Uncertainty Principle and the principle governing Gödel's undecidability or incompleteness theorem. In Foucault's version, history is a plurality of 'islands of discourse', a series of metaphors which cannot be detached from the institutionally produced languages which we bring to bear on it. There can be no recourse to a metanarrative outside history which allows us to establish any one narrative as the 'truth' of history. History, too, it would seem, is now also to be found incarcerated in the prisonhouse of language. In consequence, a theorist such as Jean Baudrillard has declared that 'we have exceeded the limit where, by the sophistication of events and information, history as such ceases to exist'.[2] Baudrillard regards such 'textuality' or aestheticization of history and knowledge as a banalization rather than democratization of art. He has been energetic in his prognosis of the imminent demise of both: for art, too, 'is dead, not only because its critical transcendence is gone, but because reality itself, entirely impregnated by an aesthetic which is inseparable from its own structure, has been confused with its own image'.[3] Criticism, literature, history, knowledge: are they simply to be reduced to moves in a kaleidoscope of shifting language games? The sub-title of this book includes the word 'contexts', but how can we legitimately talk of 'text' and 'context', or of literature and history, when we have learned that history can no longer be objectified as a neutral backdrop to be represented in and of itself? History cannot be an inert 'context', should not be a screen for the unselfconscious projection of present preoccupations, but then neither can we dress it up any longer in the Hegelian garb of '*Zeitgeist*': teleology has been banished too.

In a recent essay on literary theory and historical writing, Hayden White is anxious to assert some truths that modern historical theory has tended regularly to forget; these are, namely, that the 'history' which is the subject of all this learning is accessible only by way of language, that our experience of history is indissociable from our discourse about it, that this discourse must be written before it can be digested as 'history' and that this experience, therefore, can be as various as the different kinds of discourse met with in the history of writing itself.[4]

Logically, of course, Hayden White must submit his own argument to the terms of this definition, and we seem to be back in the same kind of endless linguistic circularity. If all experience and knowledge must be 'textualized', then it would seem that the revolution of the word has simply spilled outside of literature and flooded history, philosophy and science too. Everything is potentially opened up to endless textual reinscription – a condition of exhilarating possibility for confirmed postmodernists, but described by historical materialists such as the Marxist critic Perry Anderson as the wearisome and nihilistic spectacle of 'one void chasing another' in a return less to *history* than to a plurality of *theories* of history.

However, if we pause for a moment and consider the usual meaning of the word 'revolution', we may arrive at a definition in which textuality does not occupy the foreground. Revolution is usually understood as the overthrow from below of one political regime by another. In his history of the twentieth century, *The Age of Extremes*, Eric Hobsbawm reminds us that the literally violent and bloody revolutions, turbulences, wars and catastrophes of this century have expunged 'history', as it was ever understood in the past, far more effectively than any textualist 'revolution'. He writes:

> at the end of this century it has for the first time become possible to see what a world may be like in which the past, including the past in the present, has lost its role, in which the old maps and charts which guided human beings, singly and collectively, through life no longer represent the landscape through which we move, the sea on which we sail. In which we do not know where our journey is taking us, or even ought to take us.[5]

Hobsbawm's reading of twentieth-century history should serve to remind us that naïve conflations of the violence of war and political revolution with the idea of textual disruption or linguistic violation simply demean the former and may even produce a denial of the horrendous, experiential suffering and loss associated with the wars and major revolutions of this century.

The pervasive obsession with the notion of decentred subjectivity, for example, arises not simply from the impact of the philosophical critique of the Kantian concept of the universal transcendental subject, but also surely from the historical experience of exile, metropolitan dislocation, diasporas, and the spectacle, throughout the wars of this century, of bodies all too literally in bits. As a response to the hyper-sophistications of theory, this seems an obvious and banal point to make, but perhaps it should be made more often. Perhaps intellectuals should mind less about stating what 'ordinary' people know – and I make this point in defence of and not against intellectualism. In some of the linguistic idealisms that flourish at the moment, for example, is there not a tendency to assume that an event in a text is ontologically equivalent to an event in the world? A common strategy has been to regard the formal disruptions of the avant-garde text as bearing ontologically the same subversive status as existentially disruptive political action in the world outside. It does not seem to be entirely a coincidence that as the New Right spread its ever more invincible grip in the last decade, when socialism seemed confused and in retreat and praxis became a dirty word, that the dissent of literary intellectuals should express itself through a critical preference for textual constructivism, linguistic 'jouissance' or the idea of a sublime and unrepresentable otherness beyond text and history altogether. Once everything is seen to be linguistically determined, then the revolution of the word becomes inseparable from revolution of, and in, the world. As the idea of the creative deformation of language spreads from literature itself to literary criticism, analogy and causality might easily be conflated. Are the revolutions of the text and the revolutions in history categorically the same? No they are not (as Samuel Beckett might have put it).

Fredric Jameson has referred to this tendency as a pathology of auto-referentiality and described the current age of postmodernisms and new historicisms as one which 'has forgotten how to think historically'.[6] Certainly our conversations with the past have become more complex and more self-reflexive. How shall we assess this tendency? There are a number of ways in which these most recent intellectual shifts may be considered in a more positive light than this discussion has so far indicated. Historians such as Perry Anderson and Eric Hobsbawm, who tend either to ignore or to repudiate the post-structuralist turn in knowledge, are often pessimistic about the possibility of continued belief in any kind of political or aesthetic utopian redemption. Perry Anderson has even suggested that 'what marks the typical situation of the contemporary artist in the West is . . . the closure of horizons; without an appropriate past, or imaginable future, in an interminably recurrent present'.[7] Anderson senses that one effect of the supposed demise of grand narratives of history, such as the heroic Hegelian synthesis, is that the present seems locked into a frozen stasis, dismembered and disconnected from a meaningful past and unable to generate any vision of a redemptive future. If we believe history can never be more than a mirage, a story created within the available conventions and preoccupations of the present, then we risk destruction of the most productive tensions which generated modernist culture. This is the tension which we have seen so elegantly articulated in Baudelaire's description of the art of modernity: the tension between the claims of tradition and the imperative to make it new.

So Anderson describes pre-1945 modernist culture as flowering in the space 'between a still usable classical past, a still indeterminate technical present, and still unpredictable political future', but passing over, after 1945, into a period which saw the end of revolutionary hope, aristocratic tradition and any value not tied to late capitalist consumerism.[8] If Anderson detects a loss of depth, however, constructivism itself may provide a more optimistic way of assessing contemporary intellectual trends. The peculiar tensions of the present may turn out to be just as productive of aesthetic talent and vision as those of the past. Cultural and intellectual changes which represent loss or threat to the identity of a particular group or individual may offer undreamt-of possibility or liberation for others. The various new historicisms are themselves intellectual products not only of the gathering modernist crisis of knowledge, but also of the post-1945 fragmentation of consensus, the questioning of the goal of a 'common culture' and the recognition of an ever-widening cultural perspectivism as increasingly diverse social groups have sought to voice their own versions of 'tradition' and history. Salman Rushdie is only one of many writers for whom the condition of cultural hybridity, the state of translation, the fractured and continual reassemblings of identity politics, have produced new and liberating revisions of history:

'Outsider! Trespasser! You have no right to this subject!' . . . I know: nobody ever arrested me. Nor are they likely to. 'Poacher! Pirate! We reject your authority. We know you, with your foreign language wrapped around you like a flag: speaking about us in your forked tongue, what can you tell but lies?' I reply with more questions: is history to be considered the property of the participants solely? In what courts are such claims staked, what boundary commissions map out the territories?[9]

In Rushdie's novel, other dissident voices march in from the periphery of the story and complicate his account of history as they challenge the fixity of the (masculine) Logos as the foundation of the theocratic state. Throughout history, all cultures have renewed themselves through hybrid minglings and cross-fertilizations and such minglings have always produced howls of outrage from those who regard themselves as defenders of the pure. From the early 1960s onwards, different groups and individuals would seize upon metaphors of revision, rewriting and reclamation to describe their own social and cultural struggles. Increasingly, since the 1970s, the concept of representative democracy has come under strain as more and more social, ethnic and racial groups have claimed the right to speak for themselves and to write their own histories. For optimists, the ensuing fragmentation of both past and present is simply an effect of the release of opportunities for the negotiation of new historical identities and the construction of new selves and histories in a more genuinely democratic, if more separatist, culture. From this point of view, earlier Hegelian definitions of history or the Enlightenment ideal of universal knowledge are simply the imperialist myths of a western and white male leisure-class. But historians such as Perry Anderson or E.P. Thompson remained less convinced. The fragmentation of knowledge and value might simply reflect the growing narcissism of a society whose members only recognize the good as that which directly reflects their own sectarian interest, whether in literature, philosophy or political theory. In a series of articles written for *New Society* at the end of the 1970s, E.P. Thompson made his own position absolutely clear:

> We are approaching a state of anarchy, or arbitrary and unaccountable rule, in which the constitution, or political culture of the nation is being surreptitiously destroyed and where the British traditions of middle class and working class dissent have collapsed into local squabbles and fragmented identity politics.[10]

If the underlying economic divisions and organization of political power remain unchanged, then it might seem appropriate to continue to hold a sceptical attitude towards the capacity for aesthetic language games to undo authoritarian state politics or gross economic inequalities. Moreover, Thompson's fear is that the pluralization of cultural critique and intellectual and political opposition will simply further fragment the culture of dissent and render it even more confused and ineffectual.

What remains fairly constant, however, across these debates and, indeed, throughout the entire century, is some belief in art as an important means of self and social liberation. Even in a commercially aestheticized and textualized world, literary texts still provide a unique way of knowing and seeing. Paradoxically enough, what has emerged from this discussion is the sense that history is never simply text (though it is never simply *not* text either) and that literature, as a highly self-conscious mode of textuality, teaches us to recognize its own difference. To respond adequately both to literature and history must surely involve the acknowledgement that neither their understanding nor interpretation can simply be reduced to a 'relevance' which arises purely from present desire or even personal need. Modernism has taught us the value of cognitive estrangement, formal decreation, linguistic dissolution, the attempt to achieve, momentarily, the autonomy of a view from nowhere; postmodernism has provided another version of creative dislocation in its insistence on the views from marginals, outsiders, and the voices from the periphery. Exiles, heretics, parodists and echolalists, however, have been a strong feature of the literature of the entire century. They provide us with rich and complex ways of understanding our own histories.

In an essay on history and value, Frank Kermode has argued that

> so long as we seek value in the works of the past we shall be forced to submit the show of history to the desires of the mind . . . we shall invent new grids and impose them on the past – rewrite the past to suit our modern wishes.[11]

This seems an inevitable condition of our knowledge, but he goes on to argue that if we rest entirely satisfied with this relation between history and value, we may break 'the only strong link we have with the past – our ability to identify with the interests of our predecessors, to qualify their judgements without necessarily overthrowing them, to converse with them in a transhistorical dimension'.[12] In order to converse with the past, we must respect its strangeness yet still recognize a continuity in intellectual and aesthetic culture which ensures that the past is not so radically other that we cannot recognize it at all. The opening up of new perspectives on the past as a consequence of intellectual and cultural shifts in the present is one way of keeping the past alive in its strangeness, but only so long as we try to recognize other ways of seeing and knowing, including those ways in which the past tried to know itself. This requires a continuously strenuous effort: like trying to think oneself into the consciousness of a sixteenth-century scientist confronted with Copernicus' proposal that the earth revolves around the sun; or a mid-nineteenth-century Christian attempting to come to terms with the implications for creationism of Darwin's evolutionary thesis.

If the literature and intellectual culture of the twentieth century have made reality strange in order that we learn to see with new eyes, then criticism should try to preserve that sense of strangeness without resorting to a literal-minded antiquarianism as the only alternative to a cannibalistic cultural 'relevance'. This may require that we sometimes make an effort to suspend our present preoccupations, to entertain the possibility that not everything can be rewritten, and to recognize that, if we insist on so doing, we may risk confusing aesthetic with sociological knowledge and of assuming that what is important for one is equally valuable, and for the same reasons, for the other. In the end, and as scientists and philosophers of the twentieth century have also taught us, literary texts, like personal and cultural histories, always exist both inside and outside our frameworks of knowledge. Perhaps we will have to acknowledge, with Virginia Woolf, that however hard we try, and 'whether we call it life or spirit, truth or reality, this, the essential thing, has moved off, or on, and refuses to be contained any longer in such ill-fitting vestments as we provide'.[13]

Notes

1 Michel Foucault, *The Archaeology of Knowledge*, pp. 182–3; also see Chapter 1, 'The Unities of Discourse', for a full account of Foucault's position.

2 Jean Baudrillard, 'The Year Two Thousand Will Not Take Place', in *Futur Fall: Excursions into Postmodernity* (Sydney, Power Institute Publications, 1986), pp. 18–28.

3 Jean Baudrillard, *Simulations* (New York, Semiotext(e), 1983), pp. 151–2.

4 Hayden White, 'Figuring the Nature of the Times Deceased: Literary Theory and

Historical Writing', in Ralph Cohen, ed., *The Future of Literary Theory* (New York and London, Routledge, 1989), p. 19.

5 Eric Hobsbawm, *The Age of Extremes: The Short Twentieth Century 1914–1990* (London, Michael Joseph, 1994), p. 16.

6 Fredric Jameson, *Postmodernism or the Cultural Logic of Late Capitalism* (London and New York, Verso, 1991), p. ix.

7 Perry Anderson, *A Zone of Engagement* (London, Verso, 1992), p. 40.

8 Anderson, *A Zone of Engagement*, p. 36.

9 Salman Rushdie, *Shame* (London, Picador, 1983).

10 E.P. Thompson, *Writing by Candlelight* (London, 1980), p. 248.

11 Frank Kermode, *History and Value* (Oxford, Clarendon Press, 1988), p. 126.

12 Kermode, *History and Value*, p. 126.

13 Virginia Woolf, 'Modern Fiction', *Collected Essays*, vol. 2 (London, Hogarth Press, 1966), p. 105.

PART TWO

DOCUMENTS, ESSAYS, MANIFESTOS

SECTION ONE

MANIFESTOS AND PERIODIZATIONS

The essays in this section have been chosen as representative attempts to define from within some of the important literary and aesthetic interventions and movements of the century. The section begins with Baudelaire's commentary on 'The Exposition Universelle' of 1855 as one of the most influential precursors of the modernist concern with the challenge of modernity to traditional representative forms: Baudelaire confronts the problem of the relations between the 'transitory' and the 'eternal' and insists that, for the modern writer, 'the Beautiful is always strange'. His essay addresses issues which recur throughout the documents in this anthology: about tradition and innovation; the nature of modern life; the preoccupation with formal dissolution and reconstruction; and the limits of positivism. Pound's essay of 1913, as Woolf's of 1919, respectively laid the foundations for discussions of modern poetry and modern fiction. Clement Greenberg's essay 'Modernist Painting' (1961) represents a later retrospective theorization of the modernist aesthetic which he interprets as a logical extension of the critical premises of the Kantian Enlightenment: modern art constitutes a criticism from within of the very possibilities of the aesthetic medium itself. The debate between Alvarez and Conquest took place in the early 1960s after the publication of Alvarez's important anthology of 1962, *The New Poetry*, which claimed that, in the wake of two world wars, the concentration camps and the threat of nuclear disaster, poets must renounce the comforts of 'rational gentility' and espouse a new poetic of existential extremism. A sense of the explosion of a new and bewildering pluralism and the fragmentation of earlier social and aesthetic consensus is conveyed in David Lodge's essay of 1969. David Hare's 1978 piece usefully explores the dilemmas facing the political dramatist and provides an illuminating perspective from which to evaluate political theatre in the 1970s. The last three essays in this section, by Jencks (1977), Graff (1979) and Hassan (1987), represent different perspectives on postmodernism as the debate was poised to move out of the confines of aesthetic practice and into the much larger arena of cultural politics.

Charles Baudelaire
    'The Exposition Universelle'

Any reader who has been at all accustomed by solitude (far better than by books) to these vast contemplations will already have guessed the point that I am wanting to make; and, to cut across the periphrastics and hesitations of Style with a question which is almost equivalent to a formula, I will put it thus to any honest man, always provided that he has thought and travelled a little. Let him imagine a modern Winckelmann (we are full of them; the nation overflows with them; they are the idols of the lazy). What would *he* say, if faced with a product of China – something weird, strange, distorted in form, intense in colour and sometimes delicate to the point of evanescence? And yet such a thing is a specimen of universal beauty; but in order for it to be understood, it is necessary for the critic, for the spectator, to work a transformation in himself which partakes of the nature of a mystery – it is necessary for him, by means of a phenomenon of the will acting upon the imagination, to learn of himself to participate in the surroundings which have given birth to this singular flowering. Few men have the divine grace of cosmopolitanism in its entirety; but all can acquire it in different degrees. The best endowed in this respect are those solitary wanderers who have lived for years in the heart of forests, in the midst of illimitable prairies, with no other companion but their gun – contemplating, dissecting, writing. No scholastic veil, no university paradox, no academic utopia has intervened between them and the complex truth. They know the admirable, eternal and inevitable relationship between form and function. Such people do not criticize; they contemplate, they study.

If, instead of a pedagogue, I were to take a man of the world, an intelligent being, and transport him to a faraway country, I feel sure that, while the shocks and surprises of disembarkation might be great, and the business of habituation more or less long and laborious, nevertheless sooner or later his sympathy would be so keen, so penetrating, that it would create in him a whole new world of ideas, which would form an integral part of himself and would accompany him, in the form of memories, to the day of his death.[1] Those curiously-shaped buildings, which at first provoke his academic eye (all peoples are academic when they judge others, and barbaric when they are themselves judged); those plants and trees, which are disquieting for a mind filled with memories of its native land; those men and women, whose muscles do not pulse to the classic rhythms of his country, whose gait is not measured according to the

From Jonathan Mayne (ed.), *Art in Paris 1845–1862*, Phaidon, 1965, pp. 121–4.

accustomed beat, and whose gaze is not directed with the same magnetic power; those perfumes, which are no longer the perfumes of his mother's boudoir; those mysterious flowers, whose deep colour forces an entrance into his eye, while his glance is teased by their shape; those fruits, whose taste deludes and deranges the senses, and reveals to the palate ideas which belong to the sense of smell; – all that world of new harmonies will enter slowly into him, will patiently penetrate him, like the vapours of a perfumed Turkish bath; all that undreamt-of vitality will be added to his own vitality; several thousands of ideas and sensations will enrich his earthly dictionary, and it is even possible that, going a step too far and transforming justice into revolt, he will do like the converted Sicambrian[2] and burn what he had formerly adored – and adore what he had formerly burnt.

Or take one of those modern 'aesthetic pundits', as Heinrich Heine[3] calls them – Heine, that delightful creature, who would be a genius if he turned more often towards the divine. What would *he* say? what, I repeat, would *he* write if faced with such unfamiliar phenomena? The crazy doctrinaire of Beauty would rave, no doubt; locked up within the blinding fortress of his system, he would blaspheme both life and nature; and under the influence of his fanaticism, be it Greek, Italian or Parisian, he would prohibit that insolent race from enjoying, from dreaming or from thinking in any other ways but his very own. O ink-smudged science, bastard taste, more barbarous than the barbarians themselves! you that have forgotten the colour of the sky, the movement and the smell of animality! you whose wizened fingers, paralysed by the pen, can no longer run with agility up and down the immense keyboard of the universal *correspondences*![4]

Like all my friends I have tried more than once to lock myself up within a system in order to preach there at my ease. But a system is a kind of damnation which forces one to a perpetual recantation; it is always necessary to be inventing a new one, and the drudgery involved is a cruel punishment. Now my system was always beautiful, spacious, vast, convenient, neat and, above all, water-tight; at least so it seemed to me. But always some spontaneous, unexpected product of universal vitality would come to give the lie to my childish and superannuated wisdom – that lamentable child of Utopia! It was no good shifting or stretching my criterion – it always lagged behind universal man, and never stopped chasing after multiform and multi-coloured Beauty as it moved in the infinite spirals of life. Condemned unremittingly to the humiliation of a new conversion, I took a great decision. To escape from the horror of these philosophical apostasies, I haughtily resigned myself to modesty; I became content to *feel*; I returned to seek refuge in impeccable *naïveté*. I humbly beg pardon of the academics of all kinds who occupy the various workrooms of our artistic factory. But it is *there* that my philosophic conscience has found its rest; and at least I can declare – in so far as any man can answer for his virtues – that my mind now rejoices in a more abundant impartiality.

Anyone can easily understand that if those whose business it is to express beauty were to conform to the rules of the pundits, beauty itself would disappear from the earth, since all types, all ideas and all sensations would be fused in a vast, impersonal and monotonous unity, as immense as boredom or total negation. Variety, the *sine qua non* of life, would be effaced from life. So true is it that in the multiple productions of art there is an element of the ever-new which will eternally elude the rules and analyses of the school! That shock of surprise, which is one of the great joys produced by art and literature, is due to this very variety of types and sensations. The *aesthetic pundit* – a kind of mandarin-tyrant – always puts me in mind of a godless man who substitutes himself for God.

Notes

1 Baudelaire was doubtless thinking of his own experience, and of that of Delacroix and Decamps (both of whom had made early journeys, to Morocco and Turkey respectively, and had been indelibly affected by them). The 'journey to the Orient' was a classic Romantic experience.
2 I.e. Clovis.
3 In his *Salon* of 1831.
4 Miss Gilman points out that this is the first time that Baudelaire uses this important word in its full sense.

---

2 Ezra Pound
'A Retrospect'

There has been so much scribbling about a new fashion in poetry, that I may perhaps be pardoned this brief recapitulation and retrospect.

In the spring or early summer of 1912, 'H.D.', Richard Aldington and myself decided that we were agreed upon the three principles following:

1. Direct treatment of the 'thing' whether subjective or objective.

2. To use absolutely no word that does not contribute to the presentation.

3. As regarding rhythm: to compose in the sequence of the musical phrase, not in sequence of a metronome.

From T.S. Eliot (ed.), *Literary Essays of Ezra Pound*, Faber, pp. 3–7.

Upon many points of taste and of predilection we differed, but agreeing upon these three positions we thought we had as much right to a group name, at least as much right, as a number of French 'schools' proclaimed by Mr Flint in the August number of Harold Monro's magazine for 1911.

This school has since been 'joined' or 'followed' by numerous people who, whatever their merits, do not show any signs of agreeing with the second specification. Indeed *vers libre* has become as prolix and as verbose as any of the flaccid varieties that preceded it. It has brought faults of its own. The actual language and phrasing is often as bad as that of our elders without even the excuse that the words are shovelled in to fill a metric pattern or to complete the noise of a rhyme-sound. Whether or no the phrases followed by the followers are musical must be left to the reader's decision. At times I can find a marked metre in 'vers libres', as stale and hackneyed as any pseudo-Swinburnian, at times the writers seem to follow no musical structure whatever. But it is, on the whole, good that the field should be ploughed. Perhaps a few good poems have come from the new method, and if so it is justified.

Criticism is not a circumscription or a set of prohibitions. It provides fixed points of departure. It may startle a dull reader into alertness. That little of it which is good is mostly in stray phrases; or if it be an older artist helping a younger it is in great measure but rules of thumb, cautions gained by experience.

I set together a few phrases on practical working about the time the first remarks on imagisme were published. The first use of the word 'Imagiste' was in my note to T.E. Hulme's five poems, printed at the end of my 'Ripostes' in the autumn of 1912. I reprint my cautions from *Poetry* for March, 1913.

A few don'ts

An 'Image' is that which presents an intellectual and emotional complex in an instant of time. I use the term 'complex' rather in the technical sense employed by the newer psychologists, such as Hart, though we might not agree absolutely in our application.

It is the presentation of such a 'complex' instantaneously which gives that sense of sudden liberation; that sense of freedom from time limits and space limits; that sense of sudden growth, which we experience in the presence of the greatest works of art.

It is better to present one Image in a lifetime than to produce voluminous works.

All this, however, some may consider open to debate. The immediate necessity is to tabulate A LIST OF DON'TS for those beginning to write verses. I can not put all of them into Mosaic negative.

To begin with, consider the three propositions (demanding direct treatment, economy of words, and the sequence of the musical phrase), not as dogma – never consider anything as dogma – but as the result of long contemplation, which, even if it is some one else's contemplation, may be worth consideration.

Pay no attention to the criticism of men who have never themselves written a notable work. Consider the discrepancies between the actual writing of the Greek poets and dramatists, and the theories of the Graeco-Roman grammarians, concocted to explain their metres.

Language

Use no superfluous word, no adjective which does not reveal something.

Don't use such an expression as 'dim lands of *peace*'. It dulls the image. It mixes an abstraction with the concrete. It comes from the writer's not realizing that the natural object is always the *adequate* symbol.

Go in fear of abstractions. Do not retell in mediocre verse what has already been done in good prose. Don't think any intelligent person is going to be deceived when you try to shirk all the difficulties of the unspeakably difficult art of good prose by chopping your composition into line lengths.

What the expert is tired of today the public will be tired of tomorrow.

Don't imagine that the art of poetry is any simpler than the art of music, or that you can please the expert before you have spent at least as much effort on the art of verse as the average piano teacher spends on the art of music.

Be influenced by as many great artists as you can, but have the decency either to acknowledge the debt outright, or to try to conceal it.

Don't allow 'influence' to mean merely that you mop up the particular decorative vocabulary of some one or two poets whom you happen to admire. A Turkish war correspondent was recently caught red-handed babbling in his despatches of 'dove-grey' hills, or else it was 'pearl-pale', I can not remember.

Use either no ornament or good ornament.

Rhythm and rhyme

Let the candidate fill his mind with the finest cadences he can discover, preferably in a foreign language,[1] so that the meaning of the words may be less likely to divert his attention from the movement; e.g. Saxon charms, Hebridean Folk Songs, the verse of Dante, and the lyrics of Shakespeare – if he can dissociate the vocabulary from the cadence. Let him dissect the lyrics of Goethe coldly into their component sound values, syllables long and short, stressed and unstressed, into vowels and consonants.

It is not necessary that a poem should rely on its music, but if it does rely on its music that music must be such as will delight the expert.

Let the neophyte know assonance and alliteration, rhyme immediate and delayed, simple and polyphonic, as a musician would expect to know harmony and counterpoint and all the minutiae of his craft. No time is too great to give to these matters or to any one of them, even if the artist seldom have need of them.

Don't imagine that a thing will 'go' in verse just because it's too dull to go in prose.

Don't be 'viewy' – leave that to the writers of pretty little philosophic essays. Don't be descriptive; remember that the painter can describe a landscape much better than you can, and that he has to know a deal more about it.

When Shakespeare talks of the 'Dawn in russet mantle clad' he presents something which the painter does not present. There is in this line of his nothing that one can call description; he presents.

Consider the way of the scientists rather than the way of an advertising agent for a new soap.

The scientist does not expect to be acclaimed as a great scientist until he has *discovered* something. He begins by learning what has been discovered already. He goes from that point onward. He does not bank on being a charming fellow personally. He does not expect his friends to applaud the results of his freshman class work. Freshmen in poetry are unfortunately not confined to a definite and recognizable class room. They are 'all over the shop'. Is it any wonder 'the public is indifferent to poetry?'

Don't chop your stuff into separate *iambs*. Don't make each line stop dead at the end, and then begin every next line with a heave. Let the beginning of the next line catch the rise of the rhythm wave, unless you want a definite longish pause.

In short, behave as a musician, a good musician, when dealing with that phase of your art which has exact parallels in music. The same laws govern, and you are bound by no others.

Naturally, your rhythmic structure should not destroy the shape of your words, or their natural sound, or their meaning. It is improbable that, at the start, you will be able to get a rhythm-structure strong enough to affect them very much, though you may fall a victim to all sorts of false stopping due to line ends and cæsurae.

The musician can rely on pitch and the volume of the orchestra. You can not. The term harmony is misapplied in poetry; it refers to simultaneous sounds of different pitch. There is, however, in the best verse a sort of residue of sound which remains in the ear of the hearer and acts more or less as an organ-base.

A rhyme must have in it some slight element of surprise if it is to give pleasure; it need not be bizarre or curious, but it must be well used if used at all.

Vide further Vildrac and Duhamel's notes on rhyme in '*Technique Poétique*'.

That part of your poetry which strikes upon the imaginative *eye* of the reader will lose nothing by translation into a foreign tongue; that which appeals to the ear can reach only those who take it in the original.

Consider the definiteness of Dante's presentation, as compared with Milton's rhetoric. Read as much of Wordsworth as does not seem too unutterably dull.[2]

If you want the gist of the matter go to Sappho, Catullus, Villon, Heine when he is in the vein, Gautier when he is not too frigid; or, if you have not the tongues, seek out the leisurely Chaucer. Good prose will do you no harm, and there is good discipline to be had by trying to write it.

Translation is likewise good training, if you find that your original matter 'wobbles' when you try to rewrite it. The meaning of the poem to be translated can not 'wobble'.

If you are using a symmetrical form, don't put in what you want to say and then fill up the remaining vacuums with slush.

Don't mess up the perception of one sense by trying to define it in terms of another. This is usually only the result of being too lazy to find the exact word. To this clause there are possibly exceptions.

The first three simple prescriptions will throw out nine-tenths of all the bad poetry now accepted as standard and classic; and will prevent you from many a crime of production.

'. . . *Mais d'abord il faut être un poète*, as MM. Duhamel and Vildrac have said at the end of their little book, *Notes sur la Technique Poétique*.

Notes

1 This is for rhythm; his vocabulary must of course be found in his native tongue.
2 Vide infra.

---

3   Virginia Woolf
'Modern Fiction'

We have to admit that we are exacting, and, further, that we find it difficult to justify our discontent by explaining what it is that we exact. We frame our question differently at different times. But it reappears most persistently as we drop the finished novel on the crest of a sigh – Is it worth while? What is the point of it all? Can it be that, owing to one of those little

From *Collected Essays*, vol. ii, Hogarth Press, 1966, pp. 105–6, 108–10.

deviations which the human spirit seems to make from time to time, Mr. Bennett has come down with his magnificent apparatus for catching life just an inch or two on the wrong side? Life escapes; and perhaps without life nothing else is worth while. It is a confession of vagueness to have to make use of such a figure as this, but we scarcely better the matter by speaking, as critics are prone to do, of reality. Admitting the vagueness which afflicts all criticism of novels, let us hazard the opinion that for us at this moment the form of fiction most in vogue more often misses than secures the thing we seek. Whether we call it life or spirit, truth or reality, this, the essential thing, has moved off, or on, and refuses to be contained any longer in such ill-fitting vestments as we provide. Nevertheless, we go on perseveringly, conscientiously, constructing our two and thirty chapters after a design which more and more ceases to resemble the vision in our minds. So much of the enormous labour of proving the solidity, the likeness to life, of the story is not merely labour thrown away but labour misplaced to the extent of obscuring and blotting out the light of the conception. The writer seems constrained, not by his own free will but by some powerful and unscrupulous tyrant who has him in thrall, to provide a plot, to provide comedy, tragedy, love interest, and an air of probability embalming the whole so impeccable that if all his figures were to come to life they would find themselves dressed down to the last button of their coats in the fashion of the hour. The tyrant is obeyed; the novel is done to a turn. But sometimes, more and more often as time goes by, we suspect a momentary doubt, a spasm of rebellion, as the pages fill themselves in the customary way. Is life like this? Must novels be like this?

Look within and life, it seems, is very far from being 'like this'. Examine for a moment an ordinary mind on an ordinary day. The mind receives a myriad impressions – trivial, fantastic, evanescent, or engraved with the sharpness of steel. From all sides they come, an incessant shower of innumerable atoms; and as they fall, as they shape themselves into the life of Monday or Tuesday, the accent falls differently from of old; the moment of importance came not here but there; so that, if a writer were a free man and not a slave, if he could write what he chose, not what he must, if he could base his work upon his own feeling and not upon convention, there would be no plot, no comedy, no tragedy, no love interest or catastrophe in the accepted style, and perhaps not a single button sewn on as the Bond Street tailors would have it. Life is not a series of gig-lamps symmetrically arranged; life is a luminous halo, a semi-transparent envelope surrounding us from the beginning of consciousness to the end. Is it not the task of the novelist to convey this varying, this unknown and uncircumscribed spirit, whatever aberration or complexity it may display, with as little mixture of the alien and external as possible? We are not pleading merely for courage and sincerity; we are suggesting that the proper stuff of fiction is a little other than custom would have us believe it.

. . . the problem before the novelist at present, as we suppose it to have been in the past, is to contrive means of being free to set down what he chooses. He has to have the courage to say that what interests him is no longer 'this' but 'that': out of 'that' alone must he construct his work. For the moderns 'that', the point of interest, lies very likely in the dark places of psychology. At once, therefore, the accent falls a little differently; the emphasis is upon something hitherto ignored; at once a different outline of form becomes necessary, difficult for us to grasp, incomprehensible to our predecessors. No one but a modern, no one perhaps but a Russian, would have felt the interest of the situation which Tchekov has made into the short story which he calls 'Gusev'. Some Russian soldiers lie ill on board a ship which is taking them back to Russia. We are given a few scraps of their talk and some of their thoughts; then one of them dies and is carried away; the talk goes on among the others for a time, until Gusev himself dies, and looking 'like a carrot or a radish' is thrown overboard. The emphasis is laid upon such unexpected places that at first it seems as if there were no emphasis at all; and then, as the eyes accustom themselves to twilight and discern the shapes of things in a room we see how complete the story is, how profound, and how truly in obedience to his vision Tchekov has chosen this, that, and the other, and placed them together to compose something new. But it is impossible to say 'this is comic', or 'that is tragic', nor are we certain, since short stories, we have been taught, should be brief and conclusive, whether this, which is vague and inconclusive, should be called a short story at all.

. . . 'The proper stuff of fiction' does not exist; everything is the proper stuff of fiction, every feeling, every thought; every quality of brain and spirit is drawn upon; no perception comes amiss. And if we can imagine the art of fiction come alive and standing in our midst, she would undoubtedly bid us break her and bully her, as well as honour and love her, for so her youth is renewed and her sovereignty assured.

4 Clement Greenberg
'Modernist Painting'[1]

Modernism includes more than just art and literature. By now it includes almost the whole of what is truly alive in our culture. It happens, also, to be very much of a historical novelty. Western civilization is not the first to turn around and question its own foundations, but it is the civilization that has gone furthest in doing so. I identify Modernism with the intensification, almost the exacerbation, of this self-critical tendency that began with the philosopher Kant. Because he was the first to criticize the means itself of criticism, I conceive of Kant as the first real Modernist.

The essence of Modernism lies, as I see it, in the use of the characteristic methods of a discipline to criticize the discipline itself – not in order to subvert it, but to entrench it more firmly in its area of competence. Kant used logic to establish the limits of logic, and while he withdrew much from its old jurisdiction, logic was left in all the more secure possession of what remained to it.

The self-criticism of Modernism grows out of but is not the same thing as the criticism of the Enlightenment. The Enlightenment criticized from the outside, the way criticism in its more accepted sense does; Modernism criticizes from the inside, through the procedures themselves of that which is being criticized. It seems natural that this new kind of criticism should have appeared first in philosophy, which is critical by definition, but as the nineteenth century wore on it made itself felt in many other fields. A more rational justification had begun to be demanded of every formal social activity, and Kantian self-criticism was called on eventually to meet and interpret this demand in areas that lay far from philosophy.

We know what has happened to an activity like religion that has not been able to avail itself of 'Kantian' immanent criticism in order to justify itself. At first glance the arts might seem to have been in a situation like religion's. Having been denied by the Enlightenment all tasks they could take seriously, they looked as though they were going to be assimilated to entertainment pure and simple, and entertainment itself looked as though it was going to be assimilated, like religion, to therapy. The arts could save themselves from this leveling down only by demonstrating that the kind

From Francis Frascina and Charles Harrison (eds), *Modern Art and Modernism: A Critical Anthology*, Open University, Harper and Row, 1982, pp. 5–7.

[1] *Source: Art and Literature* no. 4, spring 1965, pp. 193–201. Reprinted by permission of the author.

of experience they provided was valuable in its own right and not to be obtained from any other kind of activity.

Each art, it turned out, had to effect this demonstration on its own account. What had to be exhibited and made explicit was that which was unique and irreducible not only in art in general, but also in each particular art. Each art had to determine, through the operations peculiar to itself, the effects peculiar and exclusive to itself. By doing this each art would, to be sure, narrow its area of competence, but at the same time it would make its possession of this area all the more secure.

It quickly emerged that the unique and proper area of competence of each art coincided with all that was unique to the nature of its medium. The task of self-criticism became to eliminate from the effects of each art any and every effect that might conceivably be borrowed from or by the medium of any other art. Thereby each art would be rendered 'pure', and in its 'purity' find the guarantee of its standards of quality as well as of its independence. 'Purity' meant self-definition, and the enterprise of self-criticism in the arts became one of self-definition with a vengeance.

Realistic, illusionist art had dissembled the medium, using art to conceal art. Modernism used art to call attention to art. The limitations that constitute the medium of painting – the flat surface, the shape of the support, the properties of pigment – were treated by the Old Masters as negative factors that could be acknowledged only implicitly or indirectly. Modernist painting has come to regard these same limitations as positive factors that are to be acknowledged openly. Manet's paintings became the first Modernist ones by virtue of the frankness with which they declared the surfaces on which they were painted. The Impressionists, in Manet's wake, abjured underpainting and glazing, to leave the eye under no doubt as to the fact that the colors used were made of real paint that came from pots or tubes. Cézanne sacrificed verisimilitude, or correctness, in order to fit drawing and design more explicitly to the rectangular shape of the canvas.

It was the stressing, however, of the ineluctable flatness of the support that remained most fundamental in the processes by which pictorial art criticized and defined itself under Modernism. Flatness alone was unique and exclusive to that art. The enclosing shape of the support was a limiting condition, or norm, that was shared with the art of the theater; color was a norm or means shared with sculpture as well as the theater. Flatness, two-dimensionality, was the only condition painting shared with no other art, and so Modernist painting oriented itself to flatness as it did to nothing else.

The Old Masters had sensed that it was necessary to preserve what is called the integrity of the picture plane: that is, to signify the enduring presence of flatness under the most vivid illusion of three-dimensional space. The apparent contradiction involved – the dialectical tension, to use a fashionable but apt phrase – was essential to the success of their art, as it is indeed to the success of all pictorial art. The Modernists have neither avoided nor resolved this contradiction; rather, they have reversed its terms. One is made aware of the flatness of their pictures before, instead of after, being made aware of what the flatness contains. Whereas one tends to see what is *in* an Old Master before seeing it as a picture, one sees a Modernist painting as a picture first. This is, of course, the best way of seeing any kind of picture, Old Master or Modernist, but Modernism imposes it as the only and necessary way, and Modernism's success in doing so is a success of self-criticism.

It is not in principle that Modernist painting in its latest phase has abandoned the representation of recognizable objects. What it has abandoned in principle is the representation of the kind of space that recognizable, three-dimensional objects can inhabit. Abstractness, or the non-figurative, has in itself still not proved to be an altogether necessary moment in the self-criticism of pictorial art, even though artists as eminent as Kandinsky and Mondrian have thought so. Representation, or illustration, as such does not abate the uniqueness of pictorial art; what does do so are the associations of the things represented. All recognizable entities (including pictures themselves) exist in three-dimensional space, and the barest suggestion of a recognizable entity suffices to call up associations of that kind of space. The fragmentary silhouette of a human figure, or of a teacup, will do so, and by doing so alienate pictorial space from the two-dimensionality which is the guarantee of painting's independence as an art. Three-dimensionality is the province of sculpture, and for the sake of its own autonomy painting has had above all to divest itself of everything it might share with sculpture. And it is in the course of its effort to do this, and not so much – I repeat – to exclude the representational or the 'literary', that painting has made itself abstract.

At the same time Modernist painting demonstrates, precisely in its resistance to the sculptural, that it continues tradition and the themes of tradition, despite all appearances to the contrary.

5   A. Alvarez
From *The New Poetry* (Introduction)

The only English writer who was able to face the more uncompromising forces at work in our time was D.H. Lawrence. And he was born in the working-class and spent most of his life outside England; so he had almost nothing to do with middle-class gentility. 'In those days', he wrote, 'they were always telling me I had genius as though to console me for not having their own incomparable advantages.'

But these forces I have invoked are beyond mere shell-shock and class guilt. They are general and concern us all. What, I suggest, has happened in the last half century is that we are gradually being made to realize that all our lives, even those of the most genteel and enislanded, are influenced profoundly by forces which have nothing to do with gentility, decency or politeness. Theologians would call these forces evil, psychologists, perhaps, libido. Either way, they are the forces of disintegration which destroy the old standards of civilization. Their public faces are those of two world wars, of the concentration camps, of genocide, and the threat of nuclear war.

I do not wish to over-dramatize the situation. War and cruelty have always existed, but those of the twentieth century are different in two ways. First, mass evil (for lack of a better term) has been magnified to match the scale of mass society. We no longer have local wars, we have world wars, which involve the civilians quite as deeply as the military. Where once, at worst, regiments of professional soldiers were wiped out, now whole cities go. Instead of the death of individuals, we have a mass extermination. Instead of individual torture and sadism, we have concentration camps run scientifically as death factories. The disintegration, to put it most mildly, has reached proportions which make it increasingly difficult to ignore. Once upon a time, the English could safely believe that Evil was something that happened on the Continent, or farther off, in the Empire where soldiers were paid to take care of it. To believe this now requires at best an extraordinary single-mindedness, at worst stupidity.

The second, and specifically modern difference in our attitude to the problem is this: the forcible recognition of a mass evil outside us has developed precisely parallel with psychoanalysis; that is, with our recognition of the ways in which the same forces are at work within us. One of the therapeutic purposes, for example, of Bruno Bettelheim's secret psychoanalytic observations when he was in Dachau and Buchenwald was to

From A. Alvarez, *The New Poetry*, Penguin, 1996, pp. 26–8.

educate himself into realizing how much of what went on around him expressed what went on inside himself. Another analyst has suggested that the guilt which seems to dog the refugees who escaped from Germany may in part be due to the fact that the Nazis fulfilled the deepest and most primitive drives of the refugees themselves, killing fathers, mothers, brothers, sisters and children. Be this as it may, it is hard to live in an age of psychoanalysis and feel oneself wholly detached from the dominant public savagery. In this way, at least, the makers of horror films are more in tune with contemporary anxiety than most of the English poets.

But as England was not affected by the concentration camps, so it has remained, on the whole, contemptuously impervious to psychology. Primitivism is only generally acknowledged in this country when it takes a peculiarly British form: the domestic sex murder. Then the gloating is public and universal. Had Freud been born in London instead of Vienna, he would probably have finished not in psychoanalysis but in criminology.

I am not suggesting that modern English poetry, to be really modern, must be concerned with psychoanalysis or with the concentration camps or with the hydrogen bomb or with any other of the modern horrors. I am not suggesting, in fact, that it *must* be anything. For poetry that feels it has to cope with pre-determined subjects ceases to be poetry and becomes propaganda. I am, however, suggesting that it drop the pretence that life, give or take a few social distinctions, is the same as ever, that gentility, decency and all the other social totems will eventually muddle through.

What poetry needs, in brief, is a new seriousness. I would define this seriousness simply as the poet's ability and willingness to face the full range of his experience with his full intelligence; not to take the easy exits of either the conventional response or choking incoherence. Believe in it or not, psychology has left its mark on poetry. First, the writer can no longer deny with any assurance the fears and desires he does not wish to face; he knows obscurely that they are there, however skilfully he manages to elude them. Second, having acknowledged their existence, he is no longer absolved from the need to use all his intelligence and skill to make poetic sense of them. Since Freud, the late Romantic dichotomy between emotion and intelligence has become totally meaningless.

6 Robert Conquest
From *New Lines II* (Introduction)

. . . to demand that each line or phrase should be highly charged is as if one insisted that a whole painting should consist of highlights. As Yeats has pointed out, in all except 'dream poetry' like Kubla Khan, 'certain words must be dull and numb'. And Wordsworth remarked that:

> not only the language of a large portion of every good poem, even of the most elevated character, must necessarily, except with reference to the metre, in no respect differ from that of good prose, but likewise that some of the most interesting parts of the best poems will be found to be strictly the language of prose when prose is well written. The truth of this assertion might be demonstrated by innumerable passages from almost all the poetical writings, even of Milton himself.

And yet it is clear that this 'degrading thirst after outrageous stimulation' (Wordsworth again) is common enough. Words often used in criticism to justify it are 'tension' and 'density', qualities supposed to be admirable in their own right, as who should say that Herbert is a better poet than Marlowe or Dryden. There is a spinsterish opposition to balance and proportion and in favour of 'brutal' frankness; and a demand for vigour is vulgarly satisfied by a plethora of kinaesthetic adjectives and images.

For there are those who treat verse as no more than a means of whipping up their emotions – (and increasingly, these days, not even as an aphrodisiac but rather as what one might call an areac, a drug for arousing feelings of violence). Some justify this on the grounds that verse should match the age. It is maintained, rather dubiously yet at least arguably, that our present situation is the most extreme, the most appalling that has ever existed. But even granting this, there is no reason whatever to draw from it the conclusion commonly seen, that poetry should 'reflect' it, or 'cope with' it by itself falling into violence and disproportion.

The 'reflection' is to be achieved in one or both of two ways: by writing on violent themes, or by giving the effect of violence to the structure of the verse by disrupting it in various ways. Of course, such disruption may be urged for other reasons. Obliquity, if one is to follow some critics, is itself a virtue, and their notion of modernity in verse may be essentially defined as finding a new way to be oblique. But not only modernity – individuality too. Their taste is so coarse that they cannot detect differences in style

From Robert Conquest, *New Lines II*, Macmillan, 1963, pp. xxii–xxvi.

unless they are of this gross and extreme nature. But, of course, any real reader of poetry can (for example) recognise the individuality of a Housman line even though it is couched in the most ordinary of metres and vocabularies.

To speak of proportion is not to say that it is the only quality needed in poetry. Baudelaire remarked on prosody fulfilling the 'immortels besoins de monotonie, de symétrie et de surprise': and several poets have spoken in terms of poetry needing to seem both inevitable and new. But if proportion by itself is insufficient, it is none the less necessary, and it is too often supposed that novelty is an adequate substitute.

One even comes across the impudent assertion that English poets were unaware of the existence of the darker elements in the human personality, and of large-scale suffering, until psychoanalysts and world wars drew attention to them, and this is compounded, with transparently spurious logic, by the notion that the way to cope with these forces is to abandon sanity and hope. Such, amongst others, are the pressures which attempt to direct poetry into the service of psychological needs of a type only peripherally relevant to art.

It seems both egotistical and insensitive to proclaim that the circumstances of modern life are so different from anything that has gone before that they open up hitherto unsuspected psychological depths to be exploited, or expose entirely new methods and attitudes, beyond such variation and novelty as have come in generation after generation in the past. All of us were brought up in the tradition of the supposed poetic revolution of the 1920s and 1930s. All our predilections and original partisanships were for this 'modernism'. It is only now, with the advantage perhaps of perspective, that the innovations of that time are seen to be peripheral additions to the main tradition of English poetry, in so far as they are valuable to all, and for the most part as wholly useless. It is natural for any period to over-rate the most 'contemporary', as they say in the furniture world. But such tastes are naturally ephemeral.

It has been common for at least thirty or forty years, though the point is now being put more and more noisily, to accuse and condemn British poets for 'insularity'. If all British poets remained totally ignorant of and unaffected by the foreign and classical cultures, this might well produce qualms – though one can see no reason why a particular poet could not write good poetry even under those conditions. But the charge, as usually stated, is something different. A poet like Byron was obviously not insular, in the sense that he had a familiar command of a number of foreign literatures. But he would be taken as insular nowadays, in the sense that he did not consciously seize on these to impose them on his extremely English verse. In this, I make no doubt he was entirely right.

For it is obtuse to imagine that work in other languages can simply be assimilated into English. Certain French poets are treated as suitable, indeed compulsory, influences on current English writing. The differences between French and English poetry are as great, as basic, as any in Europe. The likelihood of anyone truly assimilating a foreign language's verse is very, very low. This is not to reject French influences. On the contrary; it is to stigmatise as grotesquely arrogant and insensitive the notion that they can simply be picked up at will.

Rather more plausible, at first sight, is a not uncommon insistence that British poets have a duty to be influenced by American poetry. The crux is the same: no poet has a duty to be influenced by anyone at all, American, or French, Polish or Chinese, or even British. In any case, it is not American poetry which is really being held up as a model, but only a particular type of American poetry long notorious for obliquity of grammar, vocabulary, structure, and sense. (There is indeed a little verse being composed in Britain which is directly imitative of such American styles: but it is not on the whole highly thought of, except by some Americans to whom the addition of a slight British accent to run-of-the-mill pastiche appears to give it a touch of individuality.) It is not merely that a poet must use his own judgment, and not someone else's; that influences cannot just be meaningfully absorbed by an effort of will. It is equally true that the human condition from which the poetry of one country springs cannot be readily tapped by that of another. The British culture is receptive to immigration, if not to invasion: but it remains highly idiosyncratic. It is part of our experience, and for that no one else's experience, however desirable, can be a substitute.

---

7   David Lodge
'The Novelist at the Crossroads'

We seem, indeed, to be living through a period of unprecedented cultural pluralism which allows, in all the arts, an astonishing variety of styles to flourish simultaneously. Though they are in many cases radically opposed on aesthetic and epistemological grounds, no one style has managed to become dominant. In this situation, the critic has to be very fast on his feet. He is not, of course, obliged to like all the styles equally, but he must avoid the cardinal error of judging one style by criteria appropriate to another. He

From Malcolm Bradbury (ed.), *The Novel Today*, Fontana, 1977, pp. 100–2, 105–6, 108–10.

needs what Mr Scholes calls 'a highly discriminated sense of genre'. For the practising artist, however, the existence of a bewildering plurality of styles presents problems not so easily solved; and we should not be surprised that many contemporary writers manifest symptoms of extreme insecurity, nervous self-consciousness and even at times a kind of schizophrenia.

The situation of the novelist today may be compared to a man standing at a crossroads. The road on which he stands (I am thinking primarily of the English novelist) is the realistic novel, the compromise between fictional and empirical modes. In the fifties there was a strong feeling that this was the main road, the central tradition, of the English novel, coming down through the Victorians and Edwardians, temporarily diverted by modernist experimentalism, but subsequently restored (by Orwell, Isherwood, Greene, Waugh, Powell, Angus Wilson, C.P. Snow, Amis, Sillitoe, Wain, etc., etc.) to its true course. That wave of enthusiasm for the realistic novel in the fifties has, however, considerably abated. For one thing, the novelty of the social experience the fiction of that decade fed on – the break-up of a bourgeois-dominated class society – has faded. More important, the literary theorizing behind the 'Movement' was fatally thin. For example, C.P. Snow:

> Looking back, we can see what an odd affair the 'experimental' novel was. To begin with, the 'experiment' stayed remarkably constant for thirty years. Miss Dorothy Richardson was a great pioneer, so were Virginia Woolf and Joyce: but between *Pointed Roofs* in 1915 and its successors, largely American, in 1945, there was no significant development. In fact there could not be; because this method, the essence of which was to represent brute experience through the moments of sensation, effectively cut out precisely those aspects of the novel where a living tradition can be handed on. Reflection had to be sacrificed; so did moral awareness; so did the investigatory intelligence. That was altogether too big a price to pay and hence the 'experimental novel' . . . died from starvation, because its intake of human stuff was so low.

Or Kingsley Amis:

> The idea about experiment being the life-blood of the English novel is one that dies hard. 'Experiment', in this context, boils down pretty regularly to 'obtruded oddity', whether in construction – multiple viewpoints and such – or in style; it is not felt that adventurousness in subject matter or attitude or tone really counts. Shift from one scene to the next in mid-sentence, cut down on verbs or definite articles, and you are putting yourself right up in the forefront, at any rate in the eyes of those who were reared on Joyce and Virginia Woolf and take a jaundiced view of more recent developments.

Simply as literary history, Snow's comment does not survive the most cursory examination (no development between *A Portrait of the Artist* and

Finnegans Wake? Between *Pointed Roofs* and *The Sound and the Fury*?). Amis's has a certain satiric force and cogency, and is aimed at a more vulnerable target, but that kind of 'cultivated Philistinism', refreshing in its time, could not be maintained indefinitely, even by Amis, let alone anyone else.

Realistic novels continue to be written – it is easy to forget that most novels published in England still fall within this category – but the pressure of scepticism on the aesthetic and epistemological premises of literary realism is now so intense that many novelists, instead of marching confidently straight ahead, are at least considering the two routes that branch off in opposite directions from the crossroads. One of these routes leads to the non-fiction novel, and the other to what Mr Scholes calls 'fabulation'.

There are indeed good reasons for anticipating with something less than enthusiasm the disappearance of the novel and its replacement by the non-fiction novel of fabulation. Especially to anyone whose imagination has been nourished by the great realistic novelists of the past, both these side roads will seem to lead all too easily into desert or bog – self-defeating banality or self-indulgent excess. Yet, as I have already suggested, there are formidable discouragements to continuing serenely along the road of fictional realism. The novelist who has any kind of self-awareness must at least hesitate at the crossroads; and the solution many novelists have chosen in their dilemma is to *build their hesitation into the novel itself*. To the novel, the non-fiction novel, and the fabulation, we must add a fourth category: the novel which exploits more than one of these modes without fully committing itself to any, the novel-about-itself, the trick-novel, the game-novel, the puzzle-novel, the novel that leads the reader (who wishes, naïvely, only to be told what to believe) through a fairground of illusions and deceptions, distorting mirrors and trap-doors that open disconcertingly under his feet, leaving him ultimately not with any simple or reassuring message or meaning but with a paradox about the relation of art to life.

This kind of novel, which I shall call the 'problematic novel', clearly has affinities with both the non-fiction novel and fabulation, but it remains distinct precisely because it brings both into play. Mr Scholes's fabulators, for instance, play tricks on their readers, expose their fictive machinery, dally with aesthetic paradoxes, in order to shed the restricting conventions of realism, to give themselves freedom to invent and manipulate. In the kind of novel I am thinking of, however, the reality principle is never allowed to lapse entirely – indeed, it is often invoked, in the spirit of the non-fiction novel, to expose the artificiality of conventional realistic illusion. Whereas the fabulator is impatient with 'reality', and the non-fiction novelist is impatient with fiction, the kind of novelist I am talking about retains a loyalty to both, but lacks the orthodox novelist's confidence in the possibility of reconciling them. He makes the difficulty of his task, in a sense, his subject.

If the case for realism has any ideological content it is that of liberalism. The aesthetics of compromise go naturally with the ideology of compromise, and it is no coincidence that both are under pressure at the present time. The non-fiction novel and fabulation are *radical* forms which take their impetus from an extreme reaction to the world we live in – *The Armies of the Night* and *Giles Goat-boy* are equally products of the apocalyptic imagination. The assumption behind such experiments is that our 'reality' is so extraordinary, horrific or absurd that the methods of conventional realistic imitation are no longer adequate. There is no point in carefully creating fiction that gives an illusion of life when life itself seems illusory. (This argument, interestingly, was used by the Marquis de Sade, writing at the time of the French Revolution, to explain the Gothic novel and, by implication, his own pornographic contributions to the genre.) Art can no longer compete with life on equal terms, showing the universal in the particular. The alternatives are either to cleave to the particular – to 'tell it like it is' – or to abandon history altogether and construct pure fictions which reflect in an emotional or metaphorical way the discords of contemporary experience.

The realist – and liberal – answer to this case must be that while many aspects of contemporary experience encourage an extreme, apocalyptic response, most of us continue to live most of our lives on the assumption that the reality which realism imitates actually exists. History may be, in a philosophical sense, a fiction, but it does not feel like that when we miss a train or somebody starts a war. We are conscious of ourselves as unique, historic individuals, living together in societies by virtue of certain common assumptions and methods of communication; we are conscious that our sense of identity, of happiness and unhappiness, is defined by small things as well as large; we seek to adjust our lives, individually and communally, to some order or system of values which, however, we know is always at the mercy of chance and contingency. It is this sense of reality which realism imitates; and it seems likely that the latter will survive as long as the former.

Writing in 1939, at the beginning of the Second World War, George Orwell voiced many of the doubts about the future of the novel reviewed in this essay. The novel, he said in 'Inside the Whale', was inextricably tied up with liberal individualism and could not survive the era of totalitarian dictatorships he saw ahead. In his appreciation of Henry Miller's *Tropic of Cancer* he seems to endorse the confessional non-fiction novel as the only viable alternative ('Get inside the whale . . . Give yourself over to the world process, stop fighting against it or pretending you control it, simply accept it, endure it, record it. That seems to be the formula that any sensitive novelist is likely to adopt.') Orwell's prophecy was, however, incorrect. Shortly after the War there was a significant revival of the realistic novel in England, inspired partly by Orwell's own fiction of the thirties; and although none of this fiction is of the very first rank, it is not an inconsiderable body of work. Many of the most talented post-war American novelists – John Updike, Saul Bellow, Bernard Malamud and Philip Roth, for example – have worked, for the most part, within the conventions of realistic fiction. Obsequies over the novel may be as premature today as they were in 1939.

8   David Hare
'On Political Theatre'

For this is an austere and demanding medium. It is a place where the playwright's ultimate sincerity and good faith is going to be tested and judged in a way that no other medium demands. As soon as a word is spoken on stage it is tested. As soon as a line is put into the reconstruction of a particular event, it will be judged. In this way the theatre is the exact opposite art to journalism; the bad journalist throws off a series of casual and half-baked propositions, ill-considered, dashed-off, entertainment pieces to put forward a point of view which may or may not amuse, which may or may not be lasting, which may or may not be true; but were he once to hear those same words spoken out loud in a theatre he would begin to feel that terrible chill of being collectively judged and what had seemed light and trenchant and witty would suddenly seem flip and arch and silly.

Judgement. Judgement is at the heart of the theatre. A man steps forward and informs the audience of his intention to lifelong fidelity to his wife, while his hand, even as he speaks, drifts at random to the body of another woman. The most basic dramatic situation you can imagine; the gap between what he says and what we see him to be opens up, and in that gap we see something that makes theatre unique: that it exposes the difference between what a man says and what he does. That is why nothing on stage is so exciting as a great lie; why *Brassneck* never recovers as a play after its greatest liar is killed off at the end of the first act.

I would suggest crudely that one of the reasons for the theatre's possible authority, and for its recent general drift towards politics, is its unique suitability to illustrating an age in which men's ideals and men's practice bear no relation to each other; in which the public profession of, for example, socialism has often been reduced by the passage of history to wearying personal fetish, or even chronic personality disorder. The theatre

From *The Early Plays*, Faber, 1992, pp. 2–3, 5–10.

is the best way of showing the gap between what is said and what is seen to be done, and that is why, ragged and gap-toothed as it is, it has still a far healthier potential than some of the other, poorer, abandoned arts.

Must it always be, however, that Marxist drama set in Europe reflects the state of revolutionary politics with an answering sluggishness of its own? By this, I mean, that sinking of the heart when you go to a political play and find that the author really believes that certain questions have been answered even before the play has begun. Why do we so often have to endure the demeaning repetition of slogans which are seen not as transitional aids to understanding, but as ultimate solutions to men's problems? Why the insulting insistence in so much political theatre that a few gimcrack mottoes of the Left will sort out the deep problems of reaction in modern England? Why the urge to caricature? Why the deadly stiffness of limb? Brecht uncoils the great sleeping length of his mind to give us, in everything but the greatest of his writing, exactly that impression, the godlike feeling that the questions have been answered before the play has begun. Even his idea of irony is unsufferably coy. He parades it, he hangs it out to dry as if it were proof of the broadness of his mind. It should not need such demonstration.

I do understand the thinking. The Marxist playwright working in a fairly hostile medium, feels that his first job is to declare his allegiance, to show his hand if you like. He thinks that because the play itself is part of the class struggle, he must first say which side he is on and make that clear, before he proceeds to lay out the ideas of the play as fairly as he may. To me this approach is rubbish, it insults the audience's intelligence; more important it insults their experience; most important it is also a fundamental misunderstanding of what a play is. A play is not actors, a play is not a text; a play is what happens between the stage and the audience. A play is a performance. So if a play is to be a weapon in the class struggle, then that weapon is not going to be the things you are saying; it is the interaction of what you are saying and what the audience is thinking. The play is in the air. The woman in the balcony who yelled out during the famous performance of *Othello*, 'Can't you see what he's going to do, you stupid black fool?' expressed the life of that play better than any writer I ever knew; and understood the nature of performance better than the slaves of Marxist fashion.

I think that it is in some way to avoid this uncomfortable fact that dramatists have lately taken to brandishing their political credentials as frequently as possible throughout their work, and that political theatre groups have indulged in such appalling overkill, in some way to stave off failure with an audience; to flaunt your sincerity, to assert and re-assert a simple scaffolding of belief in order not to face the real and unpredictable dangers of a genuinely live performance is all a way of not being judged. It is understandable, but it is wrong. It is in no way as craven as the scaffolding you will find in West End theatres, the repeated reassurances to the audience that narrow lives are the only lives worth leading; nor in my mind is it in any way as poisonous as the upper-middle-brow, intellectual comedies which have become the snob fashion of the day, meretricious structures full of brand references to ideas at which people laugh in order to prove that they have heard of them; the pianola of chic which tinkles night and day in Shaftesbury Avenue, and which is thought to be real music in the smart Sunday papers. The English theatre loves the joker, the detached observer, the man who stands outside; no wonder, faced with this ubiquity of tat, that political theatre tends to be strident and unthinking, not in its attitude to its content, but in its distrust of the essential nature of performance itself.

When I first wrote, I wrote in the present day, I believed in a purely contemporary drama; so as I headed backwards, I worried I was avoiding the real difficulties of the day. It took me time to realize that the reason was, if you write about now, just today and nothing else, then you seem to be confronting only stasis, but if you begin to describe the undulations of history, if you write plays that cover passages of time, then you begin to find a sense of movement, of social change, if you like; and the facile hopelessness that comes from confronting the day and only the day, the room and only the room, begins to disappear and in its place the writer can offer a record of movement and change.

You will see what I am arguing. The Marxist writer spends a great deal of time rebuking societies for not behaving in the way that he expected them to; but also, furious because change is not taking the form he would like it to, he denigrates or ignores the real changes which have taken place in the last thirty years. A great empire falls apart, offering, as it collapses, a last great wash of wealth through this country, unearned, unpaid for, a shudder of plenty, which has dissolved so many of the rules which kept the game in order; while intellectuals grope wildly for an answer, any answer to the moral challenge of collectivism, the citizens have spent and spent, after the war in time of wealth, but recently in a time of encroaching impoverishment. We are living through a great, groaning, yawling festival of change – but because this is England it is not always seen on the streets. In my view it is seen in the extraordinary intensity of people's personal despair, and it is to that despair that as a historical writer I choose to address myself time and time again: in *Teeth 'n' Smiles*, in *Knuckle*, in *Plenty*.

I feel exactly as Tom Wolfe does in a marvellous account of his opportunities as a writer:

About the time I came to New York . . . the most serious novelists abandoned the richest terrain of the novel: namely, society, the social tableau, manners and morals, the whole business of the 'way we live now'. There is no novelist who captures the sixties in America or even in New York in the same sense that Thackeray was the chronicler of London in the 1840s and Balzac was the chronicler of Paris and all of France . . . That was marvellous for journalists, I tell you that. The sixties were one of the most extraordinary decades in American history in terms of manners and morals. Manners and morals *were* history in the sixties. I couldn't believe the scene I saw spread out before me. But what really amazed me as a writer I had it practically all to myself . . . As fast as I could possibly do it, I was turning out articles on this amazing spectacle I saw bubbling and screaming right there . . . and all the while I knew that some enterprising novelist was going to come along and *do* the whole marvellous scene in one gigantic bold stroke. It was so ready, so ripe – beckoning . . . and it never happened.

I can't tell you how accurately that expresses a feeling I have always had as a playwright and which I know colleagues have experienced, that sense that the greater part of the culture is simply looking at the wrong things. I became a writer by default, to fill in the gaps, to work on the areas of the fresco which were simply ignored, or appropriated for the shallowest purposes: rock music, black propaganda, gun-selling, diplomacy. And yet I cannot believe to this day that a more talented writer will not come along and *do* the whole scene. In common with other writers who look with their own eyes, I have been abused in the newspapers for being hysterical, strident and obscene, when all I was doing was observing the passing scene, its stridency, its hysteria, its obscenity, and trying to put it in a historical context which the literary community seems pathologically incapable of contemplating. In *Teeth 'n' Smiles* a girl chooses to go to prison because it will give her an experience of suffering which is bound in her eyes to be more worthwhile than the life she could lead outside: not one English critic could bring himself to mention this central event in the play, its plausibility, its implications. It was beyond their scope to engage with such an idea. And yet, how many people here have close friends who have taken control of their own lives, only to destroy them?

We are drawing close, I think, to what I hope a playwright can do. He can put people's sufferings in a historical context; and by doing that, he can help to explain their pain. But what I mean by history will not be the mechanized absolving force theorists would like it to be; it will be those strange uneasy factors that make a place here and nowhere else, make a time now and no other time. A theatre which is exclusively personal, just a place of private psychology, is inclined to self-indulgence; a theatre which is just social is inclined to unreality, to the impatient blindness I've talked about today. Yeats said, out of our quarrel with others, we make rhetoric, while out of our quarrel with ourselves, we make poetry. I value both, and value the theatre as a place where both are given weight.

I write love stories. Most of my plays are that. Over and over again I have written about romantic love, because it never goes away. And the view of the world it provides, the dislocation it offers, is the most intense experience that many people know on earth.

And I write comedy because . . . such ideas as the one I have just uttered make me laugh.

And I write about politics because the challenge of communism, in however debased and ugly a form, is to ask whether the criteria by which we have been brought up are right; whether what each of us experiences uniquely really is what makes us valuable; whether every man should really be his own cocktail; or whether our criteria could and should be collective, and if they were, whether we would be any happier. However absolute the sufferings of men in the totalitarian Soviet countries, however decadent the current life of the West, the fact is that this question has only just been asked, and we have not even the first hundredth of an answer. To give up now would be death.

---

9   Charles Jencks
From *The Language of Post-Modern Architecture*

A Radical Eclecticism would include areas of extreme simplicity and reduction, not only for their contrast in space, but also because of a dialectic in meaning over time. As opposed to the theory of Modernism, however, this reduction would never be more than momentary, or situational, depending on the particular context. It would be motivated by the original Greek meaning of eclectic – 'I select' – and follow the basically sensible course of selecting from all possible sources those elements which were most useful or pertinent *ad hoc*.

In a studio building on Cape Cod for instance, I selected elements from the existing vernacular, from traditional shingle construction and a basic catalogue of prefabricated building parts. The selection was a mixture of new and old, traditional balusters and modern pivot windows – all of which was local to the area and easy to build. The basic shell was a prefabricated garage (although finally hand-built) and the garage door was the cheapest way to get a large, framed opening (and the effect of a *baldacchino*). Since all the basic choices were absolutely minimal, inexpensive and based on builder's vernacular, the majority of the money could be

From Charles Jencks, *The Language of Post-Modern Architecture*, 5th edition, Academy Editions, 1987, pp. 128–32.

spent on articulation, on changing levels, and painting harmonic colour combinations. I wouldn't claim this studio as a model of Radical Eclecticism – the program was too limited for one thing – but it does have the mixture of languages and can be read by the local inhabitants (for instance those who built it while I wasn't there).

There are, I think, no completely convincing examples of Radical Eclecticism in existence, besides the venerable buildings of Antonio Gaudí; just hints of what it might be adumbrated by designers such as Bruno Reichlin in Switzerland, or Thomas Gordon Smith in California. In general, however, some of its aspects have now clarified.

Unlike Modernism it makes use of the full spectrum of communicational means – metaphorical and symbolic as well as spatial and formal. Like traditional eclecticism it selects the right style, or subsystem, where it is appropriate – but a Radical Eclecticism mixes these elements within one building. Thus the semantic overtones to each style are mapped to their closest functional equivalents – for instance in Thomas G. Smith's work the entrance and porch are given classical formality whereas the sides are in the vernacular of the region.

The examples cited are just individual houses and therefore too restricted in their coding and breadth of expression. At the present time a larger model is needed, greater in scope and urban – for instance an apartment house in the inner city, which could take into account the existing local codes.

Theoretically at least several of the key issues are clear. One must start by defining a basic opposition in coding between the inhabitant and professional, perhaps taking as one departure point Basil Bernstein's fundamental distinction between 'restricted' and 'elaborated' codes.[1] . . . [T]he varying codes based on semiotic groups may not be determined by class alone, but are usually a complex mixture of ethnic background, age, history and locale. The designer should logically start with an investigation of the semiotic group and always keep in his mind the varying views of the good life as seen by the people involved since architecture ultimately signifies a way of life – something not entirely understood by the Modern Movement. The training necessary for this needn't entail a degree in anthropology. Common sense, a willingness to understand the client's background plus a certain appreciation of etiquette can suffice. Social research may help. Sympathy and constant consultation are minimum requirements. The difficulty is that since continuous traditions have been broken, and the profession has its own language and ideology, one cannot assume a commonalty of values and architectural language, so an inevitable self-conscious theory must suffice to link this duality.

In any case, the designer should first study the area, the language of the tribe, and understand it fully before designing. The language may have an ethnic or cultural dimension based on the background of the inhabitants and also a purely architectural dimension – the vernacular (which has usually been disrupted, but elements of which usually exist). The kinds of thing that can be said in this traditional language will conserve the values of the local group. Indeed such a conservative approach is the *sine qua non* for any urban development, for the reasons that preservations, the 'contextualists' and Conrad Jameson advance. But this traditional base does not exhaust the questions as they sometimes argue.

In several studies concerning the way architecture is perceived I've found an underlying schizophrenia in interpretations which, I believe, parallels the essentially dual nature of the architectural language.[2] Generally speaking there are two codes, a popular, traditional one which like spoken language is slow-changing, full of clichés and rooted in family life, and secondly a modern one full of neologisms and responding to quick changes in technology, art and fashion as well as the avant-garde of architecture. One code is likely to be preferred by any individual, but quite likely both, contradictory codes exist in the same person. Since an architect is, by profession and daily work, necessarily responsive to fast-changing codes – and these of course include literal building codes – one can see why he has been alienated from the slow-changing languages, and Modernism has had such an ideological hold on his mind. It simplified his problem considerably to a professional one of communication between specialists. Architectural conferences and magazines necessarily celebrate specialist values, and architecture as an art addresses itself to an even smaller elite, the 'happy few' who are concerned to make subtle distinctions and perpetuate the art – not a minor achievement. Since there is an unbridgeable gap between the elite and popular codes, the professional and traditional values, the modern and vernacular language, and since there is no way to abolish this gap without a drastic curtailment in possibilities, a totalitarian manoeuvre, it seems desirable that architects recognise the schizophrenia and code their buildings on two levels. Partly this will parallel the 'high' and 'low' versions of classical architecture, but it will not be, as that was, an homogeneous language. Rather the double coding will be eclectic and subject to the heterogeneity that makes up any large city. Partly this is the 'inclusivism' that Venturi, Stern and Moore call for, but in addition it asks for more precise local or traditional coding than they have yet undertaken. Their work still gives priority to esoteric, fast-changing codes and treats traditional ones, often, as an opportunity for historical allusion.

Radical Eclecticism by contrast starts design from the tastes and languages prevailing in any one place and overcodes architecture (with many redundant cues) so that it can be understood and enjoyed by different taste cultures – both the inhabitants and the elite. Although it starts from these codes, it doesn't necessarily use them to send the expected messages, or ones which simply confirm the existing values. In this sense it is both contextual and dialectical, attempting to set up a discourse between different and often opposed taste cultures.

Although it is generated in participation with those who will use the building, it transcends their goals and may even criticise them. For these contrasting reasons it can be read on at least two quite distinct levels telling parallel stories which may or may not be consistent, depending on the context and building involved.

Finally Radical Eclecticism is multivalent, as against so much Modern architecture: it pulls together different kinds of meaning, which appeal to opposite faculties of the mind and body, so that they interrelate and modify each other. The taste of the building, its smell and touch, engage the sensibility as much as does the sight and contemplation. In a perfectly successful work of architecture – that of Gaudí – the meanings add up and work together in the deepest combination. We aren't there yet, but a tradition is growing which dares make this demand for the future.

Notes

1 See Basil Bernstein, *Class, Codes and Control*, vols. I & II, London, 1971–3 and Linda Clarke, 'Explorations into the nature of environmental codes', *Journal of Architectural Research*, vol. 3, no. 1, 1974.

2 The studies are admittedly very fragmentary and made with students in England, Norway and California, although several interviews at buildings were conducted in England and Holland. One study has been published, 'A Semantic Analysis of Stirling's Olivetti Centre Wing', in *AAQ*, vol. 6, no. 2, 1974, and part of another is included in my 'Architectural Sign' published in *Signs, Symbols and Architecture*, the anthology edited by Richard Bunt, Geoffrey Broadbent and myself. Supporting evidence can be found in B. Bernstein, *op. cit.* and Philip Boudon, *Lived-in Architecture: Le Corbusier's Pessac Revisited*, London, 1972, pp. 46, 65, 112.

---

10 Gerald Graff
From *Literature Against Itself*

The two postmodernisms

In carrying the logic of modernism to its extreme limits, postmodern literature poses in an especially acute fashion the critical problem raised

From Gerald Graff, *Literature Against Itself*, University of Chicago Press, 1979, pp. 55–8.

by all experimental art: does this art represent a criticism of the distorted aspects of modern life or a mere addition to it? Georg Lukács has argued persuasively that the successful presentation of distortion as such presupposes the existence of an undistorted norm. 'Literature,' he writes, 'must have a concept of the normal if it is to "place" distortion correctly, that is to say, to see it *as* distortion.'[1] If life were really a solipsistic madness, we should have no means of knowing this fact or representing it. But once the concept of the normal is rejected as a vestige of an outmoded metaphysics or patronized as a myth, the concepts of 'distortion' and 'madness' lose their meanings. This observation provides a basis for some necessary distinctions between tendencies in postmodern writing.

In Jorge Luis Borges's stories, for example, techniques of reflexiveness and self-parody suggest a universe in which human consciousness is incapable of transcending its own mythologies. This condition of imprisonment, however, though seen from the 'inside,' is presented from a tragic or tragicomic point of view that forces us to see it *as* a problem. The stories generate a pathos at the absence of a transcendent order of meanings. As Borges's narrator in 'The Library of Babel' declares, 'Let heaven exist, though my place be in hell. Let me be outraged and annihilated, but for one instant, in one being, let Your enormous Library be justified.'[2] The library contains all possible books and all possible interpretations of experience but none which can claim authority over the others; therefore, it cannot be 'justified.' Nevertheless, Borges affirms the indispensable nature of justification. As in such earlier writers as Kafka and Céline, the memory of a significant external reality that would justify human experience persists in the writer's consciousness and serves as his measure of the distorted, indeterminate world he depicts. Borges's kind of postmodern writing, even in presenting solipsistic distortion as the only possible perspective, nevertheless presents this distortion *as* distortion – that is, it implicitly affirms a concept of the normal, if only as a concept which has been tragically lost. The comic force of characters like 'Funes the Memorious' and of solipsistic worlds such as those of 'Tlön, Uqbar, Orbis Tertius' lies in the crucial fact that Borges, for all his imaginative sympathy, is *not* Funes, is not an inhabitant of Tlön, and is thus able to view the unreality of their worlds as a predicament. His work retains a link with traditional classical humanism by virtue of its sense of the pathos of this humanism's demise. The critical power of absence remains intact, giving Borges a perspective for judging the unreality of the present. His work affirms the sense of reality in a negative way by dramatizing its absence as a deprivation.

Whatever tendency toward subjectivism these Borges works may contain is further counteracted by their ability to suggest the historical and social causes of this loss of objective reality. Borges invites us to see the solipsistic plight of his characters as a consequence of the relativistic thrust of modern philosophy and modern politics. If reality has yielded to the myth-making of Tlön, as he suggests it has, 'the truth is that it longed to yield.' The mythologies of 'dialectical materialism, anti-Semitism, Nazism' were sufficient 'to entrance the minds of men.'[3] The loss of reality is made intelligible to the reader as an aspect of a social and historical evolution. At its best, the contemporary wave of self-reflexive fiction is not quite so totally self-reflexive as it is taken to be, since its very reflexivity implies a 'realistic' comment on the historical crisis which brought it about. Where such a comment is made, the conventions of anti-realism subserve a higher realism. Often, however, this fiction fails to make its reflexivity intelligible as a consequence of any recognizable cause. Estrangement from reality and meaning becomes detached from the consciousness of its causes – as in the more tediously claustrophobic and mannered experiments of Barthelme and the later Barth. Even in these works, however, the loss of reality and meaning is seen as a distortion of the human condition.

Far different is the attitude expressed in the more celebratory forms of postmodernism. Here there is scarcely any memory of an objective order of values in the past and no regret over its disappearance in the present. Concepts like 'significant external reality' and 'the human condition' figure only as symbols of the arbitrary authority and predetermination of a repressive past, and their disappearance is viewed as liberation. Dissolution of ego boundaries, seen in tragic postmodern works like *Invitation to a Beheading* as a terrifying disintegration of identity, is viewed as a bracing form of consciousness-expansion and a prelude to growth. Both art and the world, according to Susan Sontag, simply *are*. 'Both need no justification; nor could they possibly have any.'[4] The obsessive quest for justification which characterizes Borges's protagonists is thus regarded, if it is noticed at all, as a mere survival of outmoded thinking.

It is symptomatic of the critical climate that Borges has been widely read as a celebrant of apocalyptic unreality. Borges's current celebrity is predicated to a large degree on a view that sees him as a pure fabulator revelling in the happy indistinguishability of truth and fiction. Richard Poirier, for example, urges us in reading Borges to get rid of 'irrelevant distinctions between art and life, fiction and reality.'[5] But if distinctions between fiction and reality were really irrelevant, Borges's work would be pointless.

But then, in a world which simply *is*, pointlessness is truth. There is no ground for posing the question of justification as a question. We can no longer even speak of 'alienation' or 'loss' of perspective, for there never was anything to be alienated from, never any normative perspective to be lost. The realistic perspective that gives shape and point to works of tragicomic postmodernism, permitting them to present distortion *as* distortion, gives way to a celebration of *energy* – the vitalism of a world that cannot be understood or controlled. We find this celebration of energy in the poetry of the Beats, the 'Projective' poets, and other poetic continuators of the nativist line of Whitman, Williams, and Pound, in the short-lived vogue of the Living Theater, happenings, and pop art, and in a variety of artistic and musical experiments with randomness and dissonance. It is also an aspect of the writing of Mailer, Burroughs, and Pynchon, where despite the suggestion of a critical or satiric point of view, the style expresses a facile excitement with the dynamisms of technological process. Richard Poirier states the rationale for this worship of energy, making energy and literature synonymous: 'Writing is a form of energy not accountable to the orderings anyone makes of it and specifically not accountable to the liberal humanitarian values most readers want to find there.[6] Literature, in short, is closer to a physical force than to an understanding or 'criticism of life,' both of which are tame and bourgeois. This celebration of energy frequently seems to hover somewhere between revolutionary politics and sophisticated acquiescence to the agreeably meaningless surfaces of mass culture.

Notes

1 Georg Lukács, *The Meaning of Contemporary Realism*, trans. J. and N. Mander (London, Merlin Press, 1963), p.33.
2 Jorge Luis Borges, *Labyrinths: Selected Stories and Other Writings*, trans. J. Irby (New York, New Directions, 1964), p. 57.
3 Ibid., p. 17.
4 Sontag, *Against Interpretation*, p. 27.
5 Poirier, *The Performing Self*, p. 40.
6 Ibid.

11 Ihab Hassan
'Toward a Concept of Postmodernism'

My point here is double: in the question of postmodernism, there is a will and counter-will to intellectual power, an imperial desire of the mind, but this will and desire are themselves caught in a historical moment of supervention, if not exactly of obsolescence. The reception or denial of postmodernism thus remains contingent on the psychopolitics of academic life – including the various dispositions of people and power in our universities, of critical factions and personal frictions, of boundaries that arbitrarily

From Thomas Doherty (ed.), *Reader in Postmodernism*, Harvester, 1993, pp. 148–52.

include or exclude – no less than on the imperatives of the culture at large. This much, reflexivity seems to demand from us at the start.

But reflection demands also that we address a number of conceptual problems that both conceal and constitute postmodernism itself. I shall try to isolate ten of these, commencing with the simpler, moving toward the more intractable.

1. The word postmodernism sounds not only awkward, uncouth; it evokes what it wishes to surpass or suppress, modernism itself. The term thus contains its enemy within, as the terms romanticism and classicism, baroque and rococo, do not. Moreover, it denotes temporal linearity and connotes belatedness, even decadence, to which no postmodernist would admit. But what better name have we to give this curious age? The Atomic, or Space, or Television Age? These technological tags lack theoretical definition. Or shall we call it the Age of Indetermanence (indeterminacy + immanence) as I have half-antically proposed?[1] Or better still, shall we simply live and let others live to call us what they may?

2. Like other categorical terms – say poststructuralism, or modernism, or romanticism for that matter – postmodernism suffers from a certain *semantic* instability: that is, no clear consensus about its meaning exists among scholars. The general difficulty is compounded in this case by two factors: (a) the relative youth, indeed brash adolescence, of the term postmodernism and (b) its semantic kinship to more current terms, themselves equally unstable. Thus some critics mean by postmodernism what others call avant-gardism or even neo-avant-gardism, while still others would call the same phenomenon simply modernism. This can make for inspired debates.[2]

3. A related difficulty concerns the *historical* instability of many literary concepts, their openness to change. Who, in this epoch of fierce misprisions, would dare to claim that romanticism is apprehended by Coleridge, Pater, Lovejoy, Abrams, Peckham, and Bloom in quite the same way? There is already some evidence that postmodernism, and modernism even more, are beginning to slip and slide in time, threatening to make any diacritical distinction between them desperate.[3] But perhaps the phenomenon, akin to Hubble's 'red shift' in astronomy, may someday serve to measure the historical velocity of literary concepts.

4. Modernism and postmodernism are not separated by an Iron Curtain or a Chinese Wall; for history is a palimpsest, and culture is permeable to time past, time present, and time future. We are all, I suspect, a little Victorian, Modern, and Postmodern, at once. And an author may, in his or her own lifetime, easily write both a modernist and a postmodernist work. (Contrast Joyce's *Portrait of the Artist as a Young Man* with his *Finnegans*

Wake.) More generally, on a certain level of narrative abstraction, modernism itself may be rightly assimilated to romanticism, romanticism related to the Enlightenment, the latter to the Renaissance, and so back, if not to the Olduvai Gorge, then certainly to ancient Greece.

5. This means that a 'period', as I have already intimated, must be perceived in terms of *both* continuity *and* discontinuity, the two perspectives being complementary and partial. The Apollonian view, rangy and abstract, discerns only historical conjunctions; the Dionysian feeling, sensuous though nearly purblind, touches only the disjunctive moment. Thus postmodernism, by invoking two divinities at once, engages a double view. Sameness and difference, unity and rupture, filiation and revolt, all must be honored if we are to attend to history, apprehend (perceive, understand) change both as a spatial, mental structure and as a temporal, physical process, both as pattern and as unique event.

6. Thus a 'period' is generally not a period at all; it is rather both a diachronic and synchronic construct. Postmodernism, again like modernism or romanticism, is no exception; it requires *both* historical *and* theoretical definition. We would not seriously claim an inaugural 'date' for it as Virginia Woolf pertly did for modernism, though we may sometimes woefully imagine that postmodernism began 'in or about September 1939'. Thus we continually discover 'antecedents' of postmodernism – in Sterne, Sade, Blake, Lautréamont, Rimbaud, Jarry, Tzara, Hofmannsthal, Gertrude Stein, the later Joyce, the later Pound, Duchamp, Artaud, Roussel, Bataille, Broch, Queneau, and Kafka. What this really indicates is that we have created in our mind a model of postmodernism, a particular typology of culture and imagination, and have proceeded to 'rediscover' the affinities of various authors and different moments with that model. We have, that is, reinvented our ancestors – and always shall. Consequently, 'older' authors can be postmodern – Kafka, Beckett, Borges, Nabokov, Gombrowicz – while 'younger' authors need not be so – Styron, Updike, Capote, Irving, Doctorow, Gardner.

7. As we have seen, any definition of postmodernism calls upon a fourfold vision of complementarities, embracing continuity and discontinuity, diachrony and synchrony. But a definition of the concept also requires a dialectical vision, for defining traits are often antithetical, and to ignore this tendency of historical reality is to lapse into single vision and Newton's sleep. Defining traits are dialectical and also plural; to elect a single trait as an absolute criterion of postmodern grace is to make of all other writers preterites.[4] Thus we can not simply rest – as I have sometimes done – on the assumption that postmodernism is antiformal, anarchic, or decreative; for though it is indeed all these, and despite its fanatic will to unmaking, it also contains the need to discover a 'unitary sensibility' (Sontag), to 'cross

the border and close the gap' (Fiedler), and to attain, as I have suggested, an immanence of discourse, an expanded noetic intervention, a 'neo-gnostic immediacy of mind'.[5]

8. All this leads to the prior problem of periodization itself, which is also that of literary history conceived as a particular apprehension of change. Indeed, the concept of postmodernism implies some theory of innovation, renovation, novation, or simply change. But which one? Heraclitean? Viconian? Darwinian? Marxist? Freudian? Kuhnian? Derridean? Eclectic?[6] Or is a 'theory of change' itself an oxymoron best suited to ideologues intolerant of the ambiguities of time? Should postmodernism, then, be left – at least for the moment – unconceptualized, a kind of literary-historical 'difference' or 'trace'?[7]

9. Postmodernism can expand into a still larger problem: is it only an artistic tendency or also a social phenomenon, perhaps even a mutation in Western humanism? If so, how are the various aspects of this phenomenon – psychological, philosophical, economic, political – joined or disjoined? In short, can we understand postmodernism in literature without some attempt to perceive the lineaments of a postmodern society, a Toynbeean postmodernity, or future Foucauldian *episteme*, of which the literary tendency I have been discussing is but a single, elitist strain?[8]

10. Finally, though not least vexing, is postmodernism an honorific term, used insidiously to valorize writers, however disparate, whom we otherwise esteem, to hail trends, however discordant, which we somehow approve? Or is it, on the contrary, a term of opprobrium and objurgation? In short, is postmodernism a descriptive as well as evaluative or normative category of literary thought? Or does it belong, as Charles Altieri notes, to that category of 'essentially contested concepts' in philosophy that never wholly exhaust their constitutive confusions?[9]

No doubt, other conceptual problems lurk in the matter of postmodernism. Such problems, however, cannot finally inhibit the intellectual imagination, the desire to apprehend our historical presence in noetic constructs that reveal our being to ourselves. I move, therefore, to propose a provisional scheme that the literature of silence, from Sade to Beckett, seems to envisage, and do so by distinguishing, tentatively, between three modes of artistic change in the last hundred years. I call these avant-garde, modern, and postmodern, though I realize that all three have conspired together to create that 'tradition of the new' that, since Baudelaire, brought 'into being an art whose history, regardless of the credos of its practitioners, has consisted of leaps from vanguard to vanguard, and political mass movements whose aim has been the total renovation not only of social institutions but of man himself.[10]

By avant-garde, I mean those movements that agitated the earlier part of our century, including 'Pataphysics, Cubism, Futurism, Dadaism, Surrealism, Suprematism, Constructivism, Merzism, de Stijl. Anarchic, these assaulted the bourgeoisie with their art, their manifestoes, their antics. But their activism could also turn inward, becoming suicidal – as happened later to some postmodernists like Rudolf Schwartzkogler. Once full of brio and bravura, these movements have all but vanished now, leaving only their story, at once fugacious and exemplary. Modernism, however, proved more stable, aloof, hieratic, like the French Symbolism from which it derived; even its experiments now seem Olympian. Enacted by such 'individual talents' as Valéry, Proust, and Gide, the early Joyce, Yeats, and Lawrence, Rilke, Mann, and Musil, the early Pound, Eliot, and Faulkner, it commanded high authority, leading Delmore Schwartz to chant in *Shenandoah*: 'Let us consider where the great men are / Who will obsess the child when he can read . . .'. But if much of modernism appears hieratic, hypotactical, and formalist, postmodernism strikes us by contrast as playful, paratactical, and deconstructionist. In this it recalls the irreverent spirit of the avant-garde, and so carries sometimes the label of neo-avant-garde. Yet postmodernism remains 'cooler', in McLuhan's sense, than older vanguards – cooler, less cliquish, and far less aversive to the pop, electronic society of which it is a part, and so hospitable to kitsch.

Can we distinguish postmodernism further? Perhaps certain schematic differences from modernism will provide a start.

↕	↔
Modernism	Postmodernism
Romanticism/Symbolism	'Pataphysics/Dadaism
Form (conjunctive, closed)	Antiform (disjunctive, open)
Purpose	Play
Design	Chance
Hierarchy	Anarchy
Mastery/Logos	Exhaustion/Silence
Art Object/Finished Work	Process/Performance/Happening
Distance	Participation
Creation/Totalization	Decreation/Deconstruction
Synthesis	Antithesis
Presence	Absence
Centering	Dispersal
Genre/Boundary	Text/Intertext
Semantics	Rhetoric
Paradigm	Syntagm
Hypotaxis	Parataxis
Metaphor	Metonymy
Selection	Combination
Root/Depth	Rhizome/Surface
Interpretation/Reading	Against Interpretation/Misreading

Signified	Signifier
Lisible (Readerly)	*Scriptible* (Writerly)
Narrative/*Grande Histoire*	Anti-narrative/*Petite Histoire*
Master Code	Idiolect
Symptom	Desire
Type	Mutant
Genital/Phallic	Polymorphous/Androgynous
Paranoia	Schizophrenia
Origin/Cause	Difference-Differance/Trace
God the Father	The Holy Ghost
Metaphysics	Irony
Determinacy	Indeterminacy
Transcendence	Immanence

The preceding table draws on ideas in many fields – rhetoric, linguistics, literary theory, philosophy, anthropology, psychoanalysis, political science, even theology – and draws on many authors – European and American – aligned with diverse movements, groups, and views. Yet the dichotomies this table represents remain insecure, equivocal. For differences shift, defer, even collapse; concepts in any one vertical column are not all equivalent; and inversions and exceptions, in both modernism and postmodernism, abound. Still, I would submit that rubrics in the right column point to the postmodern tendency, the tendency of indetermanence, and so may bring us closer to its historical and theoretical definition.

Notes

1 *See* I. Hassan, *The Postmodern Turn*, 1987, pp. 46–83.
2 Matei Calinescu, for instance, tends to assimilate 'postmodern' to 'neo-avant-garde' and sometimes to 'avant-garde', in *Faces of Modernity: Avant-garde, decadence, kitsch*, 1977, though later he discriminates between these terms thoughtfully, in 'Avant-garde, neo-avant-garde, and post-modernism', unpublished manuscript. Miklos Szabolcsi would identify 'modern' with 'avant-garde' and call 'postmodern' the 'neo-avant-garde', in 'Avant-garde, neo-avant-garde, modernism: Questions and suggestions', *New Literary History*, 3, 1 (1971); while Paul de Man would call 'modern' the innovative element, the perpetual 'moment of crisis' in the literature of every period, in 'Literary history and literary modernity', in *Blindness and Insight*, New York, 1971, ch. 8; in a similar vein, William V. Spanos employs the term 'postmodernism' to indicate 'not fundamentally a chronological event, but rather a permanent mode of human understanding', in 'De-struction and the question of postmodern literature: Towards a definition', *Par Rapport*, 2, 2 (1979), 107. And even John Barth, as inward as any writer with postmodernism, now argues that postmodernism is a synthesis yet to come, and what we had assumed to be postmodernism all along was only late modernism, in 'The literature of replenishment: Postmodernist fiction', 1980, 65–71.
3 In my own earlier and later essays on the subject I can discern such a slight shift.

See 'POSTmodernISM', *New Literary History*, 3, 1 (1971), 5–30, 'Joyce, Beckett, and the Post-modern imagination', *TriQuarterly*, 34 (1975), and 'Culture, indeterminacy, and immanence', in *The Postmodern Turn*, pp. 46–83.

4 Though some critics have argued that postmodernism is primarily 'temporal' and others that it is mainly 'spatial', it is in the particular relation between these single categories that postmodernism probably reveals itself. See the two seemingly contradictory views of William V. Spanos, 'The detective at the boundary', in *Existentialism* 2, ed. William V. Spanos (New York, 1976), pp. 163–89; and Jürgen Peper, 'Postmodernismus: Unitary sensibility', 1977, 65–89.

5 Susan Sontag, 'One culture and the new sensibility', in *Against Interpretation*, 1967, pp. 293–304; Leslie Fiedler, 'Cross the border – close that gap', in *Collected Essays*, vol. 2, New York, 1971, pp. 461–85; and Ihab Hassan, 'The new gnosticism', *Paracriticisms: Seven speculations of the times*, Urbana, IL, 1975, ch. 6.

6 For some views of this, see Ihab Hassan and Sally Hassan, eds, *Innovation/Renovation: Recent trends and reconceptions in Western culture*, 1983.

7 At stake here is the idea of literary periodicity, challenged by current French thought. For other views of literacy and historical change, including 'hierarchic organization' of time, see Leonard Meyer, *Music, the Arts, and Ideas*, Chicago, 1967, pp. 93, 102; Calinescu, *Faces of Modernity*, pp. 147 ff; Ralph Cohen, 'Innovation and variation: Literary change and Georgic poetry', in Ralph Cohen and Murray Krieger, *Literature and History*, Los Angeles, 1974; and my *Paracriticisms*, ch. 7. A harder question is one Geoffrey Hartman asks: 'With so much historical knowledge, how can we avoid historicism, or the staging of history as a drama in which epiphanic raptures are replaced by epistemic ruptures?' Or, again, how can we 'formulate a theory of reading that would be historical rather than historicist'? *Saving the Text: Literature/Derrida/philosophy*, Baltimore, MD, 1981, p. xx.

8 Writers as different as Marshall McLuhan and Leslie Fiedler have explored the media and pop aspects of postmodernism for two decades, though their efforts are now out of fashion in some critical circles. The difference between postmodernism, as a contemporary artistic tendency, and postmodernity, as a cultural phenomenon, perhaps even an era of history, is discussed by Richard E. Palmer in 'Postmodernity and hermeneutics', 1977, 363–93.

9 Charles Altieri, 'Postmodernism: A question of definition', *Par Rapport*, 2 (1979), 90. This leads Altieri to conclude: 'The best one can do who believes himself post-modern . . . is to articulate spaces of mind in which the confusions can not paralyze because one enjoys the energies and glimpses of our condition which they produce', p. 99.

10 Harold Rosenberg, *The Tradition of the New*, New York, 1961, p. 9.

SECTION TWO

SOCIETY AND SELF

The essays collected here represent a variety of attempts to define and explore relations between self and society from a range of disciplinary and ideological perspectives. The first section focuses on analyses of urbanization and the nature and cultural impact of 'mass society' written as part of an ongoing attempt to define the nature of modernity and its relations with the postmodern. Daniel Bell's *The Cultural Contradictions of Capitalism* (1976) represents a neo-conservative critique of cultural modernism; Marshall Berman's book of 1983 is a late Marxist response which situates itself (critically) within the postmodern frame. In the chapter reproduced here from Huyssen's *After the Great Divide*, he re-examines the debates about high and mass culture in relation to the issue of gender. David Harvey's book (1989) was an important attempt to relate the economic effects of late capitalism on the subjective experience of time and space to cultural and aesthetic constructions of identity and selfhood. Francis Fukuyama's thesis of the 'end of history' first appeared as an essay in 1989 and presented in neo-Hegelian terms the argument that the universalization of liberal democracy had now brought an end to history as a narrative of ideological evolution. The essay received enormous critical attention and was expanded into a book, published in 1992, from which the extract reproduced here was taken.

Throughout the century, and particularly in relation to the two world wars, the crisis of imperialism, decolonization and changes in class relations, the problem of national identity and of the nature of 'Englishness' have been enduring preoccupations of British writers. E.M. Forster's essay of 1939 returned to his earlier concern with liberalism and national identity as the war presented new complications in the construction of that identity. It is usefully complemented from a later post-colonial perspective in the piece by Heaney (originally a lecture delivered in California in 1976). A more theoretical perspective is provided by Perry Anderson's essay of 1990 and the excerpt from Said's *Orientalism*, which established the discursive space of post-colonial theory in 1978. The excerpts from Paul Fussell (1975) and Virginia Woolf (1942) represent accounts of the two world wars, the first a retrospective analysis and the second a personal account of the experience from within.

The subsections *Narratives of the self* and *Gender and sexuality* offer reflections on the construction of identity and the idea of the modern self as a 'narrative project'. The essays in the former represent different perspectives from across the disciplines of psychoanalysis, sociology, aesthetics and social theory. They range from attempts to define a core self, whether personal or collective, to later postmodern accounts of the constructedness of identity. Each writer confronts the age-old problem of free will and determinism from within a modern vocabulary. The excerpt from Freud is taken from the 1946 edition of *Civilization and its Discontents* and, like the pieces from Lawrence and Goffman (1959), attempts to retain some notion of a core self. Woolf's essay presents an uncannily 'postmodern' sense of self as fluid and situated whereas Giddens offers an analysis of the institutional self-reflexivity of late modernism where self is as much a theoretical as a narrative project. None of these writers directly considers issues of gender (though they have plenty to say about sexuality) despite the fact that modern feminism, more than any other political or intellectual movement, has profoundly challenged historical definitions of subjective identity. The essays in the final subsection therefore represent a variety of positions from within this feminist challenge.

Probably the most important document of modern feminism was de Beauvoir's book, published by Cape in 1953. Her analysis of the construction of woman as 'other' within a pervasive dialectic of immanence and transcendence provided the touchstone for much of the feminist theory which followed. Each of the essays here represents a key moment in the subsequent history of feminist theory: Kristeva's essay of 1971 proposed the possibility of reaching beyond the contradictions of the first phases of feminism; Irigary's essay was a central document of so-called 'French feminism'; Evelyn Fox Keller's work (1985) took up object relations theory in order to challenge patriarchal constructions of knowledge in the sphere of science.

URBANIZATION AND MASS SOCIETY

12 Daniel Bell
From *The Cultural Contradictions of Capitalism*

Modern culture is defined by this extraordinary freedom to ransack the world storehouse and to engorge any and every style it comes upon. Such freedom comes from the fact that the axial principle of modern culture is the expression and remaking of the 'self' in order to achieve self-realization and self-fulfillment. And in its search, there is a denial of any limits or boundaries to experience. It is a reaching out for all experience; nothing is forbidden, all is to be explored.

Within this framework, one can discern the structural sources of tension in the society; between a social structure (primarily techno-economic) which is bureaucratic and hierarchical, and a polity which believes, formally, in equality and participation; between a social structure that is organized fundamentally in terms of roles and specialization, and a culture which is concerned with the enhancement and fulfillment of the self and the 'whole' person. In these contradictions, one perceives many of the latent social conflicts that have been expressed ideologically as alienation, depersonalization, the attack on authority, and the like. In these adversary relations, one sees the disjunction of realms.

This notion of the disjunction of realms is a general, theoretical approach to the analysis of modern society. At this point, it might be useful to define the particular terms that differentiate socio-technical, socio-economic and socio-political systems.

Industrialism is the application of energy and machinery for the mass production of goods. Both the United States and the Soviet Union, though differing markedly in other respects, are both technical and industrial societies. The phase of post-industrialism represents a shift in the kinds of work people do, from manufacturing to services (especially human and professional services) and a new centrality of theoretical knowledge in economic innovation and policy. For similar reasons, both the United States and the Soviet Union could become post-industrial societies.

Capitalism is an economic-cultural system, organized economically around the institution of property and the production of commodities and based culturally in the fact that exchange relations, that of buying and selling, have permeated most of the society. Democracy is a socio-

From Daniel Bell, *The Cultural Contradictions of Capitalism*, Heinemann, 1976, pp. 13–18, 29–30.

political system in which legitimacy lies in the consent of the governed, where the political arena is available to various contending groups, and where fundamental liberties are safeguarded.

Though capitalism and democracy historically have arisen together, and have been commonly justified by philosophical liberalism, there is nothing which makes it either theoretically or practically necessary for the two to be yoked. In modern society, the political order increasingly becomes autonomous, and the management of the techno-economic order, or the democratic planning, or the management of the economy, becomes ever more independent of capitalism.

Soviet communism, which should more correctly be called bureaucratic collectivism, is a state-directed society which has sought to fuse all realms into a single monolith and to impose a common direction, from economics to politics to culture, through a single institution, the Party. Whether the Party can maintain such monolithic control in a society that becomes increasingly differentiated, without broadening the arena of elite participation in decision making, is increasingly open to question.

These distinctions are necessary for two reasons. First, they point out the fact that the question of the movement from industrial to post-industrial society and the question of the movement from capitalism to socialism or bureaucratic collectivism are two distinct questions with respect to developments along two very different axes. The post-industrial society centers on the technology, the kind of *work* people do (though there are political implications in the relative decline of the working class), and the organization of *knowledge*. The questions of whether a system is capitalist or socialist, or capitalist or bureaucratic collectivist, are questions about the management of the *economy* and the *ethos* of the society. Second, the contradictions of capitalism of which I speak in these pages, have to do with the disjunction between the kind of organization and the norms demanded in the economic realm, and the norms of self-realization that are now central in the culture. The two realms which had historically been joined to produce a single character structure – that of the Puritan and of his calling – have now become unjoined. The principles of the economic realm and those of the culture now lead people in contrary directions. These contradictions have arisen primarily in American and other Western societies. It is not at all clear that the Communist world, with its drive for efficiency and its promise of self-realization, is immune to these contradictions. We shall have to wait and see when (or if) a consumer society is achieved in the Soviet Union. So far as Maoist China is concerned, the Russians are already the damned.

If we turn from our analytical distinctions to sociological history, we can trace this disjunction between social structure and culture in an extraordinary contrast of changing moral tempers.

The fundamental assumption of modernity, the thread that has run through Western civilization since the sixteenth century, is that the social unit of society is not the group, the guild, the tribe, or the city, but the person. The Western ideal was the autonomous man who, in becoming self-determining, would achieve freedom. With this 'new man' there was a repudiation of institutions (the striking result of the Reformation, which installed individual conscience as the source of judgment); the opening of new geographical and social frontiers; the desire, and the growing ability, to master nature and to make of oneself what one can, and even, in discarding old roots, to remake oneself altogether. What began to count was not the past but the future.

This is expressed in a twofold development. In the economy, there arises the bourgeois entrepreneur. Freed from the ascriptive ties of the traditional world, with its fixed status and checks on acquisition, he seeks his fortune by remaking the economic world. Free movement of goods and money and individual economic and social mobility become the ideal. At its extreme, laissez-faire becomes 'rampant individualism.' In the culture, we have the rise of the independent artist, released from church and princely patron, writing and painting what pleases him rather than his sponsor; the market will make him free.[1] In the development of culture, this search for independence, the will to be free not only of patron but of all conventions, finds its expression in modernism and, in its extreme form, in the idea of the untrammeled self.

The impulse driving both the entrepreneur and the artist is a restlessness to search out the new, to rework nature, and to refashion consciousness. . . .

Both impulses, historically, were aspects of the same sociological surge of modernity. Together they opened up the Western world in a radical way. Yet the extraordinary paradox is that each impulse then became highly conscious of the other, feared the other, and sought to destroy it. Radical in economics, the bourgeoisi became conservative in morals and cultural taste. The bourgeois economic impulse was organized into a highly restrictive character structure whose energies were channeled into the production of goods and into a set of attitudes toward work that feared instinct, spontaneity, and vagrant impulse. In the extreme Puritanism of America, laws were passed to constrain intemperate behavior, while in painting and literature bourgeois taste ran to the heroic and banal.

The cultural impulse – I take Baudelaire as its exemplary figure – thus turned into rage against bourgeois values. 'To be a useful man has always appeared to me as something quite hideous,' Baudelaire declared. Utility, rationalism, and materialism were barren, and the bourgeois had no spiritual life and no excesses. The 'cruel implacable regularity' of industry was what the modern business house had created: 'Mechanization will have . . . Americanized us, Progress will have well atrophied us, our entire spiritual part. . . .'[2]

What is striking is that while bourgeois society introduced a radical individualism in economics, and a willingness to tear up all traditional social relations in the process, the bourgeois class feared the radical experimental individualism of modernism in the culture. Conversely, the radical experimentalists in the culture, from Baudelaire to Rimbaud to Alfred Jarry, were willing to explore all dimensions of experience, yet fiercely hated bourgeois life. The history of this sociological puzzle, how this antagonism came about, is still to be written.[3]

The effort to find excitement and meaning in literature and art as a substitute for religion led to modernism as a cultural mode. Yet modernism is exhausted and the various kinds of post-modernism (in the psychedelic effort to expand consciousness without boundaries) are simply the decomposition of the self in an effort to erase individual ego. The idea of revolution still mesmerizes some,[4] but the real problems arise the 'day after the revolution,' when the mundane world again intrudes upon consciousness, and one finds that the moral ideas are abstract against the intractable desire for material incentives or to pass privileges on to one's children. Thus one finds a revolutionary society itself becoming bureaucratic or being enmeshed ceaselessly in the turmoil of permanent revolution.[5]

What holds one to reality, if one's secular system of meanings proves to be an illusion? I will risk an unfashionable answer – the return in Western society of some conception of religion. In his *Lettre du voyant*, Rimbaud remarked, 'Je sais qu'il faut être voyant, se faire voyant.' To be a *voyant* means to discern, on the far side of art and history, realities which the eyes of others have yet failed to see, to 'inspecter l'invisible et entendre l'inouï.'[6]

If it is true that what the poet says hearkens toward the future, then in that country where contemporary poetry has had the strongest voice, and expressed the most human anguish – in Soviet Russia – religion would have the strongest flowering in the culture, if the political shackles of the regime were undone. In the invisible writing that is soundlessly heard, the recurrent underground theme is the salvation of man through the resurrection of traditional faith.[7]

What religion can restore is the continuity of generations, returning us to the existential predicaments which are the ground of humility and care for others. Yet such a continuity cannot be manufactured, nor a cultural revolution engineered. That thread is woven out of those experiences which give one a tragic sense of life, a life that is lived on the knife-edge of finitude and freedom.

Notes

1 In the eighteenth century, the growth of publishing and the creation of a market made the writer not only independent but in some cases, such as Alexander Pope, quite wealthy. As Oliver Goldsmith wrote in 1762: 'At present the few poets of England no longer depend on the Great for subsistence, they have now no other

patrons but the public, and the public, collectively considered, is a good and generous master. . . . Every polite member of the community, by buying what a man of letters writes, contributes to reward him. The ridicule therefore of living in a garret, might have been wit in the last age, but continues such no longer, because no longer true.' Quoted in Alexander Beljame, *Men of Letters and the English Public in the XVIIIth Century* (London, Kegan Paul, 1948), p. 385; the first French edition appeared in 1881.

2 *See* César Graña, 'Bourgeois Enterprise and Modern Life,' in *Bohemian versus Bourgeois* (New York, Basic Books, 1964), especially pp. 95–8; and Joseph D. Bennett, *Baudelaire: A Criticism* (Princeton, Princeton University Press, 1944), especially chs. 2 and 3 for Baudelaire's conception of evil, which relates to the discussion that follows.

3 Is there a parallel with the Communist world? The Russian Revolution released an unprecedented burst of vitality and experimentation in all the arts. Hundreds of artists and writers took up the revolution with enthusiasm. 'Cubism and futurism were the revolutionary forms in art foreshadowing the revolution in the political and economic life of 1917,' declared Malevich. Constructivism was proclaimed the new aesthetic of Communist society. In design, painting, and sculpture there were the innovations of Tatlin, Lissitsky, Gabo, and Pevsner, as well as the abstractions of Kandinsky and Malevich. In the theater there were the stylistic experiments of Meyerhold, Tairov, and Vakhtangov. In poetry there were the triumphant futurists, such as Mayakovsky ('the streets are our brushes, the squares our palette'), and the symbolists, such as Blok and Bely (who interpreted the revolution as a religious epiphany). In fiction there was the writing of Babel and Pilnyak, Zamyatin and Bulgakov; in the cinema the films of Eisenstein and Pudovkin.

By the 1930s, it was finished. All that was left was the cold pudding of a Party-defined 'socialist realism.' Those who had created the feverish experiments were prisoners, suicides, silent, or abroad. Clearly there was a question whether, in a society so single-mindedly focused on mobilizing a populace for industrialization, the independence or the vagrant impulses of artists and writers would not be a 'diversion' from the creation of the 'new man' and the channeling of economic energies which the Party sought to direct.

4 Nadezhda Mandelstam has written of the Russian experience: 'My brother Evgeni Yakovlevich used to say that the decisive part in the subjugation of the intelligentsia was played not by terror and bribery (though, God knows, there was enough of both), but by the word "Revolution," which none of them could bear to give up. It is a word to which whole nations have succumbed, and its force was such that one wonders why our rulers still needed prisons and capital punishment.' *Hope Against Hope* (New York, Atheneum, 1970), p. 126.

5 One of the most amusing and revealing episodes of the Chinese cultural revolution was the fact that when hundreds of thousands of inspired youths flooded Peking in 1966, they found that each contingent wore button badges announcing its city, but some badges were scarcer and thus rarer than others. Immediately and spontaneously a market arose in which different badges were traded at discount. Youths proudly showed off the scarce badges they were able to get by trade – as they demonstrated against the restoration of capitalism and for the cultural revolution. See *Red Guard: The Political Biography of Dai Msiau-ai*, ed. Gordon A. Bennett and Ronald N. Montaperto (Garden City, N.Y., Doubleday Anchor, 1972), p. 99.

6 The full text of the *Lettre du voyant* is translated, awkwardly, as 'The Poet as Visionary,' in Edgell Rickword, *Rimbaud: The Boy and the Poet* (London, Background Books, 1963), pp. 153–5.

7 This is the thread which runs through the poems of *Doctor Zhivago*. In the final poem, 'Garden of Gethsemane,' Pasternak writes:

> But now the book of life has reached a page
> Which is more precious than are all the holies.
> That which was written now must be fulfilled.
> Fulfilled be it, then, Amen.

* * *

> I shall descend into my grave. And on the third day rise again.
> And, even as rafts float down a river,
> So shall the centuries drift, trailing like a caravan,
> Coming for judgment, out of the dark, to me.

And that thread is picked up by Joseph Brodsky a decade later:

> The total of all today's embraces
> gives far less of love than the outstretched arms of
> Christ on the cross. This lame poet's finding
> looms before me in Holy Week, sixty-seven,
> blocking my leap to the nineteen-nineties.

'The poems of Yurii Zhivago,' trans. Bernard Guilbert Guerney, in *Doctor Zhivago* (New York, Pantheon, 1958), pp.558–9; Joseph Brodsky, 'Adieu, Mademoiselle Véronique,' in *Selected Poems*, trans. George Kline (New York, Harper & Row, 1973), p. 136. The 'lame poet,' as the translator notes, is a direct reference to Pasternak, who walked with a slight limp.

---

13 Marshall Berman
From *All That is Solid Melts into Air*

Nakedness: the unaccommodated man

Now that we have seen Marx's 'melting' vision in action, I want to use it to explicate some the *Manifesto*'s most powerful images of modern life. In the passage below, Marx is trying to show how capitalism has transformed people's relationships with each other and with themselves. Although, in

From Marshall Berman, *All That is Solid Melts into Air*, Verso, 1983, pp. 105–7, 109–10.

Marx's syntax, 'the bourgeoisie' is the subject – in its economic activities that bring the big changes about – modern men and women of every class are objects, for all are changed:

> The bourgeoisie has torn apart the many feudal ties that bound men to their 'natural superiors,' and left no other bond between man and man than naked interest, than callous cash payment. It has drowned the heavenly ecstasies of pious fanaticism, of chivalrous enthusiasm, of philistine sentimentalism, in the icy water of egoistical calculation. . . . The bourgeoisie has stripped of its halo every occupation hitherto honored and looked up to with reverent awe. . . . The bourgeoisie has torn away from the family its sentimental veil, and turned the family relation into a pure money relation. . . . In place of exploitation veiled by religious and political illusions, it has put open, shameless, direct, naked exploitation.
>
> [475–76]

Marx's basic opposition here is between what is open or naked and what is hidden, veiled, clothed. This polarity, perennial in Eastern as well as Western thought, symbolizes everywhere a distinction between a 'real' world and an illusory one. In most ancient and medieval speculative thought, the whole world of sensuous experience appears illusory – the Hindu 'veil of Maya' – and the true world is thought to be accessible only through transcendence of bodies, space and time. In some traditions, reality is accessible through religious or philosophical meditation; in others, it will be available to us only in a future existence after death – the Pauline 'for now we see through a glass darkly, but then face to face.'

The modern transformation, beginning in the age of the Renaissance and Reformation, places both these worlds on earth, in space and time, filled with human beings. Now the false world is seen as a historical past, a world we have lost (or are in the process of losing), while the true world is in the physical and social world that exists for us here and now (or is in the process of coming into being). At this point a new symbolism emerges. Clothes become an emblem of the old, illusory mode of life; nakedness comes to signify the newly discovered and experienced truth; and the act of taking off one's clothes becomes an act of spiritual liberation, of becoming real. Modern erotic poetry elaborates this theme, as generations of modern lovers have experienced it, with playful irony; modern tragedy penetrates its awesome and fearsome depths. Marx thinks and works in the tragic tradition. For him, the clothes are ripped off, the veils are torn away, the stripping process is violent and brutal; and yet, somehow, the tragic movement of modern history is supposed to culminate in a happy end.

For Marx, writing in the aftermath of bourgeois revolutions and reactions, and looking forward to a new wave, the symbols of nakedness and unveiling regain the dialectical depth that Shakespeare gave them two centuries before. The bourgeois revolutions, in tearing away veils of 'religious and political illusion,' have left naked power and exploitation, cruelty and misery, exposed like open wounds; at the same time, they have uncovered and exposed new options and hopes. Unlike the common people of all ages, who have been endlessly betrayed and broken by their devotion to their 'natural superiors,' modern men, washed in 'the icy water of egoistical calculation,' are free from deference to masters who destroy them, animated rather than numbed by the cold. Because they know how to think of, by, and for themselves, they will demand a clear account of what their bosses and rulers are doing for them – and doing to them – and be ready to resist and rebel where they are getting nothing real in return.

Marx's hope is that once the unaccommodated men of the working class are 'forced to face . . . the real conditions of their lives and their relations with their fellow men,' they will come together to overcome the cold that cuts through them all. Their union will generate the collective energy that can fuel a new communal life. One of the *Manifesto*'s primary aims is to point the way out of the cold, to nourish and focus the common yearning for communal warmth. Because the workers can come through the affliction and the fear only by making contact with the self's deepest resources, they will be prepared to fight for collective recognition of the self's beauty and value. Their communism, when it comes, will appear as a kind of transparent garment, at once keeping its wearers warm and setting off their naked beauty, so that they can recognize themselves and each other in all their radiance.

Here, as so often in Marx, the vision is dazzling but the light flickers if we look hard. It isn't hard to imagine alternative endings to the dialectic of nakedness, endings less beautiful than Marx's but no less plausible. Modern men and women might well prefer the solitary pathos and grandeur of the Rousseauean unconditioned self, or the collective costumed comforts of the Burkean political masque, rather than the Marxian attempt to fuse the best of both. Indeed, the sort of individualism that scorns and fears connections with other people as threats to the self's integrity, and the sort of collectivism that seeks to submerge the self in a social role, may be more appealing than the Marxian synthesis, because they are intellectually and emotionally so much easier.

There is a further problem that might keep the Marxian dialectic from even getting under way. Marx believes that the shocks and upheavals and catastrophes of life in bourgeois society enable moderns, by going through them, as Lear does, to discover who they 'really are.' But if bourgeois society is as volatile as Marx thinks it is, how can its people ever settle on any real selves? With all the possibilities and necessities that bombard the self and all the desperate drives that propel it, how can anyone define definitively which ones are essential and which merely incidental? The nature of the newly naked modern man may turn out to be just as elusive and mysterious as that of the old, clothed one, maybe even more elusive, because there will no longer be any illusion of a real self underneath the masks. Thus, along with community and society, individuality itself may be melting into the modern air.

---

14   David Harvey
From *The Condition of Postmodernity*

The annihilation of space through time has radically changed the commodity mix that enters into daily reproduction. Innumerable local food systems have been reorganized through their incorporation into global commodity exchange. French cheeses, for example, virtually unavailable except in a few gourmet stores in large cities in 1970, are now widely sold across the United States. And if this is thought a somewhat elite example, the case of beer consumption suggests that the internationalization of a product that traditional location theory always taught should be highly market-oriented is now complete. Baltimore was essentially a one-beer town (locally brewed) in 1970, but first the regional beers from places like Milwaukee and Denver, and then Canadian and Mexican beers followed by European, Australian, Chinese, Polish, etc. beers became cheaper. Formerly exotic food became commonplace while popular local delicacies (in the Baltimore case, blue crabs and oysters) that were once relatively inexpensive jumped in price as they too became integrated into long-distance trading.

The market place has always been an 'emporium of styles' (to quote Raban's phrase) but the food market, just to take one example, now looks very different from what it was twenty years ago. Kenyan haricot beans, Californian celery and avocados, North African potatoes, Canadian apples, and Chilean grapes all sit side by side in a British supermarket. This variety also makes for a proliferation of culinary styles, even among the relatively poor. Such styles have always migrated, of course, usually following the migration streams of different groups before diffusing slowly through urban cultures. The new waves of immigrants (such as the Vietnamese, Koreans, Filipinos, Central Americans, etc. that have added to the older groups of Japanese, Chinese, Chicanos, and all the European ethnic groups that have also found their culinary heritage can be revived for fun and profit) make a typical United States city such as New York, Los Angeles, or San Francisco (where the last census showed the majority of the population

From David Harvey, *The Condition of Postmodernity*, Blackwell, 1989, pp. 299–305.

to be made up of minorities) as much an emporium of culinary styles as it is an emporium of the world's commodities. But here, too, there has been an acceleration, because culinary styles have moved faster than the immigration streams. It did not take a large French immigration to the United States to send the croissant rapidly spreading across America to challenge the traditional doughnut, nor did it take a large immigration of Americans to Europe to bring fast-food hamburgers to nearly all medium-sized European cities. Chinese takeaways, Italian pizza-parlours (run by a US chain), Middle Eastern felafel stalls, Japanese sushi bars . . . the list is now endless in the Western world.

The whole world's cuisine is now assembled in one place in almost exactly the same way that the world's geographical complexity is nightly reduced to a series of images on a static television screen. This same phenomenon is exploited in entertainment palaces like Epcott and Disneyworld; it becomes possible, as the US commercials put it, 'to experience the Old World for a day without actually having to go there'. The general implication is that through the experience of everything from food, to culinary habits, music, television, entertainment, and cinema, it is now possible to experience the world's geography vicariously, as a simulacrum. The interweaving of simulacra in daily life brings together different worlds (of commodities) in the same space and time. But it does so in such a way as to conceal almost perfectly any trace of origin, of the labour processes that produced them, or of the social relations implicated in their production.

The simulacra can in turn become the reality. Baudrillard (1986) in *L'Amérique* even goes so far, somewhat exaggeratedly in my view, to suggest that US reality is now constructed as a giant screen: 'the cinema is everywhere, most of all in the city, incessant and marvellous film and scenario'. Places portrayed in a certain way, particularly if they have the capacity to attract tourists, may begin to 'dress themselves up' as the fantasy images prescribe. Mediaeval castles offer mediaeval weekends (food, dress, but not of course the primitive heating arrangements). Vicarious participation in these various worlds has real effects on the ways in which these worlds get ordered. Jencks (1984, 127) proposes that the architect should be an active participant in this:

Any middle class urbanite in any large city from Teheran to Tokyo is bound to have a well-stocked, indeed over-stocked 'image bank' that is continually restuffed by travel and magazines. His *musée imaginaire* may mirror the pot-pourri of the producers but it is nonetheless natural to his way of life. Barring some kind of totalitarian reduction in the heterogeneity of production and consumption, it seems to be desirable that architects learn to use this inevitable heterogeneity of languages. Besides, it is quite enjoyable. Why, if one can afford to live in different ages and cultures, restrict oneself to the present, the locale? Eclecticism is the natural evolution of a culture with choice.

Much the same can be said of popular music styles. Commenting on how collage and eclecticism have recently come to dominate, Chambers (1987) goes on to show how oppositional and subcultural musics like reggae, Afro-American and Afro-Hispanic have taken their place 'in the museum of fixed symbolic structures' to form a flexible collage of 'the already seen, the already worn, the already played, the already heard'. A strong sense of 'the Other' is replaced, he suggests, by a weak sense of 'the others'. The loose hanging together of divergent street cultures in the fragmented spaces of the contemporary city re-emphasizes the contingent and accidental aspects of this 'otherness' in daily life. This same sensibility exists in post-modern fiction. It is, says McHale (1987), concerned with 'ontologies', with a potential as well as an actual plurality of universes, forming an eclectic and 'anarchic landscape of worlds in the plural'. Dazed and distracted characters wander through these worlds without a clear sense of location, wondering, 'Which world am I in and which of my personalities do I deploy?' Our postmodern ontological landscape, suggests McHale, 'is unprecedented in human history – at least in the degree of its pluralism'. Spaces of very different worlds seem to collapse upon each other, much as the world's commodities are assembled in the supermarket and all manner of sub-cultures get juxtaposed in the contemporary city. Disruptive spatiality triumphs over the coherence of perspective and narrative in post-modern fiction, in exactly the same way that imported beers coexist with local brews, local employment collapses under the weight of foreign competition, and all the divergent spaces of the world are assembled nightly as a collage of images upon the television screen.

There seem to be two divergent sociological effects of all of this in daily thought and action. The first suggests taking advantage of all of the divergent possibilities, much as Jencks recommends, and cultivating a whole series of simulacra as milieux of escape, fantasy, and distraction:

> All around us – on advertisement hoardings, bookshelves, record covers, television screens – these miniature escape fantasies present themselves. This, it seems, is how we are destined to live, as split personalities in which the private life is disturbed by the promise of escape routes to another reality.
> (Cohen and Taylor, 1978, quoted in McHale, 1987, 38)

From this standpoint I think we have to accept McHale's argument that postmodern fiction is mimetic of something, much as I have argued that the emphasis upon ephemerality, collage, fragmentation, and dispersal in philosophical and social thought mimics the conditions of flexible accumulation. And it should not be surprising either to see how all of this fits in with the emergence since 1970 of a fragmented politics of divergent special and regional interest groups.

But it is exactly at this point that we encounter the opposite reaction that can best be summed up as the search for personal or collective identity, the search for secure moorings in a shifting world. Place-identity, in this collage of superimposed spatial images that implode in upon us, becomes an important issue, because everyone occupies a space of individuation (a body, a room, a home, a shaping community, a nation), and how we individuate ourselves shapes identity. Furthermore, if no one 'knows their place' in this shifting collage world, then how can a secure social order be fashioned or sustained?

There are two elements within this problem that deserve close consideration. First, the capacity of most social movements to command place better than space puts a strong emphasis upon the potential connection between place and social identity. This is manifest in political action. The defensiveness of municipal socialism, the insistence on working-class community, the localization of the fight against capital, become central features of working-class struggle within an overall patterning of uneven geographical development. The consequent dilemmas of socialist or working-class movements in the face of a universalizing capitalism are shared by other oppositional groups – racial minorities, colonized peoples, women, etc. – who are relatively empowered to organize in place but disempowered when it comes to organizing over space. In clinging, often of necessity, to a place-bound identity, however, such oppositional movements become a part of the very fragmentation which a mobile capitalism and flexible accumulation can feed upon. 'Regional resistances', the struggle for local autonomy, place-bound organization, may be excellent bases for political action, but they cannot bear the burden of radical historical change alone. 'Think globally and act locally' was the revolutionary slogan of the 1960s. It bears repeating.

The assertion of any place-bound identity has to rest at some point on the motivational power of tradition. It is difficult, however, to maintain any sense of historical continuity in the face of all the flux and ephemerality of flexible accumulation. The irony is that tradition is now often preserved by being commodified and marketed as such. The search for roots ends up at worst being produced and marketed as an image, as a simulacrum or pastiche (imitation communities constructed to evoke images of some folksy past, the fabric of traditional working-class communities being taken over by an urban gentry). The photograph, the document, the view, and the reproduction become history precisely because they are so overwhelmingly present. The problem, of course, is that none of these are immune from tampering or downright faking for present purposes. At best, historical tradition is reorganized as a museum culture, not necessarily of high modernist art, but of local history, of local production, of how things once upon a time were made, sold, consumed, and integrated into a long-lost and often romanticized daily life (one from which all trace of oppressive social relations may be expunged). Through the presentation of a partially illusory past it becomes possible to signify something of local identity and perhaps to do it profitably.

The second reaction to the internationalism of modernism lies in the search to construct place and its meanings qualitatively. Capitalist hegemony over space puts the aesthetics of place very much back on the agenda. But this, as we have seen, meshes only too well with the idea of spatial differentiations as lures for a peripatetic capital that values the option of mobility very highly. Isn't this place better than that place, not only for the operations of capital but also for living in, consuming well, and feeling secure in a shifting world? The construction of such places, the fashioning of some localized aesthetic image, allows the construction of some limited and limiting sense of identity in the midst of a collage of imploding spatialities.

. . . Jameson (1988, 351), for his part, views the spatial peculiarities of post-modernism as symptoms and expressions of a new and historically original dilemma, one that involves our insertion as individual subjects into a multidimensional set of radically discontinuous realities, whose frames range from the still surviving spaces of bourgeois private life all the way to the unimaginable decentring of global capitalism itself. Not even Einsteinian relativity, or the multiple subjective worlds of the older modernists, is capable of giving any adequate figuration to this process, which in lived experience makes itself felt by the so-called death of the subject, or, more exactly, the fragmented and schizophrenic decentring and dispersion of this last. . . . And although you may not have realized it, I am talking about practical politics here: since the crisis of socialist internationalism, and the enormous strategic and tactical difficulties of coordinating local and grass-roots or neighbourhood political actions with national or international ones, such urgent political dilemmas are all immediately functions of the enormously complex new international space I have in mind.

---

15   Andreas Huyssen
From *After the Great Divide*

Here, then, some remarks about the history of the perception of mass culture as feminine. Time and again documents from the late 19th century ascribe pejorative feminine characteristics to mass culture – and by mass culture here I mean serialized feuilleton novels, popular and family maga-

From Andreas Huyssen, *After the Great Divide*, Macmillan, 1988, pp. 49–53.

zines, the stuff of lending libraries, fictional bestsellers and the like – not, however, working-class culture or residual forms of older popular or folk cultures. A few examples will have to suffice. In the preface to their novel *Germinie Lacerteux* (1865), which is usually regarded as the first naturalist manifesto, the Goncourt brothers attack what they call the false novel. They describe it as those 'spicy little works, memoirs of street-walkers, bedroom confessions, erotic smuttiness, scandals that hitch up their skirts in pictures in bookshop windows'. The true novel (*le roman vrai*) by contrast is called 'severe and pure'. It is said to be characterized by its scientificity, and rather than sentiment it offers what the authors call 'a clinical picture of love' (*une clinique de l'amour*).[1] Twenty years later, in the editorial of the first issue of Michael Georg Conrad's journal *Die Gesellschaft* (1885), which marks the beginning of 'die Moderne' in Germany, the editor states his intention to emancipate literature and criticism from the 'tyranny of well-bred debutantes and old wives of both sexes', and from the empty and pompous rhetoric of 'old wives' criticism'. And he goes on to polemicize against the then popular literary family magazines: 'The literary and artistic kitchen personnel has achieved absolute mastery in the art of economizing and imitating the famous potato banquet. . . . It consists of twelve courses each of which offers the potato in a different guise.'[2] Once the kitchen has been described metaphorically as the site of mass cultural production, we are not surprised to hear Conrad call for the reestablishment of an '*arg gefährdete Mannhaftigkeit*' (seriously threatened manliness) and for the restoration of bravery and courage (*Tapferkeit*) in thought, poetry, and criticism.

It is easy to see how such statements rely on the traditional notion that women's aesthetic and artistic abilities are inferior to those of men. Women as providers of inspiration for the artist, yes, but otherwise *Berufsverbot* for the muses,[3] unless of course they content themselves with the lower genres (painting flowers and animals) and the decorative arts. At any rate, the gendering of an inferior mass culture as feminine goes hand in hand with the emergence of a male mystique in modernism (especially in painting), which has been documented thoroughly by feminist scholarship.[4] What is interesting in the second half of the 19th century, however, is a certain chain effect of signification: from the obsessively argued inferiority of woman as artist (classically argued by Karl Scheffler in *Die Frau und die Kunst*, 1908) to the association of woman with mass culture (witness Hawthorne's 'the damned mob of scribbling women') to the identification of woman with the masses as political threat.

This line of argument invariably leads back to Nietzsche. Significantly, Nietzsche's ascription of feminine characteristics to the masses is always tied to his aesthetic vision of the artist-philosopher-hero, the suffering loner who stands in irreconcilable opposition to modern democracy and its inauthentic culture. Fairly typical examples of this nexus can be found in Nietzsche's polemic against Wagner, who becomes for him the paradigm of the decline of genuine culture in the dawning age of the masses and the feminization of culture: 'The danger for artists, for geniuses . . . is woman: adoring women confront them with corruption. Hardly any of them have character enough not to be corrupted – or 'redeemed' – when they find themselves treated like gods: soon they condescend to the level of the women.'[5] Wagner, it is implied, has succumbed to the adoring women by transforming music into mere spectacle, theater, delusion:

> I have explained where Wagner belongs – *not* in the history of music. What does he signify nevertheless in that history? *The emergence of the actor in music. . . .* One can grasp it with one's very hands: great success, success with the masses no longer sides with those who are authentic – one has to be an actor to achieve that. Victor Hugo and Richard Wagner – they signify the same thing: in declining cultures, wherever the decision comes to rest with the masses, authenticity becomes superfluous, disadvantageous, a liability. Only the actor still arouses *great* enthusiasm.[6]

And then Wagner, the theater, the mass, woman – all become a web of signification outside of, and in opposition to, true art: 'No one brings along the finest senses of his art to the theater, least of all the artist who works for the theater – solitude is lacking; whatever is perfect suffers no witnesses. In the theater one becomes people, herd, female, pharisee, voting cattle, patron, idiot – *Wagnerian.*'[7] What Nietzsche articulates here is of course not an attack on the drama or the tragedy, which to him remain some of the highest manifestations of culture. When Nietzsche calls theater a 'revolt of the masses',[8] he anticipates what the situationists would later elaborate as the society of the spectacle, and what Baudrillard chastises as the simulacrum. At the same time, it is no coincidence that the philosopher blames theatricality for the decline of culture. After all, the theater in bourgeois society was one of the few spaces which allowed women a prime place in the arts, precisely because acting was seen as imitative and reproductive, rather than original and productive. Thus, in Nietzsche's attack on what he perceives as Wagner's feminization of music, his 'infinite melody' – 'one walks into the sea, gradually loses one's secure footing, and finally surrenders oneself to the elements without reservation'[9] – an extremely perceptive critique of the mechanisms of bourgeois culture goes hand in hand with an exhibition of that culture's sexist biases and prejudices.

III

The fact that the identification of woman with mass has major political implications is easily recognized. Thus Mallarmé's quip about '*reportage universel*' (i.e., mass culture), with its not so subtle allusion to '*suffrage universel*', is more than just a clever pun. The problem goes far beyond questions of art and literature. In the late 19th century, a specific traditional male image of woman served as a receptacle for all kinds of projections, displaced fears, and anxieties (both personal and political), which were brought about by modernization and the new social conflicts, as well as by specific historical events such as the 1848 revolution, the 1870 Commune, and the rise of reactionary mass movements which, as in Austria, threatened the liberal order.[10] An examination of the magazines and the newspapers of the period will show that the proletarian and petit-bourgeois masses were persistently described in terms of a feminine threat. Images of the raging mob as hysterical, of the engulfing floods of revolt and revolution, of the swamp of big city life, of the spreading ooze of massification, of the figure of the red whore at the barricades – all of these pervade the writing of the mainstream media, as well as that of right-wing ideologues of the late 19th and early 20th centuries whose social psychology Klaus Theweleit has perceptively analysed in his study *Male Phantasies*.[11] The fear of the masses in this age of declining liberalism is always also a fear of woman, a fear of nature out of control, a fear of the unconscious, of sexuality, of the loss of identity and stable ego boundaries in the mass.

This kind of thinking is exemplified by Gustave Le Bon's enormously influential *The Crowd* (*La Psychologie des foules*, 1895), which as Freud observed in his own *Mass Psychology and Ego Analysis* (1921) merely summarizes arguments pervasive in Europe at the time. In Le Bon's study, the male fear of woman and the bourgeois fear of the masses become indistinguishable: 'Crowds are everywhere distinguished by feminine characteristics.'[12] And: 'The simplicity and exaggeration of the sentiments of crowds have for result that a throng knows neither doubt nor uncertainty. Like women, it goes at once to extremes. . . . A commencement of antipathy or disapprobation, which in the case of an isolated individual would not gain strength, becomes at once furious hatred in the case of an individual in a crowd.'[13] And then he summarizes his fears with a reference to that icon which perhaps more than any other in the 19th century – more even than the Judiths and Salomés so often portrayed on symbolist canvases – stood for the feminine threat to civilization: 'Crowds are somewhat like the sphinx of ancient fable: it is necessary to arrive at a solution of the problems offered by their psychology or to resign ourselves to being devoured by them.'[14] Male fears of an engulfing femininity are here projected onto the metropolitan masses, who did indeed represent a threat to the rational bourgeois order. The haunting specter of a loss of power combines with fear of losing one's fortified and stable ego boundaries, which represent the *sine qua non* of male psychology in that bourgeois order. We may want to relate Le Bon's social psychology of the masses back to modernism's own fears of being sphinxed. Thus the nightmare of being devoured by mass culture through co-option, commodification, and the 'wrong' kind of success is the constant fear of the modernist artist, who tries to stake out his territory by fortifying the boundaries between genuine art and inauthentic mass culture. Again, the problem is not the desire to differentiate between forms of high art and depraved forms of mass culture and its co-options. The problem is rather the persistent gendering as feminine of that which is devalued.

Notes

1 Edmond and Jules de Goncourt, *Germinie Lacerteux*, trans. Leonard Tancock (Harmondsworth, Penguin, 1984), p. 15.

2 *Die Gesellschaft*, 1, no. 1 (January 1885).

3 Cf. Cäcilia Rentmeister, 'Berufsverbot für Musen,' *Ästhetik und Kommunikation*, 25 (September 1976), 92–113.

4 Cf., for instance, the essays by Carol Duncan and Norma Broude in *Feminism and Art History*, ed. Norma Broude and Mary D. Garrard (New York, Harper & Row, 1982) or the documentation of relevant quotes by Valerie Jaudon and Joyce Kozloff, ' "Art Hysterical Notions" of Progress and Culture,' *Heresies*, 1, no. 4 (winter 1978), 38–42.

5 Friedrich Nietzsche, *The Case of Wagner*, in *The Birth of Tragedy and the Case of Wagner*, trans. Walter Kaufmann (New York, Random House, 1967), p. 161.

6 Nietzsche, *The Case of Wagner*, p. 179.

7 Friedrich Nietzsche, *Nietzsche contra Wagner*, in *The Portable Nietzsche*, ed. and trans. Walter Kaufmann (Harmondsworth and New York, Penguin, 1976), pp. 665f.

8 Nietzsche, *The Case of Wagner*, p. 183.

9 Nietzsche, *Nietzsche contra Wagner*, p. 666.

10 For a recent discussion of semantic shifts in the political and sociological discourse of masses, elites, and leaders from the late 19th century to fascism see Helmuth Berking. 'Mythos und Politik: Zur historischen Semantik des Massenbegriffs,' *Ästhetik und Kommunikation*, 56 (November 1984), 35–42.

11 An English translation of the two-volume work will soon be published by the University of Minnesota Press.

12 Gustave Le Bon, *The Crowd* (Harmondsworth and New York, Penguin, 1981), p. 39.

13 Le Bon, p. 50.

14 Le Bon, p. 102.

In its economic manifestation, liberalism is the recognition of the right of free economic activity and economic exchange based on private property and markets. Since the term 'capitalism' has acquired so many pejorative connotations over the years, it has recently become a fashion to speak of 'free-market economics' instead; both are acceptable alternative terms for economic liberalism. It is evident that there are many possible interpretations of this rather broad definition of economic liberalism, ranging from the United States of Ronald Reagan and the Britain of Margaret Thatcher to the social democracies of Scandinavia and the relatively statist regimes in Mexico and India. All contemporary capitalist states have large public sectors, while most socialist states have permitted a degree of private economic activity. There has been considerable controversy over the point at which the public sector becomes large enough to disqualify a state as liberal. Rather than try to set a precise percentage, it is probably more useful to look at what attitude the state takes *in principle* to the legitimacy of private property and enterprise. Those that protect such economic rights we will consider liberal; those that are opposed or base themselves on other principles (such as 'economic justice') will not qualify.

The present crisis of authoritarianism has not necessarily led to the emergence of liberal democratic regimes, nor are all the new democracies which have emerged secure. The newly democratic countries of Eastern Europe face wrenching transformations of their economies, while the new democracies in Latin America are hobbled by a terrible legacy of prior economic mismanagement. Many of the fast developers in East Asia, while economically liberal, have not accepted the challenge of political liberalization. The liberal revolution has left certain areas like the Middle East relatively untouched.[1] It is altogether possible to imagine states like Peru or the Philippines relapsing into some kind of dictatorship under the weight of the crushing problems they face.

But the fact that there will be setbacks and disappointments in the process of democratization, or that not every market economy will prosper, should not distract us from the larger pattern that is emerging in world history. The apparent number of choices that countries face in determining how they will organize themselves politically and economically has been *diminishing* over time. Of the different types of regimes that have emerged

From Francis Fukuyama, *The End of History and the Last Man*, Penguin, 1992, pp. 44–6.

in the course of human history, from monarchies and aristocracies, to religious theocracies, to the fascist and communist dictatorships of this century, the only form of government that has survived intact to the end of the twentieth century has been liberal democracy.

What is emerging victorious, in other words, is not so much liberal practice, as the liberal *idea*. That is to say, for a very large part of the world, there is now no ideology with pretensions to universality that is in a position to challenge liberal democracy, and no universal principle of legitimacy other than the sovereignty of the people. Monarchism in its various forms had been largely defeated by the beginning of this century. Fascism and communism, liberal democracy's main competitors up till now, have both discredited themselves. If the Soviet Union (or its successor states) fails to democratize, if Peru or the Philippines relapse into some form of authoritarianism, democracy will most likely have yielded to a colonel or bureaucrat who claims to speak in the name of the Russian, Peruvian, or Philippine people alone. Even non-democrats will have to speak the language of democracy in order to justify their deviation from the single universal standard.

It is true that Islam constitutes a systematic and coherent ideology, just like liberalism and communism, with its own code of morality and doctrine of political and social justice. The appeal of Islam is potentially universal, reaching out to all men as men, and not just to members of a particular ethnic or national group. And Islam has indeed defeated liberal democracy in many parts of the Islamic world, posing a grave threat to liberal practices even in countries where it has not achieved political power directly. The end of the Cold War in Europe was followed immediately by a challenge to the West from Iraq, in which Islam was arguably a factor.[2]

Despite the power demonstrated by Islam in its current revival, however, it remains the case that this religion has virtually no appeal outside those areas that were culturally Islamic to begin with. The days of Islam's cultural conquests, it would seem, are over: it can win back lapsed adherents, but has no resonance for young people in Berlin, Tokyo, or Moscow. And while nearly a billion people are culturally Islamic – one-fifth of the world's population – they cannot challenge liberal democracy on its own territory on the level of ideas.[3] Indeed, the Islamic world would seem more vulnerable to liberal ideas in the long run than the reverse, since such liberalism has attracted numerous and powerful Muslim adherents over the past century and a half. Part of the reason for the current fundamentalist revival is the strength of the perceived threat from liberal, Western values to traditional Islamic societies.

We who live in stable, long-standing liberal democracies face an unusual situation. In our grandparents' time, many reasonable people could foresee a radiant socialist future in which private property and capitalism had been abolished, and in which politics itself was somehow overcome. Today, by contrast, we have trouble imagining a world that is radically better than our own, or a future that is not essentially democratic and capitalist. Within that framework, of course, many things could be improved: we could house the homeless, guarantee opportunity for minorities and women, improve competitiveness, and create new jobs. We can also imagine future worlds that are significantly worse than what we know now, in which national, racial, or religious intolerance makes a comeback, or in which we are overwhelmed by war or environmental collapse. But we cannot picture to ourselves a world that is *essentially* different from the present one, and at the same time better. Other, less reflective ages also thought of themselves as the best, but we arrive at this conclusion exhausted, as it were, from the pursuit of alternatives we felt *had* to be better than liberal democracy.[4]

Notes

1 There have been pressures for greater democracy in various Middle Eastern countries like Egypt and Jordan, following the Eastern European revolutions of 1989. But in this part of the world, Islam has stood as a major barrier to democratization. As demonstrated by the Algerian municipal elections of 1990, or by Iran a decade earlier, greater democracy may not lead to greater liberalization because it brings to power Islamic fundamentalists hoping to establish some form of popular theocracy.
2 Although Iraq is an Islamic country, Sadam Hussein's Ba'ath party is an explicitly secular Arab nationalist organization. His attempts to wrap himself in the mantle of Islam after his invasion of Kuwait were hypocritical in light of his earlier efforts to portray himself as a defender of secular values against a fanatical Islamic Iran during his war with that country.
3 They can, of course, challenge liberal democracy through terrorist bombs and bullets, a significant but not vital challenge.
4 The suggestion made in my original article 'The End of History?' that there were no viable alternatives to liberal democracy drew a number of indignant responses from people who pointed to Islamic fundamentalism, nationalism, fascism, and a number of other possibilities. None of these critics believes that these alternatives are *superior* to liberal democracy, however, and in the course of the entire controversy over the article, no one that I am aware of suggested an alternative form of social organization that he or she personally believed was better.

NATIONAL IDENTITIES

17 E.M. Forster
From *Two Cheers for Democracy*

What I believe

I do not believe in Belief. But this is an age of faith, and there are so many militant creeds that, in self-defence, one has to formulate a creed of one's own. Tolerance, good temper and sympathy are no longer enough in a world which is rent by religious and racial persecution, in a world where ignorance rules, and science, who ought to have ruled, plays the subservient pimp. Tolerance, good temper and sympathy – they are what matter really, and if the human race is not to collapse they must come to the front before long. But for the moment they are not enough, their action is no stronger than a flower, battered beneath a military jack-boot. They want stiffening, even if the process coarsens them. Faith, to my mind, is a stiffening process, a sort of mental starch, which ought to be applied as sparingly as possible. I dislike the stuff. I do not believe in it, for its own sake, at all. Herein I probably differ from most people, who believe in Belief, and are only sorry they cannot swallow even more than they do. My law-givers are Erasmus and Montaigne, not Moses and St. Paul. My temple stands not upon Mount Moriah but in that Elysian Field where even the immoral are admitted. My motto is: 'Lord, I disbelieve – help thou my unbelief.'

I have, however, to live in an Age of Faith – the sort of epoch I used to hear praised when I was a boy. It is extremely unpleasant really. It is bloody in every sense of the word. And I have to keep my end up in it. Where do I start?

With personal relationships. Here is something comparatively solid in a world full of violence and cruelty. Not absolutely solid, for Psychology has split and shattered the idea of a 'Person,' and has shown that there is something incalculable in each of us, which may at any moment rise to the surface and destroy our normal balance. We don't know what we are like. We can't know what other people are like. How, then, can we put any trust in personal relationships, or cling to them in the gathering political storm? In theory we cannot. But in practice we can and do. Though A is not unchangeably A or B unchangeably B, there can still be love and loyalty between the two. For the purpose of living one has to assume that the

From E.M. Forster, *Two Cheers for Democracy*, Edward Arnold, 1951, pp. 77–9.

personality is solid, and the 'self' is an entity, and to ignore all contrary evidence. And since to ignore evidence is one of the characteristics of faith, I certainly can proclaim that I believe in personal relationships.

Starting from them, I get a little order into the contemporary chaos. One must be fond of people and trust them if one is not to make a mess of life, and it is therefore essential that they should not let one down. They often do. The moral of which is that I must, myself, be as reliable as possible, and this I try to be. But reliability is not a matter of contract – that is the main difference between the world of personal relationships and the world of business relationships. It is a matter for the heart, which signs no documents. In other words, reliability is impossible unless there is a natural warmth. Most men possess this warmth, though they often have bad luck and get chilled. Most of them, even when they are politicians, *want* to keep faith. And one can, at all events, show one's own little light here, one's own poor little trembling flame, with the knowledge that it is not the only light that is shining in the darkness, and not the only one which the darkness does not comprehend. Personal relations are despised to-day. They are regarded as bourgeois luxuries, as products of a time of fair weather which is now past, and we are urged to get rid of them, and to dedicate ourselves to some movement or cause instead. I hate the idea of causes, and if I had to choose between betraying my country and betraying my friend, I hope I should have the guts to betray my country. Such a choice may scandalise the modern reader, and he may stretch out his patriotic hand to the telephone at once and ring up the police. It would not have shocked Dante, though. Dante places Brutus and Cassius in the lowest circle of Hell because they had chosen to betray their friend Julius Caesar rather than their country Rome. Probably one will not be asked to make such an agonising choice. Still, there lies at the back of every creed something terrible and hard for which the worshipper may one day be required to suffer, and there is even a terror and a hardness in this creed of personal relationships, urbane and mild though it sounds. Love and loyalty to an individual can run counter to the claims of the State. When they do – down with the State, say I, which means that the State would down me.

This brings me along to Democracy, 'even Love, the Beloved Republic, which feeds upon Freedom and lives.' Democracy is not a Beloved Republic really, and never will be. But it is less hateful than other contemporary forms of government, and to that extent it deserves our support. It does start from the assumption that the individual is important, and that all types are needed to make a civilisation. It does not divide its citizens into the bossers and the bossed – as an efficiency-regime tends to do. The people I admire most are those who are sensitive and want to create something or discover something, and do not see life in terms of power, and such people get more of a chance under a democracy than elsewhere. They found religions, great or small, or they produce literature and art, or they do disinterested scientific research, or they may be what is called 'ordinary people,' who are creative in their private lives, bring up their children decently, for instance, or help their neighbours. All these people need to express themselves; they cannot do so unless society allows them liberty to do so, and the society which allows them most liberty is a democracy.

Democracy has another merit. It allows criticism, and if there is not public criticism there are bound to be hushed-up scandals. That is why I believe in the Press, despite all its lies and vulgarity, and why I believe in Parliament. Parliament is often sneered at because it is a Talking Shop. I believe in it *because* it is a talking shop. I believe in the Private Member who makes himself a nuisance. He gets snubbed and is told that he is cranky or ill-informed, but he does expose abuses which would otherwise never have been mentioned, and very often an abuse gets put right just by being mentioned. Occasionally, too, a well-meaning public official starts losing his head in the cause of efficiency, and thinks himself God Almighty. Such officials are particularly frequent in the Home Office. Well, there will be questions about them in Parliament sooner or later, and then they will have to mind their steps. Whether Parliament is either a representative body or an efficient one is questionable, but I value it because it criticises and talks, and because its chatter gets widely reported.

So Two cheers for Democracy: one because it admits variety and two because it permits criticism. Two cheers are quite enough: there is no occasion to give three. Only Love the Beloved Republic deserves that.

18   Perry Anderson
'A Culture in Contraflow'

Twenty years ago it was possible to take the nation – actually, the meta-national state making up the United Kingdom – as an unproblematic unit for cultural enquiry. There was a general and a specific reason for that. The economies of the West were still relatively self-contained entities across the major branches of industrial production, nowhere more so than in the publishing and broadcasting sectors; while their educational systems had few points of interchange. Particular intellectual patterns do not, however, depend only on such institutional infrastructures. They are formed by political history and social tradition. Within the set of major Western societies, Britain in the immediate post-war decades possessed a peculiarly

From *New Left Review*, 180, March/April 1990, pp. 47–50.

stable and insulated culture. Alone of them it had never known either social upheaval, foreign occupation or mass immigration – the three great solvents of fixed collective identity in the twentieth century; while unlike the few smaller European countries which had also escaped these, it had been the world's premier empire for two centuries, with all the confidence of superiority imparted by global power. These were circumstances which made British intellectual life exceptionally well defined. Even the admixture of conservative refugees who achieved post-war salience essentially confirmed rather than contested its standing dispositions. The national stamp of the prevailing outlook was one of its own proudest themes. In these conditions the frontiers of the spirit were indeed largely one with the borders of the state.

The ferment of 1968 thus represented not only a political break; in consciously forming part of an international chain of revolts, it marked a geocultural one too – of no less moment. This was the first time since the war that a significant movement within British society was directly synchronized to counterparts outside the country. The role of television in making the connexions possible was much commented upon at the time. The next two decades were to see a vast amplification of the material changes these events portended. Internationalization of the forces of production accelerated rapidly throughout the capitalist world, bypassing and diminishing the nation state. Global corporations, outsourcing their manufacturing sites, were followed by offshore credit systems and interpenetrating financial markets. Travel became a huge industry in its own right, tourism intercontinental. Similar developments in due course found spectacular expression in the fields of publishing and broadcasting themselves, with the media empires of Bertelsmann, Murdoch, Elsevier, Berlusconi, Maxwell or Hachette. In this epoch, no culture could remain national in the pristiner senses of the past.

These processes affected the whole OECD zone. Arguably, however, Britain underwent the greatest transformation in this respect. Only recently the most self-contained of the larger NATO cultures, it was now to become in some ways the least closed to the surrounding world. The terms of this change were basically set by its peculiar crossroads position: geographically part of Europe and linguistically tied to America. By the late 80s there was probably no other country where influences from both sides of the Atlantic intermingled so freely. This inrush was not simply a matter of natural–historical location, and its two currents were not equivalent in character. Political shifts, indicated above, were necessary to convert a combination of general economic forces and particular geo-cultural emplacement into specific intellectual results. The emergence of a substantial culture of the Left after 1968 was the key which principally unlocked the gates to Europe. A wide absorption of the corpus of continental Marxism was the main initial consequence: a decade later, it was easier for a student to gain exposure to its full range in England than in France or Germany, where translations were fewer. Structuralism, less affiliated in origin, was received in an overlapping intellectual milieu through the 70s. Hermeneutics and post-structuralism followed in the 80s, entering through more diffuse channels, but by and large still issuing into a public sphere whose sympathies were with socialism and now feminism. Publishing houses of the Left, NLB in the first phase and Polity in the second, were the most concentrated transmission points for this process of assimilation. But in its later stages it extended into the area of the liberal centre, as membership of the European Community became normalized. A period which began with Althusser and Gramsci, Adorno and Lacan pioneered by journals like this one, ended with Habermas and Bourdieu starring in a chastened TLS, and Derrida or Foucault admired by an LRB recanting its suspicion of deconstruction.

The Atlantic dimension

If the European influx was in the main a deliberate work of left and centre-left impulses in Britain, the American osmosis was by contrast partly an unintended consequence of the rise of the Right, although it was always a more mixed and multifaceted process. Common language and legal traditions had traditionally bound the two countries together, although in many fields the US had often enjoyed a more diverse intellectual life because of its composite immigrant background. In the fifties, Washington's imperial interest in securing London as a junior partner and staging-post led its espionage service to create *Encounter* as a conduit for the Cold War ideology of the time in the UK. Effective enough in this political role, until its cover was blown by CIA boasts in the mid sixties, the journal was more limited as a vehicle for familiarization with American culture; its format was actually more oriented to Europe, as the endangered front-line of the Cold War, than to the safe rearguard of the US. More generally, Anglo-American intellectual relations still remained uneven, often distant. In the 70s this changed. For the first time, central social disciplines became dominated by US developments. Outstanding cases in point were analytical philosophy, political theory and neoclassical economics, in each of which there was a certain traditional basis for Anglo-Saxon congruence. Although the new English Right could and did appropriate trends within these for its own purposes, naturalizing Friedman, Nozick or Buchanan, this was not the general pattern. The culture of the Centre filtered the distribution of influences, in which Rawls, Arrow or Chomsky loomed larger. In other areas American reception of European ideas predated or exceeded British, US adaptations then becoming a significant local reference in their own right, as in the Yale school of literary criticism; or formed distinctive hybrids like an existentialized neo-pragmatism. Overall, the American intelligentsia had followed a trajectory not unlike that of the British in these years – a radical breakthrough after the late 60s, a neo-conservative counter-thrust from the late seventies, with a continuing centre–liberal majority throughout. The two principal differences were the far weaker Marxist strain on the left – McCarthyism having ensured that there was no equivalent of the British Communist historians; and the more externally coloured alterations of mood in the liberal mainstream, troubled by visions of Soviet gain or US loss abroad rather than fears of trade-union militancy at home, before turning against Reagan's domestic programme in much the same way as its British counterpart did against Thatcher's. There was little potential here for comprehensive reinforcement of the radical Right in England, anyway scarcely warmed by the Presidential deficits.

In itself, of course, the general growth of the transatlantic presence within British intellectual life reflected the changing material balance between the two societies. The far greater resources and responsibilities of the hegemonic power were in due course bound to have their cultural effects. The rise of the *New York Review of Books*, from its beginnings in 1967, to become the peak literary-political periodical in the English-speaking world, with a circulation some four times that of its UK counterparts combined, was the most visible sign of the new correlation of forces. Drawing from the outset extensively on British contributors, to the point of incurring occasional reserve at home, the Manhattan fortnightly eventually achieved such international dominance that it seeded its opposite number in Bloomsbury. Given their approximate similarity of stance, the difference between the two publications said much about their respective contexts. Where its London offshoot exhibited a quirky individuality of temper, relatively indifferent to celebrity or news-value, combining independence of mind and a certain levity of interest,[1] the much wealthier New York original was more corporate and predictable in style, attached to conventional eminences, but also possessed of another political weight and sense of global priorities, as the intellectual look-out of a superpower.

This alteration in the periodical world, and its economic background, were a harbinger of wider energy transfers in the academic world. From the later 60s onwards, there had been a certain number of migrations from English to American departments. But these remained relatively isolated cases for another decade. It was not until the Conservative regime unleashed its campaign of attrition and compression against the institutions of higher education that a major exit to the United States occurred, in the 80s. By then the differentials in rewards and resources between the two university systems had increased enormously. In a federal state the Reagan administration, anyway more conscious of Japanese rivalry, had neither the same power, nor quite the same inclination, to wage a *Kulturkampf*; competitive pressures in boom conditions rather worked in the opposite direction, at certain levels creating something like an academic bull market. The economic contrast was also one of psychological climate, faculty morale often reflecting available matériel. The result of these push and pull forces was a well publicized exodus from British universities. Although often exaggerated in extent, by the end of the 80s selective departures had affected virtually all social disciplines, and different generations within them, from the retired to the rising. Prominent instances included Ricks, Kermode, MacCabe, MacIntyre, Wollheim, Miliband, Ryan, Lukes, Mann, Clark, Brewer, Hobsbawm, Schama, Sen. This was not an emigration in the traditional sense. Many of those who now worked in the US either continued to reside partly in the UK or would return there; nearly all still comprised part of the British intellectual scene, even where assimilation into the American had gone furthest. What the new phenomenon really represented was the increasing erosion of boundaries between the two. The overall process was, of course, rather like the respective visa requirements between the two countries, less than symmetrical in effect – given their discrepancy in size. In the standard hyphenation, it necessarily modified Anglo more than American culture.

The sum of these developments, coming from different horizons and having different effects, amounted to a notable mutation. Englishry in its worst, caricatural forms declined. The ferruginous philistinism and parochialism of long national tradition was discomposed. The monotone political conformities of the ordinary intelligentsia broke up. British culture became looser and more hybrid.

Notes

1 October 1987 provided a nice illustration of the contrast: the cover of the NYRB was dominated by the crash of the world's stock markets, the LRB's devoted to the fall of trees in the English storm.

---

19 Seamus Heaney
'Englands of the Mind'

It is in the context of this auditory imagination that I wish to discuss the language of Ted Hughes, Geoffrey Hill and Philip Larkin. All of them

From *Preoccupations*, Faber, 1980, pp. 150–3, 168–9.

return to an origin and bring something back, all three live off the hump of the English poetic achievement, all three, here and now, in England, imply a continuity with another England, there and then. All three are hoarders and shorers of what they take to be the real England. All three treat England as a region – or rather treat their region as England – in different and complementary ways. I believe they are afflicted with a sense of history that was once the peculiar affliction of the poets of other nations who were not themselves natives of England but who spoke the English language. The poets of the mother culture, I feel, are now possessed of that defensive love of their territory which was once shared only by those poets whom we might call colonial – Yeats, MacDiarmid, Carlos Williams. They are aware of their Englishness as deposits in the descending storeys of the literary and historical past. Their very terrain is becoming consciously precious. A desire to preserve indigenous traditions, to keep open the imagination's supply lines to the past, to receive from the stations of Anglo-Saxon confirmations of ancestry, to perceive in the rituals of show Saturdays and race-meetings and seaside outings, of church-going and marriages at Whitsun, and in the necessities that crave expression after the ritual of church-going has passed away, to perceive in these a continuity of communal ways, and a confirmation of an identity which is threatened – all this is signified by their language.

When we examine that language, we find that their three separate voices are guaranteed by three separate foundations which, when combined, represent almost the total resources of the English language itself. Hughes relies on the northern deposits, the pagan Anglo-Saxon and Norse elements, and he draws energy also from a related constellation of primitive myths and world views. The life of his language is a persistence of the stark outline and vitality of Anglo-Saxon that became the Middle English alliterative tradition and then went underground to sustain the folk poetry, the ballads, and the ebullience of Shakespeare and the Elizabethans. Hill is also sustained by the Anglo-Saxon base, but his proper guarantor is that language as modified and amplified by the vocabularies and values of the Mediterranean, by the early medieval Latin influence; his is to a certain extent a scholastic imagination founded on an England that we might describe as Anglo-Romanesque, touched by the polysyllabic light of Christianity but possessed by darker energies which might be acknowledged as barbaric. Larkin then completes the picture, because his proper hinterland is the English language Frenchified and turned humanist by the Norman conquest and the Renaissance, made nimble, melodious and plangent by Chaucer and Spenser, and besomed clean of its inkhornisms and its irrational magics by the eighteenth century.

And their Englands of the mind might be correspondingly characterized. Hughes's is a primeval landscape where stones cry out and horizons endure, where the elements inhabit the mind with a religious force, where the pebble dreams 'it is the foetus of God', 'where the staring angels go through', 'where all the stars bow down', where, with appropriately pre-Socratic force, water lies 'at the bottom of all things / utterly worn out utterly clear'. It is England as King Lear's heath which now becomes a Yorkshire moor where sheep and foxes and hawks persuade 'unaccommodated man' that he is a poor bare forked thing, kinned not in a chain but on a plane of being with the animals themselves. There monoliths and lintels. The air is menaced by God's voice in the wind, by demonic protean crow-shapes; and the poet is a wanderer among the ruins, cut off by catastrophe from consolation and philosophy. Hill's England, on the other hand, is more hospitable to the human presence. The monoliths make way for the keeps and chantries if also for the beheading block. The heath's loneliness is kept at bay by the natural magic of the grove and the intellectual force of the scholar's cell. The poet is not a wanderer but a clerk or perhaps an illuminator or one of a guild of masters: he is in possession of a history rather than a mythology; he has a learned rather than an oral tradition. There are wars, but there are also dynasties, ideas of inheritance and order, possibilities for the 'true governaunce of England'. His elegies are not laments for the irrevocable dispersal of the *comitatus* and the ring-giver in the hall, but solemn requiems for Plantagenet kings whose murderous wars are set in a great pattern, to be understood only when 'the sea / Across daubed rocks evacuates its dead'. And Larkin's England similarly reflects features from the period that his language is hived off. His trees and flowers and grasses are neither animistic, nor hallowed by half-remembered druidic lore; they are emblems of mutability. Behind them lies the sensibility of troubadour and courtier. 'Cut grass lies frail; / Brief is the breath / Mown stalks exhale'; his landscape is dominated neither by the untamed heath nor the totemistic architectures of spire and battlement but by the civic prospects, by roofs and gardens and prospects where urban and pastoral visions interact as 'postal districts packed like squares of wheat'. The poet is no longer a bardic remnant nor an initiate in curious learning nor a jealous master of the secrets of a craft; he is a humane and civilized member of the customs service or the civil service or, indeed, the library service. The moon is no longer his white goddess but his poetic property, to be image rather than icon: 'high and preposterous and separate', she watches over unfenced existence, over fulfilment's desolate attic, over an England of department stores, canals and floatings of industrial froth, explosions in mines, effigies in churches, secretaries in offices; and she hauls tides of life where only one ship is worth celebration, not a *Golden Hind* or a *Victory*, but 'black- / Sailed unfamiliar, towing at her back / A huge and birdless silence.'

Larkin's England of the mind is in many ways continuous with the England of Rupert Brooke's 'Grantchester' and Edward Thomas's 'Adlestrop', an England of customs and institutions, industrial and domestic, but also an England whose pastoral hinterland is threatened by the very success of those institutions. Houses and roads and factories mean that a certain England is 'Going, Going':

> It seems, just now,
> To be happening so very fast;
> Despite all the land left free
> For the first time I feel somehow
> That it isn't going to last,
>
> That before I snuff it, the whole
> Boiling will be bricked in
> Except for the tourist parts –
> First slum of Europe: a role
> It won't be so hard to win,
> With a cast of crooks and tarts.
>
> And that will be England gone,
> The shadows, the meadows, the lanes,
> The guildhalls, the carved choirs.
> There'll be books; it will linger on
> In galleries; but all that remains
> For us will be concrete and tyres.

I think that sense of an ending has driven all three of these writers into a kind of piety towards their local origins, has made them look in, rather than up, to England. The loss of imperial power, the failure of economic nerve, the diminished influence of Britain inside Europe, all this has led to a new sense of the shires, a new valuing of the native English experience. Donald Davie, for example, has published a book of poems, with that very title, *The Shires*, which attempts to annex to his imagination by personal memory or historical meditation or literary connections, each shire of England. It is a book at once intimate and exclusive, a topography of love and impatience, and it is yet another symptom that English poets are being forced to explore not just the matter of England, but what is the matter with England. I have simply presumed to share in that exploration through the medium which England has, for better or worse, impressed upon us all, the English language itself.

The Beckman Lecture, given at the University of
California, Berkeley, May 1976

20 Edward Said
From *Orientalism*

In the *Prison Notebooks* Gramsci says: 'The starting-point of critical elaboration is the consciousness of what one really is, and is "knowing thyself" as a product of the historical process to date, which has deposited in you an infinity of traces, without leaving an inventory.' The only available English translation inexplicably leaves Gramsci's comment at that, whereas in fact Gramsci's Italian text concludes by adding, 'therefore it is imperative at the outset to compile such an inventory.'[1]

Much of the personal investment in this study derives from my awareness of being an 'Oriental' as a child growing up in two British colonies. All of my education, in those colonies (Palestine and Egypt) and in the United States, has been Western, and yet that deep early awareness has persisted. In many ways my study of Orientalism has been an attempt to inventory the traces upon me, the Oriental subject, of the culture whose domination has been so powerful a factor in the life of all Orientals. This is why for me the Islamic Orient has had to be the center of attention. Whether what I have achieved is the inventory prescribed by Gramsci is not for me to judge, although I have felt it important to be conscious of trying to produce one. Along the way, as severely and as rationally as I have been able, I have tried to maintain a critical consciousness, as well as employing those instruments of historical, humanistic, and cultural research of which my education has made me the fortunate beneficiary. In none of that, however, have I ever lost hold of my cultural reality of, the personal involvement in having been constituted as, 'an Oriental.'

The historical circumstances making such a study possible are fairly complex, and I can only list them schematically here. Anyone resident in the West since the 1950s, particularly in the United States, will have lived through an era of extraordinary turbulence in the relations of East and West. No one will have failed to note how 'East' has always signified danger and threat during this period, even as it has meant the traditional Orient as well as Russia. In the universities a growing establishment of area-studies programs and institutes has made the scholarly study of the Orient a branch of national policy. Public affairs in this country include a healthy interest in the Orient, as much for its strategic and economic importance as for its traditional exoticism. If the world has become immediately accessible to a Western citizen living in the electronic age, the Orient

From Edward Said, *Orientalism*, Penguin, 1985, pp. 25–8.

too has drawn nearer to him, and is now less a myth perhaps than a place crisscrossed by Western, especially American, interests.

One aspect of the electronic, postmodern world is that there has been a reinforcement of the stereotypes by which the Orient is viewed. Television, the films, and all the media's resources have forced information into more and more standardized molds. So far as the Orient is concerned, standardization and cultural stereotyping have intensified the hold of the nineteenth-century academic and imaginative demonology of 'the mysterious Orient.' This is nowhere more true than in the ways by which the Near East is grasped. Three things have contributed to making even the simplest perception of the Arabs and Islam into a highly politicized, almost raucous matter: one, the history of popular anti-Arab and anti-Islamic prejudice in the West, which is immediately reflected in the history of Orientalism; two, the struggle between the Arabs and Israeli Zionism, and its effects upon American Jews as well as upon both the liberal culture and the population at large; three, the almost total absence of any cultural position making it possible either to identify with or dispassionately to discuss the Arabs or Islam. Furthermore, it hardly needs saying that because the Middle East is now so identified with Great Power politics, oil economics, and the simpleminded dichotomy of freedom-loving, democratic Israel and evil, totalitarian, and terroristic Arabs, the chances of anything like a clear view of what one talks about in talking about the Near East are depressingly small.

My own experiences of these matters are in part what made me write this book. The life of an Arab Palestinian in the West, particularly in America, is disheartening. There exists here an almost unanimous consensus that politically he does not exist, and when it is allowed that he does, it is either as a nuisance or as an Oriental. The web of racism, cultural stereotypes, political imperialism, dehumanizing ideology holding in the Arab or the Muslim is very strong indeed, and it is this web which every Palestinian has come to feel as his uniquely punishing destiny. It has made matters worse for him to remark that no person academically involved with the Near East – no Orientalist, that is – has ever in the United States culturally and politically identified himself wholeheartedly with the Arabs; certainly there have been identifications on some level, but they have never taken an 'acceptable' form as has liberal American identification with Zionism, and all too frequently they have been radically flawed by their association either with discredited political and economic interests (oil-company and State Department Arabists, for example) or with religion.

The nexus of knowledge and power creating 'the Oriental' and in a sense obliterating him as a human being is therefore not for me an exclusively academic matter. Yet it is an *intellectual* matter of some very obvious importance. I have been able to put to use my humanistic and political concerns for the analysis and description of a very worldly matter, the rise, development, and consolidation of Orientalism. Too often literature and culture are presumed to be politically, even historically innocent; it has regularly seemed otherwise to me, and certainly my study of Orientalism has convinced me (and I hope will convince my literary colleagues) that society and literary culture can only be understood and studied together. In addition, and by an almost inescapable logic, I have found myself writing the history of a strange, secret sharer of Western anti-Semitism. That anti-Semitism and, as I have discussed it in its Islamic branch, Orientalism resemble each other very closely is a historical, cultural, and political truth that needs only to be mentioned to an Arab Palestinian for its irony to be perfectly understood. But what I should like also to have contributed here is a better understanding of the way cultural domination has operated. If this stimulates a new kind of dealing with the Orient, indeed if it eliminates the 'Orient' and 'Occident' altogether, then we shall have advanced a little in the process of what Raymond Williams has called the 'unlearning' of 'the inherent dominative mode.'[2]

Notes

1 Antonio Gramsci, *The Prison Notebooks: Selections*, trans. and ed. Quintin Hoare and Geoffrey Nowell Smith (New York, International Publishers, 1971), p. 324. The full passage, unavailable in the Hoare and Smith translation, is to be found in Gramsci, *Quaderni del Carcere*, ed. Valentino Gerratana (Turin, Einaudi Editore, 1975), 2: 1363.
2 Raymond Williams, *Culture and Society, 1780–1950* (London, Chatto & Windus, 1958), p. 376.

WAR

21 Paul Fussell
From *The Great War and Modern Memory*

Survivals

Nobody alive during the war, whether a combatant or not, ever got over its special diction and system of metaphor, its whole jargon of techniques and tactics and strategy. (One reason we can use a term like *tactics* so readily, literally or in metaphors, is that the Great War taught it to us.) And often what impressed itself so deeply was something more than language. Not a few works written during the war, and written about matters far distant from the war, carry more of the war about them than is always recognized. Strachey's *Eminent Victorians*, published in 1918, is an example. Strachey was working on it all during the long years of heartbreaking frontal assaults on the German line, and the repeated and costly aborting of these attacks seems to have augmented his appreciation of the values of innuendo and the oblique, of working up on a position by shrewd man-euver. In working up on the Victorians, the 'direct method,' as he says in his Preface, won't do: 'It is not by the direct method of a scrupulous narration that the explorer of the past can hope to depict [the Victorian Age]. If he is wise, he will adopt a subtler strategy. He will attack his subject in unex-pected places; he will fall upon the flank, or the rear. . . . '[1] (We may be reminded of I.A. Richards blowing up the Hindenburg Line in 1926.) In the same way we can observe how Strachey's impatience with Haig's Scottish rigidity and faith in a Haig-like God underlies some of the acerbity with which he treats the last of his Eminent Victorians, General Gordon, slaugh-tered at Khartoum for his stubbornness and megalomania.

Data entering the consciousness during the war emerge long afterward as metaphor. Blunden conceives of memory itself as very like a trench system, with main stems and lesser branches, as well as 'saps' for reaching minor 'positions': 'Let the smoke of the German breakfast fires, yes, and the savor of their coffee, rise in these pages [of *Undertones of War*], and be kindly mused upon in our neighboring saps of retrogression.'[2] In 1948 Sassoon, searching for a figure to indicate the relation of his wartime poems to their context of civilian complacency, chooses to see them as Very lights, 'rockets sent up to illuminate the darkness.'[3] Stephen Spender reports on

From Paul Fussell, *The Great War and Modern Memory*, Oxford University Press, 1977, pp. 187–90.

his father's 'fairly extensive vocabulary of military metaphor.' He remembers: 'Whenever one of us asked him a favor, he would hold his head down with a butting gesture, and, looking up from under his shaggy sandy eyebrows, say: "You are trying to get round my flank." '[4] One result of the persistence of Great War rhetoric is that the contours of the Second War tend to merge with those of the First. In 1940 eighteen-year-old Colin Perry was observing the London Blitz from the perspective of Great War memoirs, of which he was a devotee. As he says, 'I like reading books about the last war in this one.'[5] The result was a conflation of wars through language, or, as one might put it, the perception of one Great War running from 1914 to 1945. On one occasion Perry spent a weekend at St. Albans after a long period in bombed London. His respite over, he had to re-enter the world of the Blitz. Or, in his words for returning to London, 'We went up the line again at about 3 on the Sunday afternoon.' Another time Perry tells us that the town of Mitcham was severely bombed: indeed, it 'caught a packet.'[6] A character in *Journey's End* couldn't put it more precisely.

Even if now attenuated and largely metaphorical, the diction of war resides everywhere just below the surface of modern experience. American football has its two-platoon system, and medical research aspires to breakthroughs. One says, 'We were bombarded with forms' or 'We've had a barrage of complaints today' without, of course, any sharp awareness that one is recalling war and yet with a sense that such figures are somehow most appropriate to the modern situation. The word *crummy*, felt to apply to numerous phenomena of the modern industrial environment ('This is a crummy town'), is a Great War word, originally meaning itchy because lousy. And there is the word *lousy* itself, without which, it sometimes seems, modern life could hardly be conducted. Before the war *keepsake* was the English word for a small thing kept for remembrance; after the British had lived in France for so long, the word became *souvenir*, which has now virtually ousted *keepsake*. Popular discussion of economics relies heavily on terms like *sector* ('The public vs. the private sector'), and the conduct of labor politics would be a very different thing without the military jargon (like *rank and file*) which it appropriated from the war.

Of the *trench* words like *trenchmouth*, *trenchfoot*, *trenchknife*, and *trenchcoat*, only *trench fever* has not survived. *Trenchcoat* (originally *Burberry*) has recently spawned the adjective *trenchy* to describe a style in women's fashions: 'This year it's the trenchy look.' In the *Sunday Times Magazine* for August 8, 1971, a caption celebrating the vogue of the trenchy announced that 'Fashion Goes Over the Top.' That phrase is now also attached to charity drives without much residue of its original meaning: 'Help our fund drive over the top!' The most torpid television talk programs have sensed the need for stirring titles drawn from the war, like 'Firing Line' for William F. Buckley's interview program and the rather complex pun 'Behind the Lines' for a 1970 series of programs analyzing the press.

The phrase No Man's Land has haunted the imagination for sixty years, although its original associations with fixed positions and static warfare are eroding. One of the photographs in Jacques Nobécourt's *Hitler's Last Gamble: The Battle of the Bulge* (1967) shows three German soldiers in snow-capes kneeling in a snow-covered open field with a pine forest in the distant background. The caption reads, 'A German patrol in no-man's land,' but there's really no parallel at all since the picture is taken in the open in broad daylight with no damage visible anywhere – even the pine trees are unscarred – and with no identifiable direction in which danger is conceived to lie. As it detaches itself further and further from its original associations, the phrase No Man's Land becomes available for jokes, like the title of Tony Parker's book of popular sociology, *In No Man's Land: Some Unmarried Mothers* (1972).

And a *French 75* is now a drink consisting of three parts champagne and one of cognac.

Notes

1 1918; 1948, p. 6.
2 *Undertones of War*, p. 231.
3 Bergonzi, *Heroes' Twilight*, p. 127.
4 *World Within World* (1951), p. 7.
5 *Boy in the Blitz*, p. 36.
6 Ibid., pp. 172, 175.

---

22 Virginia Woolf
'Thoughts on Peace in an Air Raid'*

The Germans were over this house last night and the night before that. Here they are again. It is a queer experience, lying in the dark and listening to the zoom of a hornet which may at any moment sting you to death. It is a sound that interrupts cool and consecutive thinking about peace. Yet it is a sound – far more than prayers and anthems – that should compel one to think about peace. Unless we can think peace into existence we – not this one body in this one bed but millions of bodies yet to be born – will lie in the same darkness and hear the same death rattle overhead. Let us think

From *The Death of the Moth and Other Essays*, Hogarth Press, 1942, pp. 154–7.
* Written in August 1940, for an American symposium on current matters concerning women.

what we can do to create the only efficient air-raid shelter while the guns on the hill go pop pop pop and the searchlights finger the clouds and now and then, sometimes close at hand, sometimes far away, a bomb drops.

Up there in the sky young Englishmen and young German men are fighting each other. The defenders are men, the attackers are men. Arms are not given to Englishwomen either to fight the enemy or to defend herself. She must lie weaponless to-night. Yet if she believes that the fight going on up in the sky is a fight by the English to protect freedom, by the Germans to destroy freedom, she must fight, so far as she can, on the side of the English. How far can she fight for freedom without firearms? By making arms, or clothes or food. But there is another way of fighting for freedom without arms; we can fight with the mind. We can make ideas that will help the young Englishman who is fighting up in the sky to defeat the enemy.

But to make ideas effective, we must be able to fire them off. We must put them into action. And the hornet in the sky rouses another hornet in the mind. There was one zooming in *The Times* this morning – a woman's voice saying, 'Women have not a word to say in politics.' There is no woman in the Cabinet; nor in any responsible post. All the idea makers who are in a position to make ideas effective are men. That is a thought that damps thinking, and encourages irresponsibility. Why not bury the head in the pillow, plug the ears, and cease this futile activity of idea-making? Because there are other tables besides officer tables and conference tables. Are we not leaving the young Englishman without a weapon that might be of value to him if we give up private thinking, tea-table thinking, because it seems useless? Are we not stressing our disability because our ability exposes us perhaps to abuse, perhaps to contempt? 'I will not cease from mental fight,' Blake wrote. Mental fight means thinking against the current, not with it.

That current flows fast and furious. It issues in a spate of words from the loudspeakers and the politicians. Every day they tell us that we are a free people, fighting to defend freedom. That is the current that has whirled the young airman up into the sky and keeps him circling there among the clouds. Down here, with a roof to cover us and a gas mask handy, it is our business to puncture gas bags and discover seeds of truth. It is not true that we are free. We are both prisoners to-night – he boxed up in his machine with a gun handy; we lying in the dark with a gas mask handy. If we were free we should be out in the open, dancing, at the play, or sitting at the window talking together. What is it that prevents us? 'Hitler!' the loud-speakers cry with one voice. Who is Hitler? What is he? Aggressiveness, tyranny, the insane love of power made manifest, they reply. Destroy that, and you will be free.

The drone of the planes is now like the sawing of a branch overhead. Round and round it goes, sawing and sawing at a branch directly above the house. Another sound begins sawing its way in the brain. 'Women of ability' – it was Lady Astor speaking in *The Times* this morning – 'are held down because of a subconscious Hitlerism in the hearts of men.' Certainly we are held down. We are equally prisoners to-night – the Englishmen in their planes, the Englishwomen in their beds. But if he stops to think he may be killed; and we too. So let us think for him. Let us try to drag up into consciousness the subconscious Hitlerism that holds us down. It is the desire for aggression; the desire to dominate and enslave. Even in the darkness we can see that made visible. We can see shop windows blazing; and women gazing; painted women; dressed-up women; women with crimson lips and crimson fingernails. They are slaves who are trying to enslave. If we could free ourselves from slavery we should free men from tyranny. Hitlers are bred by slaves.

A bomb drops. All the windows rattle. The anti-aircraft guns are getting active. Up there on the hill under a net tagged with strips of green and brown stuff to imitate the hues of autumn leaves guns are concealed. Now they all fire at once. On the nine o'clock radio we shall be told 'Forty-four enemy planes were shot down during the night, ten of them by anti-aircraft fire.' And one of the terms of peace, the loudspeakers say, is to be disarmament. There are to be no more guns, no army, no navy, no air force in the future. No more young men will be trained to fight with arms. That rouses another mind-hornet in the chambers of the brain – another quotation. 'To fight against a real enemy, to earn undying honour and glory by shooting total strangers, and to come home with my breast covered with medals and decorations, that was the summit of my hope. . . . It was for this that my whole life so far had been dedicated, my education, training, everything. . . . '

Those were the words of a young Englishman who fought in the last war. In the face of them, do the current thinkers honestly believe that by writing 'Disarmament' on a sheet of paper at a conference table they will have done all that is needful? Othello's occupation will be gone; but he will remain Othello. The young airman up in the sky is driven not only by the voices of loudspeakers; he is driven by voices himself – ancient instincts, instincts fostered and cherished by education and tradition. Is he to be blamed for those instincts? Could we switch off the maternal instinct at the command of a table full of politicians? Suppose that imperative among the peace terms was: 'Child-bearing is to be restricted to a very small class of specially selected women,' would we submit? Should we not say, 'The maternal instinct is a woman's glory. It was for this that my whole life has been dedicated, my education, training, everything. . . . ' But if it were necessary, for the sake of humanity, for the peace of the world, that childbearing should be restricted, the maternal instinct subdued, women would attempt it. Men would help them. They would honour them for their refusal to bear children. They would give them other openings for their creative power. That too must make part of our fight for freedom. We must help the young Englishmen to root out from themselves the love of medals and decorations. We must create more honourable activities for those who try to conquer in themselves their fighting instinct, their subconscious Hitlerism. We must compensate the man for the loss of his gun.

The sound of sawing overhead has increased. All the searchlights are erect. They point at a spot exactly above this roof. At any moment a bomb may fall on this very room. One, two, three, four, five, six . . . the seconds pass. The bomb did not fall. But during those seconds of suspense all thinking stopped. All feeling, save one dull dread, ceased. A nail fixed the whole being to one hard board. The emotion of fear and of hate is therefore sterile, unfertile. Directly that fear passes, the mind reaches out and instinctively revives itself by trying to create. Since the room is dark it can create only from memory. It reaches out to the memory of other Augusts – in Bayreuth, listening to Wagner; in Rome, walking over the Campagna; in London. Friends' voices come back. Scraps of poetry return. Each of those thoughts, even in memory, was far more positive, reviving, healing and creative than the dull dread made of fear and hate. Therefore if we are to compensate the young man for the loss of his glory and of his gun, we must give him access to the creative feelings. We must make happiness. We must free him from the machine. We must bring him out of his prison into the open air. But what is the use of freeing the young Englishman if the young German and the young Italian remain slaves?

The searchlights, wavering across the flat, have picked up the plane now. From this window one can see a little silver insect turning and twisting in the light. The guns go pop pop pop. Then they cease. Probably the raider was brought down behind the hill. One of the pilots landed safe in a field near here the other day. He said to his captors, speaking fairly good English, 'How glad I am that the fight is over!' Then an Englishman gave him a cigarette, and an Englishwoman made him a cup of tea. That would seem to show that if you can free the man from the machine, the seed does not fall upon altogether stony ground. The seed may be fertile.

At last all the guns have stopped firing. All the searchlights have been extinguished. The natural darkness of a summer's night returns. The innocent sounds of the country are heard again. An apple thuds to the ground. An owl hoots, winging its way from tree to tree. And some half-forgotten words of an old English writer come to mind: 'The huntsmen are up in America. . . . ' Let us send these fragmentary notes to the huntsmen who are up in America, to the men and women whose sleep has not yet been broken by machine-gun fire, in the belief that they will rethink them generously and charitably, perhaps shape them into something serviceable. And now, in the shadowed half of the world, to sleep.

NARRATIVES OF THE SELF

23 Sigmund Freud
From *Civilization and its Discontents*

First of all, I suspect the reader feels that the discussion about the sense of guilt oversteps its proper boundaries in this essay and takes up too much space, so that the rest of the subject-matter, which is not always closely connected with it, gets pushed on one side. This may have spoilt the composition of the work; but it faithfully corresponds to my intention to represent the sense of guilt as the most important problem in the evolution of culture, and to convey that the price of progress in civilization is paid in forfeiting happiness through the heightening of the sense of guilt.[1]

. . . The development of the individual is ordered according to the programme laid down by the pleasure-principle, namely, the attainment of happiness, and to this main objective it holds firmly; the incorporation of the individual as a member of a community, or his adaptation to it, seems like an almost unavoidable condition which has to be filled before he can attain this objective of happiness. If he could achieve it without fulfilling this condition it would perhaps be better. To express it differently, we may say: individual development seems to us a product of the interplay of two trends, the striving for happiness, generally called 'egoistic', and the impulse towards merging with others in the community, which we call 'altruistic'. Neither of these descriptions goes far beneath the surface. In individual development, as we have said, the main accent falls on the egoistic trend, the striving for happiness; while the other tendency, which may be called the 'cultural' one, usually contents itself with instituting restrictions. But things are different in the development of culture: here far the most important aim is that of creating a single unity out of individual men and women, while the objective of happiness, though still present, is pushed into the background; it almost seems as if humanity could be most successfully united into one great whole if there were no need to trouble about the happiness of individuals. The process of development in individuals must therefore be admitted to have its special features which are not repeated in the cultural evolution of humanity; the two processes

From Sigmund Freud, *Civilization and its Discontents*, 3rd edition, Hogarth Press, 1946, pp. 123, 134–40, 143–4.

only necessarily coincide in so far as the first also includes the aim of incorporation into the community.

. . . So in every individual the two trends, one towards personal happiness and the other towards unity with the rest of humanity, must contend with each other; so must the two processes of individual and of cultural development oppose each other and dispute the ground against each other. This struggle between individual and society, however, is not derived from the antagonism of the primal instincts, Eros and Death, which are probably irreconcilable; it is a dissension in the camp of the libido itself, comparable to the contest between the ego and its objects for a share of the libido; and it does eventually admit of a solution in the individual, as we may hope it will also do in the future of civilization – however greatly it may oppress the lives of individuals at the present time.

The analogy between the process of cultural evolution and the path of individual development may be carried further in an important respect. It can be maintained that the community, too, develops a super-ego, under whose influence cultural evolution proceeds. It would be an enticing task for an authority on human systems of culture to work out this analogy in specific cases. I will confine myself to pointing out certain striking details. The super-ego of any given epoch of civilization originates in the same way as that of an individual; it is based on the impression left behind them by great leading personalities, men of outstanding force of mind, or men in whom some one human tendency has developed in unusual strength and purity, often for that reason very disproportionately. In many instances the analogy goes still further, in that during their lives – often enough, even if not always – such persons are ridiculed by others, ill-used or even cruelly done to death, just as happened with the primal father who also rose again to become a deity long after his death by violence. The most striking example of this double fate is the figure of Jesus Christ, if indeed it does not itself belong to the realm of mythology which called it into being out of a dim memory of that primordial event. Another point of agreement is that the cultural super-ego, just like that of an individual, sets up high ideals and standards, and that failure to fulfil them is punished by both with 'anxiety of conscience'. In this particular, indeed, we come across the remarkable circumstance that the mental processes concerned here are actually more familiar to us and more accessible to consciousness when they proceed from the group than they can be in the individual. In the latter, when tension arises, the aggressions of the super-ego voicing its noisy reproaches are all that is perceived, while its injunctions themselves often remain unconscious in the background. If we bring them to the knowledge of consciousness we find that they coincide with the demands of the prevailing cultural super-ego. At this point the two processes, that of the evolution of the group and the development of the individual, are always firmly mortised together, so to speak. Consequently many of the effects and properties of the super-ego can be more easily detected through its operations in the group than in the individual.

The cultural super-ego has elaborated its ideals and erected its standards. Those of its demands which deal with the relations of human beings to one another are comprised under the name of ethics. The greatest value has at all times been set upon systems of ethics, as if men had expected them in particular to achieve something especially important. And ethics does in fact deal predominantly with the point which is easily seen to be the sorest of all in any scheme of civilization. Ethics must be regarded therefore as a therapeutic effort: as an endeavour to achieve something through the standards imposed by the super-ego which had not been attained by the work of civilization in other ways. We already know – it is what we have been discussing – that the question is how to dislodge the greatest obstacle to civilization, the constitutional tendency in men to aggressions against one another; and for that very reason the commandment to love one's neighbour as oneself – probably the most recent of the cultural super-ego's demands – is especially interesting to us. In our investigations and our therapy of the neuroses we cannot avoid finding fault with the super-ego of the individual on two counts: in commanding and prohibiting with such severity it troubles too little about the happiness of the ego, and it fails to take into account sufficiently the difficulties in the way of obeying it – the strength of instinctual cravings in the id and the hardships of external environment. Consequently in our therapy we often find ourselves obliged to do battle with the super-ego and work to moderate its demands. Exactly the same objections can be made against the ethical standards of the cultural super-ego. It, too, does not trouble enough about the mental constitution of human beings; it enjoins a command and never asks whether or not it is possible for them to obey it. It presumes, on the contrary, that a man's ego is psychologically capable of anything that is required of it – that his ego has unlimited power over his id. This is an error; even in so-called normal people the power of controlling the id cannot be increased beyond certain limits. If one asks more of them, one produces revolt or neurosis in individuals or makes them unhappy. The command to love our neighbours as ourselves is the strongest defence there is against human aggressiveness and it is a superlative example of the unpsychological attitude of the cultural super-ego. The command is impossible to fulfil; such an enormous inflation of love can only lower its value and not remedy the evil. Civilization pays no heed to all this; it merely prates that the harder it is to obey the more laudable the obedience. . . .

The fateful question of the human species seems to me to be whether and to what extent the cultural process developed in it will succeed in mastering the derangements of communal life caused by the human instinct of aggression and self-destruction. In this connection, perhaps the phase through which we are at this moment passing deserves special interest. Men have brought their powers of subduing the forces of nature to such a pitch that by using them they could now very easily exterminate one another to the last man. They know this – hence arises a great part of their current unrest, their dejection, their mood of apprehension. And now it may be expected that the other of the two 'heavenly forces', eternal Eros, will put forth his strength so as to maintain himself alongside of his equally immortal adversary.

24   D.H. Lawrence
'Psychoanalysis and the Unconscious'

The amazingly difficult and vital business of human relationship has been almost laughably underestimated in our epoch. All this nonsense about love and unselfishness, more crude and repugnant than savage fetish-worship. Love is a thing to be *learned*, through centuries of patient effort. It is a difficult, complex maintenance of individual integrity throughout the incalculable processes of interhuman-polarity. Even on the first great plane of consciousness, four prime poles in each individual, four powerful circuits possible between two individuals, and each of the four circuits to be established to perfection and yet maintained in pure equilibrium with all the others. Who can do it? Nobody. Yet we have all got to do it, or else suffer ascetic tortures of starvation and privation or of distortion and overstrain and slow collapse into corruption. The whole of life is one long, blind effort at an established polarity with the outer universe, human and non-human; and the whole of modern life is a shrieking failure. It is our own fault.

The actual evolution of the individual psyche is a result of the interaction between the individual and the outer universe. Which means that just as a child in the womb grows as a result of the parental blood-stream which

From John Lucas (ed.), *D.H. Lawrence: Selected Poetry and Non-Fictional Prose*, Routledge, 1990, pp. 86–90.

nourishes the vital quick of the foetus, so does every man and woman grow and develop as a result of the polarized flux between the spontaneous self and some other self or selves. It is the circuit of vital flux between itself and another being or beings which brings about the development and evolution of every individual psyche and physique. This is a law of life and creation, from which we cannot escape. Ascetics and voluptuaries both try to dodge this main condition, and both succeed perhaps for a generation. But after two generations all collapses. Man doth not live by bread alone. He lives even more essentially from the nourishing creative flow between himself and another or others.

This is the reality of the extra-individual circuits of polarity, those established between two or more individuals. But a corresponding reality is that of the internal, purely individual polarity – the polarity within a man himself of his upper and lower consciousness, and his own voluntary and sympathetic modes. Here is a fourfold interaction within the self. And from this fourfold reaction within the self results that final manifestation which we know as *mind*, mental consciousness.

The brain is, if we may use the word, the terminal instrument of the dynamic consciousness. It transmutes what is a creative flux into a certain fixed cipher. It prints off, like a telegraph instrument, the glyphs and graphic representations which we call percepts, concepts, ideas. It produces a new reality – the ideal. The idea is another static entity, another unit of the mechanical-active and materio-static universe. It is thrown off from life, as leaves are shed from a tree, or as feathers fall from a bird. Ideas are the dry, unliving, insentient plumage which intervenes between us and the circum-ambient universe, forming at once an insulator and an instrument for the subduing of the universe. The mind is the instrument of instruments; it is not a creative reality.

Once the mind is awake, being in itself a finality, it feels very assured. 'The word became flesh, and began to put on airs,' says Norman Douglas wittily. It is exactly what happens. Mentality, being automatic in its principle like the machine, begins to assume life. It begins to affect life, to pretend to make and unmake life. 'In the beginning was the Word.' This is the presumptuous masquerading of the mind. The Word cannot be the beginning of life. It is the *end* of life, that which falls shed. The mind is the dead end of life. But it has all the mechanical force of the non-vital universe. It is a great dynamo of super-mechanical force. Given the *will* as accomplice, it can even arrogate its machine-motions and automatizations over the whole of life, till every tree becomes a clipped teapot and every man a useful mechanism. So we see the brain, like a great dynamo and accumulator, accumulating *mechanical* force and presuming to apply this mechanical force-control to the living unconscious, subjecting everything spontaneous to certain machine-principles called ideals or ideas.

And the human will assists in this humiliating and sterilizing process. We don't know what the human will is. But we do know that it is a certain faculty belonging to every living organism, the faculty for self-determination. It is a strange faculty of the soul itself, for its own direction. The will is indeed the faculty which every individual possesses from the very moment of conception, for exerting a certain control over the vital and automatic processes of his own evolution. It does not depend originally on mind. Originally it is a purely spontaneous control-factor of the living unconscious. It seems as if, primarily, the will and the conscience were identical, in the premental state. It seems as if the will were given as a great balancing faculty, the faculty whereby automatization is *prevented* in the evolving psyche. The *spontaneous* will reacts at once against the exaggeration of any one particular circuit of polarity. Any vital circuit – a fact known to psychoanalysis. And against this automatism, this degradation from the spontaneous-vital reality into the mechanic-material reality, the human soul must always struggle. And the will is the power which the unique self possesses to right itself from automatism.

Sometimes, however, the free psyche really collapses, and the will *identifies* itself with an automatic circuit. Then a complex is set up, a paranoia. Then incipient madness sets in. If the identification continues, the derangement becomes serious. There may come sudden jolts of dislocation of the whole psychic flow, like epilepsy. Or there may come any of the known forms of primary madness.

The second danger is that the will shall identify itself with the mind and become an instrument of the mind. The same process of automatism sets up, only now it is slower. The mind proceeds to assume control over every organic-psychic circuit. The spontaneous flux is destroyed, and a certain automatic circuit substituted. Now an automatic establishment of the psyche must, like the building of a machine, proceed according to some definite fixed scheme, based upon certain fixed principles. And it is here that ideals and ideas enter. They are the machine-plan and the machine-principles of an automatized psyche.

So, humanity proceeds to derange itself, to automatize itself from the mental consciousness. It is a process of derangement, just as the fixing of the will upon any other primary process is a derangement. It is a long, slow development in madness. Quite justly do the advanced Russian and French writers acclaim madness as a great goal. It is the genuine goal of self-automatism, mental-conscious supremacy.

True, we must all develop into mental consciousness. But mental-consciousness is not a goal; it is a cul-de-sac. It provides us only with endless *appliances* which we can use for the all-too-difficult business of coming to our spontaneous-creative fullness of being. It provides us with means to adjust ourselves to the external universe. It gives us further means for subduing the external, materio-mechanical universe to our great end of creative life. And it gives us plain indications of how to avoid falling into automatism, hints for the *applying* of the will, the loosening of false, automatic fixations, the brave adherence to a profound soul-impulse. This is the use of the mind – a great indicator and instrument. The mind as author and director of life is anathema.

So, the few things we have to say about the unconscious end for the moment. There is almost nothing said. Yet it is a beginning. Still remain to be revealed the other great centres of the unconscious. We know four: two pairs. In all there are seven planes. That is, there are six dual centres of spontaneous polarity, and then the final one. That is, the great upper and lower consciousness is only just broached – the further heights and depths are not even hinted at. Nay, in public it would hardly be allowed us to hint at them. There is so much to know, and every step of the progress in knowledge is a death to the human idealism which governs us now so ruthlessly and vilely. It must die, and we *will* break free. But what tyranny is so hideous as that of an automatically ideal humanity?

25 Virginia Woolf 'Street Haunting'

Passing, glimpsing, everything seems accidentally but miraculously sprinkled with beauty, as if the tide of trade which deposits its burden so punctually and prosaically upon the shores of Oxford Street had this night cast up nothing but treasure. With no thought of buying, the eye is sportive and generous; it creates; it adorns; it enhances. Standing out in the street, one may build up all the chambers of an imaginary house and furnish them at one's will with sofa, table, carpet. That rug will do for the hall. That alabaster bowl shall stand on a carved table in the window. Our merry-making shall be reflected in that thick round mirror. But, having built and furnished the house, one is happily under no obligation to possess it; one can dismantle it in the twinkling of an eye, and build and furnish another house with other chairs and other glasses. Or let us indulge ourselves at the antique jewellers, among the trays of rings and the hanging necklaces. Let us choose those pearls, for example, and then imagine how, if we put them on, life would be changed. It becomes instantly between two and three in the morning; the lamps are burning very white in the deserted streets of Mayfair. Only motor-cars are abroad at this hour, and one has a sense of emptiness, of airiness, of secluded gaiety. Wearing pearls, wearing silk, one steps out on to a balcony which overlooks the gardens of sleeping Mayfair.

From *The Death of the Moth and Other Essays*, Hogarth Press, 1942, pp. 23–4, 27–9.

There are a few lights in the bedrooms of great peers returned from Court, of silk-stockinged footmen, of dowagers who have pressed the hands of statesmen. A cat creeps along the garden wall. Love-making is going on sibilantly, seductively in the darker places of the room behind thick green curtains. Strolling sedately as if he were promenading a terrace beneath which the shires and counties of England lie sun-bathed, the aged Prime Minister recounts to Lady So-and-So with the curls and the emeralds the true history of some great crisis in the affairs of the land. We seem to be riding on the top of the highest mast of the tallest ship; and yet at the same time we know that nothing of this sort matters; love is not proved thus, nor great achievements completed thus; so that we sport with the moment and preen our feathers in it lightly, as we stand on the balcony watching the moonlit cat creep along Princess Mary's garden wall.

But what could be more absurd? It is, in fact, on the stroke of six; it is a winter's evening; we are walking to the Strand to buy a pencil. How, then, are we also on a balcony, wearing pearls in June? What could be more absurd? Yet it is nature's folly, not ours. When she set about her chief masterpiece, the making of man, she should have thought of one thing only. Instead, turning her head, looking over her shoulder, into each one of us she let creep instincts and desires which are utterly at variance with his main being, so that we are streaked, variegated, all of a mixture; the colours have run. Is the true self this which stands on the pavement in January, or that which bends over the balcony in June? Am I here, or am I there? Or is the true self neither this nor that, neither here nor there, but something so varied and wandering that it is only when we give the rein to its wishes and let it take its way unimpeded that we are indeed ourselves? Circumstances compel unity; for convenience sake a man must be a whole. The good citizen when he opens his door in the evening must be banker, golfer, husband, father; not a nomad wandering the desert, a mystic staring at the sky, a debauchee in the slums of San Francisco, a soldier heading a revolution, a pariah howling with scepticism and solitude. When he opens his door, he must run his fingers through his hair and put his umbrella in the stand like the rest.

But we are come to the Strand now, and as we hesitate on the curb, a little rod about the length of one's finger begins to lay its bar across the velocity and abundance of life. 'Really I must – really I must' – that is it. Without investigating the demand, the mind cringes to the accustomed tyrant. One must, one always must, do something or other; it is not allowed one simply to enjoy oneself. Was it not for this reason that, some time ago, we fabricated the excuse, and invented the necessity of buying something? But what was it? Ah, we remember, it was a pencil. Let us go then and buy this pencil. But just as we are turning to obey the command, another self disputes the right of the tyrant to insist. The usual conflict comes about. Spread out behind the rod of duty we see the whole breadth of the river

Thames – wide, mournful, peaceful. And we see it through the eyes of somebody who is leaning over the Embankment on a summer evening, without a care in the world. Let us put off buying the pencil; let us go in search of this person – and soon it becomes apparent that this person is ourselves. For if we could stand there where we stood six months ago, should we not be again as we were then – calm, aloof, content? Let us try then. But the river is rougher and greyer than we remembered. The tide is running out to sea. It brings down with it a tug and two barges, whose load of straw is tightly bound down beneath tarpaulin covers. There is, too, close by us, a couple leaning over the balustrade with the curious lack of self-consciousness lovers have, as if the importance of the affair they are engaged on claims without question the indulgence of the human race. The sights we see and the sounds we hear now have none of the quality of the past; nor have we any share in the serenity of the person who, six months ago, stood precisely where we stand now. His is the happiness of death; ours the insecurity of life. He has no future; the future is even now invading our peace. It is only when we look at the past and take from it the element of uncertainty that we can enjoy perfect peace. As it is, we must turn, we must cross the Strand again, we must find a shop where, even at this hour, they will be ready to sell us a pencil.

It is always an adventure to enter a new room; for the lives and characters of its owners have distilled their atmosphere into it, and directly we enter it we breast some new wave of emotion. Here, without a doubt, in the stationer's shop people had been quarrelling. Their anger shot through the air. They both stopped; the old woman – they were husband and wife evidently – retired to a back room; the old man whose rounded forehead and globular eyes would have looked well on the frontispiece of some Elizabethan folio, stayed to serve us. 'A pencil, a pencil,' he repeated, 'certainly, certainly.' He spoke with the distraction yet effusiveness of one whose emotions have been roused and checked in full flood. He began opening box after box and shutting them again. He said that it was very difficult to find things when they kept so many different articles. He launched into a story about some legal gentleman who had got into deep waters owing to the conduct of his wife. He had known him for years; he had been connected with the Temple for half a century, he said, as if he wished his wife in the back room to overhear him. He upset a box of rubber bands. At last, exasperated by his incompetence, he pushed the swing door open and called out roughly: 'Where d'you keep the pencils?' as if his wife had hidden them. The old lady came in. Looking at nobody, she put her hand with a fine air of righteous severity upon the right box. There were pencils. How then could he do without her? Was she not indispensable to him? In order to keep them there, standing side by side in forced neutrality, one had to be particular in one's choice of pencils; this was too soft, that too hard. They stood silently looking on. The longer they stood there, the calmer they grew; their heat was going down, their anger disappearing.

Now, without a word said on either side, the quarrel was made up. The old man, who would not have disgraced Ben Jonson's title-page, reached the box back to its proper place, bowed profoundly his good-night to us, and they disappeared. She would get out her sewing; he would read his newspaper; the canary would scatter them impartially with seed. The quarrel was over.

In these minutes in which a ghost has been sought for, a quarrel composed, and a pencil bought, the streets had become completely empty. Life had withdrawn to the top floor, and lamps were lit. The pavement was dry and hard; the road was of hammered silver. Walking home through the desolation one could tell oneself the story of the dwarf, of the blind men, of the party in the Mayfair mansion, of the quarrel in the stationer's shop. Into each of these lives one could penetrate a little way, far enough to give oneself the illusion that one is not tethered to a single mind, but can put on briefly for a few minutes the bodies and minds of others. One could become a washerwoman, a publican, a street singer. And what greater delight and wonder can there be than to leave the straight lines of personality and deviate into those footpaths that lead beneath brambles and thick tree trunks into the heart of the forest where live those wild beasts, our fellow men?

That is true: to escape is the greatest of pleasures; street haunting in winter the greatest of adventures. Still as we approach our own doorstep again, it is comforting to feel the old possessions, the old prejudices, fold us round; and the self, which has been blown about at so many street corners, which has battered like a moth at the flame of so many inaccessible lanterns, sheltered and enclosed. Here again is the usual door; here the chair turned as we left it and the china bowl and the brown ring on the carpet. And here – let us examine it tenderly, let us touch it with reverence – is the only spoil we have retrieved from all the treasures of the city, a lead pencil.

26 Erving Goffman
From *The Presentation of Self in Everyday Life*

Personality – interaction – society

In recent years there have been elaborate attempts to bring into one framework the concepts and findings derived from three different areas of inquiry: the individual personality, social interaction, and society. I would like to suggest here a simple addition to these inter-disciplinary attempts.

When an individual appears before others, he knowingly and unwittingly projects a definition of the situation, of which a conception of himself is an important part. When an event occurs which is expressively incompatible with this fostered impression, significant consequences are simultaneously felt in three levels of social reality, each of which involves a different point of reference and a different order of fact.

First, the social interaction, treated here as a dialogue between two teams, may come to an embarrassed and confused halt; the situation may cease to be defined, previous positions may become no longer tenable, and participants may find themselves without a charted course of action. The participants typically sense a false note in the situation and come to feel awkward, flustered, and, literally, out of countenance. In other words, the minute social system created and sustained by orderly social interaction becomes disorganized. These are the consequences that the disruption has from the point of view of social interaction.

Secondly, in addition to these disorganizing consequences for action at the moment, performance disruptions may have consequences of a more far-reaching kind. Audiences tend to accept the self projected by the individual performer during any current performance as a responsible representative of his colleague-grouping, of his team, and of his social establishment. Audiences also accept the individual's particular performance as evidence of his capacity to perform the routine and even as evidence of his capacity to perform any routine. In a sense these larger social units – teams, establishments, etc. – become committed every time the individual performs his routine; with each performance the legitimacy of these units will tend to be tested anew and their permanent reputation put at stake. This kind of commitment is especially strong during some performances. Thus, when a surgeon and his nurse both turn from the operating-table and the anaesthetized patient accidentally rolls off the table

From Erving Goffman, *The Presentation of the Self in Everyday Life*, Penguin, 1959, pp. 234–6, 244–7.

to his death, not only is the operation disrupted in an embarrassing way, but the reputation of the doctor, as a doctor and as a man, and also the reputation of the hospital may be weakened. These are the consequences that disruptions may have from the point of view of social structure.

Finally, we often find that the individual may deeply involve his ego in his identification with a particular part, establishment, and group, and in his self-conception as someone who does not disrupt social interaction or let down the social units which depend upon that interaction. When a disruption occurs, then, we may find that the self-conceptions around which his personality has been built may become discredited. These are consequences that disruptions may have from the point of view of individual personality.

Performance disruptions, then, have consequences at three levels of abstraction: personality, interaction, and social structure. While the likelihood of disruption will vary widely from interaction to interaction, and while the social importance of likely disruptions will vary widely from interaction to interaction, still it seems that there is no interaction in which the participants do not take an appreciable chance of being slightly embarrassed or a slight chance of being deeply humiliated. Life may not be much of a gamble, but interaction is. Further, in so far as individuals make efforts to avoid disruptions or to correct for ones not avoided, these efforts, too, will have simultaneous consequences at the three levels. Here, then, we have one simple way of articulating three levels of abstraction and three perspectives from which social life has been studied.

Staging and the self

The general notion that we make a presentation of ourselves to others is hardly novel; what ought to be stressed in conclusion is that the very structure of the self can be seen in terms of how we arrange for such performances in our Anglo-American society.

In this report, the individual was divided by implication into two basic parts: he was viewed as a *performer*, a harried fabricator of impressions involved in the all-too-human task of staging a performance, he was viewed as a *character*, a figure, typically a fine one, whose spirit, strength, and other sterling qualities the performance was designed to evoke. The attributes of a performer and the attributes of a character are of a different order, quite basically so, yet both sets have their meaning in terms of the show that must go on.

First, character. In our society the character one performs and one's self are somewhat equated, and this self-as-character is usually seen as something housed within the body of its possessor, especially the upper parts thereof, being a nodule, somehow, in the psychobiology of personality. I suggest that this view is an implied part of what we are all trying to present, but provides, just because of this, a bad analysis of the presentation. In this report the performed self was seen as some kind of image, usually creditable, which the individual on stage and in character effectively attempts to induce others to hold in regard to him. While this image is entertained *concerning* the individual, so that a self is imputed to him, this self itself does not derive from its possessor, but from the whole scene of his action, being generated by that attribute of local events which renders them interpretable by witnesses. A correctly staged and performed scene leads the audience to impute a self to a performed character, but this imputation – this self – is a *product* of a scene that comes off, and is not a *cause* of it. The self, then, as a performed character, is not an organic thing that has a specific location, whose fundamental fate is to be born, to mature, and to die; it is a dramatic effect arising diffusely from a scene that is presented, and the characteristic issue, the crucial concern, is whether it will be credited or discredited.

In analysing the self, then, we are drawn from its possessor, from the person who will profit or lose most by it, for he and his body merely provide the peg on which something of collaborative manufacture will be hung for a time. And the means for producing and maintaining selves do not reside inside the peg; in fact these means are often bolted down in social establishments. There will be a back region with its tools for shaping the body, and a front region with its fixed props. There will be a team of persons whose activity on stage and in conjunction with available props will constitute the scene from which the performed character's self will emerge, and another team, the audience, whose interpretative activity will be necessary for this emergence. The self is a product of all of these arrangements, and in all of its parts bears the marks of this genesis.

The whole machinery of self-production is cumbersome, of course, and sometimes breaks down, exposing its separate components: back region control; team collusion; audience tact; and so forth. But, well oiled, impressions will flow from it fast enough to put us in the grip of one of our types of reality – the performance will come off and the firm self accorded each performed character will appear to emanate intrinsically from its performer.

Let us turn now from the individual as character performed to the individual as performer. He has a capacity to learn, this being exercised in the task of training for a part. He is given to having fantasies and dreams, some that pleasurably unfold a triumphant performance, others full of anxiety and dread that nervously deal with vital discreditings in a public front region. He often manifests a gregarious desire for team-mates and audiences, a tactful considerateness for their concerns; and he has a capacity for deeply felt shame, leading him to minimize the chances he takes of exposure.

These attributes of the individual *qua* performer are not merely a depicted effect of particular performances; they are psychobiological in nature, and yet they seem to arise out of intimate interaction with the contingencies of staging performances.

And now a final comment. In developing the conceptual framework employed in this report, some language of the stage was used. I spoke of performers and audiences; of routines and parts; of performances coming off or falling flat; of cues, stage settings and backstage; of dramaturgical needs, dramaturgical skills, and dramaturgical strategies. Now it should be admitted that this attempt to press a mere analogy so far was in part a rhetoric and a manoeuvre.

The claim that all the world's a stage is sufficiently commonplace for readers to be familiar with its limitations and tolerant of its presentation, knowing that at any time they will easily be able to demonstrate to themselves that it is not to be taken too seriously. An action staged in a theatre is a relatively contrived illusion and an admitted one; unlike ordinary life, nothing real or actual can happen to the performed characters – although at another level of course something real and actual can happen to the reputation of performers *qua* professionals whose everyday job is to put on theatrical performances.

And so here the language and mask of the stage will be dropped. Scaffolds, after all, are to build other things with, and should be erected with an eye to taking them down. This report is not concerned with aspects of theatre that creep into everyday life. It is concerned with the structure of social encounters – the structure of those entities in social life that come into being whenever persons enter one another's immediate physical presence. The key factor in this structure is the maintenance of a single definition of the situation, this definition having to be expressed, and this expression sustained in the face of a multitude of potential disruptions.

A character staged in a theatre is not in some ways real, nor does it have the same kind of real consequences as does the thoroughly contrived character performed by a confidence man; but the *successful* staging of either of these types of false figures involves use of *real* techniques – the same techniques by which everyday persons sustain their real social situations. Those who conduct face-to-face interaction on a theatre's stage must meet the key requirement of real situations: they must expressively sustain a definition of the situation; but this they do in circumstances that have facilitated their developing an apt terminology for the interactional tasks that all of us share.

Anthony Giddens
From *Modernity and Self-Identity*

Modernity is a post-traditional order, but not one in which the sureties of tradition and habit have been replaced by the certitude of rational knowledge. Doubt, a pervasive feature of modern critical reason, permeates into everyday life as well as philosophical consciousness, and forms a general existential dimension of the contemporary social world. Modernity institutionalises the principle of radical doubt and insists that all knowledge takes the form of hypotheses: claims which may very well be true, but which are in principle always open to revision and may have at some point to be abandoned. Systems of accumulated expertise – which form important disembedding influences – represent multiple sources of authority, frequently internally contested and divergent in their implications. In the settings of what I call 'high' or 'late' modernity – our present-day world – the self, like the broader institutional contexts in which it exists, has to be reflexively made. Yet this task has to be accomplished amid a puzzling diversity of options and possibilities.

In circumstances of uncertainty and multiple choice, the notions of trust and risk have particular application. Trust, I argue, is a crucial generic phenomenon of personality development as well as having distinctive and specific relevance to a world of disembedding mechanisms and abstract systems. In its generic manifestations, trust is directly linked to achieving an early sense of ontological security. Trust established between an infant and its caretakers provides an 'inoculation' which screens off potential threats and dangers that even the most mundane activities of day-to-day life contain. Trust in this sense is basic to a 'protective cocoon' which stands guard over the self in its dealings with everyday reality. It 'brackets out' potential occurrences which, were the individual seriously to contemplate them, would produce a paralysis of the will, or feelings of engulfment. In its more specific guise, trust is a medium of interaction with the abstract systems which both empty day-to-day life of its traditional content and set up globalising influences. Trust here generates that 'leap into faith' which practical engagement demands.

Modernity is a risk culture. I do not mean by this that social life is inherently more risky than it used to be; for most people in the developed societies that is not the case. Rather, the concept of risk becomes fundamental to the way both lay actors and technical specialists organise the social world. Under conditions of modernity, the future is continually

From Anthony Giddens, *Modernity and Self-Identity*, Polity Press, 1991, pp. 2–9.

drawn into the present by means of the reflexive organisation of knowledge environments. A territory, as it were, is carved out and colonised. Yet such colonisation by its very nature cannot be complete: thinking in terms of risk is vital to assessing how far projects are likely to diverge from their anticipated outcomes. Risk assessment invites precision, and even quantification, but by its nature is imperfect. Given the mobile character of modern institutions, coupled to the mutable and frequently controversial nature of abstract systems, most forms of risk assessment, in fact, contain numerous imponderables.

Modernity reduces the overall riskiness of certain areas and modes of life, yet at the same time introduces new risk parameters largely or completely unknown to previous eras. These parameters include high-consequence risks: risks deriving from the globalised character of the social systems of modernity. The late modern world – the world of what I term high modernity – is apocalyptic, not because it is inevitably heading towards calamity, but because it introduces risks which previous generations have not had to face. However much there is progress towards international negotiation and control of armaments, so long as nuclear weapons remain, or even the knowledge necessary to build them, and so long as science and technology continue to be involved with the creation of novel weaponry, the risk of massively destructive warfare will persist. Now that nature, as a phenomenon external to social life, has in a certain sense come to an 'end' – as a result of its domination by human beings – the risks of ecological catastrophe form an inevitable part of our horizon of day-to-day life. Other high-consequence risks, such as the collapse of global economic mechanisms, or the rise of totalitarian superstates, are an equally unavoidable part of our contemporary experience.

In high modernity, the influence of distant happenings on proximate events, and on intimacies of the self, becomes more and more commonplace. The media, printed and electronic, obviously play a central role in this respect. Mediated experience, since the first experience of writing, has long influenced both self-identity and the basic organisation of social relations. With the development of mass communication, particularly electronic communication, the interpenetration of self-development and social systems, up to and including global systems, becomes ever more pronounced. The 'world' in which we now live is in some profound respects thus quite distinct from that inhabited by human beings in previous periods of history. It is in many ways a single world, having a unitary framework of experience (for instance, in respect of basic axes of time and space), yet at the same time one which creates new forms of fragmentation and dispersal. A universe of social activity in which electronic media have a central and constitutive role, nevertheless, is not one of 'hyperreality', in Baudrillard's sense. Such an idea confuses the pervasive impact of mediated experience with the internal referentiality of the social systems of modernity – the fact that these systems become largely autonomous and determined by their own constitutive influences.

In the post-traditional order of modernity, and against the backdrop of new forms of mediated experience, self-identity becomes a reflexively organised endeavour. The reflexive project of the self, which consists in the sustaining of coherent, yet continuously revised, biographical narratives, takes place in the context of multiple choice as filtered through abstract systems. In modern social life, the notion of lifestyle takes on a particular significance. The more tradition loses its hold, and the more daily life is reconstituted in terms of the dialectical interplay of the local and the global, the more individuals are forced to negotiate lifestyle choices among a diversity of options. Of course, there are standardising influences too – most notably, in the form of commodification, since capitalistic production and distribution form core components of modernity's institutions. Yet because of the 'openness' of social life today, the pluralisation of contexts of action and the diversity of 'authorities', lifestyle choice is increasingly important in the constitution of self-identity and daily activity. Reflexively organised life-planning, which normally presumes consideration of risks as filtered through contact with expert knowledge, becomes a central feature of the structuring of self-identity.

At one pole of the interaction between the local and the global stands what I call the 'transformation of intimacy'. Intimacy has its own reflexivity and its own forms of internally referential order. Of key importance here is the emergence of the 'pure relationship' as prototypical of the new spheres of personal life. A pure relationship is one in which external criteria have become dissolved: the relationship exists solely for whatever rewards that relationship as such can deliver. In the context of the pure relationship, trust can be mobilised only by a process of mutual disclosure. Trust, in other words, can by definition no longer be anchored in criteria outside the relationship itself – such as criteria of kinship, social duty or traditional obligation. Like self-identity, with which it is closely intertwined, the pure relationship has to be reflexively controlled over the long term, against the backdrop of external transitions and transformations.

Pure relationships presuppose 'commitment', which is a particular species of trust. Commitment in turn has to be understood as a phenomenon of the internally referential system: it is a commitment to the relationship as such, as well as to the other person or persons involved. The demand for intimacy is integral to the pure relationship, as a result of the mechanisms of trust which it presumes. It is hence a mistake to see the contemporary 'search for intimacy', as many social commentators have done, only as a negative reaction to a wider, more impersonal social universe. Absorption within pure relationships certainly may often be a mode of defence against an enveloping outside world; but such relationships are thoroughly permeated by mediated influences coming from large-scale social systems, and usually actively organise those influences within the sphere of such relationships. In general, whether in personal life or in broader social milieux, processes of reappropriation and empowerment intertwine with expropriation and loss.

The reflexivity of the self, in conjunction with the influence of abstract systems, pervasively affects the body as well as psychic processes. The body is less and less an extrinsic 'given', functioning outside the internally referential systems of modernity, but becomes itself reflexively mobilized. What might appear as a wholesale movement towards the narcissistic cultivation of bodily appearance is in fact an expression of a concern lying much deeper actively to 'construct' and control the body. Here there is an integral connection between bodily development and lifestyle – manifest, for example, in the pursuit of specific bodily regimes. Yet much more wide-ranging factors are important, too, as a reflection of the socialising of biological mechanisms and processes. In the spheres of biological reproduction, genetic engineering and medical interventions of many sorts, the body is becoming a phenomenon of choices and options. These do not affect the individual alone: there are close connections between personal aspects of bodily development and global factors. Reproductive technologies and genetic engineering, for example, are parts of more general processes of the transmutation of nature into a field of human action.

Personal meaninglessness – the feeling that life has nothing worthwhile to offer – becomes a fundamental psychic problem in circumstances of late modernity. We should understand this phenomenon in terms of a repression of moral questions which day-to-day life poses, but which are denied answers. 'Existential isolation' is not so much a separation of individuals from others as a separation from the moral resources necessary to live a full and satisfying existence. The reflexive project of the self generates programmes of actualisation and mastery. But as long as these possibilities are understood largely as a matter of the extension of the control systems of modernity to the self, they lack moral meaning. 'Authenticity' becomes both a pre-eminent value and a framework for self-actualisation, but represents a morally stunted process.

   Yet the repression of existential questions is by no means complete and in high modernity, where systems of instrumental control have become more nakedly exposed than ever before and their negative consequences more apparent, many forms of counter-reaction appear. It becomes more and more apparent that lifestyle choices, within the settings of local–global interrelations, raise moral issues which cannot simply be pushed to one side. Such issues call for forms of political engagement which the new social movements both presage and serve to help initiate. 'Life politics' – concerned with human self-actualisation, both on the level of the individual and collectively – emerges from the shadow which 'emancipatory politics' has cast.

GENDER AND SEXUALITY

28 Simone de Beauvoir
From *The Second Sex*

The myth of woman plays a considerable part in literature; but what is its importance in daily life? To what extent does it affect the customs and conduct of individuals? In replying to this question it will be necessary to state precisely the relations this myth bears to reality.

There are different kinds of myths. This one, the myth of woman, sublimating an immutable aspect of the human condition – namely, the 'division' of humanity into two classes of individuals – is a static myth. It projects into the realm of Platonic ideas a reality that is directly experienced or is conceptualized on a basis of experience; in place of fact, value, significance, knowledge, empirical law, it substitutes a transcendental Idea, timeless, unchangeable, necessary. This idea is indisputable because it is beyond the given: it is endowed with absolute truth. Thus, as against the dispersed, contingent, and multiple existences of actual women, mythical thought opposes the Eternal Feminine, unique and changeless. If the definition provided for this concept is contradicted by the behaviour of flesh-and-blood women, it is the latter who are wrong: we are told not that Femininity is a false entity, but that the women concerned are not feminine. The contrary facts of experience are impotent against the myth. In a way, however, its source is in experience. Thus it is quite true that woman is other than man, and this alterity is directly felt in desire, the embrace, love; but the real relation is one of reciprocity; as such it gives rise to authentic drama. Through eroticism, love, friendship, and their alternatives, deception, hate, rivalry, the relation is a struggle between conscious beings each of whom wishes to be essential, it is the mutual recognition of free beings who confirm one another's freedom, it is the vague transition from aversion to participation. To pose Woman is to pose the absolute Other, without reciprocity, denying against all experience that she is a subject, a fellow human being.

In actuality, of course, women appear under various aspects; but each of the myths built up around the subject of woman is intended to sum her up *in toto*; each aspires to be unique. In consequence, a number of incompatible myths exist, and men tarry musing before the strange incoherencies manifested by the idea of Femininity. As every woman has a share in a majority

From Simone de Beauvoir, *The Second Sex*, tr. H.M. Parshley, Penguin, 1972, pp. 282–5.

of these archetypes – each of which lays claim to containing the sole Truth of woman – men of today also are moved again in the presence of their female companions to an astonishment like that of the old sophists who failed to understand how man could be blond and dark at the same time! Transition towards the absolute was indicated long ago in social phenomena: relations are easily congealed in classes, functions in types, just as relations, to the childish mentality, are fixed in things. Patriarchal society, for example, being centred upon the conservation of the patrimony, implies necessarily, along with those who own and transmit wealth, the existence of men and women who take property away from its owners and put it into circulation. The men – adventurers, swindlers, thieves, speculators – are generally repudiated by the group; the women, employing their erotic attraction, can induce young men and even fathers of families to scatter their patrimonies, without ceasing to be within the law. Some of these women appropriate their victims' fortunes or obtain legacies by using undue influence; this role being regarded as evil, those who play it are called 'bad women'. But the fact is that quite to the contrary they are able to appear in some other setting – at home with their fathers, brothers, husbands, or lovers – as guardian angels; and the courtesan who 'plucks' rich financiers is, for painters and writers, a generous patroness. It is easy to understand in actual experience the ambiguous personality of Aspasia or Mme de Pompadour. But if woman is depicted as the Praying Mantis, the Mandrake, the Demon, then it is most confusing to find in woman also the Muse, the Goddess Mother, Beatrice.

As group symbols and social types are generally defined by means of antonyms in pairs, ambivalence will seem to be an intrinsic quality of the Eternal Feminine. The saintly mother has for correlative the cruel stepmother, the angelic young girl has the perverse virgin: thus it will be said sometimes that Mother equals Life, sometimes that Mother equals Death, that every virgin is pure spirit or flesh dedicated to the devil.

Evidently it is not reality that dictates to society or to individuals their choice between the two opposed basic categories; in every period, in each case, society and the individual decide in accordance with their needs. Very often they project into the myth adopted the institutions and values to which they adhere. Thus the paternalism that claims woman for hearth and home defines her as sentiment, inwardness, immanence. In fact every existent is at once immanence and transcendence; when one offers the existent no aim, or prevents him from attaining any, or robs him of his victory, then his transcendence falls vainly into the past – that is to say, falls back into immanence. This is the lot assigned to woman in the patriarchate; but it is in no way a vocation, any more than slavery is the vocation of the slave. The development of this mythology is to be clearly seen in Auguste Comte. To identify Woman with Altruism is to guarantee to man absolute rights in her devotion, it is to impose on women a categorical imperative. The myth must not be confused with the recognition of significance;

significance is immanent in the object; it is revealed to the mind through a living experience; whereas the myth is a transcendent Idea that escapes the mental grasp entirely. When in *L'Age d'homme* Michel Leiris describes his vision of the feminine organs, he tells us things of significance and elaborates no myth. Wonder at the feminine body, dislike for menstrual blood, come from perceptions of a concrete reality. There is nothing mythical in the experience that reveals the voluptuous qualities of feminine flesh, and it is not an excursion into myth if one attempts to describe them through comparisons with flowers or pebbles. But to say that Woman is Flesh, to say that the Flesh is Night and Death, or that it is the splendour of the Cosmos, is to abandon terrestrial truth and soar into an empty sky. For man also is flesh for woman; and woman is not merely a carnal object; and the flesh is clothed in special significance for each person and in each experience. And likewise it is quite true that woman – like man – is a being rooted in nature; she is more enslaved to the species than is the male, her animality is more manifest; but in her as in him the given traits are taken on through the fact of existence, she belongs also to the human realm. To assimilate her to Nature is simply to act from prejudice.

Few myths have been more advantageous to the ruling caste than the myth of woman: it justifies all privileges and even authorizes their abuse. Men need not bother themselves with alleviating the pains and the burdens that physiologically are women's lot, since these are 'intended by Nature'; men use them as a pretext for increasing the misery of the feminine lot still further, for instance by refusing to grant to woman any right to sexual pleasure, by making her work like a beast of burden.[1]

Note

1 Cf. Balzac: *Physiology of Marriage*: 'Pay no attention to her murmurs, her cries, her pains; *nature has made her for our use* and for bearing everything: children, sorrows, blows and pains inflicted by man. Do not accuse yourself of hardness. In all the codes of so-called civilized nations, man has written the laws that ranged woman's destiny under this bloody epigraph: "*Vae victis!* Woe to the weak!"'

29 Evelyn Fox Keller
From *Reflections on Gender and Science*

Schrödinger (1967) has identified the two fundamental tenets of science as the beliefs that nature is (1) objectifiable and (2) knowable.[1] The first refers to the assumption of an objective reality, split off from and having an existence totally independent of us as observers. This is the principle that embodies the radical dichotomy between subject and object characteristic of the classical stance. It contains within it the implicit assumption that reality outside us is composed of objects – a rider which, although not logically necessary, is in practice an almost inevitable concomitant, if not precursor, of the classical view. The reason for this conjunction is, no doubt, that a world composed of clearly delineated objects both invites and facilitates the schism in which the subject is severed from even its own corporeal, objective existence. It is the move that is usually held responsible for, in the words of Koyré (1968), 'the splitting of our world in two.'

But a world view that posits a total separation between us as subject and reality as object is by itself of no interest to science since it permits no knowledge. Science is born out of the addition of Schrödinger's second tenet – out of the confidence that nature, so objectified, is indeed knowable. Not only is a connection between us as knowers and the reality to be known here posited, but the connection posited is of an extraordinarily special nature. For most scientists it implies a congruence between our scientific minds and the natural world – not unlike Plato's assumption of kinship between mind and form – that permits us to read the laws of reality without distortion, without error, and without omission. Belief in the knowability of nature is implicitly a belief in a one-to-one correspondence between theory and reality. What makes the resultant knowledge 'objective' is, perhaps even more than the ostensible split between subject and object, the separation within ourselves on which it is based. Scientific knowledge is made objective first by being dissociated from other modes of knowledge that are affectively tinged and hence tainted and, second, by being transcendentally wedded to the objects of nature. This felicitous marriage between the scientific mind and nature is consummated, not by worldly intercourse, but by a form of direct communion with nature, or with God, for which the scientific mind is uniquely, and unquestionably, equipped.[2]

The loneliness that others might find in a world in which subject and

From Evelyn Fox Keller, *Reflections on Gender and Science*, Yale University Press, 1985, pp. 141–3, 147–9.

object are split apart is mitigated, for the scientist, by his special access to the transcendent link between the two. The conflicting impulses implicit in these two components of objectivism find exquisite resolution in the classical Newtonian world view. Their intermingling confounds our efforts to sort out the dual aims of power and transcendence evident in the scientific endeavor; it leads simultaneously to the romantic view of the scientist as religious mystic – celibate, austere, and removed from the world of the senses – and to the technological view of science as dedicated to mastery, control, and the domination of nature. . . .

. . . The strong positivist ethos surrounding contemporary science makes it possible for some, perhaps most, physicists to limit the definition of reality to the body of theoretical and empirical knowledge at our disposal and to declare as meaningless all questions about the actual nature of the systems being studied and our relation to those systems. Without embarking on a critique of this position, I wish only to point out what is fairly obvious, namely, that it provides an extraordinarily convenient cover under which all sorts of prior beliefs about the world and its relation to science can, and do, subterraneously reside. It is too bad that we do not permit the child similar license to respond to Piaget's telling questions (questions that cannot be handled within an existing cognitive paradigm) by saying simply, 'Your questions are meaningless.'

At this point it must be asked why the classical paradigm is so difficult to give up in toto. Piaget attributes cognitive repression to the familiarity and success of older, established structures, and no doubt he is at least partly right. Certainly, the classical tenets of science have proved extraordinarily successful, and continue, in most areas of science, to do so. It seems, however, that the confusion that has for so long been evidenced in discussions about quantum mechanics, and the intense emotion such discussions can evoke, suggest that more is at stake than simply the comfort and success of an older paradigm. The great weakness of Piaget's developmental system is his failure to include any consideration of the impact of affective components on the developmental process. Egocentricity, omnipotence, and object permanence are all terms with profound meaning in the domain of affective relations as well as of cognitive relations. Although some attempt has been made to integrate the psychoanalytic understanding of affective development with Piaget's understanding of cognitive development, this remains an area in need of more research. A few comments may nevertheless be in order.

We know both from Piaget and from psychoanalysis that the capacity for objective thought and perception is not inborn but, rather, is acquired as part of the long and painful struggle for psychic autonomy – a state never entirely free of ambiguity and tension. The internal pressure to delineate self from other (a pressure exacerbated by the historical emphasis on ego autonomy) leaves us acutely vulnerable to anxiety about wishes or experiences that might threaten that delineation. We know further that such anxiety can sometimes be allayed by the imposition of an excessively delineated structure on one's emotional and cognitive environment. It would seem, therefore, that objectification in science may serve a related function. The severance of subject from object, as well as the insistence on the premise that science is affect-free, may derive in part from a heavily affect-laden motive for separateness and may serve to buttress a sense of autonomy. If so, then the continuing adherence to the belief in the objectifiability of nature would be assisted by the emotional functions served by this belief.

Similarly, the attachment to the premise that nature is 'knowable' can also be viewed in psychological terms. The ideal of a perfect congruence between us as knowers and an objective reality to be known is strikingly reminiscent of other ideas – ubiquitous among children – which we call magical. It represents a continuing belief in omniscience, now translated out of the domain of magic into the domain of science. Based on a vision of transcendent union with nature, it satisfies a primitive need for connection denied in another realm. As such, it militates against the acceptance of a more realistic, more mature, and more humble relation to the world in which the boundaries between subject and object are acknowledged to be never quite rigid and in which knowledge of any sort is never quite total. In such a frame, I suggest that the antinomies of quantum mechanics would no longer be so problematic.

Both tenets, knowability and objectifiability, need to be relinquished. The testimony of quantum mechanics is eloquent: however successful these tenets have been in the past, they are no longer adequate. Yet this testimony remains obscured by interpretations that implicitly attempt to retain some residue of the classical paradigm. Each of the two dominant schools of interpretation – the statistical and the Copenhagen – suffers from inadequacies that are evident to proponents of the other, and debate between the two continues. The failure to reach a resolution of this debate reflects the difficulties even quantum physicists have in completely relinquishing some adherence to at least one of the two basic premises of classical physics: the objectifiability and knowability of nature. The vision implicit in quantum mechanics still awaits representation in a cognitive paradigm yet more radical than any that the conventional interpretations have offered us.

Notes

1 Objectifiable, here and elsewhere, means both objective, i.e. independent of our cognizance, and objectlike, hence having a well-defined position in space and time. As remarked earlier, these two meanings are almost always conjoined.

2 Newton, e.g., was sometimes quite explicit in articulating the consonance between scientific thought and God's 'Sensorium': 'There is a Being incorporeal, living, intelligent, omnipresent who in infinite space, as it were in his sensory, sees things

intimately . . . of which things the images only . . . are there seen and beheld by that which in us perceives and thinks' (*Opticks*, 3rd ed., London, 1921, p. 344).

30 Julia Kristeva 'Women's Time'

In the name of the father, the son . . . and the woman?

These few elements of the manifestations by the new generation of women in Europe seem to me to demonstrate that, beyond the sociopolitical level where it is generally inscribed (or inscribes itself), the women's movement – in its present stage, less aggressive but more artful – is situated within the very framework of the religious crisis of our civilization.

I call 'religion' this phantasmic necessity on the part of speaking beings to provide themselves with a *representatation* (animal, female, male, parental, etc.) in place of what constitutes them as such, in other words, symbolization – the double articulation and syntactic sequence of language, as well as its preconditions or substitutes (thoughts, affects, etc.). The elements of the current practice of feminism that we have just brought to light seem precisely to constitute such a representation which makes up for the frustrations imposed on women by the anterior code (Christianity or its lay humanist variant). The fact that this new ideology has affinities, often revindicated by its creators, with so-called matriarchal beliefs (in other words, those beliefs characterizing matrilinear societies) should not overshadow its radical novelty. This ideology seems to me to be part of the broader antisacrificial current which in animating our culture and which, in its protest against the constraints of the sociosymbolic contract, is no less exposed to the risks of violence and terrorism. At this level of radicalism, it is the very principle of sociality which is challenged.

Certain contemporary thinkers consider, as is well known, that modernity is characterized as the first epoch in human history in which human beings attempt to live without religion. In its present form, is not feminism in the process of becoming one?

Or is it, on the contrary and as avant-garde feminists hope, that having started with the idea of difference, feminism will be able to break free of its belief in Woman, Her power, Her writing, so as to channel this demand for

From Robyn Warhol and Diane Price Herndl (eds), *Feminisms*, Rutgers University Press, 1991, pp. 457–9.

difference into each and every element of the female whole, and, finally, to bring out the singularity of each woman, and beyond this, her multiplicities, her plural languages, beyond the horizon, beyond sight, beyond faith itself?

A factor for ultimate mobilization? Or a factor for analysis?

Imaginary support in a technocratic era where all narcissism is frustrated? Or instruments fitted to these times in which the cosmos, atoms, and cells – our true contemporaries – call for the constitution of a fluid and free subjectivity?

The question has been posed. Is to pose it already to answer it?

Another generation is another space

If the preceding can be *said* – the question whether all this is *true* belongs to a different register – it is undoubtedly because it is now possible to gain some distance on these two preceding generations of women. This implies, of course, that a *third* generation is now forming, at least in Europe. I am not speaking of a new group of young women (though its importance should not be underestimated) or of another 'mass feminist movement' taking the torch passed on from the second generation. My usage of the word 'generation' implies less a chronology than a *signifying space*, a both corporeal and desiring mental space. So it can be argued that as of now a third attitude is possible, thus a third generation, which does not exclude – quite to the contrary – the *parallel* existence of all three in the same historical time, or even that they be interwoven one with the other.

In this third attitude, which I strongly advocate – which I imagine? – the very dichotomy man/woman as an opposition between two rival entities may be understood as belonging to *metaphysics*. What can 'identity,' even 'sexual identity,' mean in a new theoretical and scientific space where the very notion of identity is challenged?[1] I am not simply suggesting a very hypothetical bisexuality which, even if it existed, would only, in fact, be the aspiration toward the totality of one of the sexes and thus an effacing of difference. What I mean is, first of all, the demassification of the problematic of *difference*, which would imply, in a first phase, an apparent de-dramatization of the 'fight to the death' between rival groups and thus between the sexes. And this not in the name of some reconciliation – feminism has at least had the merit of showing what is irreducible and even deadly in the social contract – but in order that the struggle, the implacable difference, the violence be conceived in the very place where it operates with the maximum intransigence, in other words, in personal and sexual identity itself, so as to make it disintegrate in its very nucleus.

It necessarily follows that this involves risks not only for what we understand today as 'personal equilibrium' but also for social equilibrium itself, made up as it now is of the counterbalancing of aggressive and murderous forces massed in social, national, religious, and political groups. But is it not the insupportable situation of tension and explosive risk that the existing 'equilibrium' presupposes which leads some of those who suffer from it to divest it of its economy, to detach themselves from it, and to seek another means of regulating difference? `

To restrict myself here to a personal level, as related to the question of women, I see arising, under the cover of a relative indifference toward the militance of the first and second generations, an attitude of retreat from sexism (male as well as female) and, gradually, from any kind of anthropomorphism. The fact that this might quickly become another form of spiritualism turning its back on social problems, or else a form of repression[2] ready to support all status quos, should not hide the radicalness of the process. This process could be summarized as an *interiorization of the founding separation of the sociosymbolic contract*, as an introduction of its cutting edge into the very interior of every identity whether subjective, sexual, ideological, or so forth. This in such a way that the habitual and increasingly explicit attempt to fabricate a scapegoat victim as foundress of a society or a countersociety may be replaced by the analysis of the potentialities of *victim/executioner* which characterize each identity, each subject, each sex.

What discourse, if not that of a religion, would be able to support this adventure which surfaces as a real possibility, after both the achievements and the impasses of the present ideological reworkings, in which feminism has participated? It seems to me that the role of what is usually called 'aesthetic practices' must increase not only to counterbalance the storage and uniformity of information by present-day mass media, data-bank systems, and, in particular, modern communications technology, but also to demystify the identity of the symbolic bond itself, to demystify, therefore, the *community* of language as a universal and unifying tool, one which totalizes and equalizes. In order to bring out – along with the *singularity* of each person and, even more, along with the multiplicity of every person's possible identifications (with atoms, for example, stretching from the family to the stars) – the *relativity of his/her symbolic as well as biological existence*, according to the variation in his/her specific symbolic capacities. And in order to emphasize the *responsibility* which all will immediately face of putting this fluidity into play against the threats of death which are unavoidable whenever an inside and an outside, a self and an other, one group and another, are constituted. At this level of interiorization with its social as well as individual stakes, what I have called 'aesthetic practices' are undoubtedly nothing other than the modern reply to the eternal question of morality. At least, this is how we might understand an ethics which, conscious of the fact that its order is sacrificial, reserves part of the burden for each of its adherents, therefore declaring them guilty while immediately affording them the possibility for *jouissance*, for various productions, for a life made up of both challenges and differences.

Spinoza's question can be taken up again here: Are women subject to ethics? If not to that ethics defined by classical philosophy – in relationship to which the ups and downs of feminist generations seem dangerously precarious – are women not already participating in the rapid dismantling that our age is experiencing at various levels (from wars to drugs to artificial insemination) and which poses the *demand* for a new ethics? The answer to Spinoza's question can be affirmative only at the cost of considering feminism as but a *moment* in the thought of that anthropomorphic identity which currently blocks the horizon of the discursive and scientific adventure of our species.

Translated by Alice Jardine and Harry Blake

Notes

1 *See* Seminar on *Identity* directed by Lévi-Strauss (Paris, Grasset & Fasquelle, 1977).
2 Repression (*le refoulement* or *Verdrangung*) as distinguished from the foreclosure (*la foreclusion* or *Verwerfung*) evoked earlier in the article (*see* LaPlanche and Pontalis). – AJ.

31   Luce Irigaray
'Sexual Difference'

Sexual difference is one of the important questions of our age, if not in fact the burning issue. According to Heidegger, each age is preoccupied with one thing, and one alone. Sexual difference is probably that issue in our own age which could be our salvation on an intellectual level.

For the work of sexual difference to take place, a revolution in thought and ethics is needed. We must re-interpret the whole relationship between the subject and discourse, the subject and the world, the subject and the cosmic, the microcosmic and the macrocosmic. And the first thing to say is that, even when aspiring to a universal or neutral state, this subject has always been written in the masculine form, as man, despite the fact that, at least in French, 'man' is a sexed and not a neutral noun.

It is man who has been the subject of discourse, whether in the field of

From Toril Moi (ed.), Seán Hand (tr.), *French Feminist Thought*, Blackwell, 1987, pp. 118–20, 124–5.

theory, morality or politics. And the gender of God, the guardian of every subject and discourse, is always *paternal and masculine* in the West. For women, there remain the so-called minor art-forms: cooking, knitting, sewing and embroidery; and in exceptional cases, poetry, painting and music. Whatever their importance, these arts today do not lay down the law, at least not overtly.

We are, of course, presently bearing witness to a certain reversal of values: manual labour and art are both being revalorized. But the relationship of these arts to sexual difference is never really thought through, and properly sorted out, although on occasion it is all related to the classstruggle.

In order to live and think through this difference, we must reconsider the whole question of *space* and *time*.

In the beginning was space and the creation of space, as stated in every theogony. The gods or God first of all creates *space*. And time is there, more or less at the service of space. During the first few days the gods or God organize a world by separating the elements. This world is then peopled, and a rhythmical pattern is established among its inhabitants. God then becomes time itself, lavishing or exteriorizing itself in space or place.

Philosophy confirms this genealogy of the task of the gods or God. Time becomes *interior* to the subject, and space *exterior* (this is developed by Kant in the *Critique of Pure Reason*). The subject, the master of time, becomes the axis, managing the affairs of the world. Beyond him lies the eternal instant of God, who brings about the passage between time and space.

Could it be that this order becomes inverted in sexual difference, such that femininity is experienced as a space that often carries connotations of the depths of night (God being space and light), while masculinity is conceived of in terms of time?

The transition to a new age in turn necessitates a new perception and a new conception of *time and space*, our *occupation of place*, and the different *envelopes known as identity*.[1] It assumes and entails an evolution or transformation of forms, of the relationship of *matter* to *form* and of the interval *between* the two. This trilogy gives us our notion of place. Each age assigns limits to this trinity, be they *matter, form, interval* or *power, act, intermediate – interval*.

Desire occupies or designates the place of the *interval*. A permanent definition of desire would put an end to desire. Desire requires a sense of attraction: a change in the interval or the relations of nearness or distance between subject and object.

The transition to a new age coincides with a change in the economy of desire, necessitating a different relationship between man and god(s), man and man, man and the world, man and woman. Our own age, which is often felt to be the one in which the problem of desire has been brought to the fore, frequently theorizes about this desire on the basis of certain observations about a moment of tension, situated in historical time, whereas desire ought to be thought of as a dynamic force whose changing form can be traced in the past and occasionally the present, but never predicted. Our age will only realize the dynamic potential in desire if the latter is referred back to the economy of the *interval*, that is if it is located in the attractions, tensions, and acts between *form* and *matter*, or characterized as the *residue* of any creation or work, which lies *between* what is already identified and what has still to be identified, etc.

To arrive at the constitution of an ethics of sexual difference, we must at least return to what is for Descartes the first passion: *wonder*.[2] This passion is not opposed to, or in conflict with, anything else, and exists always as though for the first time. Man and woman, woman and man are therefore always meeting as though for the first time since they cannot stand in for one another. I shall never take the place of a man, never will a man take mine. Whatever identifications are possible, one will never exactly fill the place of the other – the one is irreducible to the other:

> When our first encounter with some object surprises us and we find it novel, or very different from what we formerly knew or from what we supposed it ought to be, this causes us to wonder and to be astonished at it. Since all this may happen before we know whether or not the object is beneficial to us, I regard wonder as the first of all the passions. It has no opposite, for, if the object before us has no characteristics that surprise us, we are not moved by it at all and we consider it without passion.[3]

Who or what the other is, I never know. But this unknowable other is that which differs sexually from me. This feeling of wonder, surprise and astonishment in the face of the unknowable ought to be returned to its proper place: the realm of sexual difference. The passions have either been repressed, stifled and subdued, or else reserved for God. Sometimes a sense of wonder is bestowed upon a work of art. But it is never found in the *gap between man and woman*. This space was filled instead with attraction, greed, possession, consummation, disgust, etc., and not with that wonder which sees something as though always for the first time, and never seizes the other as its object. Wonder cannot seize, possess or subdue such an object. The latter, perhaps, remains subjective and free?

This has never happened between the sexes. Wonder might allow them to retain an autonomy based on their difference, and give them a space of freedom or attraction, a possibility of separation or alliance.

All this would happen even before becoming engaged, during their first encounter, which would confirm their difference. The *interval* would never be crossed. There would be no consummation. Such an idea is a delusion. One sex is never entirely consummated or consumed by another. There is always a *residue*.

Notes

1 Irigaray's text has *enveloppe/envelopper* in this and subsequent passages. We have decided to translate 'envelope' and 'envelop', although this translation risks losing something of the concrete sense of enfolding, wrapping, covering, englobing, etc., associated with the French words. While the philosophical idea under discussion is that of the relationship between the container and the contained, there may also be an illusion to certain psychoanalytic theories of an early 'skin-ego', conceptualized as a 'psychic envelope' (Bion, Winnicott, Anzieu). – Ed.

2 The original French expression is *admiration*.

3 René Descartes, *The Passions of the Soul*, article 53 in *The Philosophical Writings of Descartes*, vol. I, tr. J. Cottingham, R. Stoothoff, D. Murdoch, Cambridge, Cambridge University Press, 1985, p. 350.

SECTION THREE
ART, BELIEF AND VALUE

The essays gathered in this section address the relations between literature and value, whether that relationship exists primarily within a framework of spiritual belief or of political or ethical commitment. Some of the essays are written from within orthodox frameworks of belief, but none of them suggests that the relationship between art and belief is simple or straightforward. All in various ways question or problematize Enlightenment concepts of rationality, though some of them develop or expand Enlightenment ideas. The essays in the first part respond to a sense of crisis in inherited belief systems, a crisis which can be seen to arise very often from specific historical events of the twentieth century: the experience of war, of the Holocaust, of exile, dispossession and suffering. The essays by Bataille (1957), Steiner (1967), Benjamin (from *Illuminations*, 1968), address the problem of the nature of artistic representation in the wake of historical events whose violence has blasted apart traditional notions of temporal continuity, historical progress and of rational truth or justice. In different ways, each speaks with a Messianic voice or in an apocalyptic mode. The essays by Zora Neale Hurston and C.S. Lewis represent more affirmative though very different ways of understanding relations between literature and spirituality.

The essays which follow under the heading of 'Commitment' are concerned with the problem of the writer's relation to more specifically political commitments. Those by Adorno (1965) and Williams (1979) examine the issue of formal autonomy and offer different perspectives on that question of 'relevance' in art first raised in the debates over modernism between Brecht and Lukács. Implicitly, they raise issues about the relationship between collective politics and the individual voice which are also reflected in the focus on relations between tradition and originality in essays in the third subsection, *Myth, tradition and innovation*, by T.S. Eliot, Samuel Beckett, C.G. Jung and Renato Poggioli. Eliot's essay of 1919 introduces the terms of this discussion (see my introduction). Beckett's essay of 1929 appeared in the same collection as Jolas' 'The Revolution of Language and James Joyce' and represents an attempt to develop Jolas' reading of Joyce by examining his 'individual talent' in relation to the self-constituted 'tradition' of Dante, Bruno and Vico. Jung's essay of 1933 reveals the similarities between Eliot's attempt to develop the concept of an aesthetic 'tradition' and Jung's own theory of a 'collective unconscious'. Finally, Pogioli (1962, tr. 1968) argues for the centrality of criticism itself in constructing 'tradition' in the modern period.

The last section here, on 'Aesthetics and Ethics', presents a more purely philosophical approach to the problem of literature and ethics. Nietzsche's writing had established the framework for modernist and postmodernist discussions in this area. In questioning the philosophical ideal of 'truth' and in arguing that all knowledge claims or universal ethics are always disguised manifestations of desire, of the will-to-power, Nietzsche had undermined the Kantian separation of the realms of art, knowledge and morality. The excerpt from Moore's *Principia Ethica* (1903) offers a definition of the 'good' which became central to Bloomsbury aesthetics (see my introduction), but which is rejected by MacIntyre in *After Virtue* (1981) as an example of inauthentic emotivism. MacIntyre criticizes the assumption that the rejection of Kantian universalism must entail only the choice between an emotivist or nihilist alternative. He argues that, if we cannot find universal rational grounds for an objective system of value, this does not mean that we are forced to accept the various irrationalist alternatives which have followed upon Nietzsche's critique of metaphysics. Instead, he argues for the rehabilitation of a notion of 'practical wisdom' grounded in cultural traditions rather than abstract rules. If MacIntyre seeks a way out of the 'postmodern condition', Lyotard's piece (1988) develops his earlier argument from *The Postmodern Condition* and shows that incommensurability can no more be overcome in the sphere of judgement than in that of knowledge.

THE SACRED AND PROFANE

32　Zora Neale Hurston
'Spirituals and Neo-Spirituals'

The real spirituals are not really just songs. They are unceasing variations around a theme.

Contrary to popular belief their creation is not confined to the slavery period. Like the folk-tales, the spirituals are being made and forgotten every day. There is this difference: the makers of the songs of the present go about from town to town and church to church singing their songs. Some are printed and called ballads, and offered for sale after the services at ten or fifteen cents each. Others just go about singing them in competition with other religious minstrels. The lifting of the collection is the time for the song battles. Quite a bit of rivalry develops.

These songs, even the printed ones, do not remain long in their original form. Every congregation that takes it up alters it considerably. For instance, *The Dying Bed Maker*, which is easily the most popular of the recent compositions, has been changed to *He's a Mind Regulator* by a Baptist church in New Orleans.

The idea that the whole body of spirituals are 'sorrow songs' is ridiculous. They cover a wide range of subjects from a peeve at gossipers to Death and Judgment.

The nearest thing to a description one can reach is that they are Negro religious songs, sung by a group, and a group bent on expression of feelings and not on sound effects.

There never has been a presentation of genuine Negro spirituals to any audience anywhere. What is being sung by the concert artists and glee clubs are the works of Negro composers or adapters *based* on the spirituals. Under this head come the works of Harry T. Burleigh, Rosamond Johnson, Lawrence Brown, Nathaniel Dett, Hall Johnson and Work. All good work and beautiful, but *not* the spirituals. These neo-spirituals are the outgrowth of the glee clubs. Fisk University boasts perhaps the oldest and certainly the most famous of these. They have spread their interpretation over America and Europe. Hampton and Tuskegee have not been unheard. But with all the glee clubs and soloists, there has not been one genuine spiritual presented.

From Bonnie Kime Scott (ed.), *Gender and Modernism*, Indiana University Press, 1990, pp. 188–91.

To begin with, Negro spirituals are not solo or quartette material. The jagged harmony is what makes it, and it ceases to be what it was when this is absent. Neither can any group be trained to reproduce it. Its truth dies under training like flowers under hot water. The harmony of the true spiritual is not regular. The dissonances are important and not to be ironed out by the trained musician. The various parts break in at any old time. Falsetto often takes the place of regular voices for short periods. Keys change. Moreover, each singing of the piece is a new creation. The congregation is bound by no rules. No two times singing is alike, so that we must consider the rendition of a song not as a final thing, but as a mood. It won't be the same thing next Sunday.

Negro songs to be heard truly must be sung by a group, and a group bent on expression of feelings and not on sound effects.

Glee clubs and concert singers put on their tuxedos, bow prettily to the audience, get the pitch and burst into magnificent song – but not *Negro* song. The real Negro singer cares nothing about pitch. The first notes just burst out and the rest of the church join in – fired by the same inner urge. Every man trying to express himself through song. Every man for himself. Hence the harmony and disharmony, the shifting keys and broken time that make up the spiritual.

I have noticed that whenever an untampered-with congregation attempts the renovated spirituals, the people grow self-conscious. They sing sheepishly in unison. None of the glorious individualistic flights that make up their own songs. Perhaps they feel on strange ground. Like the unlettered parent before his child just home from college. At any rate they are not very popular.

This is no condemnation of the neo-spirituals. They are a valuable contribution to the music and literature of the world. But let no one imagine that they are the songs of the people, as sung by them.

The lack of dialect in the religious expression – particularly in the prayers – will seem irregular.

The truth is, that the religious service is a conscious art expression. The artist is consciously creating – carefully choosing every syllable and every breath. The dialect breaks through only when the speaker has reached the emotional pitch where he loses all self-consciousness.

In the mouth of the Negro the English language loses its stiffness, yet conveys its meaning accurately. 'The booming bounderries of this whirling world' conveys just as accurate a picture as mere 'boundaries,' and a little music is gained besides. 'The rim bones of nothing' is just as truthful as 'limitless space.'

Negro singing and formal speech are breathy. The audible breathing is part of the performance and various devices are resorted to to adorn the breath taking. Even the lack of breath is embellished with syllables. This is, of course, the very antithesis of white vocal art. European singing is considered good when each syllable floats out on a column of air, seeming not to have any mechanics at all. Breathing must be hidden. Negro song ornaments both the song and the mechanics. It is said of a popular preacher, 'He's got a good straining voice.' I will make a parable to illustrate the difference between Negro and European.

A white man built a house. So he got it built and he told the man: 'Plaster it good so that nobody can see the beams and uprights.' So he did. Then he had it papered with beautiful paper, and painted the outside. And a Negro built him a house. So when he got the beams and all in, he carved beautiful grotesques over all the sills and stanchions, and beams and rafters. So both went to live in their houses and were happy.

The well-known 'ha!' of the Negro preacher is a breathing device. It is the tail end of the expulsion just before inhalation. Instead of permitting the breath to drain out, when the wind gets too low for words, the remnant is expelled violently. Example: (inhalation) 'And oh!'; (full breath) 'my Father and my wonder-working God'; (explosive exhalation) 'ha!'

Chants and hums are not used indiscriminately as it would appear to a casual listener. They have a definite place and time. They are used to 'bear up' the speaker. As Mama Jane of Second Zion Baptist Church, New Orleans, explained to me: 'What point they come out on, you bear 'em up.'

For instance, if the preacher should say: 'Jesus will lead us,' the congregation would bear him up with: 'I'm got my ha-hands in my Jesus' hands.' If in prayer or sermon, the mention is made of nailing Christ to the cross: 'Didn't Calvary tremble when they nailed him down.'

There is no definite post-prayer chant. One may follow, however, because of intense emotion. A song immediately follows prayer. There is a pre-prayer hum which depends for its material upon the song just sung. It is usually a pianissimo continuation of the song without words. If some of the people use the words it is done so indistinctly that they would be hard to catch by a person unfamiliar with the song.

As indefinite as hums sound, they also are formal and can be found unchanged all over the South. The Negroized white hymns are not exactly sung. They are converted into a barbaric chant that is not a chant. It is a sort of liquefying of words. These songs are always used at funerals and on any solemn occasion. The Negro has created no songs for death and burials, in spite of the sombre subject matter contained in some of the spirituals. Negro songs are one and all based on a dance-possible rhythm. The heavy interpretations have been added by the more cultured singers. So for funerals fitting white hymns are used.

Beneath the seeming informality of religious worship there is a set formality. Sermons, prayers, moans, and testimonies have their definite forms. The individual may hang as many new ornaments upon the traditional form as he likes, but the audience would be disagreeably surprised if the form were abandoned. Any new and original elaboration is welcomed, however, and this brings out the fact that all religious expression among Negroes is regarded as art, and ability is recognized as definitely as in any other art. The beautiful prayer receives the accolade as well as the beautiful song. It is merely a form of expression which people generally are not accustomed to think of as art. Nothing outside of the Old Testament is as rich in figure as a Negro prayer. Some instances are unsurpassed anywhere in literature.

There is a lively rivalry in the technical artistry of all of these fields. It is a special honor to be called upon to pray over the covered communion table, for the greatest prayer-artist present is chosen for this, a lively something spreads over the church as he kneels, and the 'bearing up' hum precedes him. It continues sometimes through the introduction, but ceases as he makes the complimentary salutation to the deity. This consists in giving to God all the titles that form allows.

The introduction to the prayer usually consists of one or two verses of some well-known hymn. 'O, that I knew a secret place' seems to be the favorite. There is a definite pause after this, then follows an elaboration of all or parts of the Lord's Prayer. Follows after that what I call the setting, that is, the artist calling attention to the physical situation of himself and the church. After the dramatic setting, the action begins.

There are certain rhythmic breaks throughout the prayer, and the church 'bears him up' at every one of these. There is in the body of the prayer an accelerando passage where the audience takes no part. It would be like applauding in the middle of a solo at the Metropolitan. It is here that the artist comes forth. He adorns the prayer with every sparkle of earth, water and sky, and nobody wants to miss a syllable. He comes down from this height to a slower tempo and is borne up again. The last few sentences are unaccompanied, for here again one listens to the individual's closing peroration. Several may join in the final amen. The best figure that I can think of is that the prayer is an obbligato over and above the harmony of the assembly.

---

33   C.S. Lewis
From *An Experiment in Criticism*

The nearest I have yet got to an answer is that we seek an enlargement of our being. We want to be more than ourselves. Each of us by nature sees the whole world from one point of view with a perspective and a selectiveness

From C.S. Lewis, *An Experiment in Criticism*, Cambridge University Press, 1961, pp. 137–41.

peculiar to himself. And even when we build disinterested fantasies, they are saturated with, and limited by, our own psychology. To acquiesce in this particularity on the sensuous level – in other words, not to discount perspective – would be lunacy. We should then believe that the railway line really grew narrower as it receded into the distance. But we want to escape the illusions of perspective on higher levels too. We want to see with other eyes, to imagine with other imaginations, to feel with other hearts, as well as with our own. We are not content to be Leibnitzian monads. We demand windows. Literature as Logos is a series of windows, even of doors. One of the things we feel after reading a great work is 'I have got out'. Or from another point of view, 'I have got in'; pierced the shell of some other monad and discovered what it is like inside.

Good reading, therefore, though it is not essentially an affectional or moral or intellectual activity, has something in common with all three. In love we escape from our self into one other. In the moral sphere, every act of justice or charity involves putting ourselves in the other person's place and thus transcending our own competitive particularity. In coming to understand anything we are rejecting the facts as they are for us in favour of the facts as they are. The primary impulse of each is to maintain and aggrandise himself. The secondary impulse is to go out of the self, to correct its provincialism and heal its loneliness. In love, in virtue, in the pursuit of knowledge, and in the reception of the arts, we are doing this. Obviously this process can be described either as an enlargement or as a temporary annihilation of the self. But that is an old paradox; 'he that loseth his life shall save it'.

We therefore delight to enter into other men's beliefs (those, say, of Lucretius or Lawrence) even though we think them untrue. And into their passions, though we think them depraved, like those, sometimes, of Marlowe or Carlyle. And also into their imaginations, though they lack all realism of content.

This must not be understood as if I were making the literature of power once more into a department within the literature of knowledge – a department which existed to gratify our rational curiosity about other people's psychology. It is not a question of knowing (in that sense) at all. It is *connaître* not *savoir*; it is *erleben*; we become these other selves. Not only nor chiefly in order to see what they are like but in order to see what they see, to occupy, for a while, their seat in the great theatre, to use their spectacles and be made free of whatever insights, joys, terrors, wonders or merriment those spectacles reveal. Hence it is irrelevant whether the mood expressed in a poem was truly and historically the poet's own or one that he also had imagined. What matters is his power to make us live it. I doubt whether Donne the man gave more than playful and dramatic harbourage to the mood expressed in *The Apparition*. I doubt still more whether the real Pope, save while he wrote it, or even then more than dramatically, felt what he expresses in the passage beginning 'Yes, I am proud'.[1] What does it matter?

This, so far as I can see, is the specific value or good of literature considered as Logos: it admits us to experiences other than our own. They are not, any more than our personal experiences, all equally worth having. Some, as we say, 'interest' us more than others. The causes of this interest are naturally extremely various and differ from one man to another; it may be the typical (and we say 'How true!') or the abnormal (and we say 'How strange!'); it may be the beautiful, the terrible, the awe-inspiring, the exhilarating, the pathetic, the comic, or the merely piquant. Literature gives the *entrée* to them all. Those of us who have been true readers all our life seldom fully realise the enormous extension of our being which we owe to authors. We realise it best when we talk with an unliterary friend. He may be full of goodness and good sense but he inhabits a tiny world. In it, we should be suffocated. The man who is contented to be only himself, and therefore less a self, is in prison. My own eyes are not enough for me, I will see through those of others. Reality, even seen through the eyes of many, is not enough. I will see what others have invented. Even the eyes of all humanity are not enough. I regret that the brutes cannot write books. Very gladly would I learn what face things present to a mouse or a bee; more gladly still would I perceive the olfactory world charged with all the information and emotion it carries for a dog.

Literary experience heals the wound, without undermining the privilege, of individuality. There are mass emotions which heal the wound; but they destroy the privilege. In them our separate selves are pooled and we sink back into sub-individuality. But in reading great literature I become a thousand men and yet remain myself. Like the night sky in the Greek poem, I see with a myriad eyes, but it is still I who see. Here, as in worship, in love, in moral action, and in knowing, I transcend myself; and am never more myself than when I do.

Notes

1 *Epilogue to the Satires*, dia. II, l. 208.

34 Georges Bataille
From *Literature and Evil*

Liberty and Evil

To reveal Evil in liberty goes totally against a conventional and widespread way of thought. To start with, Sartre will deny that liberty must necessarily be Evil. But he endows 'productive society' with a worth, before acknowledging its relative nature: yet this worth is relative to consumption. It is essentially relative to unproductive consumption, that is to say, to destruction. If we seek the coherence of these representations, it soon transpires that liberty, even after the potential relationship with Good has been taken into account, is, as Blake said of Milton, 'of the Devil's party without knowing it'. Submission and obedience, on the other hand, are on the side of Good. Liberty is always open to revolt, while Good is closed as a rule. Sartre himself talks of Evil in terms of liberty: 'nothing of what *is*,' he says[1] with reference to the 'experience of Evil', 'can define or limit me: yet I exist, I shall be the icy breath which will annihilate all life. So I will be *above* the essence: I do what I like, I do what I like to myself . . . ' In all events nobody can proceed, as Sartre would apparently like to proceed, from liberty to the traditional concept of Good corresponding to utility.[2]

Only one path leads from the rejection of servitude to the free limitations of sovereign humour: this path, which Sartre does not mention, is the path of *communication*. It is only if *liberty*, the *transgression of laws* and *sovereign consumption* are envisaged in their true form that the foundations of a moral code are revealed for those people who are not entirely regulated by necessity and who do not want to renounce the fullness which they have glimpsed.

Authentic communication, the impenetrability of all 'that is', and sovereignty

The interesting aspect of Jean Genet's work does not reside in its poetic power, but in the lesson we can learn from its weaknesses. Similarly, Sartre's study is based less on a perfect understanding than on a determination to search for the areas of darkness.

There is a cold and fragile quality in Genet's writing which does not necessarily prevent us from admiring it, but which makes us hesitate to agree with him. Genet himself would reject agreement if, by some indefen-

From Georges Bataille, *Literature and Evil*, tr. Alistair Hamilton, Calder and Boyars, 1973, pp. 168–75.

sible error, we wanted to agree with him. Since this communication fades away just when literature needs it, it leaves the impression of a grimace. It matters little if the mere sensation that there is something lacking reminds us of authentic communication. In the depression resulting from these inadequate exchanges, where a glassy barrier is maintained between the reader and the author, I am sure about one thing: humanity is not composed of isolated beings but of communication between them. Never are we revealed, even to ourselves, other than in a network of communications with others. We bathe in communication, we are reduced to this incessant communication whose absence we feel, even in the depths of solitude, like the suggestion of multiple possibilities, like the expectation of the moment when it will solve itself in a cry heard by others. In ourselves human existence is nothing but shouts, a cruel spasm, a giggling fit where agreement is born from a consciousness which is at last shared between the impenetrability of ourselves and that of others.[3]

Communication, in my sense of the word, is never stronger than when communication, in the weak sense, the sense of profane language or, as Sartre says, of prose which makes us and the others appear penetrable, fails and becomes the equivalent of darkness. There are various ways in which we talk in order to convince people to agree with us.[4] We want to establish humble truths which coordinate our attitudes and activity with those of our fellow human beings. This incessant effort to situate ourselves in the world with clarity and distinction would be apparently impossible if we were not first bound to one another by the feeling of *common subjectivity*, impenetrable in itself, and for which the world of distinct objects is impenetrable.

It is essential to understand the distinction between two sorts of communication, but this is difficult: they intermingle in that the emphasis is not on powerful communication. Even Sartre is a little confused about this. He saw, as he insists in *La Nausée*, the impenetrable nature of objects: in no wise do objects communicate with us. But he has not precisely defined the difference between object and subject. Subjectivity is clear in his eyes: it is that which is clear. On the one hand he seems inclined to minimise the importance of this intelligibility of the objects which we perceive according to the purpose we attribute to them; on the other, he does not pay enough attention to those moments of a subjectivity *which is always given us in the consciousness of other subjectivities*, to those moments when subjectivity seems unintelligible in relation to the intelligibility of customary objects and, more generally, of the objective world. He cannot overlook this appearance, but he turns away from the moments when we too are nauseated by it because, in the instant when intelligibility appears to us, it adopts an unsurmountable and scandalous quality in its turn. Finally, what *is*, for us, is scandal. Consciousness of being is the scandal of consciousness, and we cannot – indeed, we must not – be surprised.

But we must not be taken in by words. Scandal is the same thing as consciousness: a consciousness without scandal is alienated consciousness

– a consciousness, experience proves it, of clear and distinct objects, intelligible, or thought to be so. The passage from intelligibility to unintelligibility, from that which, no longer being knowable, suddenly no longer seems tolerable to us, is certainly at the origin of this feeling of scandal, but it is less a question of difference of level than of an experience 'given' in the major communication of beings. The scandal is the *instantaneous* fact that consciousness is consciousness of another consciousness, that is, the look of another look. In this way it is an intimate glow, removed from that which usually attaches consciousness to the lasting and peaceful intelligibility of objects.

If this is clear, we see that there is a fundamental distinction between *feeble communication*, the basis of profane society (of active society – in the sense in which activity merges with productivity) and *powerful communication* which abandons the consciousnesses that reflect each other, to that impenetrability which they 'ultimately' are. At the same time we can see that powerful communication is primary, it is a simple 'given', the supreme appearance of existence, which reveals itself to us in the multiplicity of consciousnesses and in their communicability. The habitual activity of beings – what we call 'our occupation' – separates them from the privileged moments of powerful communication which is based on the emotions of sensuality, festivity, drama, love, separation and death. These moments are by no means equal among themselves: we often look for them for themselves, but they only have a significance in the instant at which they appear, and it is contradictory to plan their repetition. We cannot obtain them by our own feeble means. But this does not matter: we cannot do without the reappearance, however agonising, of the instant when their impenetrability reveals itself to the consciousnesses which unite and penetrate each other unlimitedly. It is better to cheat than to be lacerated too cruelly or too definitively. With the scandal which we want to cause at all costs, but from which we also want to escape, we maintain an indefectible, but as painless as possible, a bond, in the form of religion or art (art which has inherited a part of the powers of religion). Literary expression always raises the problem of *communication*, and is indeed poetry or nothing – nothing but the quest for particular agreements or the teaching of those minor truths to which Sartre refers when he talks of prose.[5]

Sovereignty betrayed

There is no difference between this powerful communication and what I call sovereignty. *In the instant* in which it occurs communication presupposes the sovereignty of the individuals communicating with each other, just as sovereignty presupposes communication: either it is deliberately communicable, or it is not sovereign. We must insist that sovereignty is always communication, and that communication, in the powerful sense, is always sovereign. If we bide by this point of view, Genet's experience is of exemplary interest.

In order to convey the sense of this experience, which is not only that of a writer but that of a man who has broken every law of society – every taboo on which society is based – I should start with the human aspect of sovereignty and communication. In as far as it differs from animality, humanity is based on the observance of taboos, some of which are universal: the prohibition of incest, of contact with menstrual blood, of obscenity, murder and the consumption of human flesh; in the first place the dead are the objects of taboos which vary according to time and place, but which nobody should infringe.

Communication or sovereignty are 'given' whenever life is determined by certain general interdicts, as well as by countless local taboos. These different limitations infringe to various extents the fullness of sovereignty, so we must not be surprised if the quest for sovereignty is connected with the infringement of one or more interdicts. In Egypt, for example, the sovereign was exempt from the prohibition of incest. Similarly, the sovereign operation, sacrifice, has a criminal quality: to put the victim to death is to break a law which is valid in other circumstances. On a more general level behaviour contrary to profane laws is allowed, and sometimes even ordained, during those sovereign periods of festivity. The creation of a sovereign (or sacred) element, therefore, of an institutional figure or of a sacrificial victim, depends on the negation of some interdict, the general observation of which makes us human beings, as opposed to animals. This means that sovereignty, in that humanity tends towards it, requires us to situate ourselves 'above the essence' which constitutes it. It also means that major communication can only take place on one condition – that we resort to Evil, that is to say to violation of the law.[6]

Genet has a classical attitude in that he searches for sovereignty in Evil and that Evil does indeed provide him with those ecstatic moments when our very being seems to fall apart and, though it survives, escapes from the essence which limits it. But Genet refuses to communicate. By so doing he never reaches the sovereign moment, the moment when he would at last cease bringing everything back to his own obsession with isolation, or, as Sartre says, simply with 'being'. It is to the extent in which he abandons himself *completely* to Evil that communication escapes him. Everything becomes clear at this point. What holds Genet down is the solitude into which he shuts himself and where whatever subsists of other people is always vague and indifferent. He does the Evil to which he resorted in order to exist sovereignly for his own *benefit* alone. The Evil required by sovereignty is necessarily limited. Sovereignty itself limits it. It sets itself in opposition to all that enslaves it in as far as it is communication. It opposes itself with that sovereign instinct which expresses a sacred aspect of morality.

I admit that Genet wanted to become *sacred*. I admit that, in him, the *taste* for Evil went beyond personal interest, that he wanted Evil for a spiritual value, and that he lived his experience without flinching. No vulgar motive would account for his failure, but, as in a dungeon guarded more closely than real prisons, a ghastly destiny enclosed him within himself, at the depths of his mistrust. He never yielded completely to the irrational impulses which unite beings, but which unite them on the condition that they shed the suspicions and diffidence bred in the difference between each being. Sartre has given us a good account of this sullen sadness with which Genet is contorted.

A somewhat exaggerated literary admiration has not prevented Sartre from passing judgment on Genet. Indeed, it has enabled him to do so, and this judgment is of an astringent severity, tempered by a profound sympathy. Sartre insists on this point: although Genet, tormented by the contradictions of his desire for the worst, seeks 'the impossible Nullity',[7] he finally demands *being* for his existence. He wants to *seize* his existence. He must arrive at the *being*, he wants the *being* of *things* for himself . . . 'This existence' would have 'to be without risking its being: it would have to be *in itself*'.[8] Genet wants to 'petrify himself'. And, if it is true, as Sartre says it is, that Genet is searching for the point which Breton defined, in one of the best approaches to sovereignty, as the point 'where life and death, the real and the imaginary, past and future, the communicable and the incommunicable, the high and the low are no longer perceived in contradiction to one another . . . ', there must be a fundamental alteration. Indeed, Sartre adds: 'Breton hopes, if not to "see" the surreal, at least to merge with it in an indistinction where vision and being are all one . . . ' But 'Genet's sanctity' is 'Breton's surreal understood as the inaccessible and substantial reverse of existence . . . '[9] It is sovereignty *confiscated*, the dead sovereignty of him whose solitary desire for sovereignty is the betrayal of sovereignty.

Notes

1 *Saint Genet*. The italics are Sartre's.
2 The greatest difficulty encountered by Sartre in his philosophical studies is connected with his inability to pass from a moral of liberty to a common morality which binds individuals to each other in a system of obligations. Only a morality of communication – and loyalty based on communication – goes beyond utilitarian morality. But for Sartre, communication is not a basis; if he sees its possibilities it is through the opacity which beings present to each other. For him, it is the isolated being that is fundamental, not the multiplicity of beings in *communication*. So we await from him a work on morals which was announced after the war. Only the honest *Saint Genet* can give us an idea of what is in store for us. But *Saint Genet*, however rich, is by no means conclusive.
3 Where, we should add, sharing is possible. I must here pass over the deeper aspect of communication which depends on the paradoxical significance of tears. And yet I should observe that tears undoubtedly represent the height of commu-

nicative emotion and communication, but that Genet's coldness is at the opposite pole to this extreme emotion.

4 See *Saint Genet*.

5 Ibid.

6 I have frequently dwelt on the essential theme of law and transgression. The theory of transgression is primarily due to Marcel Mauss whose essays dominate modern sociology. Marcel Mauss, unwilling to formulate his ideas too definitely, has merely expressed them periodically in his lecture courses. But the theory of transgression has been the object of a brilliant study by one of his pupils. *See* Roger Caillois, *L'Homme et le Sacré*, enlarged edition with three appendices on sex, games, and war in their relationship to the sacred, published by Gallimard in 1950. Unfortunately Caillois' work has not yet attained the authority which it deserves, especially abroad. In this book I have shown that the distinction between law and transgression has dominated modern society no less than it dominated primitive society. It will soon appear that, whenever it is based on the interdict which opposes it to animal life, human life, at all times and in every form, is doomed, outside the domain of work, to the transgression which determines the transition from animal to man. (*See* my article in *Critique*, 1956, no. 111/112, August–September, 1956).

7 The term is Genet's and is quoted by Sartre (*Saint Genet*). In my opinion the quest for the 'impossible Nullity' is the form which the quest for sovereignty took in Genet's case.

8 Sartre, op. cit. The italics are Sartre's.

9 Ibid. My italics.

35 George Steiner
From *Language and Silence*

The retreat from the word

The Apostle tells us that in the beginning was the Word. He gives us no assurance as to the end.

It is appropriate that he should have used the Greek language to express the Hellenistic conception of the *Logos*, for it is to the fact of its Greco-Judaic inheritance that Western civilization owes its essentially verbal character. We take this character for granted. It is the root and bark of our experience and we cannot readily transpose our imaginings outside it. We live inside the act of discourse. But we should not assume that a verbal matrix is the

From George Steiner, *Langage and Silence*, Penguin, 1979, pp. 31–3, 51–3, 56.

only one in which the articulations and conduct of the mind are conceivable. There are modes of intellectual and sensuous reality founded not on language, but on other communicative energies such as the icon or the musical note. And there are actions of the spirit rooted in silence. It is difficult to *speak* of these, for how should speech justly convey the shape and vitality of silence? But I can cite examples of what I mean.

In certain Oriental metaphysics, in Buddhism and Taoism, the soul is envisioned as ascending from the gross impediments of the material, through domains of insight that can be rendered by lofty and precise language, towards ever deepening silence. The highest, purest reach of the contemplative act is that which has learned to leave language behind it. The ineffable lies beyond the frontiers of the word. It is only by breaking through the walls of language that visionary observance can enter the world of total and immediate understanding. Where such understanding is attained, the truth need no longer suffer the impurities and fragmentation that speech necessarily entails. It need not conform to the naïve logic and linear conception of time implicit in syntax. In ultimate truth, past, present and future are simultaneously comprised. It is the temporal structure of language that keeps them artificially distinct. That is the crucial point.

The holy man, the initiate, withdraws not only from the temptations of worldly action; he withdraws from speech. His retreat into the mountain cave or monastic cell is the outward gesture of his silence. Even those who are only novices on this arduous road are taught to distrust the veil of language, to break through it to the more real. The Zen *koan* – you know the sound of two hands clapping, what is the sound of one? – is a beginner's exercise in the retreat from the word.

The Western tradition also knows transcendences of language towards silence. The Trappist ideal goes back to abandonments of speech as ancient as those of the Stylites and Desert Fathers. St John of the Cross expresses the austere exaltation of the contemplative soul as it breaks loose from the moorings of common verbal understanding:

> Entréme donde no supe,
> Y quedéme no sabiendo,
> Toda sciencia trascendiendo.

But to the Western point of view, this order of experience inevitably carries a flavour of mysticism. And whatever our lip service (itself a revealing word) to the sanctity of the mystic vocation, the commanding Western attitude is that of Cardinal Newman's quip, that mysticism begins in mist and ends in schism. Very few Western poets – perhaps only Dante – have persuaded the imagination of the authority of transrational experience. We accept, at the lambent close of the *Paradiso*, the blindness of eye and understanding before the totality of vision. But Pascal is nearer the mainstream of classic Western feeling when he says that the silence of cosmic space strikes terror. To the Taoist that selfsame silence conveys tranquillity and the intimation of God.

The primacy of the word, of that which can be spoken and communicated in discourse, was characteristic of the Greek and Judaic genius and carried over into Christianity. The classic and the Christian sense of the world strive to order reality within the governance of language. Literature, philosophy, theology, law, the arts of history, are endeavours to enclose within the bounds of rational discourse the sum of human experience, its recorded past, its present condition and future expectations. The code of Justinian, the *Summa* of Aquinas, the world chronicles and compendia of medieval literature, the *Divina Commedia*, are attempts at total containment. They bear solemn witness to the belief that all truth and realness – with the exception of a small, queer margin at the very top – can be housed inside the walls of language.

This belief is no longer universal. . . .

What is, perhaps, the dominant school in contemporary literature has made a virtue of necessity. The style of Hemingway and of his myriad imitators is a brilliant response to the diminution of linguistic possibility. Sparse, laconic, highly artificial in its conventions of brevity and understatement, that style sought to reduce the ideal of Flaubert – *le mot juste* – to a scale of basic language. One may admire it or not. But, undeniably, it is based on a most narrow conception of the resources of literacy. Moreover, the technical mastery of a Hemingway tends to blur a crucial distinction: simple words can be used to express complex ideas and feelings, as in Tacitus, the Book of Common Prayer, or Swift's *Tale of a Tub*; or they can be used to express states of consciousness that are themselves rudimentary. By retrenching language to a kind of powerful, lyric shorthand, Hemingway narrows the compass of observed and rendered life. He is often charged with his monotonous adherence to hunters, fishermen, bullfighters or alcoholic soldiers. But this constancy is a necessary result of the available medium. How could Hemingway's language convey the inward life of more manifold or articulate characters? Imagine trying to translate the consciousness of Raskolnikov into the vocabulary of 'The Killers'. Which is not to deny the perfection of that grim snapshot. But *Crime and Punishment* gathers into itself a sum of life entirely beyond Hemingway's thin medium.

The thinning out of language has condemned much of recent literature to mediocrity. There are various reasons why *The Death of a Salesman* falls short of the discernible reach of Arthur Miller's talent. But an obvious one is the paucity of its language. The brute snobbish fact is that men who die speaking as does Macbeth are more tragic than those who sputter platitudes in the style of Willy Loman. Miller has learned much from Ibsen; but he has failed to hear behind Ibsen's realistic conventions the constant beat of poetry.

Language seeks vengeance on those who cripple it. A striking example occurs in O'Neill, a dramatist committed, in a sombre and rather moving way, to the practice of bad writing. Interspersed in the sodden morass of *A Long Day's Journey into Night*, there are passages from Swinburne. The lines are flamboyant, romantic verbiage. They are meant to show up the adolescent inadequacies of those who recite them. But, in fact, when the play is performed, the contrary occurs. The energy and glitter of Swinburne's language burn a hole in the surrounding fabric. They elevate the action above its paltry level and instead of showing up the character show up the playwright. Modern authors rarely quote their betters with impunity.

But amid the general retreat or flight from the word in literature, there have been a number of brilliant rearguard actions. I shall cite only a few instances, limiting myself to English.

No doubt the most exuberant counter-attack any modern writer has launched against the diminution of language is that of James Joyce. After Shakespeare and Burton, literature has known no greater gourmand of words. As if aware of the fact that science had torn from language many of its former possessions and outer provinces, Joyce chose to annex a new kingdom below ground. *Ulysses* caught in its bright net the live tangle of subconscious life; *Finnegans Wake* mines the bastions of sleep. Joyce's work, more than any since Milton, recalls to the English ear the wide magnificence of its legacy. It marshals great battalions of words, calling back to the ranks words long asleep or rusted, and recruiting new ones by stress of imaginative need.

Yet when we look back upon the battle so decisively won, we can attribute to it little positive consequence, and scarcely any wider richening. There have been no genuine successors to Joyce in English; perhaps there can be none to a talent so exhaustive of its own potential. What counts more: the treasures which Joyce brought back to language from his wide-ranging forays remain piled glitteringly around his own labours. They have not passed into currency. They have caused none of that general quickening of the spirit of speech which follows on Spenser and Marlowe. I do not know why. Perhaps the action was fought too late; or perhaps the privacies and parts of incoherence in *Finnegans Wake* have proved too obstructive. As it stands, Joyce's performance is a monument rather than a living force.

The poet of the *Pervigilium Veneris* wrote in a darkening time, amid the breakdown of classic literacy. He knew that the Muses can fall silent:

> perdidi musam tacendo, nec me Apollo respicit:
> sic Amyclas, cum tacerent, perdidit silentium.

'To perish by silence': that civilization on which Apollo looks no more shall not long endure.

36 Walter Benjamin
'Theses on the Philosophy of History'

To articulate the past historically does not mean to recognize it 'the way it really was' (Ranke). It means to seize hold of a memory as it flashes up at a moment of danger. Historical materialism wishes to retain that image of the past which unexpectedly appears to man singled out by history at a moment of danger. The danger affects both the content of the tradition and its receivers. The same threat hangs over both: that of becoming a tool of the ruling classes. In every era the attempt must be made anew to wrest tradition away from a conformism that is about to overpower it. The Messiah comes not only as the redeemer, he comes as the subduer of Antichrist. Only that historian will have the gift of fanning the spark of hope in the past who is firmly convinced that *even the dead* will not be safe from the enemy if he wins. And this enemy has not ceased to be victorious.

> Consider the darkness and the great cold
> In this vale which resounds with misery.
> – Brecht, *The Threepenny Opera*

To historians who wish to relive an era, Fustel de Coulanges recommends that they blot out everything they know about the later course of history. There is no better way of characterizing the method with which historical materialism has broken. It is a process of empathy whose origin is the indolence of the heart, *acedia*, which despairs of grasping and holding the genuine historical image as it flares up briefly. Among medieval theologians it was regarded as the root cause of sadness. Flaubert, who was familiar with it, wrote, 'Peu de gens devineront combien il a fallu être triste pour resusciter Carthage.'[1] The nature of this sadness stands out more clearly if one asks with whom the adherents of historicism actually empathize. The answer is inevitable: with the victor. And all rulers are the heirs of those who conquered before them. Hence, empathy with the victor invariably benefits the rulers. Historical materialists know what that means. Whoever has emerged victorious participates to this day in the triumphal procession in which the present rulers step over those who are lying prostrate. According to traditional practice, the spoils are carried along in the procession. They are called cultural treasures, and a historical materialist views them with cautious detachment. For without exception

From S. Bronner and D. Kellner (eds), *Critical Theory and Society: A Reader*, Routledge, pp. 256–9, 262.

the cultural treasures he surveys have an origin which he cannot contemplate without horror. They owe their existence not only to the efforts of the great minds and talents who have created them, but also to the anonymous toil of their contemporaries. There is no document of civilization which is not at the same time a document of barbarism. And just as such a document is not free of barbarism, barbarism taints also the manner in which it was transmitted from one owner to another. A historical materialist therefore dissociates himself from it as far as possible. He regards it as his task to brush history against the grain.

The tradition of the oppressed teaches us that the 'state of emergency' in which we live is not the exception but the rule. We must attain to a conception of history that is in keeping with this insight. Then we shall clearly realize that it is our task to bring about a real state of emergency, and this will improve our position in the struggle against fascism. One reason why fascism has a chance is that in the name of progress its opponents treat it as a historical norm. The current amazement that the things we are experiencing are 'still' possible in the twentieth century is not philosophical. This amazement is not the beginning of knowledge – unless it is the knowledge that the view of history which gives rise to it is untenable.

> Mein Flügel ist zum Schwung bereit,
> ich kehrte gern zurück,
> denn blieb ich auch lebendige Zeit,
> ich hätte wenig Glück.
> – Gerhard Scholem, 'Gruss vom Angelus'[2]

A Klee painting named *Angelus Novus* shows an angel looking as though he is about to move away from something he is fixedly contemplating. His eyes are staring, his mouth is open, his wings are spread. This is how one pictures the angel of history. His face is turned toward the past. Where we perceive a chain of events, he sees one single catastrophe which keeps piling wreckage upon wreckage and hurls it in front of his feet. The angel would like to stay, awaken the dead, and make whole what has been smashed. But a storm is blowing from Paradise; it has got caught in his wings with such violence that the angel can no longer close them. This storm irresistibly propels him into the future to which his back is turned, while the pile of debris before him grows skyward. This storm is what we call progress.

The themes which monastic discipline assigned to friars for meditation were designed to turn them away from the world and its affairs. The thoughts which we are developing here originate from similar considerations. At a moment when the politicians in whom the opponents of fascism had placed their hopes are prostrate and confirm their defeat by betraying their own cause, these observations are intended to disentangle the political worldlings from the snares in which the traitors have entrapped them. Our consideration proceeds from the insight that the politicians' stubborn faith in progress, their confidence in their 'mass basis,' and, finally, their servile integration in an uncontrollable apparatus have been three aspects of the same thing. It seeks to convey an idea of the high price our accustomed thinking will have to pay for a conception of history that avoids any complicity with the thinking to which these politicians continue to adhere.

Historicism contents itself with establishing a causal connection between various moments in history. But no fact that is a cause is for that very reason historical. It became historical posthumously, as it were, through events that may be separated from it by thousands of years. A historian who takes this as his point of departure stops telling the sequence of events like the beads of a rosary. Instead, he grasps the constellation which his own era has formed with a definite earlier one. Thus, he establishes a conception of the present as the 'time of the now' which is shot through with chips of Messianic time.

The soothsayers who found out from time what it had in store certainly did not experience time as either homogeneous or empty. Anyone who keeps this in mind will perhaps get an idea of how past times were experienced in remembrance – namely, in just the same way. We know that the Jews were prohibited from investigating the future. The Torah and the prayers instruct them in remembrance, however. This stripped the future of its magic, to which all those succumb who turn to the soothsayers for enlightenment. This does not imply, however, that for the Jews the future turned into homogeneous, empty time. For every second of time was the strait gate through which the Messiah might enter.

Notes

1 'Few will be able to guess how sad one had to be in order to resuscitate Carthage.'
2 'My wing is ready for flight, / I would like to turn back. / If I stayed timeless time, / I would have little luck.'

37 Edward Bond
'On Violence' (Preface)

Violence is a biological mechanism which evolved before human beings evolved, and which has been inherited by them. It first occurred in animals lower than human beings in the order of biological organisation. When these animals are threatened, and have no alternative, they may violently attack whatever is threatening them. It is a last defence, used in a crisis, and its value for primitive animals is clear: it helps to ensure the continuation of their species. But for human beings the opposite is true. Violence threatens the continuation of our species, at least in a civilised form. How has this happened and what must we do about it?

The idea that human beings are necessarily violent is a political device, the modern equivalent of the doctrine of original sin. For a long time this doctrine helped to enforce acceptance of the existing social order. For reasons the church could not explain everyone was born to eternal pain after death unless the church saved them. It carefully monopolised all the sacraments which were the only means to salvation. To be saved a man had to accept the church's teaching on the way secular society should be organised; if that society ever needed restraining or reforming, the only ways of doing this that the church permitted were admonishment and excommunication. Leaders of church and state often came from the same families; and before a poor man was elevated to any rank in the church he had to accept its teaching on secular society. Those who wouldn't, whether clerical or lay, were handed over to the state to be tortured and burned. This vividly demonstrated to everyone else the eternal hell in which all dissent would be punished. God is a secular mechanism, a device of class-rule.

But because the idea of god is incompatible with modern science, science has been mis-used to formulate the doctrine of necessary human violence. This is a political invention, not a scientific discovery. The man who cries wolf must constantly shout louder, and, in an analogous way, capitalism has had to drag its hell up out of the ground and set it in our midst. If men are necessarily violent they will always endanger one another, so there must be a strong authority that will use violence to control violence. This authority is the ruling class. It maintains its existence by using violence and being able to organise it politically. The rest doesn't necessarily follow, but in practice it always does: as the ruling class best understands the human

From Edward Bond, *Plays One*, Methuen, 1991, pp. 9–15, 17.

condition, its members are the best and most intelligent of human beings, and they are therefore acting only for the common good when they control and monopolise for themselves education, information, art, money, living space, medicine and everything else desirable.

Plato wanted his rulers to knowingly lie. The members of our ruling class are not liars but – worse – fools who believe their own mythology. In ignorance they teach an intellectual corruption, and it is accepted in naïvety. The consequences are heard in bar room chatter, 'We throw babies against the wall because we're animals at heart', and seen in the conservative MP who, some time about 1970, wanted young offenders publicly exhibited in cages.

The ruling mythology has a spurious plausibility. As evidence there are the mountains of bodies from twentieth-century wars, the world-litter of H-bombs, and the increasing aggression of affluent society (which is seen as a very special proof of the incorrigibility of the *need* to be violent). No one could deny that human beings can be violent. But the argument is about why they are violent. Human violence is contingent not necessary, and occurs in situations that can be identified and prevented. These are situations in which people are at such physical and emotional risk that their life is neither natural nor free. I don't want to try to describe these situations in detail here, but as freedom and natural living are so often misunderstood I must point out a few things to make my view clear. Firstly, it is as natural to live in a city as in the country; whether one is wise to live in a particular city or village depends on what sort of city or village it is. Secondly, mutually sharing common social obligations and restraints is not a repression of our natural egotism; on the contrary, at their best these social bonds are not just the condition of human freedom, they are the essence of it. Thirdly, we create our subjective selves through our objective social relations, and our self-consciousness is not primarily the fruit of private introspection but of social interaction. Fourthly, I am not substituting one absurdity for another by claiming that although people are not innately evil they *are* innately good. Human nature is not fixed at birth, it is created through our relation to the culture of our society. It could be said that every child is born an orphan and must be adopted by its society. The only innate part of our nature can be seen as the capacity for this social, cultural adoption; it is our natural biological expectation of society. As human nature is created by society in this way, it is possible for us to bring up people to be, within reasonable limits, good. All that is necessary is a culture which is sufficiently rational. Abolishing violence would not in itself create this society; the truth is that violence can only be abolished as part of the creation of this society. However, I don't want to go further into these points now. I only want to make clear that the cause and solution of the problem of human violence lie not in our instincts but in our social relationships. Violence is not an instinct we must forever repress because it threatens civilised social relationships; we are violent because we have not yet made those relationships civilised.

Fortunately the causes of human violence can be easily summed up. It occurs in situations of injustice. It is caused not only by physical threats, but even more significantly by threats to human dignity. That is why, in spite of all the physical benefits of affluence, violence flourishes under capitalism. There will always be minor human aggressions; even in Utopia people will fall in love with the wrong person, forget proper gratitude, lose their temper; but whenever there is serious and constant violence, that is a sign of the presence of some major social injustice. Violence can't be contained by an equal or even greater force of counter-violence; it can't be sublimated in games; it can't be controlled by a drug in the water supply (because this would also remove the creative tensions necessary to any society); it will only stop when we live in a just society in which all people are equal in all significant respects. Human beings are much more likely to be violent than many other animals, but in a curious way this is a necessary part of their ethical development: no human society can be a lasting or stable home for injustice. Class society must be violent, but it must also create the frustration, stimulation, aggression and – if necessary – physical violence that are the means by which it can change into a classless society. The only alternatives to this – which in the last few years technology has made possible – are the destruction of our species or, perhaps even worse, its dehumanisation.

Violence is getting cheaper nowadays – cheaper, because it is usually punished lightly. (Political violence is sometimes an exception, for obvious reasons.) By keeping it cheap capitalism shows its self-serving wisdom. If it punished it severely it would provoke even greater unrest and violence. This would show that the scapegoat device no longer contains violence (not least because we are no longer a sacramental society) and this is the real reason why Tory governments don't after all put offenders in public cages. But more important, in an effort to free itself from the increasing barbarism that severer punishments would provoke, capitalism would have to look again at the causes of violence. Capitalism can't do this because its political ethos is competitiveness, and it cannot afford to admit that under the pressure of economic struggle this leads not only to commercial aggression between firms but also to commercial aggression by firms against the public. This is seen in the way that commerce often misuses technology and industry so that they exacerbate social problems, instead of solving them and helping to create a humane society. Of course, I don't mean that our class-society should punish criminals more severely; on the contrary, it is a mark of its decadence that it no longer has the moral right, and probably not even the political authority, to deal with violence – with hooliganism, vandalism and crime – any more than it has the intellectual vitality to understand it. It's easy to see that capitalism has made its ethos of violence very readily available on TV, but sometimes it's not noticed that it sells it at very reduced prices in its courts. Capitalism has made violence a cheap consumer commodity.

We have to understand that not only is capitalism destructive in war *and* peace, but that it is *as* destructive in peace as in war. Its peacetime destructiveness is caused not so much by naked force as by its false culture. This false culture is hidden by its interpretation of culture – they come to the same thing – but its destructiveness can be clearly seen in its waste of life, resources and human energy. Worse, it is an intellectual attack on mankind. Culture is the way we live, and when it is nihilistic, cynical or despairing, then there are waste and violence at all the stages of our life and in all our relationships. Nehru said it cost a lot of money to keep Gandhi poor; we can add that it takes a lot of violence to keep a capitalist peace, and that under capitalism war can never lead to peace. Using violence to create socialism out of capitalism would not mean introducing violence into the peaceful politics of a world of law and order; whenever you walk quietly down the orderly street of a capitalist society you are surrounded by the hidden debris of waste and destruction and are already involved in a prolonged act of communal violence. Violence is not a function of human nature but of human societies.

COMMITMENT

38 Theodor Adorno
'Commitment'

Since Sartre's essay *What is Literature?* there has been less theoretical debate about committed and autonomous literature. Nevertheless, the controversy over commitment remains urgent, so far as anything that merely concerns the life of the mind can be today, as opposed to sheer human survival. Sartre was moved to issue his manifesto because he saw – and he was certainly not the first to do so – works of art displayed side by side in a pantheon of optional edification, decaying into cultural commodities. In such coexistence, they desecrate each other. If a work, without its author necessarily intending it, aims at a supreme effect, it cannot really tolerate a neighbour beside it. This salutary intolerance holds not only for individual works, but also for aesthetic genres or attitudes such as those once symbolized in the now half-forgotten controversy over commitment.

There are two 'positions on objectivity' which are constantly at war with one another, even when intellectual life falsely presents them as at peace. A work of art that is committed strips the magic from a work of art that is content to be a fetish, an idle pastime for those who would like to sleep through the deluge that threatens them, in an apoliticism that is in fact deeply political. For the committed, such works are a distraction from the battle of real interests, in which no one is any longer exempt from the conflict between the two great blocs. The possibility of intellectual life itself depends on this conflict to such an extent that only blind illusion can insist on rights that may be shattered tomorrow. For autonomous works of art, however, such considerations, and the conception of art which underlies them, are themselves the spiritual catastrophe of which the committed keep warning. Once the life of the mind renounces the duty and liberty of its own pure objectification, it has abdicated. Thereafter, works of art merely assimilate themselves to the brute existence against which they protest, in forms so ephemeral (the very charge made against autonomous works by committed writers) that from their first day they belong to the seminars in which they inevitably end. The menacing thrust of the antithesis is a reminder of how precarious the position of art is today. Each of the two alternatives negates itself with the other. Committed art, necessarily detached as art from reality, cancels the distance between the two. 'Art

From Theodor Adorno, *Aesthetics and Politics*, foreword by F. Jameson, Verso, 1980, pp. 177–8, 180–3, 188–9, 193–5.

for art's sake' denies by its absolute claims that ineradicable connection with reality which is the polemical *a priori* of the attempt to make art autonomous from the real. Between these two poles the tension in which art has lived in every age till now is dissolved.

In aesthetic theory, 'commitment' should be distinguished from 'tendency'. Committed art in the proper sense is not intended to generate ameliorative measures, legislative acts or practical institutions – like earlier propagandist plays against syphilis, duels, abortion laws or borstals – but to work at the level of fundamental attitudes. For Sartre its task is to awaken the free choice of the agent which makes authentic existence possible at all, as opposed to the neutrality of the spectator. But what gives commitment its aesthetic advantage over tendentiousness also renders the content to which the artist commits himself inherently ambiguous. In Sartre the notion of choice – originally a Kierkegaardian category – is heir to the Christian doctrine 'He who is not with me is against me', but now voided of any concrete theological content. What remains is merely the abstract authority of a choice enjoined, with no regard for the fact that the very possibility of choosing depends on what can be chosen. The archetypal situation always cited by Sartre to demonstrate the irreducibility of freedom merely underlines this. Within a predetermined reality, freedom becomes an empty claim: Herbert Marcuse has exposed the absurdity of the philosophical theorem that it is always possible inwardly either to accept or to reject martyrdom.[1] Yet this is precisely what Sartre's dramatic situations are designed to demonstrate. But his plays are nevertheless bad models of his own existentialism, because they display in their respect for truth the whole administered universe which his philosophy ignores: the lesson we learn from them is one of unfreedom. Sartre's theatre of ideas sabotages the aims of his categories. This is not a specific shortcoming of his plays. It is not the office of art to spotlight alternatives, but to resist by its form alone the course of the world, which permanently puts a pistol to men's heads. In fact, as soon as committed works of art do instigate decisions at their own level, the decisions themselves become interchangeable. Because of this ambiguity, Sartre has with great candour confessed that he expects no real changes in the world from literature – a scepticism which reflects the historical mutations both of society and of the practical function of literature since the days of Voltaire. The principle of commitment thus slides towards the proclivities of the author, in keeping with the extreme subjectivism of Sartre's philosophy, which for all its materialist undertones still echoes German speculative idealism. In his literary theory the work of art becomes an appeal to subjects, because it is itself nothing other than a declaration by a subject of his own choice or failure to choose.

Brecht, in some of his plays, such as the dramatization of Gorky's *The Mother* or *The Measures Taken*, bluntly glorifies the Party. But at times, at

least according to his theoretical writings, he too wanted to educate spec-
tators to a new attitude that would be distanced, thoughtful, experimental,
the reverse of illusory empathy and identification. In tendency to abstraction, his plays after *Saint Joan* trump those of Sartre. The difference is that
Brecht, more consistent than Sartre and a greater artist, made this abstraction into the formal principle of his art, as a didactic poetics that eliminates
the traditional concept of dramatic character altogether. He realized that
the surface of social life, the sphere of consumption, which includes the
psychologically motivated actions of individuals, conceals the essence of
society – which, as the law of exchange, is itself abstract. Brecht rejected
aesthetic individuation as an ideology. He therefore sought to translate the
true hideousness of society into theatrical appearance, by dragging it
straight out of its camouflage. The people on his stage shrink before our
eyes into the agents of social processes and functions, which indirectly and
unknowingly they are in empirical reality. Brecht no longer postulates, like
Sartre, an identity between living individuals and the essence of society, let
alone any absolute sovereignty of the subject. Nevertheless, the process of
aesthetic reduction that he pursues for the sake of political truth, in fact gets
in its way. For this truth involves innumerable mediations, which Brecht
disdains. What is artistically legitimate as alienating infantilism – Brecht's
first plays came from the same milieu as Dada – becomes merely infantile
when it starts to claim theoretical or social validity. Brecht wanted to reveal
in images the inner nature of capitalism. In this sense his aim was indeed
what he disguised it as against Stalinist terror – realistic. He would have
refused to deprive social essence of meaning by taking it as it appeared,
imageless and blind, in a single crippled life. But this burdened him with
the obligation of ensuring that what he intended to make unequivocally
clear was theoretically correct. His art, however, refused to accept this *quid
pro quo*: it both presents itself as didactic, and claims aesthetic dispensation
from responsibility for the accuracy of what it teaches.

I have no wish to soften the saying that to write lyric poetry after Auschwitz is barbaric; it expresses in negative form the impulse which inspires
committed literature. The question asked by a character in Sartre's play
Morts sans Sépulture, 'Is there any meaning in life when men exist who beat
people until the bones break in their bodies?', is also the question whether
any art now has a right to exist; whether intellectual regression is not
inherent in the concept of committed literature because of the regression
of society. But Enzensberger's retort also remains true, that literature must
resist this verdict; in other words, be such that its mere existence after
Auschwitz is not a surrender to cynicism. Its own situation is one of
paradox, not merely the problem of how to react to it. The abundance of
real suffering tolerates no forgetting; Pascal's theological saying, *On ne doit
plus dormir*, must be secularized. Yet this suffering, what Hegel called
consciousness of adversity, also demands the continued existence of art

while it prohibits it; it is now virtually in art alone that suffering can still find its own voice, consolation, without immediately being betrayed by it. The most important artists of the age have realized this. The uncompromising radicalism of their works, the very features defamed as formalism, give them a terrifying power, absent from helpless poems to the victims of our time. But even Schoenberg's *Survivor of Warsaw* remains trapped in the aporia to which, autonomous figuration of heteronomy raised to the intensity of hell, it totally surrenders. There is something embarrassing in Schoenberg's composition – not what arouses anger in Germany, the fact that it prevents people from repressing from memory what they at all costs want to repress – but the way in which, by turning suffering into images, harsh and uncompromising though they are, it wounds the shame we feel in the presence of the victims. For these victims are used to create something, works of art, that are thrown to the consumption of a world which destroyed them. The so-called artistic representation of the sheer physical pain of people beaten to the ground by rifle-butts contains, however remotely, the power to elicit enjoyment out of it. The moral of this art, not to forget for a single instant, slithers into the abyss of its opposite. The aesthetic principle of stylization, and even the solemn prayer of the chorus, make an unthinkable fate appear to have had some meaning; it is transfigured, something of its horror is removed. This alone does an injustice to the victims; yet no art which tried to evade them could confront the claims of justice. Even the sound of despair pays its tribute to a hideous affirmation. Works of less than the highest rank are also willingly absorbed as contributions to clearing up the past. When genocide becomes part of the cultural heritage in the themes of committed literature, it becomes easier to continue to play along with the culture which gave birth to murder.

. . . This is why today autonomous rather than committed art should be encouraged in Germany. Committed works all too readily credit themselves with every noble value, and then manipulate them at their ease. Under fascism too, no atrocity was perpetrated without a moral veneer. Those who trumpet their ethics and humanity in Germany today are merely waiting for a chance to persecute those whom their rules condemn, and to exercise the same inhumanity in practice of which they accuse modern art in theory. In Germany, commitment often means bleating what everyone is already saying or at least secretly wants to hear. The notion of a 'message' in art, even when politically radical, already contains an accommodation to the world: the stance of the lecturer conceals a clandestine entente with the listeners, who could only be rescued from deception by refusing it.

The type of literature that, in accordance with the tenets of commitment but also with the demands of philistine moralism, exists for man, betrays him by traducing that which could help him, if only it did not strike a pose of helping him. But any literature which therefore concludes that it can be a law unto itself, and exist only for itself, degenerates into ideology no less.

Art, which even in its opposition to society remains a part of it, must close its eyes and ears against it: it cannot escape the shadow of irrationality. But when it appeals to this unreason, making it a *raison d'être*, it converts its own malediction into a theodicy. Even in the most sublimated work of art there is a hidden 'it should be otherwise'. When a work is merely itself and no other thing, as in a pure pseudo-scientific construction, it becomes bad art – literally pre-artistic. The moment of true volition, however, is mediated through nothing other than the form of the work itself, whose crystallization becomes an analogy of that other condition which should be. As eminently constructed and produced objects, works of art, including literary ones, point to a practice from which they abstain: the creation of a just life. This mediation is not a compromise between commitment and autonomy, nor a sort of mixture of advanced formal elements with an intellectual content inspired by genuinely or supposedly progressive politics. The content of works of art is never the amount of intellect pumped into them: if anything, it is the opposite.

Nevertheless, an emphasis on autonomous works is itself socio-political in nature. The feigning of a true politics here and now, the freezing of historical relations which nowhere seem ready to melt, oblige the mind to go where it need not degrade itself. Today every phenomenon of culture, even if a model of integrity, is liable to be suffocated in the cultivation of kitsch. Yet paradoxically in the same epoch it is to works of art that has fallen the burden of wordlessly asserting what is barred to politics. Sartre himself has expressed this truth in a passage which does credit to his honesty.[2] This is not a time for political art, but politics has migrated into autonomous art, and nowhere more so than where it seems to be politically dead. An example is Kafka's allegory of toy guns, in which an idea of non-violence is fused with a dawning awareness of the approaching paralysis of politics. Paul Klee too has a place in any debate about committed and autonomous art; for his work, *écriture par excellence*, had its roots in literature and would not have been what it was without them – or if it had not consumed them. During the First World War or shortly after, Klee drew cartoons of Kaiser Wilhelm as an inhuman iron-eater. Later, in 1920, these became – the development can be shown quite clearly – the *Angelus Novus*, the angel of the machine, who, though he no longer bears any emblem of caricature or commitment, flies far beyond both. The machine angel's enigmatic eyes force the onlooker to try to decide whether he is announcing the culmination of disaster or salvation hidden within it. But, as Walter Benjamin, who owned the drawing, said, he is the angel who does not give, but takes.

Translated by Francis McDonagh

Notes

1 Reference to Marcuse's essay 'Sartre's Existentialism', included in *Studies in Critical Philosophy*, NLB, London, 1972, pp. 157–90.
2 See Jean-Paul Sartre, *L'Existentialisme est un Humanisme*, Paris, 1946, p. 105.

The voices came and were silenced; came again and were partly silenced; came again and . . .

In the years that have passed since I wrote *Modern Tragedy* there has been more than enough evidence of the centrality of its themes. At the point where I ended, with the children of the struggle facing its men turned to stone, an extraordinary history was about to begin. There was to be the liberation and repression of the Prague Spring. There were to be new voices, some desperate, some hysterical, some lucidly challenging, within the nominally post-revolutionary regimes. But the history was to be more than this. The children of an indifferent affluence were to become, for a decade, the children of struggle, above all in resistance to the violent assault on Vietnam. In 1965, at the beginning of those years, I argued that 'Korea, Suez, the Congo, Cuba, Vietnam, are names of our struggle'. That perspective was verified, and it came to include new names: Czecho-slovakia, Chile, Zimbabwe, Iran, Kampuchea. The struggle to make such connections, as a way of resolving rather than confirming a general dis-order, was remarkably widened and deepened. But there can also be no doubt that this extending and complex revolution, and the extended and very bitter resistance to it, have still to be seen in a tragic perspective. It is not only the weight of the continuing suffering. It is also the intricacy of the relations between action and consequence.

These are matters of contemporary history, to be specifically as well as generally addressed. What I here feel most need to add is a note on one particular cultural consequence. My central argument, it will be remem-bered, was on the deep relations between the actual forms of our history and the tragic forms within which these are perceived, articulated and reshaped. What I have now to note is a strengthening of one of these forms, which in cultures like my own has become temporarily dominant and indeed, at times, overwhelming.

In its most general sense this can be expressed, simply, as a widespread loss of the future. It is remarkable how quickly this mood has developed. It can be observed most evidently in the very centres of orthodox opinion. In the early nineteen sixties, when I was writing *Modern Tragedy*, there were many voices of protest and warning, and some of despair, but the prevail-ing official mood was one of calmly and happily extending prospects: a

From P. Pinkney (ed.), *The Politics of Modernism*, Verso, 1989, pp. 95–7, 102–5.

managed affluence; managed consensus; managed and profitable transitions from colonialism; even managed violence, the 'balance of terror'. Some scraps of this repertory survive here and there, as electoral gestures. But the dominant messages from the centres are now again of danger and conflict, with accompanying calculations of temporary advantage or containment but also with deeper rhythms of shock and loss. Managed affluence has slid into an anxiously managed but perhaps unmanageable depression. Some political consensus has held but the social consensus underlying it has been visibly breaking down, and especially at the level of everyday life. Managed transitions from colonialism have been profitably achieved but are increasingly and fiercely being fought in a hundred fields. The balance of terror is still there, and is yet more terrifying, but its limited and enclosed stabilities are increasingly threatened by the surges of wider actions. It is then not surprising that the dominant messages are of danger and conflict, and that the dominant forms are of shock and loss.

Yet these rhythms are familiar in history. They can be traced, with some accuracy, to a dying social order and a dying class. The particular forms of that kind of tragedy, their kind of tragedy, are now everywhere around us. They are outnumbered, it is true, by alternative responses within the same structure of feeling. There is a seemingly endless flow of colourful retrospect, simple idealizations of a happy and privileged past, most of which are not even nostalgic – an attitude which predicates a present – but merely temporary alternatives to the pain of any kind of connection. There is also a flow, touching some real nerves, of a new and dangerous form of legitimated violence by the forces of order: the rationally penetrating detective and the exposed and unorthodox private eye have in the last ten years been largely replaced, in the dominant centres of mass dramatic production, by the hard police officer, indistinguishable physically and ethically from those he is hunting and punishing, but with the formal advantage that he is taken to be on the side of the law, of things as they are or should be. This connects explicitly with the harder political gestures, in this place and that becoming more than gestures, of a new and deliberate constitutional authoritarianism. These flows continue compulsively, but beyond their wistfulness or their stylish recklessness, disturbing even those to whom they are necessary, there is a graver, more authentic sound: the loss of hope; the slowly settling loss of any acceptable future.

When a social order is dying, it grieves for itself, but at that very time it might be expected that all those who have suffered under it can at last release quite opposite feelings: of relief, at least; or of confident reconstruction; or of rejoicing. And indeed we have heard all those voices, at a certain distance, and are glad to have heard them. But at the slow turning point of a culture like my own, in the very cultures that are the rich expressions of this lived and now dying order, our feelings are necessarily more intricate and more involved. These feelings are coming through in overlapping phases.

This is the structural reality of the very active, very diverse but curiously decentred culture of our period. The phases then need description.

But is not the end of hope the very root of tragedy? This book was written, against specific ideological pressures in Cambridge, and against the wider pressures of a dominant period of a culture, to break down that rhetorical question to the historical and continuing diversity of tragic theory and practice. That sense of diversity, of authentic tragic variations, is still my main emphasis, as the pressures towards simplification and reduction have continued to work through. But there is now this difference: that there is what seems to me a much wider gap between the realized and demonstrated historical and cultural diversity and the now apparently blank page of the future. The very forms of our struggle for a future, under conditions only partly and at times quite indistinctly of our own making, have entered, as I argued and as subsequent history has confirmed, a tragic dimension. But for much longer than now seems reasonable or even possible, we have endured disorder, and entered the struggle against disorder, with very simple convictions of the kind of future order towards which this struggle was directed. This trap has now been sprung.

Not, of course, for the first time. There were specifically tragic historical moments, of this general kind, in the late nineteen twenties, in the late nineteen thirties, and in the early and middle nineteen fifties. A foreseen future was falsified, and the consequence lent tragic depth to what were already the pains of struggle. The overwhelming historical example was of course what happened to the Russian Revolution. I see now, rereading *Modern Tragedy*, how much of that specific experience was still shaping my ideas, and not only explicitly. It is an experience that still reverberates, in an ageing generation and in other generations, as its details are relentlessly documented. To try to evade that experience remains unforgivable. But I have felt in myself, and noticed very clearly in others, a kind of fixing of vision on that intense and terrible experience which induces – and by many is intended to induce – a very deep stasis. Its sheer magnitude and importance can come to cancel the dynamics of what is now, after all, a very long and extended history. There are then moments, readily recognizable to an analyst of dramatic forms, when the real events of the Stalinist terror come to function as a dumb show, to be ritually and statically displayed before each new act and scene. It is certainly impossible to respect those who will not look, or who say merely that they have seen it before, just as it is impossible not to despise those who attempt to cover that tragic history with mere apologetics. But I find it also increasingly difficult to respect all those who gaze so fixedly on this scene that they fail to notice, in any adequate way, the turbulent actions that have begun and are continuing elsewhere. By the very fact of isolating that terrible moment they begin the conversion of an action into a dumb show. And this process is quite radically connected with one deep form of the tragedy of non-communication.

It is not only that caught in struggles elsewhere, demanding active attention and engagement, people can be ritually terrified by the unceasing production of the dumb show. It is that while that action, even in its most vivid and speaking forms, preoccupies our ideas and our feelings, there is not enough left in us to live where we are, except in the reduced forms of stasis and incommunicability. Certainly the experience of Stalinism has radically reduced the confidence of many of those who are most actively confronting the destructive and dying order of imperialism and capitalism. But it seems to be false to believe that the observable loss of hope, the felt loss of a future in our own time, can be merely rendered back to those other events. In some morbid cases this may indeed be so. But in many cases it has become an evasion, of a kind common in tragic actions, of our own real situations and relations. Many vigorous and admirable people, in new kinds of dramatic production, are now attempting to counter the stasis with active discovery and rediscovery of alternative real pasts. There have been significant and understandable new connections with periods of our own popular struggles, and especially with some of the most heroic and invigorating periods. But this also, while incomparably better than the forms of reduction and stasis, can sometimes be seen as one of the more active forms of the loss of a future. For there is a sense in which the reproduction of struggle is not primarily, whatever may be claimed, a production of struggle. The few real cases of forms of dramatic *connection* of past and present and future struggles are not only exceptionally valuable in themselves; they allow us to see the difference between this and mere reproduction.

Tragedy can inhere in so many shapes of the historical process: in the failed revolution; in the deep divisions and contradictions of a time of shock and loss; in the deadlock or stalemate of a blocked and apparently static period. But it is in the overlap of the last two of these areas, in cultures like my own, that we now find ourselves. The forms of deadlock and much more commonly of stalemate are now being intensively practised, in deepening modes of reduction and stasis (ironically, sometimes as proud alternatives to realism, which they damagingly are; or, more plausibly, to Naturalism, which while it was usually static, though hardly ever as fundamentally static as some of these new forms, was never, in the central sense, reduced, but at its best was always extending, exploring and inquiring). The forms of division and contradiction are also now extensively practised, but in majority in ways that confirm and stabilize, wryly specify or rhetorically universalize, the very forms of division and contradiction to which they are addressed.

It is here that the loss of a future is most keenly felt. It has been argued that it is time now to move from a tragic to a utopian mode, and there is some strength in this; it is a classical form of invigoration and hopeful protest; it is also, at any time, a necessary mode of one area of social thought. But it is not, when we look into it, a question of this or that prescription. The fact is that neither the frankly utopian form, nor even the more qualified outlines of practicable futures, which are now so urgently needed, can begin to flow until we have faced, at the necessary depth, the divisions and contradictions which now inhibit them.

This can be done, of course, in other than tragic modes: by theoretical analysis of the most general kind, and by many kinds of specific analysis and action. Without these it is difficult to believe that we could ever gather the materials to find our ways beyond the present and paralysing sense of loss. It is easy to gather a kind of energy from the rapid disintegration of an old, destructive and frustrating order. But these negative energies can be quickly checked by a sobering second stage, in which what we want to become, rather than what we do not now want to be, remains a so largely unanswered question. To the significant degree that our reasons for not answering or trying to answer this question are connected with the now painful divisions and contradictions – as painful to try to shift as to experience – it seems inevitable that a tragic stress must still be made, but in that form which follows the whole action and which is thus again profoundly dynamic.

This is of course much easier to project than to do, but it is in fact far from easy, under current pressures and limits, even to project it. Yet one immediately available way of creating some conditions for its projection, and perhaps for its performance, is now, as when I was first writing, to push past the fixed forms in the only way that is possible, by trying to understand their intricate and diverse formations, and then to see through and beyond them, the elements of new dynamic formations.

MYTH, TRADITION AND INNOVATION

40   T.S. Eliot
'Tradition and the Individual Talent'

In English writing we seldom speak of tradition, though we occasionally apply its name in deploring its absence. We cannot refer to 'the tradition' or to 'a tradition'; at most, we employ the adjective in saying that the poetry of So-and-so is 'traditional' or even 'too traditional.' Seldom, perhaps, does the word appear except in a phrase of censure. If otherwise, it is vaguely approbative, with the implication, as to the work approved, of some pleasing archæological reconstruction. You can hardly make the word agreeable to English ears without this comfortable reference to the reassuring science of archæology.

Certainly the word is not likely to appear in our appreciations of living or dead writers. Every nation, every race, has not only its own creative, but its own critical turn of mind; and is even more oblivious of the shortcomings and limitations of its critical habits than of those of its creative genius. We know, or think we know, from the enormous mass of critical writing that has appeared in the French language the critical method or habit of the French; we only conclude (we are such unconscious people) that the French are 'more critical' than we, and sometimes even plume ourselves a little with the fact, as if the French were the less spontaneous. Perhaps they are; but we might remind ourselves that criticism is as inevitable as breathing, and that we should be none the worse for articulating what passes in our minds when we read a book and feel an emotion about it, for criticizing our own minds in their work of criticism. One of the facts that might come to light in this process is our tendency to insist, when we praise a poet, upon those aspects of his work in which he least resembles anyone else. In these aspects or parts of his work we pretend to find what is individual, what is the peculiar essence of the man. We dwell with satisfaction upon the poet's difference from his predecessors, especially his immediate predecessors; we endeavour to find something that can be isolated in order to be enjoyed. Whereas if we approach a poet without this prejudice we shall often find that not only the best, but the most individual parts of his work may be those in which the dead poets, his ancestors, assert their immortality most vigorously. And I do not mean the impressionable period of adolescence, but the period of full maturity.

From T.S. Eliot, *The Sacred Wood*, Methuen, 1960, pp. 47–53.

Yet if the only form of tradition, of handing down, consisted in following the ways of the immediate generation before us in a blind or timid adherence to its successes, 'tradition' should positively be discouraged. We have seen many such simple currents soon lost in the sand; and novelty is better than repetition. Tradition is a matter of much wider significance. It cannot be inherited, and if you want it you must obtain it by great labour. It involves, in the first place, the historical sense, which we may call nearly indispensable to anyone who would continue to be a poet beyond his twenty-fifth year; and the historical sense involves a perception, not only of the pastness of the past, but of its presence; the historical sense compels a man to write not merely with his own generation in his bones, but with a feeling that the whole of the literature of Europe from Homer and within it the whole of the literature of his own country has a simultaneous existence and composes a simultaneous order. This historical sense, which is a sense of the timeless as well as of the temporal and of the timeless and of the temporal together, is what makes a writer traditional. And it is at the same time what makes a writer most acutely conscious of his place in time, of his contemporaneity.

No poet, no artist of any art, has his complete meaning alone. His significance, his appreciation is the appreciation of his relation to the dead poets and artists. You cannot value him alone; you must set him, for contrast and comparison, among the dead. I mean this as a principle of æsthetic, not merely historical, criticism. The necessity that he shall conform, that he shall cohere, is not one-sided; what happens when a new work of art is created is something that happens simultaneously to all the works of art which preceded it. The existing monuments form an ideal order among themselves, which is modified by the introduction of the new (the really new) work of art among them. The existing order is complete before the new work arrives; for order to persist after the supervention of novelty, the *whole* existing order must be, if ever so slightly, altered; and so the relations, proportions, values of each work of art toward the whole are readjusted; and this is conformity between the old and the new. Whoever has approved this idea of order, of the form of European, of English literature, will not find it preposterous that the past should be altered by the present as much as the present is directed by the past. And the poet who is aware of this will be aware of great difficulties and responsibilities.

In a peculiar sense he will be aware also that he must inevitably be judged by the standards of the past. I say judged, not amputated, by them; not judged to be as good as, or worse or better than, the dead; and certainly not judged by the canons of dead critics. It is a judgment, a comparison, in which two things are measured by each other. To conform merely would be for the new work not really to conform at all; it would not be new, and would therefore not be a work of art. And we do not quite say that the new is more valuable because it fits in; but its fitting in is a test of its value – a test, it is true, which can only be slowly and cautiously applied, for we are none of us infallible judges of conformity. We say: it appears to conform, and is perhaps individual, or it appears individual, and may conform; but we are hardly likely to find that it is one and not the other.

To proceed to a more intelligible exposition of the relation of the poet to the past: he can neither take the past as a lump, an indiscriminate bolus, nor can he form himself wholly on one or two private admirations, nor can he form himself wholly upon one preferred period. The first course is inadmissible, the second is an important experience of youth, and the third is a pleasant and highly desirable supplement. The poet must be very conscious of the main current, which does not at all flow invariably through the most distinguished reputations. He must be quite aware of the obvious fact that art never improves, but that the material of art is never quite the same. He must be aware that the mind of Europe – the mind of his own country – a mind which he learns in time to be much more important than his own private mind – is a mind which changes, and that this change is a development which abandons nothing *en route*, which does not superannuate either Shakespeare, or Homer, or the rock drawing of the Magdalenian draughtsmen. That this development, refinement perhaps, complication certainly, is not, from the point of view of the artist, any improvement. Perhaps not even an improvement from the point of view of the psychologist or not to the extent which we imagine; perhaps only in the end based upon a complication in economics and machinery. But the difference between the present and the past is that the conscious present is an awareness of the past in a way and to an extent which the past's awareness of itself cannot show.

Some one said: 'The dead writers are remote from us because we *know* so much more than they did.' Precisely, and they are that which we know.

I am alive to a usual objection to what is clearly part of my programme for the *métier* of poetry. The objection is that the doctrine requires a ridiculous amount of erudition (pedantry), a claim which can be rejected by appeal to the lives of poets in any pantheon. It will even be affirmed that much learning deadens or perverts poetic sensibility. While, however, we persist in believing that a poet ought to know as much as will not encroach upon his necessary receptivity and necessary laziness, it is not desirable to confine knowledge to whatever can be put into a useful shape for examinations, drawing-rooms, or the still more pretentious modes of publicity. Some can absorb knowledge, the more tardy must sweat for it. Shakespeare acquired more essential history from Plutarch than most men could from the whole British Museum. What is to be insisted upon is that the poet must develop or procure the consciousness of the past and that he should continue to develop this consciousness throughout his career.

What happens is a continual surrender of himself as he is at the moment to something which is more valuable. The progress of an artist is a continual self-sacrifice, a continual extinction of personality.

There remains to define this process of depersonalization and its relation to the sense of tradition. It is in this depersonalization that art may be said to approach the condition of science. I shall, therefore, invite you to consider, as a suggestive analogy, the action which takes place when a bit of finely filiated platinum is introduced into a chamber containing oxygen and sulphur dioxide.

---

41 Samuel Beckett
'Dante, Bruno, Vico, Joyce'

The danger is in the neatness of identifications. The conception of Philosophy and Philology as a pair of nigger minstrels out of the Teatro dei Piccoli is soothing, like the contemplation of a carefully folded ham-sandwich. Giambattista Vico himself could not resist the attractiveness of such coincidence of gesture. He insisted on complete identification between the philosophical abstraction and the empirical illustration, thereby annulling the absolutism of each conception – hoisting the real unjustifiably clear of its dimensional limits, temporalizing that which is extratemporal. And now here am I, with my handful of abstractions, among which notably: a mountain, the coincidence of contraries, the inevitability of cyclic evolution, a system of Poetics, and the prospect of self-extension in the world of Mr. Joyce's *Work in Progress*. There is the temptation to treat every concept like 'a bass dropt neck fust in till a bung crate', and make a really tidy job of it. Unfortunately such an exactitude of application would imply distortion in one of two directions. Must we wring the neck of a certain system in order to stuff it into a contemporary pigeon-hole, or modify the dimensions of that pigeon-hole for the satisfaction of the analogymongers? Literary criticism is not book-keeping.

His [Vico's] exposition of the ineluctable circular progression of Society was completely new, although the germ of it was contained in Giordano Bruno's treatment of identified contraries. But it is in Book 2, described by himself as '*tutto il corpo . . . la chiave maestra . . . dell'opera*', that appears the unqualified originality of his mind; here he evolved a theory of the origins of poetry and language, the significance of myth, and the nature of barbaric civilization that must have appeared nothing less than an impertinent

From Samuel Beckett, *Our Exagmination Round His Factification for Incamination of Work in Progress*, Faber, 1972, pp. 3–14.

outrage against tradition. These two aspects of Vico have their reverbera-
tions, their reapplications – without, however, receiving the faintest explicit
illustration – in *Work in Progress*.

It is first necessary to condense the thesis of Vico, the scientific historian.
In the beginning was the thunder: the thunder set free Religion, in its most
objective and unphilosophical form – idolatrous animism: Religion produced Society, and the first social men were the cave-dwellers, taking
refuge from a passionate Nature: this primitive family life receives its first
impulse towards development from the arrival of terrified vagabonds:
admitted, they are the first slaves: growing stronger, they exact agrarian
concessions, and a despotism has evolved into a primitive feudalism: the
cave becomes a city, and the feudal system a democracy: then an anarchy:
this is corrected by a return to monarchy: the last stage is a tendency
towards interdestruction: the nations are dispersed, and the Phoenix of
Society arises out of their ashes. To this six-termed social progression
corresponds a six-termed progression of human motives: necessity, utility,
convenience, pleasure, luxury, abuse of luxury: and their incarnate manifestations: Polyphemus, Achilles, Caesar and Alexander, Tiberius, Caligula
and Nero. At this point Vico applies Bruno – though he takes very good
care not to say so – and proceeds from rather arbitrary data to philosophical abstraction. There is no difference, says Bruno, between the smallest
possible chord and the smallest possible arc, no difference between the
infinite circle and the straight line. The maxima and minima of particular
contraries are one and indifferent. Minimal heat equals minimal cold.
Consequently transmutations are circular. The principle (minimum) of
one contrary takes its movement from the principle (maximum) of another.
Therefore not only do the minima coincide with the minima, the maxima
with the maxima, but the minima with the maxima in the succession of
transmutations. Maximal speed is a state of rest. The maximum of corruption and the minimum of generation are identical: in principle, corruption
is generation. And all things are ultimately identified with God, the universal monad, Monad of monads. From these considerations Vico evolved a
Science and Philosophy of History. . . . It follows that History is neither to
be considered as a formless structure, due exclusively to the achievements
of individual agents, nor as possessing reality apart from and independent
of them, accomplished behind their backs in spite of them, the work of
some superior force, variously known as Fate, Chance, Fortune, God. Both
these views, the materialistic and the transcendental, Vico rejects in favour
of the rational. Individuality is the concretion of universality, and every
individual action is at the same time superindividual. The individual and
the universal cannot be considered as distinct from each other. History,
then, is not the result of Fate or Chance – in both cases the individual would
be separated from his product – but the result of a Necessity that is not
Fate, of a Liberty that is not Chance (compare Dante's 'yoke of liberty').
This force he called Divine Providence, with his tongue, one feels, very

much in his cheek. And it is to this Providence that we must trace the three institutions common to every society: Church, Marriage, Burial. This is not Bossuet's Providence, transcendental and miraculous, but immanent and the stuff itself of human life, working by natural means. Humanity is its work in itself. God acts on her, but by means of her. Humanity is divine, but no man is divine. This social and historical classification is clearly adapted by Mr. Joyce as a structural convenience – or inconvenience. His position is in no way a philosophical one. It is the detached attitude of Stephen Dedalus in *Portrait of the Artist . . .* who describes Epictetus to the Master of Studies as 'an old gentleman who said that the soul is very like a bucketful of water'. The lamp is more important than the lamp-lighter. By structural I do not only mean a bold outward division, a bare skeleton for the housing of material. I mean the endless substantial variations on these three beats, and interior intertwining of these three themes into a decoration of arabesques – decoration and more than decoration. Part 1 is a mass of past shadow, corresponding therefore to Vico's first human institution, Religion, or to his Theocratic age, or simply to an abstraction – Birth. Part 2 is the lovegame of the children, corresponding to the second institution, Marriage, or to the Heroic age, or to an abstraction – Maturity. Part 3 is passed in sleep, corresponding to the third institution, Burial, or to the Human age, or to an abstraction – Corruption. Part 4 is the day beginning again, and corresponds to Vico's Providence, or to the transition from the Human to the Theocratic, or to an abstraction – Generation. Mr. Joyce does not take birth for granted, as Vico seems to have done. So much for the dry bones. The consciousness that there is a great deal of the unborn infant in the lifeless octogenarian, and a great deal of both in the man at the apogee of his life's curve, removes all the stiff interexclusiveness that is often the danger in neat construction. Corruption is not excluded from Part 1 nor maturity from Part 3. . . .

Vico rejected the three popular interpretations of the poetic spirit, which considered poetry as either an ingenious popular expression of philosophical conceptions, or an amusing social diversion, or an exact science within the reach of everyone in possession of the recipe. Poetry, he says, was born of curiosity, daughter of ignorance. The first men had to create matter by the force of their imagination, and 'poet' means 'creator'. Poetry was the first operation of the human mind, and without it thought could not exist. Barbarians, incapable of analysis and abstraction, must use their fantasy to explain what their reason cannot comprehend. Before articulation comes song; before abstract terms, metaphors. The figurative character of the oldest poetry must be regarded, not as sophisticated confectionery, but as evidence of a poverty-stricken vocabulary and of a disability to achieve abstraction. Poetry is essentially the antithesis of Metaphysics: Metaphysics purge the mind of the senses and cultivate the disembodiment of the spiritual; Poetry is all passion and feeling and animates the inanimate;

Metaphysics are most perfect when most concerned with universals;
Poetry, when most concerned with particulars. Poets are the sense, philosophers the intelligence of humanity. Considering the Scholastics' axiom:
'niente è nell'intelleto che prima non sia nel senso', it follows that poetry is a
prime condition of philosophy and civilization. The primitive animistic
movement was a manifestation of the *'forma poetica dello spirito'*.

His treatment of the origin of language proceeds along similar lines. Here
again he rejected the materialistic and transcendental views: the one declaring that language was nothing but a polite and conventional symbolism;
the other, in desperation, describing it as a gift from the Gods. As before,
Vico is the rationalist, aware of the natural and inevitable growth of language. In its first dumb form, language was gesture. If a man wanted to say
'sea', he pointed to the sea. With the spread of animism this gesture was
replaced by the word: 'Neptune'. He directs our attention to the fact that
every need of life, natural, moral and economic, has its verbal expression in
one or other of the 30 000 Greek divinities. This is Homer's 'language of the
Gods'. Its evolution through poetry to a highly civilized vehicle, rich in
abstract and technical terms, was as little fortuitous as the evolution of
society itself. Words have their progressions as well as social phases. . . .

. . . Thus Vico asserts the spontaneity of language and denies the dualism
of poetry and language. Similarly, poetry is the foundation of writing.
When language consisted of gesture, the spoken and the written were
identical. Hieroglyphics, or sacred language, as he calls it, were not the
invention of philosophers for the mysterious expression of profound
thought, but the common necessity of primitive peoples. Convenience
only begins to assert itself at a far more advanced stage of civilization, in
the form of alphabetism. Here Vico, implicitly at least, distinguishes
between writing and direct expression. In such direct expression, form
and content are inseparable. Examples are the medals of the Middle
Ages, which bore no inscription and were a mute testimony to the feeble-
ness of conventional alphabetic writing: and the flags of our own day. As
with Poetry and Language, so with Myth. Myth, according to Vico, is
neither an allegorical expression of general philosophical axioms (Conti,
Bacon), nor a derivative from particular peoples, as for instance the
Hebrews or Egyptians, nor yet the work of isolated poets, but an historical
statement of fact, of actual contemporary phenomena, actual in the sense
that they were created out of necessity by primitive minds, and firmly
believed. Allegory implies a threefold intellectual operation: the construction of a message of general significance, the preparation of a fabulous
form, and an exercise of considerable technical difficulty in uniting the two,
an operation totally beyond the reach of the primitive mind. Moreover, if
we consider the myth as being essentially allegorical, we are not obliged to
accept the form in which it is cast as a statement of fact. But we know that
the actual creators of these myths gave full credence to their face-value.

Jove was no symbol: he was terribly real. It was precisely their superficial metaphorical character that made them intelligible to people incapable of receiving anything more abstract than the plain record of objectivity.

Such is a painful exposition of Vico's dynamic treatment of Language, Poetry and Myth. He may still appear as a mystic to some: if so, a mystic that rejects the transcendental in every shape and form as a factor in human development, and whose Providence is not divine enough to do without the cooperation of Humanity.

On turning to the *Work in Progress* we find that the mirror is not so convex. Here is direct expression – pages and pages of it. And if you don't understand it, Ladies and Gentlemen, it is because you are too decadent to receive it. You are not satisfied unless form is so strictly divorced from content that you can comprehend the one almost without bothering to read the other. This rapid skimming and absorption of the scant cream of sense is made possible by what I may call a continuous process of copious intellectual salivation. The form that is an arbitrary and independent phenomenon can fulfil no higher function than that of stimulus for a tertiary or quartary conditioned reflex of dribbling comprehension. When Miss Rebecca West clears her decks for a sorrowful deprecation of the Narcisstic element in Mr. Joyce by the purchase of 3 hats, one feels that she might very well wear her bib at all her intellectual banquets, or alternatively, assert a more noteworthy control over her salivary glands than is possible for Monsieur Pavlo's unfortunate dogs. The title of this book is a good example of a form carrying a strict inner determination. It should be proof against the usual volley of cerebral sniggers: and it may suggest to some a dozen incredulous Joshuas prowling around the Queen's Hall, springing their tuning-forks lightly against finger-nails that have not yet been refined out of existence. Mr. Joyce has a word to say to you on the subject: 'Yet to concentrate solely on the literal sense or even the psychological content of any document to the sore neglect of the enveloping facts themselves circumstantiating it is just as harmful; etc.' And another: 'Who in his hearts doubts either that the facts of feminine clothiering are there all the time or that the feminine fiction, stranger than the facts, is there also at the same time, only a little to the rere? Or that one may be separated from the orther? Or that both may be contemplated simultaneously? Or that each may be taken up in turn and considered apart from the other?'

Here form *is* content, content *is* form. You complain that this stuff is not written in English. It is not written at all. It is not to be read – or rather it is not only to be read. It is to be looked at and listened to. His writing is not *about* something; *it is that something itself*. (A fact that has been grasped by an eminent English novelist and historian whose work is in complete opposition to Mr. Joyce's.) When the sense is sleep, the words go to sleep. (See the end of *Anna Livia*.) When the sense is dancing, the words dance. Take the passage at the end of Shaun's pastoral: 'To stirr up love's young fizz I tilt with this bridle's cup champagne, dimming douce from her

peepair of hideseeks tight squeezed on my snowybreasted and while my
pearlies in their sparkling wisdom are nippling her bubblets I swear (and
let you swear) by the bumper round of my poor old snaggletooth's solid-
bowel I ne'er will prove I'm untrue to (theare!) you liking so long as my
hole looks. Down.' The language is drunk. The very words are tilted and
effervescent. How can we qualify this general esthetic vigilance without
which we cannot hope to snare the sense which is for ever rising to the
surface of the form and becoming the form itself?

42   Renato Poggioli
From *The Theory of the Avant-Garde*

The overcoming of the avant-garde

Fortunately, the most recent avant-garde seems definitely to have freed
itself of the dross of that ridiculous and cheapened modernism which
afflicted Western culture just before and after the First World War. Still,
strange to say, the more literal and ingenuous-minded observers believe
they see in exactly this cure for the modernistic malady what they call the
crisis of avant-gardism. Other observers (in this case the less perceptive
ones) go so far as to affirm that the process in which we are assisting is the
liquidation, or at least the overcoming, of the avant-garde. Our task in these
final pages is to criticize that view. It is obvious that the very dialectic of
movements and the effect of fashion cause every avant-garde to be able (or
to pretend to be able) to transcend not only the academy and tradition but
also the avant-garde preceding it. Sometimes a movement fools itself into
believing it attains the peak and end point of all avant-gardism in its own
action, believing that it realizes and represents, all by itself, the ultimate
intention and the ultimate stage of avant-gardism. The Italian Novecento
movement thought as much, if we are to believe a declaration of Bontempelli, its coryphaeus. After paying homage 'to those brilliant avant-gardes
by whom, in an earlier time, we all were nourished,' Bontempelli in fact
treats them as a starting point; the point of arrival, which the Novecento
was held to have reached, would consist in inaugurating and commencing
the 'third period,' when the avant-garde spirit, certain that it had wholly

From Renato Poggioli, *The Theory of the Avant-Garde*, Harvard University Press, 1968, pp. 220–5.

fulfilled its mission, would cease to function as the presupposition of present and future creation.

When we look more closely, we shall see how avant-gardistic is the idea of the advent of a new golden age through the mediation of the avant-garde. If such an idea makes any sense, it would be as the implicit prophecy of a future culture in which avant-gardism would itself be tradition and would become, instead of the exception, the rule. Basically what is now happening is only a transference of this kind. The crisis of avant-gardism is not, so to speak, a crisis of rule, but only of succession: the king is dead, long live the king! More ingenuous observers see denials and betrayals where there is only a simple change of names and personalities, at most a change of emblems and banners. To tell the truth, transference of power cannot be effected without some defections and secessions; no doubt we have been present at a recrudescence of legitimist nostalgias, the attempt to restore dynasties long since dethroned. We certainly cannot deny that in the latest days there have been recalls to the ancient order, or returns to other and more solemn traditions. But if we look carefully, we see that these recalls to order and returns to tradition come more from the desire to consolidate the modern revolution in art than from the desire to organize a coup d'état or restore the *ancien régime*. Even in the case of T.S. Eliot, the most symptomatic and significant case, we have in fact only the theoretical reinvocation of an historical classicism now irrevocably lost. Just so, whereas that reinvocation has exercised a valid function in the critical field, it has not in the least worked for the creation of art or even for the mere practice of art: a judgment that holds also in the particular case of Eliot himself as an artist.

Besides, even Eliot realized that it could not be otherwise, as may be seen from a passage in his essay on Baudelaire where, after condemning the romantic and inferior modernism which disfigures Baudelaire's work, he ends up admitting, 'It must not be forgotten that a poet in a romantic age [or, we might add, in a modern age] cannot be a "classical" poet except in tendency.' The same reservation is found in Eliot's essay on Joyce's *Ulysses*, formulated by means of the following alternative: 'One can be "classical," in a sense, by turning away from nine-tenths of the material which lies at hand and selecting only mummified stuff from a museum – or one can be classical in tendency by doing the best he can with the material at hand.' Obviously the first is the negative solution of the epigones who fool themselves into believing they have attained to antique grandeur by denying their own Zeitgeist; the second is the progressive solution of the artist who accepts (as Ortega puts it) 'the imperative of the work imposed by the period.' But all this means that a modern classicism, albeit theoretically conceivable, is impossible in the face of effective aesthetic achievement – a truth Eliot again confesses in the Joyce article when he observes, 'It is much easier to be a classicist in literary criticism than in creative art.'

This predestined historical dialectic had already been perceived even by

Eliot's teacher, the critic T.E. Hulme, failed prophet of a new poetry of which he himself said: 'Although it will be classical it will be different because it has passed through a romantic period.' Thus, as we have already seen, nothing is more romantic and modern than Valéry's definition of the classical writer as one constantly flanked by a critic: a definition much more suitably applied to three modern masters (rather than to the authentic or ancient classics), Baudelaire, Mallarmé, and Valéry – that is to say, the three classics of avant-garde poetry. This observation reconfirms what we have already said concerning the extraordinary importance assumed by criticism in modern art, where it functions not as an exterior canon but as an integral law. If this is so, it really means that, in modern poetry and art, classicism can operate only as a retrospective utopia, as a logical counterbalance to the futuristic utopia. In any case, the frequency within the recent avant-garde of positions such as Eliot's, along with the rehabilitation and renewal of the very concept of tradition, has certainly contributed to making new movements and manifestoes more rare and scarce. Thus the appearance of a series of new poetics, neoclassical on the surface, has devaluated experiment as an end in itself. But all this indicates fundamentally that an ingenuous and exacerbated modernism is giving way before a more profound and truer sense of our own modernity.

If there has been an overcoming, it consists of the felicitous transition of the avant-garde in the strictest sense to an avant-garde in the broad sense; of a defeat in the letter and a victory in the spirit of avant-gardism. The onetime fever is, bit by bit, yielding to a controlled lucidity. To those who look on with eyes not befogged by partisan ideologies, this transition appears as clear progress; to those who continue to keep faith in a no longer pragmatic rhetoric, for whom the reading of history is not only useless but noxious, it appears as regression or even as a return of the reactionary. The transition now under way lies in the working of a mutation, not a negation. The modern spirit certainly cannot enslave itself to the conservative instinct. For it, not to renew itself means to die. Otherwise what would happen to it is what the critic Piccone Stella claimed had finished off futurism: 'Believing itself always in the avant-garde, in effect it remained in the rear-guard.' The case of futurism, because of the ambition of its programs and the extravagance of its claims, the vanity of its works and its incapacity to transform the letter into the spirit, its own attempt to survive itself, proves – as an extreme example – that each specific avant-garde is destined to last only a morning. When a specific avant-garde which has had its day insists on repeating the promises it cannot now keep, it transforms itself without further ado into its own opposite. Then, as happened with futurism, the movement becomes an academy. But this does not mean that the same fate menaces avant-gardism in general; it does not annul the validity of the much vaster ideals that such groups proclaimed. If the real futurism is dead forever, ideal futurism is still living, precisely because it renews itself in the consciousness of each successive avant-garde. This is because, as Stephen Spender said in an essay significantly entitled *What's Modern in Modern Poetry*, 'we who live in 1948 are not as futurist as the Futurists in 1909 thought we would be.'

In that way Bontempelli was partially right when he affirmed that the periods of avant-gardism (by which we understand those phases that are truly in crises) correspond to 'dead periods, of fragmentary production, decadence and preparation.' Right, if for no other reason than his involuntary emphasis on the practical and psychological, if not the creative and aesthetic, importance of the agonistic movement. The same paradoxical juxtaposition of two antithetical concepts, preparation and decadence, indicates that the historical dialectic of avant-garde crisis is resolved in a synthesis of the notions of decay and growth. The cultural phase of the present, what Bontempelli calls the third period, can then be defined, using other images from pathology in a neutral way, as the period when the avant-garde mentality is moving from the epidemic stage into the endemic and chronic. That overcoming of the avant-garde which can appear a real thing in an episodic and anecdotal perspective no longer appears so when contemplated in less superficial or relativist dimensions. As far as the immediate future goes, it does not seem predictable or possible that a mentality which has now predominated for almost a century in the art of the West, which has become more diffuse and less intense, growing more effective in inverse proportion to the decrease in its radical and aggressive tendencies, can disappear. Thanks precisely to this extension of the concept, we now see works and artists whose greatness and modernity cannot be doubted, and whose modernism may easily be denied, re-entering with full rights into the *idea* of the avant-garde. This is a question of works and artists for whom originality of message counts more than novelty of experiment, who subordinate experiment to experience and, precisely because of this, now seem to have issued from the margins rather than the center of the avant-garde. Not only Eliot and Pound, Joyce and Bely, Stravinsky and Picasso, Klee and Henry Moore, but also Yeats and Saint-John Perse, Pasternak and Blok, Ungaretti and Montale, Guillén and García Lorca, Despiau and Rouault, all these, both groups, prove that the modern genius is essentially avant-gardistic.

But that does not mean (indeed means the very opposite) that the supporters and enthusiasts of avant-garde art are right in believing that it is enough to say 'avant-garde art' to mean art without an adjective. Such a claim is no less ridiculous than their adversaries' claim that it is enough to say 'avant-garde' to deny *a priori* any aesthetic value. To be sure, the second position has less validity than the first; the adversaries of the avant-garde do not realize that the doors upon which they pound are closed forever, even if a few not ignoble talents still seek to open them. On the other side, the left wing of contemporary artistic opinion refuses to recognize that rhetorical and programmatic avant-gardism is now an all-too-open door, and it leads only to a void and a desert. Precisely because it has almost become a main thoroughfare, the avant-garde ought to lead the artist up to that narrow gate which opens onto the paradise of art. Empty exaltation as well as empty protest serve nothing; the only valid opinion, the only one worthy of acceptance, accepts the aesthetic condition which history assigns. It is not the business of the artist or the critic to idolize or reject what Ortega felicitously called the imperative of the work of one's own time. Thus it is in a spirit quite different from that inspiring fanatic supporters and fanatic attackers, by disdaining the bravos of the one and the catcalls of the other, that this essay ends with an affirmation, once more, that the avant-garde is a law of nature for contemporary and modern art.

The validity of such an opinion cannot be confirmed or weakened by quantitative criteria, by the statistical calculation of how many supporters there are and how very, very many adversaries. In any case, the very multitude of adversaries, both relatively and absolutely greater than in any other controversy in the history of culture, underlines the singular novelty of the phenomenon here described.

---

43   C.G. Jung
'Psychology and Literature'

It is not alone the creator of this kind of art who is in touch with the night-side of life, but the seers, prophets, leaders and enlighteners also. However dark this nocturnal world may be, it is not wholly unfamiliar. Man has known of it from time immemorial – here, there, and everywhere; for primitive man today it is an unquestionable part of his picture of the cosmos. It is only we who have repudiated it because of our fear of super-stition and metaphysics, and because we strive to construct a conscious world that is safe and manageable in that natural law holds in it the place of statute law in a commonwealth. Yet, even in our midst, the poet now and then catches sight of the figures that people the night-world – the spirits, demons and gods. He knows that a purposiveness out-reaching human ends is the life-giving secret for man; he has a presentiment of incompre-hensible happenings in the pleroma. In short, he sees something of that psychic world that strikes terror into the savage and the barbarian.

From the very first beginnings of human society onward man's efforts to give his vague intimations a binding form have left their traces. Even in the

From C.G. Jung, *Modern Man in Search of a Soul*, Ark, 1985, pp. 188–92.

Rhodesian cliff-drawings of the Old Stone Age there appears, side by side with the most amazingly life-like representations of animals, an abstract pattern – a double cross contained in a circle. This design has turned up in every cultural region, more or less, and we find it today not only in Christian churches, but in Tibetan monasteries as well. It is the so-called sun-wheel, and as it dates from a time when no one had thought of wheels as a mechanical device, it cannot have had its source in any experience of the external world. It is rather a symbol that stands for a psychic happening; it covers an experience of the inner world, and is no doubt as lifelike a representation as the famous rhinoceros with the tick-birds on its back. There has never been a primitive culture that did not possess a system of secret teaching, and in many cultures this system is highly developed. The men's councils and the totem-clans preserve this teaching about hidden things that lie apart from man's daytime existence – things which, from primeval times, have always constituted his most vital experiences. Knowledge about them is handed on to younger men in the rites of initiation. The mysteries of the Græco-Roman world performed the same office, and the rich mythology of antiquity is a relic of such experiences in the earliest stages of human development.

It is therefore to be expected of the poet that he will resort to mythology in order to give his experience its most fitting expression. It would be a serious mistake to suppose that he works with materials received at second-hand. The primordial experience is the source of his creativeness; it cannot be fathomed, and therefore requires mythological imagery to give it form. In itself it offers no words or images, for it is a vision seen 'as in a glass, darkly'. It is merely a deep presentiment that strives to find expression. It is like a whirlwind that seizes everything within reach and, by carrying it aloft, assumes a visible shape. Since the particular expression can never exhaust the possibilities of the vision, but falls far short of it in richness of content, the poet must have at his disposal a huge store of materials if he is to communicate even a few of his intimations. What is more, he must resort to an imagery that is difficult to handle and full of contradictions in order to express the weird paradoxicality of his vision. Dante's presentiments are clothed in images that run the gamut of Heaven and Hell; Goethe must bring in the Blocksberg and the infernal regions of Greek antiquity; Wagner needs the whole body of Nordic myth; Nietzsche returns to the hieratic style and recreates the legendary seer of prehistoric times; Blake invents for himself indescribable figures, and Spitteler borrows old names for new creatures of the imagination. And no intermediate step is missing in the whole range from the ineffably sublime to the perversely grotesque.

Psychology can do nothing towards the elucidation of this colourful imagery except bring together materials for comparison and offer a terminology for its discussion. According to this terminology, that which appears in the vision is the collective unconscious. We mean by collective unconscious, a certain psychic disposition shaped by the forces of heredity; from it consciousness has developed. In the physical structure of the body we find traces of earlier stages of evolution, and we may expect the human psyche also to conform in its make-up to the law of phylogeny. It is a fact that in eclipses of consciousness – in dreams, narcotic states and cases of insanity – there come to the surface psychic products or contents that show all the traits of primitive levels of psychic development. The images themselves are sometimes of such a primitive character that we might suppose them derived from ancient, esoteric teaching. Mythological themes clothed in modern dress also frequently appear. What is of particular importance for the study of literature in these manifestations of the collective unconscious is that they are compensatory to the conscious attitude. This is to say that they can bring a one-sided, abnormal, or dangerous state of consciousness into equilibrium in an apparently purposive way. In dreams we can see this process very clearly in its positive aspect. In cases of insanity the compensatory process is often perfectly obvious, but takes a negative form. There are persons, for instance, who have anxiously shut themselves off from all the world only to discover one day that their most intimate secrets are known and talked about by everyone.[1]

If we consider Goethe's *Faust*, and leave aside the possibility that it is compensatory to his own conscious attitude, the question that we must answer is this: In what relation does it stand to the conscious outlook of his time? Great poetry draws its strength from the life of mankind, and we completely miss its meaning if we try to derive it from personal factors. Whenever the collective unconscious becomes a living experience and is brought to bear upon the conscious outlook of an age, this event is a creative act which is of importance to everyone living in that age. A work of art is produced that contains what may truthfully be called a message to generations of men. So *Faust* touches something in the soul of every German. So also Dante's fame is immortal, while *The Shepherd of Hermas* just failed of inclusion in the New Testament canon. Every period has its bias, its particular prejudice and its psychic ailment. An epoch is like an individual; it has its own limitations of conscious outlook, and therefore requires a compensatory adjustment. This is effected by the collective unconscious in that a poet, a seer or a leader allows himself to be guided by the unexpressed desire of his times and shows the way, by word or deed, to the attainment of that which everyone blindly craves and expects – whether this attainment results in good or evil, the healing of an epoch or its destruction.

It is always dangerous to speak of one's own times, because what is at stake in the present is too vast for comprehension. A few hints must therefore suffice. Francesco Colonna's book is cast in the form of a dream, and is the apotheosis of natural love taken as a human relation; without countenancing a wild indulgence of the senses, he leaves completely aside the Christian sacrament of marriage. The book was written in 1453. Rider

Haggard, whose life coincides with the flowering-time of the Victorian era, takes up this subject and deals with it in his own way; he does not cast it in the form of a dream, but allows us to feel the tension of moral conflict. Goethe weaves the theme of Gretchen-Helen-Mater-Gloriosa like a red thread into the colourful tapestry of Faust. Nietzsche proclaims the death of God, and Spitteler transforms the waxing and waning of the gods into a myth of the seasons. Whatever his importance, each of these poets speaks with the voice of thousands and ten thousands, foretelling changes in the conscious outlook of his time.

Note

1 *See* my article: 'Mind and the Earth', in *Contributions to Analytical Psychology.* Kegan Paul, Trench, Trubner & Co., London, 1928.

44   G.E. Moore
From *Principia Ethica*

Our first conclusion as to the subject-matter of Ethics is, then, that there is a simple, indefinable, unanalysable object of thought by reference to which it must be defined. By what name we call this unique object is a matter of indifference, so long as we clearly recognise what it is and that it does differ from other objects. The words which are commonly taken as the signs of ethical judgments all do refer to it; and they are expressions of ethical judgments solely because they do so refer. But they may refer to it in two different ways, which it is very important to distinguish, if we are to have a complete definition of the range of ethical judgments. Before I proceeded to argue that there was such an indefinable notion involved in ethical notions, I stated that it was necessary for Ethics to enumerate all true universal judgments, asserting that such and such a thing was good, whenever it occurred. But, although all such judgments do refer to that unique notion which I have called 'good', they do not all refer to it in the same way. They may either assert that this unique property does always attach to the thing in question, or else they may assert only that the thing in question is *a cause or necessary condition* for the existence of other things to which this unique property does attach. The nature of these two species of universal ethical judgments is extremely different; and a great part of the difficulties which are met with in ordinary ethical speculation are due to the failure to distinguish them clearly. Their difference has, indeed, received expression in ordinary language by the contrast between the terms 'good as means' and 'good in itself', 'value as a means' and 'intrinsic value.' But these terms are apt to be applied correctly only in the more obvious instances; and this seems to be due to the fact that the distinction between the conceptions which they denote has not been made a separate object of investigation.

I may, however, state two general principles, closely connected with the results of this chapter, the recognition of which would seem to be of great importance for the investigation of what things are truly beautiful. The first of these is (1) a definition of beauty, of what is meant by saying that a thing is truly beautiful. The naturalistic fallacy has been quite as commonly

From G.E. Moore, *Principia Ethica*, Cambridge University Press, 1959, pp. 21, 201–2.

committed with regard to beauty as with regard to good: its use has introduced as many errors into Aesthetics as into Ethics. It has been even more commonly supposed that the beautiful may be *defined* as that which produces certain effects upon our feelings; and the conclusion which follows from this – namely, that judgments of taste are merely *subjective* – that precisely the same thing may, according to circumstances, be *both* beautiful *and* not beautiful – has very frequently been drawn. The conclusions of this chapter suggest a definition of beauty, which may partially explain and entirely remove the difficulties which have led to this error. It appears probable that the beautiful should be *defined* as that of which the admiring contemplation is good in itself. That is to say: To assert that a thing is beautiful is to assert that the cognition of it is an essential element in one of the intrinsically valuable wholes we have been discussing; so that the question whether it is *truly* beautiful or not depends upon the *objective* question whether the whole in question is or is not truly good, and does not depend upon the question whether it would or would not excite particular feelings in particular persons. This definition has the double recommendation that it accounts both for the apparent connection between goodness and beauty and for the no less apparent difference between these two conceptions. It appears, at first sight, to be a strange coincidence, that there should be two *different* objective predicates of value, 'good' and 'beautiful,' which are nevertheless so related to one another that whatever is beautiful is also good. But, if our definition be correct, the strangeness disappears; since it leaves only one *unanalysable* predicate of value, namely 'good,' while 'beautiful,' though not identical with, is to be defined by reference to this, being thus, at the same time, different from and necessarily connected with it. In short, on this view, to say that a thing is beautiful is to say, not indeed that it is *itself* good, but that it is a necessary element in something which is: to prove that a thing is truly beautiful is to prove that a whole, to which it bears a particular relation as a part, is truly good. And in this way we should explain the immense predominance, among objects commonly considered beautiful, of *material* objects – objects of the external senses; since these objects, though themselves having, as has been said, little or no intrinsic value, are yet essential constituents in the largest group of wholes which have intrinsic value. These wholes themselves may be, and are, also beautiful; but the comparative rarity with which we regard them as themselves *objects* of contemplation seems sufficient to explain the association of beauty with external objects.

And secondly (2) it is to be observed that beautiful objects are themselves, for the most part, organic unities, in this sense, that they are wholes of great complexity, such that the contemplation of any part, by itself, may have no value, and yet that, unless the contemplation of the whole includes the contemplation of that part, it will lose in value. From this it follows that there can be no single criterion of beauty. It will never be true to say: This object owes its beauty *solely* to the presence of this characteristic; nor yet that: Wherever this characteristic is present, the object must be beautiful. All that can be true is that certain objects are beautiful, *because* they have certain characteristics, in the sense that they would not be beautiful *unless* they had them. And it may be possible to find that certain characteristics are more or less universally present in all beautiful objects, and are, in this sense, more or less important conditions of beauty. But it is important to observe that the very qualities which differentiate one beautiful object from all others are, if the object be truly beautiful, as *essential* to its beauty as those which it has in common with ever so many others. The object would no more have the beauty it has, without its specific qualities, than without those that are generic; and the generic qualities, *by themselves*, would fail, as completely, to give beauty, as those which are specific.

45   Jean-François Lyotard
From *The Differend*

1. You are informed that human beings endowed with language were placed in a situation such that none of them is now able to tell about it. Most of them disappeared then, and the survivors rarely speak about it. When they do speak about it, their testimony bears only upon a minute part of this situation. How can you know that the situation itself existed? That it is not the fruit of your informant's imagination? Either the situation did not exist as such. Or else it did exist, in which case your informant's testimony is false, either because he or she should have disappeared, or else because he or she should remain silent, or else because, if he or she does speak, he or she can bear witness only to the particular experience he had, it remaining to be established whether this experience was a component of the situation in question.

2. 'I have analyzed thousands of documents. I have tirelessly pursued specialists and historians with my questions. I have tried in vain to find a single former deportee capable of proving to me that he had really seen, with his own eyes, a gas chamber' (Faurisson in Pierre Vidal-Naquet, 1981: 81). To have 'really seen with his own eyes' a gas chamber would be the condition which gives one the authority to say that it exists and to persuade the unbeliever. Yet it is still necessary to prove that the gas chamber was

From Jean-François Lyotard, *The Differend*, Manchester University Press, 1988, pp. 3–6.

used to kill at the time it was seen. The only acceptable proof that it was used to kill is that one died from it. But if one is dead, one cannot testify that it is on account of the gas chamber. – The plaintiff complains that he has been fooled about the existence of gas chambers, fooled that is, about the so-called Final Solution. His argument is: in order for a place to be identified as a gas chamber, the only eyewitness I will accept would be a victim of this gas chamber; now, according to my opponent, there is no victim that is not dead; otherwise, this gas chamber would not be what he or she claims it to be. There is, therefore, no gas chamber.

3. Can you give me, says an editor defending his or her profession, the title of a work of major importance which would have been rejected by every editor and which would therefore remain unknown? Most likely, you do not know any masterpiece of this kind because, if it does exist, it remains unknown. And if you think you know one, since it has not been made public, you cannot say that it is of major importance, except in your eyes. You do not know of any, therefore, and the editor is right. – This argument takes the same form as those in the preceding numbers. Reality is not what is 'given' to this or that 'subject,' it is a state of the referent (that about which one speaks) which results from the effectuation of establishment procedures defined by a unanimously agreed-upon protocol, and from the possibility offered to anyone to recommence this effectuation as often as he or she wants. The publishing industry would be one of these protocols, historical inquiry another.

4. Either the Ibanskian[1] witness is not a communist, or else he is. If he is, he has no need to testify that Ibanskian society is communist, since he admits that the communist authorities are the only ones competent to effectuate the establishment procedures for the reality of the communist character of that society. He defers to them then just as the layperson defers to the biologist or to the astronomer for the affirmation of the existence of a virus or a nebula. If he ceases to give his agreement to these authorities, he ceases to be a communist. We come back then to the first case: he is not a communist. This means that he ignores or wishes to ignore the establishment procedures for the reality of the communist character of Ibanskian society. There is, in this case, no more credit to be accorded his testimony than to that of a human being who says he has communicated with Martians. 'There is therefore nothing surprising in the fact that the [Ibanskian] State regards opposition activity in general as a criminal activity on the same level as robbery, gangsterism, speculation and so on. . . . It is a non-political society' (Zinoviev, 1977: 600–1). More exactly, it is a learned State (Châtelet, 1981), it knows no reality other than the established one, and it holds the monopoly on procedures for the establishment of reality.

5. The difference, though, between communism, on the one hand, and a virus or a nebula, on the other hand, is that there are means to observe the latter – they are objects of cognition – while the former is the object of an idea of historical–political reason, and this object is not observable (Kant Notice 4 § 1). There are no procedures, defined by a protocol unanimously approved and renewable on demand, for establishing in general the reality of the object of an idea. For example, even in physics, there exists no such protocol for establishing the reality of the universe, because the universe is the object of an idea. As a general rule, an object which is thought under the category of the whole (or of the absolute) is not an object of cognition (whose reality could be subjected to a protocol, etc.). The principle affirming the contrary could be called totalitarianism. If the requirement of establishing the reality of a phrase's referent according to the protocol of cognition is extended to any given phrase, especially to those phrases that refer to a whole, then this requirement is totalitarian in its principle. That's why it is important to distinguish between phrase regimens, and this comes down to limiting the competence of a given tribunal to a given kind of phrase.

6. The plaintiff's conclusion (No. 2) should have been that since the only witnesses are the victims, and since there are no victims but dead ones, no place can be identified as a gas chamber. He should not have said that there are none, but rather that his opponent cannot prove that there are any, and that should have been sufficient to confound the tribunal. It is up to the opponent (the victim) to adduce the proof of the wrong done to him or her!

7. This is what a wrong [*tort*] would be: a damage [*dommage*] accompanied by the loss of the means to prove the damage. This is the case if the victim is deprived of life, or of all his or her liberties, or of the freedom to make his or her ideas or opinions public, or simply of the right to testify to the damage, or even more simply if the testifying phrase is itself deprived of authority (Nos. 24–27). In all of these cases, to the privation constituted by the damage there is added the impossibility of bringing it to the knowledge of others, and in particular to the knowledge of a tribunal. Should the victim seek to bypass this impossibility and testify anyway to the wrong done to him or to her, he or she comes up against the following argumentation: either the damages you complain about never took place, and your testimony is false; or else they took place, and since you are able to testify to them, it is not a wrong that has been done to you, but merely a damage, and your testimony is still false.

8. Either you are the victim of a wrong, or you are not. If you are not, you are deceived (or lying) in testifying that you are. If you are, since you can bear witness to this wrong, it is not a wrong, and you are deceived (or lying) in testifying that you are the victim of a wrong. Let p be: you are the victim of a wrong; *not p*: you are not; Tp: phrase p is true; Fp: it is false. The

argument is, either *p* or *not-p*; if *not-p*, then *Fp*; if *p*, then *not-p*, then *Fp*. The ancients called this argument a dilemma. It contains the mechanism of the *double bind* as studied by the Palo Alto School,[2] it is a linchpin of Hegelian dialectical logic (Hegel Notice, § 2). This mechanism consists in applying to two contradictory propositions, *p* and *not-p*, two logical operators: exclusion (*either . . . , or*) and implication (*if . . . , then*). So, at once [(*either p or not-p*) and (*if p, then not-p*)]. It's as if you said both, *either it is white, or it is not white*; and *if it is white, it is not white*.

Notes

1 The term is from Alexander Zinoviev's satirical novel *The Yawning Heights*, set in a fictitious locale – Ibansk – whose name is a derivative of Ivan, the stereotypical Russian name. –Tr.
2 The foremost member of which was, of course, Gregory Bateson. –Tr.

46 Alasdair MacIntyre
From *After Virtue*

For it was Nietzsche's historic achievement to understand more clearly than any other philosopher – certainly more clearly than his counterparts in Anglo-Saxon emotivism and continental existentialism – not only that what purported to be appeals to objectivity were in fact expressions of subjective will, but also the nature of the problems that this posed for moral philosophy. It is true that Nietzsche, as I shall later argue, illegitimately generalized from the condition of moral judgment in his own day to the nature of morality as such; and I have already said justifiably harsh words about Nietzsche's construction of that at once absurd and dangerous fantasy, the *Übermensch*. But it is worth noting how even that construction began from a genuine insight.

In a famous passage in *The Gay Science* (section 335) Nietzsche jeers at the notion of basing morality on inner moral sentiments, on conscience, on the one hand, or on the Kantian categorical imperative, on universalizability, on the other. In five swift, witty and cogent paragraphs he disposes of both what I have called the Enlightenment project to discover rational foundations for an objective morality and of the confidence of the everyday moral

From Alasdair MacIntyre, *After Virtue*, 2nd ed., Duckworth, 1985, pp. 113–14, 117–19.

agent in post-Enlightenment culture that his moral practice and utterance are in good order. But Nietzsche then goes on to confront the problem that this act of destruction has created. The underlying structure of his argument is as follows: if there is nothing to morality but expressions of will, my morality can only be what my will creates. There can be no place for such fictions as natural rights, utility, the greatest happiness of the greatest number. I myself must now bring into existence 'new tables of what is good'. 'We, however, *want to become those we are* – human beings who are new, unique, incomparable, who give themselves laws, who create themselves' (p. 266). The rational and rationally justified autonomous moral subject of the eighteenth century is a fiction, an illusion; so, Nietzsche resolves, let will replace reason and let us make ourselves into autonomous moral subjects by some gigantic and heroic act of the will, an act of the will that by its quality may remind us of that archaic aristocratic self-assertiveness which preceded what Nietzsche took to be the disaster of slave-morality and which by its effectiveness may be the prophetic precursor of a new era. The problem then is how to construct in an entirely original way, how to invent a new table of what is good and a law, a problem which arises for each individual. This problem would constitute the core of a Nietzschean moral philosophy. For it is in his relentlessly serious pursuit of the problem, not in his frivolous solutions that Nietzsche's greatness lies, the greatness that makes him *the* moral philosopher *if* the only alternatives to Nietzsche's moral philosophy turn out to be those formulated by the philosophers of the Enlightenment and their successors.

In another way too Nietzsche is *the* moral philosopher of the present age. For I have already argued that the present age is in its presentation of itself to itself dominantly Weberian; and I have also noticed that Nietzsche's central thesis was presupposed by Weber's central categories of thought. Hence Nietzsche's prophetic irrationalism – irrationalism because Nietzsche's problems remain unsolved and his solutions defy reason – remains immanent in the Weberian managerial forms of our culture. Whenever those immersed in the bureaucratic culture of the age try to think their way through to the moral foundations of what they are and what they do, they will discover suppressed Nietzschean premises. And consequently it is possible to predict with confidence that in the apparently quite unlikely contexts of bureaucratically managed modern societies there will periodically emerge social movements informed by just that kind of prophetic irrationalism of which Nietzsche's thought is the ancestor. Indeed just because and insofar as contemporary Marxism is Weberian in substance we can expect prophetic irrationalisms of the Left as well as of the Right. . . .

. . . Nietzsche rarely reflects explicitly to Aristotle except on aesthetic questions. He *does* borrow the name and notion of 'the great-souled man' from the *Ethics*, although it becomes in the context of his theory something quite other than it was in Aristotle's. But his interpretation of the history of morality makes it quite clear that the Aristotelian account of ethics and politics would have to rank for Nietzsche with all those degenerate disguises of the will to power which follow from the false turning taken by Socrates.

Yet it is not of course just that Nietzsche's moral philosophy is false if Aristotle's is true and *vice versa*. In a much stronger sense Nietzsche's moral philosophy is matched specifically against Aristotle's by virtue of the historical role which each plays. For, as I argued earlier, it was because a moral tradition of which Aristotle's thought was the intellectual core was repudiated during the transitions of the fifteenth to seventeenth centuries that the Enlightenment project of discovering new rational secular foundations for morality had to be undertaken. And it was because that project failed, because the views advanced by its most intellectually powerful protagonists, and more especially by Kant, could not be sustained in the face of rational criticism that Nietzsche and all his existentialist and emotivist successors were able to mount their apparently successful critique of all previous morality. Hence the defensibility of the Nietzschean position turns *in the end* on the answer to the question: was it right in the first place to reject Aristotle? For if Aristotle's position in ethics and politics – or something very like it – could be sustained, the whole Nietzschean enterprise would be pointless. This is because the power of Nietzsche's position depends upon the truth of one central thesis: that all rational vindications of morality manifestly fail and that *therefore* belief in the tenets of morality needs to be explained in terms of a set of rationalizations which conceal the fundamentally non-rational phenomena of the will. My own argument obliges me to agree with Nietzsche that the philosophers of the Enlightenment never succeeded in providing grounds for doubting his central thesis; his epigrams are even deadlier than his extended arguments. But, if my earlier argument is correct, that failure itself was nothing other than an historical sequel to the rejection of the Aristotelian tradition. And thus the key question does indeed become: can Aristotle's ethics, or something very like it, after all be vindicated?

It is an understatement to call this a large and complex question. For the issues which divide Aristotle and Nietzsche are of a number of very different kinds. At the level of philosophical theory there are questions in politics and in philosophical psychology as well as in moral theory; and what confront each other are not in any case merely two theories, but the theoretical specification of two different ways of life. The role of Aristotelianism in my argument is not entirely due to its historical importance. In the ancient and medieval worlds it was always in conflict with other standpoints, and the various ways of life of which it took itself to be the best theoretical interpreter had other sophisticated theoretical protagonists. It is true that no doctrine vindicated itself in so wide a variety of contexts as did Aristotelianism: Greek, Islamic, Jewish and Christian; and that when modernity made its assaults on an older world its most perceptive exponents understood that it was Aristotelianism that had to be overthrown. But all these historical truths, crucial as they are, are unimportant compared with the fact that Aristotelianism is *philosophically* the most powerful of pre-modern modes of moral thought. If a premodern view of morals and politics is to be vindicated against modernity, it will be in *something like* Aristotelian terms or not at all.

What then the conjunction of philosophical and historical argument reveals is that *either* one must follow through the aspirations and the collapse of the different versions of the Enlightenment project until there remains only the Nietzschean diagnosis and the Nietzschean problematic *or* one must hold that the Enlightenment project was not only mistaken, but should never have been commenced in the first place. There is no third alternative and more particularly there is no alternative provided by those thinkers at the heart of the contemporary conventional curriculum in moral philosophy, Hume, Kant and Mill. It is no wonder that the teaching of ethics is so often destructive and skeptical in its effects upon the minds of those taught.

But *which* ought we to choose? And *how* ought we to choose? It is yet another of Nietzsche's merits that he joins to his critique of Enlightenment moralities a sense of their failure to address adequately, let alone to answer, the question: what sort of person am I to become? This is in a way an inescapable question in that an answer to it is given *in practice* in each human life. But for characteristically modern moralities it is a question to be approached only by indirection. The primary question from their standpoint has concerned rules: what rules ought we to follow? And why ought we to obey them? And that this has been the primary question is unsurprising when we recall the consequences of the expulsion of Aristotelian teleology from the moral world. Ronald Dworkin has recently argued that the central doctrine of modern liberalism is the thesis that questions about the *good life for man* or the ends of human life are to be regarded from the public standpoint as systematically unsettlable. On these individuals are free to agree or to disagree. The rules of morality and law hence are not to be derived from or justified in terms of some more fundamental conception of the good for man. In arguing thus Dworkin has, I believe, identified a stance characteristic not just of liberalism, but of modernity. Rules become the primary concept of the moral life. Qualities of character then generally come to be prized only because they will lead us to follow the right set of rules. 'The virtues are sentiments, that is, related families of dispositions and propensities regulated by a higher-order desire, in this case a desire to act from the corresponding moral principles,' asserts John Rawls, one of the latest moral philosophers of modernity (1971, p. 192), and elsewhere he defines 'the fundamental moral virtues' as 'strong and normally effective desires to act on the basic principles of right' (p. 436).

Hence on the modern view the justification of the virtues depends upon some prior justification of rules and principles; and if the latter become radically problematic, as they have, so also must the former. Suppose however that in articulating the problems of morality the ordering of evaluative concepts has been misconceived by the spokesmen of modernity and more particularly of liberalism; suppose that we need to attend to *virtues* in the first place in order to understand the function and authority of rules; we ought then to begin the enquiry in the quite different way from that in which it is begun by Hume or Diderot or Kant or Mill. On this interestingly Nietzsche and Aristotle agree.

SECTION FOUR
THEORIES AND VARIETIES OF KNOWLEDGE

Bergson's essay was first published in French in 1889 and his concept of *durée* represented an attempt to offer an alternative epistemology which would exist outside the deterministic confines of mechanistic science (see my introductory discussion). The essay probably represents the most influential modern attempt to read art as a form of knowledge. Rorty's neo-pragmatist alternative (1982) and Foucault's concept of the *episteme* (first published in French in 1969) break with the idealist tradition in arguing for the culturally situated nature of knowledge and the role of institutional discourses in framing what is to be regarded as 'truth'. Similar themes recur in the essays collected in the next section on 'Philosophies of science and critiques of method'. Heisenberg's essay, from *Philosophic Problems of Nuclear Science* (1952), examines the implications of quantum physics as they bear on the methodological and epistemological assumptions of classic realist science (see Introduction to Section II). Kuhn's book of 1962 had an enormous impact on assumptions about 'objectivity' in science and together with Gadamer's work and Feyerabend's *Against Method* (1975) produced a further assault on classic realism. Popper's work (1972) endeavours to defend 'objectivity' while recognizing the claims of the New Science and its philosophical implications. In various ways, each of these writers suggests that the boundaries between scientific and artistic endeavour are less absolute than was once assumed.

The section on 'Time and space' suggests further ways in which philosophy, science and literature have impinged on each other in the last century. The excerpt from Bradley (1903) is included as an example of an absolute idealism which argues for the containment of time within a realm of 'truth' which is timeless (see my introduction). Lewis's famous assault on Joyce (1927) accused him of subservience to an insidious Bergsonian 'time philosophy' intended to demonstrate subjective freedom but actually confirming the existence of a world of dead and mechanical matter. Lewis produced a bizarre conflation of Einstein, Bergson, Whitehead and Alexander in order to mount his assault on modern writers such as Proust, Stein and Joyce. The excerpt from Heidegger's 'The Age of the World Picture' (first delivered as a lecture in 1938) attempts to offer a critique of the way in which modern science represents nature as an inert object by assuming the position of the scientist as a mastering 'subject' disconnected from what it beholds. Modern knowledge is thus conceived in terms of a universalizing abstraction which denies temporality and inserts an absolute division between subject and object. The excerpt from David Harvey (1989) offers a socio-economic analysis of how late capitalism produced a space–time compression which has radically changed those relations between the local and the global central to our conceptualization of identity.

Though all of these essays address the implications for knowledge and representation of modern ideas of space and time, the writers in the section entitled 'Representation and the image' focus specifically on the nature of the aesthetic as it exists within the new frameworks of knowledge. Bell's position (1913) is discussed extensively in my introduction for it was one of the most influential statements of the theory of aesthetic autonomy. Langer's theory of 'symbolic transformation' (1942) is another meditation on the limitations of rationalist theories of knowledge and explores the importance of the aesthetic as an alternative form of meaning which is presentational, performative and symbolic rather than reductively discursive or analytic. In effect, her work reformulates the problem of mind in terms of myth, symbol, ritual and feeling. Alain Robbe-Grillet's essay 'Nature, Humanism, Tragedy' (1958) represents a position diametrically opposed to that of Langer's. For him, what must be repudiated is precisely our misguided attempt to anthropomorphize nature and he calls for a new art in which the writer might become more like the classic scientist even as science is infiltrated by the demand to acknowledge its connections with the aesthetic.

EPISTEMOLOGIES

47   Henri Bergson
From *Time and Free Will*

Hence there are finally two different selves, one of which is, as it were, the external projection of the other, its spatial and, so to speak, social representation. We reach the former by deep introspection, which leads us to grasp our inner states as living things, constantly *becoming*, as states not amenable to measure, which permeate one another and of which the succession in duration has nothing in common with juxtaposition in homogeneous space. But the moments at which we thus grasp ourselves are rare, and that is just why we are rarely free. The greater part of the time we live outside ourselves, hardly perceiving anything of ourselves but our own ghost, a colourless shadow which pure duration projects into homogeneous space. Hence our life unfolds in space rather than in time; we live for the external world rather than for ourselves; we speak rather than think; we 'are acted' rather than act ourselves. To act freely is to recover possession of oneself, and to get back into pure duration.

Kant's great mistake was to take time as a homogeneous medium. He did not notice that real duration is made up of moments inside one another, and that when it seems to assume the form of a homogeneous whole, it is because it gets expressed in space. Thus the very distinction which he makes between space and time amounts at bottom to confusing time with space, and the symbolical representation of the ego with the ego itself. He thought that consciousness was incapable of perceiving psychic states otherwise than by juxtaposition, forgetting that a medium in which these states are set side by side and distinguished from one another is of course space, and not duration. He was thereby led to believe that the same states can recur in the depths of consciousness, just as the same physical phenomena are repeated in space; this at least is what he implicitly admitted when he ascribed to the causal relation the same meaning and the same function in the inner as in the outer world. Thus freedom was made into an incomprehensible fact. And yet, owing to his unlimited though unconscious confidence in this inner perception whose scope he tried to restrict, his belief in freedom remained unshakable. He therefore raised it to the sphere of noumena; and as he had confused duration with space, he made

From Henri Bergson, *Time and Free Will*, Allen and Unwin, 1921, pp. 231–40.

this genuine free self, which is indeed outside space, into a self which is supposed to be outside duration too, and therefore out of the reach of our faculty of knowledge. But the truth is that we perceive this self whenever, by a strenuous effort of reflection, we turn our eyes from the shadow which follows us and retire into ourselves. Though we generally live and act outside our own person, in space rather than in duration, and though by this means we give a handle to the law of causality, which binds the same effects to the same causes, we can nevertheless always get back into pure duration, of which the moments are internal and heterogeneous to one another, and in which a cause cannot repeat its effect since it will never repeat itself.

In this very confusion of true duration with its symbol both the strength and the weakness of Kantianism reside. Kant imagines on the one side 'things in themselves' and on the other a homogeneous Time and Space, through which the 'things in themselves' are refracted: thus are supposed to arise on the one hand the phenomenal self – a self which consciousness perceives – and, on the other, external objects. Time and space on this view would not be any more in us than outside us; the very distinction of outside and inside would be the work of time and space. This doctrine has the advantage of providing our empirical thought with a solid foundation, and of guaranteeing that phenomena, as phenomena, are adequately knowable. Indeed, we might set up these phenomena as absolute and do without the incomprehensible 'things in themselves,' were it not that the Practical Reason, the revealer of duty, came in, like the Platonic reminiscence, to warn us that the 'thing in itself' exists, invisible but present. The controlling factor in the whole of this theory is the very sharp distinction between the matter of consciousness and its form, between the homogeneous and the heterogeneous, and this vital distinction would probably never have been made unless time also had been regarded as a medium indifferent to what fills it.

But if time, as immediate consciousness perceives it, were, like space, a homogeneous medium, science would be able to deal with it, as it can with space. Now we have tried to prove that duration, as duration, and motion, as motion, elude the grasp of mathematics: of time everything slips through its fingers but simultaneity, and of movement everything but immobility. This is what the Kantians and even their opponents do not seem to have perceived: in this so-called phenomenal world, which, we are told, is a world cut out for scientific knowledge, all the relations which cannot be translated into simultaneity, i.e. into space, are scientifically unknowable.

In the second place, in a duration assumed to be homogeneous, the same states could occur over again, causality would imply necessary determination, and all freedom would become incomprehensible. Such, indeed, is the result to which the *Critique of Pure Reason* leads. But instead of concluding from this that real duration is heterogeneous, which, by clearing up the second difficulty, would have called his attention to the first, Kant preferred to put freedom outside time and to raise an impassable barrier between the world of phenomena, which he hands over root and branch to our understanding, and the world of things in themselves, which he forbids us to enter.

But perhaps this distinction is too sharply drawn and perhaps the barrier is easier to cross than he supposed. For if perchance the moments of real duration, perceived by an attentive consciousness, permeated one another instead of lying side by side, and if these moments formed in relation to one another a heterogeneity within which the idea of necessary determination lost every shred of meaning, then the self grasped by consciousness would be a free cause, we should have absolute knowledge of ourselves, and, on the other hand, just because this absolute constantly commingles with phenomena and, while filling itself with them, permeates them, these phenomena themselves would not be as amenable as is claimed to mathematical reasoning.

So we have assumed the existence of a homogeneous Space and, with Kant, distinguished this space from the matter which fills it. With him we have admitted that homogeneous space is a 'form of our sensibility': and we understand by this simply that other minds, e.g. those of animals, although they perceive objects, do not distinguish them so clearly either from one another or from themselves. This intuition of a homogeneous medium, an intuition peculiar to man, enables us to externalize our concepts in relation to one another, reveals to us the objectivity of things, and thus, in two ways, on the one hand by getting everything ready for language, and on the other by showing us an external world, quite distinct from ourselves, in the perception of which all minds have a common share, foreshadows and prepares the way for social life.

Over against this homogeneous space we have put the self as perceived by an attentive consciousness, a living self, whose states, at once undistinguished and unstable, cannot be separated without changing their nature, and cannot receive a fixed form or be expressed in words without becoming public property. How could this self, which distinguishes external objects so sharply and represents them so easily by means of symbols, withstand the temptation to introduce the same distinctions into its own life and to replace the interpenetration of its psychic states, their wholly qualitative multiplicity, by a numerical plurality of terms which are distinguished from one another, set side by side, and expressed by means of words? In place of a heterogeneous duration whose moments permeate one another, we thus get a homogeneous time whose moments are strung on a spatial line. In place of an inner life whose successive phases, each unique of its kind, cannot be expressed in the fixed terms of language, we get a self which can be artificially reconstructed, and simple psychic states which can be added to and taken from one another just like the letters of the alphabet in forming words. Now, this must not be thought to be a mode of symbolical representation only, for immediate intuition and discursive thought are one in concrete reality, and the very mechanism by which we only meant at first to explain our conduct will end by also controlling it. Our psychic states, separating then from each other, will get solidified; between our ideas, thus crystallized, and our external movements we shall witness permanent associations being formed; and little by little, as our consciousness thus imitates the process by which nervous matter procures reflex actions, automatism will cover over freedom.[1] It is just at this point that the associationists and the determinists come in on the one side, and the Kantians on the other. As they look at only the commonest aspect of our conscious life, they perceive clearly marked states, which can recur in time like physical phenomena, and to which the law of causal determination applies, if we wish, in the same sense as it does to nature. As, on the other hand, the medium in which these psychic states are set side by side exhibits parts external to one another, in which the same facts seem capable of being repeated, they do not hesitate to make time a homogeneous medium and treat it as space. Henceforth all difference between duration and extensity, succession and simultaneity, is abolished: the only thing left is to turn freedom out of doors, or, if you cannot entirely throw off your traditional respect for it, to escort it with all due ceremony up to the supratemporal domain of 'things in themselves,' whose mysterious threshold your consciousness cannot cross. But, in our view, there is a third course which might be taken, namely, to carry ourselves back in thought to those moments of our life when we made some serious decision, moments unique of their kind, which will never be repeated – any more than the past phases in the history of a nation will ever come back again. We should see that if these past states cannot be adequately expressed in words or artificially reconstructed by a juxtaposition of simpler states, it is because in their dynamic unity and wholly qualitative multiplicity they are phases of our real and concrete duration, a heterogeneous duration and a living one. We should see that, if our action was pronounced by us to be free, it is because the relation of this action to the state from which it issued could not be expressed by a law, this psychic state being unique of its kind and unable ever to occur again. We should see, finally, that the very idea of necessary determination here loses every shred of meaning, that there cannot be any question either of foreseeing the act before it is performed or of reasoning about the possibility of the contrary action once the deed is done, for to have all the conditions given is, in concrete duration, to place oneself at the very moment of the act and not to foresee it. But we should also understand the illusion which makes the one party think that they are compelled to deny freedom, and the others that they must define it. It is because the transition is made by imperceptible steps from concrete duration, whose elements permeate one another, to symbolical duration, whose moments are set side by side, and consequently from free activity to conscious automatism. It is because, although we are free whenever we are willing to get back into ourselves, it seldom happens that we are willing. It is because, finally, even in the cases where the action is freely performed, we cannot reason about it without setting out its conditions externally to one another, therefore in space and no longer in pure duration. The problem of freedom has thus sprung from a misunderstanding: it has been to the moderns what the paradoxes of the Eleatics were to the ancients, and, like these paradoxes, it has its origin in the illusion through which we confuse succession and simultaneity, duration and extensity, quality and quantity.

Note

1 Renouvier has already spoken of these voluntary acts which may be compared to reflex movements, and he has restricted freedom to moments of crisis. But he does not seem to have noticed that the process of our free activity goes on, as it were, unknown to ourselves, in the obscure depths of our consciousness at every moment of duration, that the very feeling of duration comes from this source, and that without this heterogeneous and continuous duration, in which our self evolves, there would be no moral crisis. The study, even the close study, of a given free action will thus not settle the problem of freedom. The whole series of our heterogeneous states of consciousness must be taken into consideration. In other words, it is in a close analysis of the idea of duration that the key to the problem must be sought.

---

48   Richard Rorty
From *Consequences of Pragmatism*

'Value-free' social science and hermeneutic social science

There has recently been a reaction against the idea that students of man and society will be 'scientific' only if they remain faithful to the Galilean model – if they find 'value-neutral,' purely descriptive terms in which to state their predictive generalizations, leaving evaluation to 'policy-makers.' This has led to a revival of Dilthey's notion that to understand human beings 'scientifically' we must apply non-Galilean, 'hermeneutic' methods. From the point of view I wish to suggest, the whole idea of 'being scientific' or of choosing between 'methods' is confused. Consequently, the question about whether social scientists should seek value-neutrality along Galilean lines,

From Richard Rorty, *Consequences of Pragmatism*, Harvester, 1991, pp. 195–8, 203–8.

or rather should try for something more cozy, Aristotelian, and 'softer' – a distinctive 'method of the human sciences' – seems to me misguided.

One reason this quarrel has developed is that it has become obvious that *whatever* terms are used to describe human beings *become* 'evaluative' terms. The suggestion that we segregate the 'evaluative' terms in a language and use their absence as one criterion for the 'scientific' character of a discipline or a theory cannot be carried out. For there is no way to prevent anybody using *any* term 'evaluatively.' If you ask somebody whether he is using 'repression' or 'primitive' or 'working class' normatively or descriptively, he might be able to answer in the case of a given statement, made on a given occasion. But if you ask him whether he uses the term only when he is describing, only when he is engaging in moral reflection, or both, the answer is almost always going to be 'both.' Further – and this is the crucial point – unless the answer *is* 'both,' it is just not the sort of term which will do us much good in social science. Predictions will do 'policy-making' no good if they are not phrased in the terms in which policy can be formulated.

Suppose we picture the 'value-free' social scientist walking up to the divide between 'fact' and 'value' and handing his predictions to the policy-makers who live on the other side. They will not be of much use unless they contain some of the terms which the policy-makers use among themselves. What the policy-makers would like, presumably, are rich juicy predictions like 'If basic industry is socialized, the standard of living will [or won't] decline,' 'If literacy is more widespread, more [or fewer] honest people will be elected to office,' and so on. They would like hypothetical sentences whose consequents are phrased in terms which might occur in morally urgent recommendations. When they get predictions phrased in the sterile jargon of 'quantified' social sciences ('maximizes satisfaction,' 'increases conflict,' etc.), they either tune out, or, more dangerously, begin to use the jargon in moral deliberation. The desire for a new, 'interpretive' social science seems to me best understood as a reaction against the temptation to formulate social policies in terms so thin as barely to count as 'moral' at all – terms which never stray far from definitional links with 'pleasure,' 'pain,' and 'power.'

The issue between those who hanker after 'objective,' 'value-free,' 'truly scientific' social science and those who think this should be replaced with something more hermeneutical is misdescribed as a quarrel about 'method.' A quarrel about method requires a common goal, and disagreement about the means for reaching it. But the two sides to this quarrel are not disagreeing about how to get more accurate predictions of what will happen if certain policies are adopted. Neither side is very good at making such predictions, and if anybody ever did find a way of making them both sides would be equally eager to incorporate this strategy in their view. The nature of the quarrel is better, but still misleadingly, seen as one between the competing goals of 'explanation' and 'understanding.' As this contrast has developed in the recent literature, it is a contrast between the sort of jargon which permits Galilean-style generalizations, and Hempelian specification of confirming and disconfirming instances of such generalizations, and the sort which sacrifices this virtue for the sake of describing in roughly the same vocabulary as one evaluates (a 'teleological' vocabulary, crudely speaking).

This contrast is real enough. But it is not an issue to be resolved, only a difference to be lived with. The idea that explanation and understanding are opposed ways of doing social science is as misguided as the notion that microscopic and macroscopic descriptions of organisms are opposed ways of doing biology. There are lots of things you want to do with bacteria and cows for which it is very useful to have biochemical descriptions of them; there are lots of things you want to do with them for which such descriptions would be merely a nuisance. Similarly, there are lots of things you want to do with human beings for which descriptions of them in non-evaluative, 'inhuman' terms are very useful; there are others (e.g. thinking of them as your fellow-citizens) in which such descriptions are not. 'Explanation' is merely the sort of understanding one looks for when one wants to predict and control. It does not contrast with something else called 'understanding' as the abstract contrasts with the concrete, or the artificial with the natural, or the 'repressive' with the 'liberating.' To say that something is better 'understood' in one vocabulary than another is always an ellipsis for the claim that a description in the preferred vocabulary is more useful for a certain purpose. If the purpose is prediction, then one will want one sort of vocabulary. If it is evaluation, one may or may not want a different sort of vocabulary. (In the case of evaluating artillery fire, for example, the predictive vocabulary of ballistics will do nicely. In the case of evaluating human character, the vocabulary of stimulus and response is beside the point.)

To sum up this point: there are two distinct requirements for the vocabulary of the social sciences:

(1) It should contain descriptions of situations which facilitate their prediction and control
(2) It should contain descriptions which help one decide what to do.

Value-free social science assumed that a thin 'behavioristic' vocabulary met the first requirement. This assumption has not panned out very well; the last fifty years of research in the social sciences have not notably increased our predictive abilities. But even if it *had* succeeded in offering predictions, this would not *necessarily* have helped fulfill the second requirement. It would not necessarily have been useful in deciding what to do. The debate between friends of value-freedom and friends of hermeneutics has often taken for granted that neither requirement can be satisfied unless the other is also. Friends of hermeneutics have protested that Behaviorese was inappropriate for 'understanding' people – meaning that it could not catch what they were 'really' doing. But this is a misleading way of saying it is not a good vocabulary for moral reflection. We just don't want to be the sort of policy-makers who use those terms for deciding what to do to our fellow-humans. Conversely, friends of value-freedom, insisting that as soon as social science finds its Galileo (who is somehow known in advance to be a behaviorist) the first requirement will be satisfied, have argued that it is our duty to start making policy decisions in suitably thin terms – so that our 'ethics' may be 'objective' and 'scientifically based.' For only in that way will we be able to make maximal use of all those splendid predictions which will shortly be coming our way. Both sides make the same mistake in thinking that there is some intrinsic connection between the two requirements. It is a mistake to think that when we know how to deal justly and honorably with a person or a society we *thereby* know how to predict and control him or her or it, and a mistake to think that ability to predict and control is *necessarily* an aid to such dealing.

To be told that only a certain vocabulary is *suited* to human beings or human societies, that only *that* vocabulary permits us to 'understand' them, is the seventeenth-century myth of Nature's Own Vocabulary all over again. If, with Dewey, one sees vocabularies as instruments for coping with things rather than representations of their intrinsic natures, then one will not think that there is an intrinsic connection, nor an intrinsic *lack* of connection, between 'explanation' and 'understanding' – between being able to predict and control people of a certain sort and being able to sympathize and associate with them, to view them as fellow-citizens. One will not think that there are two 'methods' – one for explaining some-body's behavior and another for understanding his nature.

Ungrounded hope: Dewey vs. Foucault

The burden of my argument so far has been that if we get rid of traditional notions of 'objectivity' and 'scientific method' we shall be able to see the social sciences as continuous with literature – as interpreting other people to us, and thus enlarging and deepening our sense of community. We shall see the anthropologists and historians as having made it possible for us – educated, leisured policy-makers of the West – to see any exotic specimen of humanity as also 'one of us.' We shall see the sociologists as having done the same for the poor (and various other sorts of nearby outsiders), and the psychologists as having done the same for the eccentric and the insane. This is not all that the social sciences have done, but it is perhaps the most important thing. If we emphasize this side of their achievement, then we shall not object to their sharing a narrative and anecdotal style with the novelist and the journalist. We shall not worry about how this style is related to the 'Galilean' style which 'quantified behavioral science' has tried to emulate. We shall not think either style particularly appropriate or inappropriate to the study of man. For we shall not think that 'the study of man' or 'the human sciences' have a nature, any more than we think that man does. When the notion of knowledge as representation goes, then the notion of inquiry as split into discrete sectors with discrete subject matters goes. The lines between novels, newspaper articles, and sociological research get blurred. The lines between subject matters are drawn by reference to current practical concerns, rather than putative ontological status.

Once this pragmatist line is adopted, however, there are still two ways to go. One can emphasize, as Dewey did, the moral importance of the social sciences – their role in widening and deepening our sense of community and of the possibilities open to this community. Or one can emphasize, as Michel Foucault does, the way in which the social sciences have served as instruments of 'the disciplinary society,' the connection between knowledge and power rather than that between knowledge and human solidarity. Much present-day concern about the status and the role of the social sciences comes out of the realization that in addition to broadening the sympathies of the educated classes, the social sciences have also helped them manipulate all the other classes (not to mention, so to speak, helping them manipulate themselves). Foucault's is the best account of this dark side of the social sciences. Admirers of Habermas and of Foucault join in thinking of the 'interpretive turn' in the social sciences as a turn against their use as 'instruments of domination,' as tools for what Dewey called 'social engineering.' This has resulted in a confusing quasi-politicization of what was already a factitious 'methodological' issue. In this final section, I want to argue that one should not attribute undue importance to the 'Galilean-vs.-hermeneutic' or 'explanation-vs.-understanding' contrasts by seeing them as parallel with the contrast between 'domination' and 'emancipation.' We should see Dewey and Foucault as differing not over a theoretical issue, but over what we may hope.

Dewey and Foucault make exactly the same criticism of the tradition. They agree, right down the line, about the need to abandon traditional notions of rationality, objectivity, method, and truth. They are both, so to speak, 'beyond method.' They agree that rationality is what history and society make it – that there is no overarching ahistorical structure (the Nature of Man, the laws of human behavior, the Moral Law, the Nature of Society) to be discovered. They share the Whewellian and Kuhnian notion of Galilean Science – as exemplifying the power of new vocabularies rather than offering the secret of scientific success. But Dewey emphasizes that this move 'beyond method' gives mankind an opportunity to grow up, to be free to make itself, rather than seeking direction from some imagined outside source (one of the ahistorical structures mentioned above). His experimentalism asks us to see knowledge-claims as proposals about what actions to try out next:

The elaborate systems of science are born not of reason but of impulses at first slight and flickering; impulses to handle, to move about, to hunt, to uncover, to mix things separated and divide things combined, to talk and to listen. Method is their effectual organization into continuous dispositions of inquiry, development, and testing. . . . Reason, the rational attitude, is the resulting disposition. . . . [1]

Foucault also moves beyond the traditional ideals of method and rationality as antecedent constraints upon inquiry, but he views this move as the Nietzschean realization that all knowledge-claims are moves in a power-game. 'We are subject to the production of truth through power, and we cannot exercise power except through the production of truth.[2]

Here we have two philosophers saying the same thing but putting a different spin on it. The same phenomenon is found in their respective predecessors. James and Nietzsche (as Arthur Danto has pointed out[3]) developed the same criticisms of traditional notions of truth, and the same 'pragmatic' (or 'perspectivalist') alternative. James jovially says that 'ideas become true just insofar as they help us to get into satisfactory relation with other parts of our experience,'[4] and Dewey follows this up when he says that 'rationality is the attainment of a working harmony among diverse desires.'[5] Nietzsche says that 'the criterion of truth resides in the enhancement of the feeling of power'[6] and that

[the] mistake of philosophy is that, instead of seeing logic and the categories of reasons as means for fixing up the world for utilitarian ends . . . one thinks that they give one a criterion of truth about *reality*.[7]

Foucault follows this up by saying that 'we should not imagine that the world presents us with a legible face . . . [we] must conceive discourse as a violence that we do to things.'[8] The arguments which James and Dewey on the one hand, and Nietzsche and Foucault on the other, present for these identical views are as similar as the tone of each is different. Neither pair has any arguments except the usual 'idealist' ones, familiar since Kant, against the notion of knowledge as a correspondence to nonrepresentations (rather than coherence among representations). These are the arguments in whose direction I gestured in the first section of this paper, when I said that all attempts to cash Galileo's metaphor of Nature's Own Language had failed. Since the cash-value of a philosophical conclusion is the pattern of argument around it, I do not think that we are going to find any *theoretical* differences which divide these two pairs of philosophers from each other.

Is the difference then *merely* one of tone – an ingenuous Anglo-Saxon pose as opposed to a self-dramatizing Continental one? The difference could be better put in terms of something like 'moral outlook.' One is reminded of the famous passage in Wittgenstein:

If good or bad willing changes the world, it can only change the limits of the world, not the facts; not the things that can be expressed in language. In brief, the world must thereby become quite another. It must so to speak wax or wane as a whole. The world of the happy is quite another than that of the unhappy.[9]

But again, 'good and bad willing,' 'happy and unhappy' are not right for the opposition we are trying to describe. 'Hopeful' and 'hopeless' are a bit better. Ian Hacking winds up a discussion of Foucault by saying:

'What is man?' asked Kant. 'Nothing,' says Foucault. 'For what then may we hope?' asks Kant. Does Foucault give the same *nothing* in reply? To think so is to misunderstand Foucault's reply to the question about Man. Foucault said that the concept Man is a fraud, not that you and I are as nothing. Likewise the concept Hope is all wrong. The hopes attributed to Marx and Rousseau are perhaps part of that very concept Man, and they are a sorry basis for optimism. Optimism, pessimism, nihilism and the like are all concepts that make sense only within the idea of a transcendental or enduring subject. Foucault is not in the least incoherent about all this. If we're not satisfied, it should not be because he is pessimistic. It is because he has given no surrogate for whatever it is that springs eternal in the human breast.[10]

What Foucault doesn't give us is what Dewey wanted to give us – a kind of hope which doesn't *need* reinforcement from 'the idea of a transcendental or enduring subject.' Dewey offered ways of using words like 'truth,' 'rationality,' 'progress,' 'freedom,' 'democracy,' 'culture,' 'art,' and the like which presupposed neither the ability to use the familiar vocabulary of what Foucault calls 'the classic age,' nor that of the nineteenth-century French intellectuals (the vocabulary of 'man and his doubles').

Foucault sees no middle ground, in thinking about the social sciences, between the 'classic' Galilean conception of 'behavioral sciences' and the French notion of *'sciences de l'homme.'* It was just such a middle ground that Dewey proposed, and which inspired the social sciences in America before the failure of nerve which turned them 'behavioral.' More generally, the recent reaction in favor of hermeneutical social sciences which I discussed earlier has taken for granted that if we don't want something like Parsons, we have to take something like Foucault; i.e., that overcoming the deficiencies of Weberian *Zweckrationalität* requires going all the way, repudiating the 'will to truth.' What Dewey suggested was that we keep the will to truth and the optimism that goes with it, but free them from the behaviorist notion that Behaviorese is Nature's Own Language *and* from the notion of man as 'transcendental or enduring subject.' For, in Dewey's hands, the will to truth is not the urge to dominate but the urge to create, to 'attain working harmony among diverse desires.'

This may sound too pat, too good to be true. I suggest that the reason we find it so is that we are convinced that liberalism requires the notion of a common human nature, or a common set of moral principles which binds us all, or some other descendent of the Christian notion of the Brotherhood of Man. So we have come to see liberal social hope – such as Dewey's – as inherently self-deceptive and philosophically naive. We think that, once we have freed ourselves from the various illusions which Nietzsche diagnosed, we *must* find ourselves all alone, without the sense of community which liberalism requires. Perhaps, as Hacking says, Nietzsche and Foucault are not saying that you and I are as nothing, but they do seem to hint that you and I together, as *we*, aren't much – that human solidarity goes when God and his doubles go. Man as Hegel thought of him, as the Incarnation of the Idea, doubtless does have to go. The proletariat as the Redeemed Form of Man has to go, too. But there seems no particular reason why, after dumping Marx, we have to keep on repeating all the nasty things about bourgeois liberation which he taught us to say. There is no inferential connection between the disappearance of the transcendental subject – of 'man' as something having a nature which society can repress or understand – and the disappearance of human solidarity. Bourgeois liberalism seems to me the best example of this solidarity we have yet achieved, and Deweyan pragmatism the best articulation of it.[11]

The burden of my argument here is that we should see Dewey as having already gone the route Foucault is traveling, and as having arrived at the point Foucault is still trying to reach – the point at which we can make philosophical and historical ('genealogical') reflection useful to those, in Foucault's phrase, 'whose fight is located in the fine meshes of the webs of power.'[12] Dewey spent his life trying to lend a hand in these little fights, and in the course of doing so he worked out the vocabulary and rhetoric of American 'pluralism.' This rhetoric made the first generation of American social scientists think of themselves as apostles of a new form of social life. Foucault does not, as far as I can see, do more than update Dewey by warning that the social scientists have often been, and are always likely to be, co-opted by the bad guys. Reading Foucault reinforces the disillusion which American intellectuals have suffered during the last few decades of watching the 'behavioralized' social sciences team up with the state.

The reason why it may appear that Foucault has something new and distinctive to add to Dewey is that he is riding the crest of a powerful but vaguely-defined movement which I have elsewhere[12] described as 'textualism' – the movement which suggests, as Foucault puts it at the end of *The Order of Things*, that 'Man is in the process of perishing as the being of language continues to shine ever brighter upon our horizon.'[13] Another reason is that Foucault is attempting to transform political discourse by seeing 'power' as not intrinsically repressive – because, roughly, there is no naturally good self to repress. But Dewey, it seems to me, had already grasped both points. Foucault's vision of discourse as a network of power-relations isn't very different from Dewey's vision of it as instrumental, as one element in the arsenal of tools people use for gratifying, synthesizing, and harmonizing their desires. Dewey had learned from Hegel what

Foucault learns from Nietzsche – that there is nothing much to 'man' except one more animal, until culture, the meshes of power, begin to shape him into something else. For Dewey too there is nothing Rousseauian to be 'repressed'; 'repression' and 'liberation' are just names for the sides of the structures of power we like and the sides we don't like. Once 'power' is freed from its connotation of 'repression,' then Foucault's 'structures of power' will not seem much different from Dewey's 'structures of culture.' 'Power' and 'culture' are equipollent indications of the social forces which make us more than animals – and which, when the bad guys take over, can turn us into something worse and more miserable than animals.

These remarks are not meant to downgrade Foucault – who seems to me one of the most interesting philosophers alive – but just to insist that we go slow about assuming that the discovery of things like 'discourse,' 'textuality,' 'speech-acts,' and the like have radically changed the philosophical scene. The current vogue of 'hermeneutics' is going to end soon, and badly, if we advertise these new notions as more than they are – namely, one more jargon which tries to get out from under some of the mistakes of the past. Dewey had his own jargon – popular at the time, but now a bit musty – for the same purpose. But the difference in jargon should not obscure the common aim. This is the attempt to free mankind from Nietzsche's 'longest lie,' the notion that outside the haphazard and perilous experiments we perform there lies something (God, Science, Knowledge, Rationality, or Truth) which will, if only we perform the correct rituals, step in to save us. Although Foucault and Dewey are trying to do the same thing, Dewey seems to me to have done it better, simply because his vocabulary allows room for unjustifiable hope, and an ungroundable but vital sense of human solidarity.

Notes

1 John Dewey, *Human Nature and Conduct* (New York, Modern Library, 1930), p. 196.
2 Michel Foucault, *Power/Knowledge* (Brighton, Harvester Books, 1980) p. 93).
3 Arthur Danto, *Nietzsche as Philosopher* (New York, Macmillan, 1965), chap. 3.
4 William James, *Pragmatism* (New York, Longmans Green, 1947), p. 58.
5 Dewey, *op. cit.*, p. 196.
6 Friedrich Nietzsche, *The Will to Power*, trans. Kaufmann (New York, Random House, 1967), p. 290.
7 Nietzsche, *Werke*, ed. Schlechta, III, p. 318.
8 Foucault, *The Archaeology of Knowledge* (New York, Harper and Row, 1972), p. 229.
9 Ludwig Wittgenstein, *Tractatus Logico-Philosophicus* 6.42.
10 Ian Hacking, review of Foucault's *Power/Knowledge*, in *New York Review of Books*, April 1981.
11 Dewey seems to me the twentieth-century counterpart of John Stuart Mill, whose attempt to synthesize Coleridge with Bentham is paralleled by Dewey's

attempt to synthesize Hegel with Mill himself. In a brilliant critique of liberalism, John Dunn describes Mill as attempting to combine the 'two possible radical intellectual strategies open to those who aspire to rescue liberalism as a coherent political option':

> One is to shrink liberalism to a more or less pragmatic and sociological doctrine about the relations between types of political and social order and the enjoyment of political liberties. The version of liberalism which embraces this option is usually today termed 'pluralism,' a conception . . . which is still in effect the official intellectual ideology of American society. The second possible radical strategy is simply to repudiate the claims of sociology, to take an epistemological position of such stark scepticism that the somewhat over-rated causal status of sociology can safely be viewed with limited scorn.
> (*Western Political Values in the Face of the Future* [Cambridge, Cambridge University Press, 1979], pp. 47–48)

Dunn thinks Mill's attempt to 'integrate intellectual traditions so deeply and explicitly inimical to one another' failed, and that modern pluralism fails also:

> Modern pluralism is thus at least sufficiently sociologically self-aware not to blanch from the insight that a liberal polity is the political form of bourgeois capitalist society. But the price which it has paid, so far pretty willingly, for this self-awareness, is the surrender of any plausible overall intellectual frame, uniting epistemology, psychology and political theory, which explains and celebrates the force of such political commitment.
> *(Ibid.,* p. 49)

My view is that such an overall intellectual frame was exactly what Dewey gave us, and that he did so precisely by carrying out Mill's combination of strategies. (For some links between Rawls [who is Dunn's favorite example of modern pluralism] and Dewey, see Rawls's Dewey Lectures, 'Kantian Constructivism in Moral Theory,' *Journal of Philosophy* LXXVII (1980): 515–72. Note esp. p. 542, on a conception of justice which swings free of religious, philosophical or moral doctrines, and *Weltanschauungen* generally. See also p. 519 for Rawls's repudiation of an 'epistemological problem,' and his doctrine of 'moral facts' as 'constructed.') Dunn seems to me right in saying that liberalism has little useful to say about contemporary global politics, but wrong in pinning the blame for this on its lack of a philosophical synthesis of the old, Kantian, unpragmatic sort. On my view, we should be more willing than we are to celebrate bourgeois capitalist society as the best polity actualized so far, while regretting that it is irrelevant to most of the problems of most of the population of the planet.

12 See Essay 9 in *Consequences of Pragmatism* [from which this extract is taken].

13 Foucault, *The Order of Things* (New York, Random House, 1973), p. 386.

49 Michel Foucault
From *The Archaeology of Knowledge*

The analysis of discursive formations, of positivities, and knowledge in their relations with epistemological figures and with the sciences is what has been called, to distinguish it from other possible forms of the history of the sciences, the analysis of the *episteme*. This episteme may be suspected of being something like a world-view, a slice of history common to all branches of knowledge, which imposes on each one the same norms and postulates, a general stage of reason, a certain structure of thought that the men of a particular period cannot escape – a great body of legislation written once and for all by some anonymous hand. By *episteme*, we mean, in fact, the total set of relations that unite, at a given period, the discursive practices that give rise to epistemological figures, sciences, and possibly formalized systems; the way in which, in each of these discursive formations, the transitions to epistemologization, scientificity, and formalization are situated and operate; the distribution of these thresholds, which may coincide, be subordinated to one another, or be separated by shifts in time; the lateral relations that may exist between epistemological figures or sciences in so far as they belong to neighbouring, but distinct, discursive practices. The episteme is not a form of knowledge (*connaissance*) or type of rationality which, crossing the boundaries of the most varied sciences, manifests the sovereign unity of a subject, a spirit, or a period; it is the totality of relations that can be discovered, for a given period, between the sciences when one analyses them at the level of discursive regularities.

The description of the episteme presents several essential characteristics therefore: it opens up an inexhaustible field and can never be closed; its aim is not to reconstitute the system of postulates that governs all the branches of knowledge (*connaissances*) of a given period, but to cover an indefinite field of relations. Moreover, the episteme is not a motionless figure that appeared one day with the mission of effacing that all preceded it: it is a constantly moving set of articulations, shifts, and coincidences that are established, only to give rise to others. As a set of relations between sciences, epistemological figures, positivities, and discursive practices, the episteme makes it possible to grasp the set of constraints and limitations which, at a given moment, are imposed on discourse: but this limitation is not the negative limitation that opposes knowledge (*connaissance*) to ignorance, reasoning to imagination, armed experience to fidelity to appearances, and fantasy to inferences and deductions; the episteme is not what

From Michel Foucault, *The Archaeology of Knowledge*, Tavistock, 1972, pp. 191–2, 194–5.

may be known at a given period, due account taken of inadequate techniques, mental attitudes, or the limitations imposed by tradition; it is what, in the positivity of discursive practices, makes possible the existence of epistemological figures and sciences. Lastly, we see that the analysis of the episteme is not a way of returning to the critical question ('given the existence of something like a science, what is its legitimacy?'); it is a questioning that accepts the fact of science only in order to ask the question what it is for that science to be a science. In the enigma of scientific discourse, what the analysis of the episteme questions is not its right to be a science, but the fact that it exists. And the point at which it separates itself off from all the philosophies of knowledge (*connaissance*) is that it relates this fact not to the authority of an original act of giving, which establishes in a transcendental subject the fact and the right, but to the processes of a historical practice.

It seems to me that one might also carry out an analysis of the same type on political knowledge. One would try to show whether the political behaviour of a society, a group, or a class is not shot through with a particular, describable discursive practice. This positivity would obviously not coincide either with the political theories of the period or with economic determinations: it would define the element in politics that can become an object of enunciation, the forms that this enunciation may take, the concepts that are employed in it, and the strategic choices that are made in it. Instead of analysing this knowledge – which is always possible – in the direction of the episteme that it can give rise to, one would analyse it in the direction of behaviour, struggles, conflicts, decisions, and tactics. One would thus reveal a body of political knowledge that is not some kind of secondary theorizing about practice, nor the application of theory. Since it is regularly formed by a discursive practice that is deployed among other practices and is articulated upon them, it is not an expression that more or less adequately 'reflects' a number of 'objective data' or real practices. It is inscribed, from the outset, in the field of different practices in which it finds its specificity, its functions, and its network of dependences. If such a description were possible, there would be no need of course to pass through the authority of an individual or collective consciousness in order to grasp the place of articulation of a political practice and theory; there would be no need to try to discover to what extent this consciousness may, on the one hand, express silent conditions, and, on the other, show that it is susceptible to theoretical truths; one would not need to pose the psychological problem of an act of consciousness (*prise de conscience*); instead, one would analyse the formation and transformations of a body of knowledge. The question, for example, would not be to determine from what moment a revolutionary consciousness appears, nor the respective roles of economic conditions and theoretical elucidations in the genesis of this consciousness; it would not attempt to retrace the general, and exemplary, biography of revolutionary man, or to find the origins of his project; but it would try to explain the formation of a discursive practice and a body of revolutionary knowledge that are expressed in behaviour and strategies, which give rise to a theory of society, and which operate the interference and mutual transformation of that behaviour and those strategies.

To the questions posed above – Is archaeology concerned only with sciences? Is it always an analysis of scientific discourse? – we can now give a reply, in each case in the negative. What archaeology tries to describe is not the specific structure of science, but the very different domain of *knowledge*. Moreover, although it is concerned with knowledge in its relation to epistemological figures and the sciences, it may also question knowledge in a different direction and describe it in a different set of relations. The orientation towards the episteme has been the only one to be explored so far. The reason for this is that, because of a gradient that no doubt characterizes our cultures, discursive formations are constantly becoming epistemologized. It is by questioning the sciences, their history, their strange unity, their dispersion, and their ruptures, that the domain of positivities was able to appear; it is in the interstice of scientific discourses that we were able to grasp the play of discursive formations. It is hardly surprising, therefore, that the most fruitful region, the one most open to archaeological description, should have been that 'Classical' age, which from the Renaissance to the nineteenth century saw the epistemologization of so many positivities; nor is it surprising that the discursive formations and specific regularities of knowledge are outlined precisely where the levels of scientificity and formalization were most difficult to attain. But that was no more than a preferential point of attack; it is not, for archaeology, an obligatory domain.

PHILOSOPHIES OF SCIENCE AND CRITIQUES OF METHOD

50 Werner Heisenberg
'Changes in the Foundations of Exact Science'

These special questions of the theory of perception are already connected with the second great problem facing physical theory: that of giving information about the more general interrelations of nature, of which we, ourselves, are part. Science cannot evade this issue if it is to remain true to itself. We need only recollect here, that some of the first representatives of early natural philosophy in antiquity were at the same time centres of religious movements. It is to be expected that the present changes in the scientific concept of the universe will exert their influence upon the wider fields of the world of ideas, when we consider that the changes at the end of the Renaissance transformed the cultural life of the succeeding epochs. The very recent transformations, though not comparable with those at the beginning of modern times, may nevertheless suffice to replace the views, which we may call the scientific concepts of the universe of the nineteenth century, by something new and different. I should like to elaborate this point a little. The scientific views which have become the axiomatic basis of all scientific investigation during the last century, have only assumed gradually, since the beginning of modern times, the rigid forms familiar to us. It was a fundamentally new discovery which gave scientific development its new power. A whole field of reality was found, altogether beyond the appreciation of the Middle Ages during which supernatural revelation was the centre of all thought. Man came up against that objective reality which was free from all doubt and which could be experienced by observation and experiment. The attempt to separate the general from the scientific in objective reality had become the subject of human endeavour, and was a natural consequence of this discovery. A group of axioms emerged from the mass of specific results as the real nucleus of the new science and appeared, as though of a necessity, to be at the root of all scientific investigations. The influence of this new reality was soon exerted in philosophy also, and the foundations of the new understanding of nature appeared as parts of great philosophic systems. Just as, in antiquity, Geometry served as an example of consistency to philosophic thought, so,

From *Philosophic Problems of Nuclear Science*, Faber, 1952, pp. 21–5.

under the influence of science, were born new philosophic systems. And just as in science, one or several truths recognized as unimpeachable were made the basis of all further deductions, so the same system was used in philosophy (the systems of Descartes and Spinoza will serve as examples). Even Kant's philosophy, intended as a critique of premature dogmatization in scientific concepts, could not prevent the torpescence of the scientific concept of the universe – it may even be said that it encouraged it. For, once the main reasoning of classical physics had been accepted as the *a priori* of physical investigations, the belief arose, through an obvious though false extrapolation, that it was absolute, i.e. valid for all time, and could never be modified as a result of new experiences.

Thus was formed the solid framework of classical physics, and thus arose the conception of a material world in time and space comparable to a machine which, once set in motion, continues to run, governed by immutable laws. The fact that this machine as well as the whole of science were themselves only products of the human mind appeared irrelevant and of no consequence for an understanding of nature. Only the extension of scientific methods of thought far beyond their legitimate limits of application led to the much deplored division in the world of ideas between the field of science on the one side and the fields of religion and art on the other. Exact science, convinced of the general validity and applicability of scientific principles, interfered in other spheres of intellectual life and thus threatened its own status. Since, however, its power was insufficient to give full expression to these other fields, almost impassable frontiers arose, as in self-defence, between them and science.

The scientific concept of the universe of the nineteenth century, born under these circumstances, is called rational, since its centre, classical physics, can be built up from a small number of axioms capable of rational analysis, and since it rests on belief in the possibility of a rational analysis of all reality. It must, however, be stressed that the hope of gaining an understanding of the whole world from a small part of it can never be supported rationally. Now, the changes in the foundations of science forced upon us by nature in such a marvellous way through atomic phenomena leave classical physics untouched, but they show that scientific systems – like classical mechanics or other parts of classical physics – must always be complete in order to be correct. Hence the extension of scientific investigation to new fields of experience does not mean the application of previously known laws to new subjects. I should like to return again to the analogy I used before, between the discovery of the spherical shape of the earth and the conclusions of modern physics. As long as the earth was taken to be a large disc, there could be hope that the man who had travelled to the end of the world would be able to explain all the things on it. This hope was shattered for ever with the discoveries of Columbus, though they only changed our views about certain parts previously unknown.

Now that we know all our journeying can only bring us back to our starting point, we realize that we are unable to reach full understanding no matter how far we travel. The infinity of the universe lies outside this path. In quite a similar way modern physics has shown that the structure of classical physics – as that of modern physics – is complete in itself. Classical physics extends just as far as the conceptions which form its basis can be applied. But these conceptions already fail us when applied to the processes of nuclear physics, and much more so in the case of all fields of science which are even further removed from classical physics. Thus the hope of understanding all aspects of intellectual life on the principles of classical physics is no more justified than the hope of the traveller who believes he will have obtained the answer to all problems once he has journeyed to the end of the world.

Yet the misunderstanding, that the transformations in exact science have brought to light certain limits to the application of rational thinking, must immediately be countered. A narrower field of application is given to certain ways of thought only, and not to rational thought in general. The discovery that the earth is not the world, but only a small and discrete part of the world, has enabled us to relegate to its proper position the illusory 'end of the world' concept, and instead to map the whole surface of the earth accurately. In a similar way modern physics has purged classical physics of its arbitrary belief in its unlimited application. It has shown that some parts of our science, e.g. mechanics, electricity, quantum theory, present scientific systems complete in themselves, rational, and capable of complete investigation. They state their respective natural laws, probably correctly, for all time. The essence of this statement is given by the phrase 'completeness in itself' (*Abgeschlössenheit*). The most important new result of nuclear physics was the recognition of the possibility of applying quite different types of natural laws, without contradiction, to one and the same physical event. This is due to the fact that within a system of laws which are based on certain fundamental ideas only certain quite definite ways of asking questions make sense, and thus, that such a system is separated from others which allow different questions to be put. Thus, the transition in science from previously investigated fields of experience to new ones will never consist simply of the application of already known laws to these new fields. On the contrary, a really new field of experience will always lead to the crystallization of a new system of scientific concepts and laws. They will be no less capable of rational analysis than the old ones but their nature will be fundamentally different. It is for this reason that modern physics adopts an attitude very different from classical physics towards all those fields not yet included in its investigations. . . .

Thus contemporary science, to-day much more than at any previous time, has been forced by nature herself to pose again the old question of the possibility of comprehending reality by mental processes, and to answer it in a slightly different way. Previously the example of science could lead to philosophic systems which assumed a certain truth – like the 'cogito, ergo sum' of Descartes – as the starting point from which all questions of 'Weltanschauung' could be attacked. But now nature, through the medium of modern physics, has reminded us very clearly that we should never hope for such a firm basis for the comprehension of the whole field of 'things perceptible'. Rather when faced with essentially new intellectual challenges should we continually follow the example of Columbus, who possessed the courage to leave the known world in the almost insane hope of finding land again beyond the sea.

---

51 Karl Popper
From *Objective Knowledge*

The commonsense problem of induction

The commonsense theory of knowledge (which I have also dubbed 'the bucket theory of the mind') is the theory most famous in the form of the assertion that 'there is nothing in our intellect which has not entered it through the senses'. (I have tried to show that this view was first formulated by Parmenides – in a satirical vein: Most mortals have nothing in their erring intellect unless it got there through their erring senses.[1])

However, we do have *expectations*, and we strongly *believe in certain regularities* (laws of nature, theories). This leads to the commonsense problem of induction (which I will call '*Cs*'):

Cs How can these expectations and beliefs have arisen?

The commonsense answer is: Through *repeated* observations made in the past: we believe that the sun will rise tomorrow because it has done so in the past.

In the commonsense view it is simply taken for granted (without any problems being raised) that our belief in regularities is justified by those repeated observations which are responsible for its genesis. (Genesis *cum* justification – both due to repetition – is what philosophers since Aristotle and Cicero have called '*epagōgē*' or '*induction*'.)[2]

From Karl Popper, *Objective Knowledge*, Clarendon, Oxford, 1972, pp. 3–5, 7, 13–5, 20, 23–5, 29–31.

Hume's two problems of induction

Hume was interested in the status of human *knowledge* or, as he might have said, in the question of whether any of our beliefs – and which of them – can be *justified* by sufficient reasons.[3]

He raised two problems: a logical problem (H_L) and a psychological problem (H_{Ps}). One of the important points is that his two answers to these two problems in some way clash with each other.

Hume's logical problem is:[4]

H_L Are we justified in reasoning from [repeated] instances of which we have experience to other instances [conclusions] of which we have no experience?

Hume's answer to H_L is: No, however great the number of repetitions.

Hume also showed that the logical situation remained *exactly the same* if in H_L the word *'probable'* is inserted before 'conclusions', or if the words 'to instances' are replaced by 'to the *probability* of instances'.

Hume's psychological problem is:[5]

H_{Ps} Why, nevertheless, do all reasonable people expect, and *believe*, that instances of which they have no experience will conform to those of which they have experience? That is, Why do we have expectations in which we have great confidence?

Hume's answer to H_{Ps} is: Because of 'custom or habit'; that is, because we are conditioned, by *repetitions* and by the mechanism of the association of ideas; a mechanism without which, Hume says, we could hardly survive.

Important consequences of Hume's results

By these results Hume himself – one of the most rational minds ever – was turned into a sceptic and, at the same time, into a believer: a believer in an irrationalist epistemology. His result that repetition has no power whatever as an argument, although it dominates our cognitive life or our 'understanding', led him to the conclusion that argument or reason plays only a minor role in our understanding. Our 'knowledge' is unmasked as being not only of the nature of belief, but of rationally indefensible belief – of *an irrational faith.*[6]

. . . Russell says about Hume's treatment of induction: 'Hume's philosophy . . . represents the bankruptcy of eighteenth-century reasonableness' and, 'It is therefore important to discover whether there is any answer to Hume within a philosophy that is wholly or mainly *empirical*. If not, *there is no intellectual difference between sanity and insanity.* The lunatic who believes that he is a poached egg is to be condemned solely on the ground that he is in a minority. . . . '

Russell goes on to assert that if induction (or the principle of induction) is rejected, 'every attempt to arrive at general scientific laws from particular observations is fallacious, and Hume's scepticism is inescapable for an empiricist'.[7]

Thus Russell stresses the clash between Hume's answer to H_L and (a) rationality, (b) empiricism, and (c) scientific procedures.

I formulated Hume's logical problem of induction as follows:

L_1 Can the claim that an explanatory universal theory is true be justified by 'empirical reasons'; that is, by assuming the truth of certain test statements or observation statements (which, it may be said, are 'based on experience')?

My answer to the problem is the same as Hume's: No, it cannot; no number of true test statements would justify the claim that an explanatory universal theory is true.[8]

But there is a second logical problem, L_2, which is a generalization of L_1. It is obtained from L_1 merely by replacing the words 'is true' by the words 'is true or that it is false':

L_2 Can the claim that an explanatory universal theory is true or that it is false be justified by 'empirical reasons'; that is, can the assumption of the truth of test statements justify either the claim that a universal theory is true or the claim that it is false?

To this problem, my answer is positive: Yes, *the assumption of the truth of test statements sometimes allows us to justify the claim that an explanatory universal theory is false.*

The theoretician, I will assume, is essentially interested in truth, and especially in finding true theories. But when he has fully digested the fact that we can never justify empirically – that is, by test statements – the claim that a scientific theory is true, and that we are therefore at best always faced with the question of preferring, tentatively, some guesses to others, then he may consider, from the point of view of a seeker for true theories, the questions: *What principles of preference should we adopt? Are some theories 'better' than others?*

The theoretician will for several reasons be interested in non-refuted theories, especially because some of them *may* be true. He will prefer a non-refuted theory to a refuted one, provided it explains the successes and failures of the refuted theory.

But the new theory may, like all non-refuted theories, be false. The theoretician will therefore try his best to detect any false theory among the set of non-refuted competitors; he will try to 'catch' it. That is, he will, with respect to any given non-refuted theory, try to think of cases or situations in which it is likely to fail, if it is false. Thus he will try to construct *severe* tests, and *crucial* test situations. This will amount to the construction of a falsifying law; that is, a law which may perhaps be of such a low level of universality that it may not be able to explain the successes of the theory to be tested, but which will, nevertheless, suggest a *crucial experiment*: an experiment which may refute, depending on its outcome, either the theory to be tested or the falsifying theory.

By this method of elimination, we may hit upon a true theory. But in no case can the method *establish* its truth, even if it is true; for the number of *possibly* true theories remains infinite, at any time and after any number of crucial tests. (This is another way of stating Hume's negative result.) The actually proposed theories will, of course, be finite in number; and it may well happen that we refute all of them, and cannot think of a new one.

. . . The fundamental difference between my approach and the approach for which I long ago introduced the label 'inductivist' is that I lay stress on *negative arguments*, such as negative instances or counter-examples, refutations, and attempted refutations – in short, criticism – while the inductivist lays stress on *'positive instances'*, from which he draws 'non-demonstrative inferences',[9] and which he hopes will guarantee the *'reliability'* of the conclusions of these inferences. In my view, all that can possibly be *'positive'* in our scientific knowledge is positive *only* in so far as certain theories are, at a certain moment of time, preferred to others in the light of our *critical* discussion which consists of attempted refutations, including empirical tests. Thus even what may be called 'positive' is so *only* with respect to *negative methods*.

Background to my restatement of Hume's psychological problem of induction

Historically, I found my new solution to Hume's psychological problem of induction before my solution to the logical problem: it was here that I first noticed that induction – the formation of a belief by repetition – is a myth. It was first in animals and children, but later also in adults, that I observed the immensely powerful *need for regularity* – the need which makes them seek for regularities; which makes them sometimes experience regularities even where there are none; which makes them cling to their expectations dogmatically; and which makes them unhappy and may drive them to despair and to the verge of madness if certain assumed regularities break down. When Kant said that our intellect imposes its laws upon nature, he was right – except that he did not notice how often our intellect fails in the attempt: the regularities we try to impose are *psychologically a priori*, but there is not the slightest reason to assume that they are *a priori valid*, as Kant thought. The need to try to impose such regularities upon our environment is, clearly, inborn, and based on drives, or instincts. There is the general need for a world that conforms to our expectations; and there are many more specific needs, for example the need for regular social response, or the need for learning a language with rules for descriptive (and other) statements. This led me first to the conclusion that expectations may arise without, or before, any repetition; and later to a logical analysis which showed that they could not arise otherwise because repetition presupposes similarity, and similarity presupposes a point of view – a theory, or an expectation.

Thus I decided that Hume's inductive theory of the formation of beliefs could not possibly be true, *for logical reasons*. This led me to see that logical considerations may be transferred to psychological considerations; and it led me further to the heuristic conjecture that, quite generally, what holds in logic also holds – provided it is properly transferred – in psychology. (This heuristic principle is what I now call the 'principle of transference'.) I suppose it was largely this result which made me give up psychology and turn to the logic of discovery.

I used to take pride in the fact that I am not a belief philosopher: I am primarily interested in ideas, in theories, and I find it comparatively unimportant whether or not anybody 'believes' in them. And I suspect that the interest of philosophers in belief results from that mistaken philosophy which I call 'inductivism'. They are theorists of knowledge, and starting from subjective experiences they fail to distinguish between objective and subjective knowledge. This leads them to believe in belief as the genus of which knowledge is a species ('justification' or perhaps a 'criterion of truth' such as clarity and distinctness, or vivacity,[10] or 'sufficient reason', providing the specific difference).

This is why, like E.M. Forster, I do not believe in belief.

I saw that what has to be given up is the *quest for justification*, in the sense of the justification of the claim that a theory is true. *All theories are hypotheses*; all *may* be overthrown.

This led me to the view that all languages are theory-impregnated; which meant, of course, a radical revision of empiricism. It also made me look upon the critical attitude as characteristic of the rational attitude; and it led me to see the significance of the argumentative (or critical) function of language; to the idea of deductive logic as the organon of criticism, and to stressing the retransmission of falsity from the conclusion to the premises (a corollary of the transmission of truth from the premises to the conclusion). And it further led me to realize that only a *formulated* theory (in contradistinction to a believed theory) can be objective, and to the idea that it is this formulation or objectivity that makes criticism possible.

Notes

1 *See* my *Conjectures and Refutations* (C. & R.) Addendum 8 to the third edn., 1969, esp. pp. 408–12.
2 Cicero, *Topica*, X. 42; cp. *De inventione*, Book I; xxxi. 51 to xxxv. 61.

3 *See* David Hume, *Enquiry Concerning Human Understanding*, ed. L.A. Selby-Bigge, Oxford, 1927, Section V, Part I, p. 46. (Cp. *C. & R.*, p. 21.)

4 Hume, *Treatise on Human Nature*, ed. Selby-Bigge, Oxford, 1888, 1960, Book I, Part III, section vi, p. 91; Book I, Part III, section xii, p. 139. *See also* Kant, *Prolegomena*, pp. 14 f., where he calls the problem of the existence of *a priori* valid statements 'Hume's problem'. To my knowledge I was the first to call the problem of induction 'Hume's problem'; though of course there may have been others. I did so in 'Ein Kriterium des empirischen Charakters theoretischer Systeme', *Erkenntnis*, 3, 1933, pp. 426 f., and in *Logik der Forschung* (Vienna, Julius Springer Verlag, 1934), section 4, p. 7, where I wrote: 'If, following Kant, we call the problem of induction "Hume's problem", we might call the problem of demarcation "Kant's problem".' This very brief remark of mine (supported by a few remarks such as on p. 29 of *On the Logic of Scientific Discovery* (London, Hutchinson, 1959), that Kant took the principle of induction as '*a priori* valid') contained hints of an important historical interpretation of the relationship between Kant, Hume, and the problem of induction.

5 *See Treatise*, pp. 91, 139.

6 Since Hume, many disappointed inductivists have become irrationalists (just as have many disappointed Marxists).

7 The quotations are from Bertrand Russell, *A History of Western Philosophy*, London, 1946, pp. 698 f. (The italics are mine.)

8 An explanatory theory goes essentially beyond even an infinity of universal test statements; even a law of low universality does so.

9 C.G. Hempel, 'Recent Problems of Induction', in R.G. Colodny (ed.), *Mind and Cosmos*, Pittsburgh University Press, 1966, p. 112.

10 *See* Hume, *Treatise*, p. 265.

52 Thomas Kuhn
The Structure of Scientific Revolutions

We have already seen several reasons why the proponents of competing paradigms must fail to make complete contact with each other's viewpoints. Collectively these reasons have been described as the incommensurability of the pre- and postrevolutionary normal-scientific traditions, and we need only recapitulate them briefly here. In the first place, the proponents of competing paradigms will often disagree about the list of problems that any candidate for paradigm must resolve. Their standards or

From Thomas Kuhn, *The Structure of Scientific Revolutions*, 2nd ed., University of Chicago Press, 1970, pp. 148–52.

their definitions of science are not the same. Must a theory of motion explain the cause of the attractive forces between particles of matter or may it simply note the existence of such forces? Newton's dynamics was widely rejected because, unlike both Aristotle's and Descartes's theories, it implied the latter answer to the question. When Newton's theory had been accepted, a question was therefore banished from science. That question, however, was one that general relativity may proudly claim to have solved. Or again, as disseminated in the nineteenth century, Lavoisier's chemical theory inhibited chemists from asking why the metals were so much alike, a question that phlogistic chemistry had both asked and answered. The transition to Lavoisier's paradigm had, like the transition to Newton's, meant a loss not only of a permissible question but of an achieved solution. That loss was not, however, permanent either. In the twentieth century questions about the qualities of chemical substances have entered science again, together with some answers to them.

More is involved, however, than the incommensurability of standards. Since new paradigms are born from old ones, they ordinarily incorporate much of the vocabulary and apparatus, both conceptual and manipulative, that the traditional paradigm had previously employed. But they seldom employ these borrowed elements in quite the traditional way. Within the new paradigm, old terms, concepts, and experiments fall into new relationships one with the other. The inevitable result is what we must call, though the term is not quite right, a misunderstanding between the two competing schools. The laymen who scoffed at Einstein's general theory of relativity because space could not be 'curved' – it was not that sort of thing – were not simply wrong or mistaken. Nor were the mathematicians, physicists, and philosophers who tried to develop a Euclidean version of Einstein's theory.[1] What had previously been meant by space was necessarily flat, homogeneous, isotropic, and unaffected by the presence of matter. If it had not been, Newtonian physics would not have worked. To make the transition to Einstein's universe, the whole conceptual web whose strands are space, time, matter, force, and so on, had to be shifted and laid down again on nature whole. Only men who had together undergone or failed to undergo that transformation would be able to discover precisely what they agreed or disagreed about. Communication across the revolutionary divide is inevitably partial. Consider, for another example, the men who called Copernicus mad because he proclaimed that the earth moved. They were not either just wrong or quite wrong. Part of what they meant by 'earth' was fixed position. Their earth, at least, could not be moved. Correspondingly, Copernicus' innovation was not simply to move the earth. Rather, it was a whole new way of regarding the problems of physics and astronomy, one that necessarily changed the meaning of both 'earth' and 'motion.'[2] Without those changes the concept of a moving earth was mad. On the other hand, once they had been made and understood, both

Descartes and Huyghens could realize that the earth's motion was a question with no content for science.[3]

These examples point to the third and most fundamental aspect of the incommensurability of competing paradigms. In a sense that I am unable to explicate further, the proponents of competing paradigms practice their trades in different worlds. One contains constrained bodies that fall slowly, the other pendulums that repeat their motions again and again. In one, solutions are compounds, in the other mixtures. One is embedded in a flat, the other in a curved, matrix of space. Practicing in different worlds, the two groups of scientists see different things when they look from the same point in the same direction. Again, that is not to say that they can see anything they please. Both are looking at the world, and what they look at has not changed. But in some areas they see different things, and they see them in different relations one to the other. That is why a law that cannot even be demonstrated to one group of scientists may occasionally seem intuitively obvious to another. Equally, it is why, before they can hope to communicate fully, one group or the other must experience the conversion that we have been calling a paradigm shift. Just because it is a transition between incommensurables, the transition between competing paradigms cannot be made a step at a time, forced by logic and neutral experience. Like the gestalt switch, it must occur all at once (though not necessarily in an instant) or not at all.

How, then, are scientists brought to make this transposition? Part of the answer is that they are very often not. Copernicanism made few converts for almost a century after Copernicus' death. Newton's work was not generally accepted, particularly on the Continent, for more than half a century after the *Principia* appeared.[4] Priestley never accepted the oxygen theory, nor Lord Kelvin the electromagnetic theory, and so on. The difficulties of conversion have often been noted by scientists themselves. Darwin, in a particularly perceptive passage at the end of his *Origin of Species*, wrote: 'Although I am fully convinced of the truth of the views given in this volume . . . , I by no means expect to convince experienced naturalists whose minds are stocked with a multitude of facts all viewed, during a long course of years, from a point of view directly opposite to mine. . . . [B]ut I look with confidence to the future, – to young and rising naturalists, who will be able to view both sides of the question with impartiality.'[5] And Max Planck, surveying his own career in his *Scientific Autobiography*, sadly remarked that 'a new scientific truth does not triumph by convincing its opponents and making them see the light, but rather because its opponents eventually die, and a new generation grows up that is familiar with it.'[6]

These facts and others like them are too commonly known to need further emphasis. But they do need re-evaluation. In the past they have most often been taken to indicate that scientists, being only human, cannot always admit their errors, even when confronted with strict proof. I would argue, rather, that in these matters neither proof nor error is at issue. The transfer of allegiance from paradigm to paradigm is a conversion experience that cannot be forced. Lifelong resistance, particularly from those whose productive careers have committed them to an older tradition of normal science, is not a violation of scientific standards but an index to the nature of scientific research itself. The source of resistance is the assurance that the older paradigm will ultimately solve all its problems, that nature can be shoved into the box the paradigm provides. Inevitably, at times of revolution, that assurance seems stubborn and pigheaded as indeed it sometimes becomes. But it is also something more. That same assurance is what makes normal or puzzle-solving science possible. And it is only through normal science that the professional community of scientists succeeds, first, in exploiting the potential scope and precision of the older paradigm and, then, in isolating the difficulty through the study of which a new paradigm may emerge.

Notes

1 For lay reactions to the concept of curved space, *see* Philipp Frank, *Einstein, His Life and Times*, trans. and ed. G. Rosen and S. Kusaka (New York, 1947), pp. 142–6. For a few of the attempts to preserve the gains of general relativity within a Euclidean space, *see* C. Nordmann, *Einstein and the Universe*, trans. J. McCabe (New York, 1922), chap. ix.

2 T.S. Kuhn, *The Copernican Revolution* (Cambridge, Mass., 1957), chaps. iii, iv, and vii. The extent to which heliocentrism was more than a strictly astronomical issue is a major theme of the entire book.

3 Max Jammer, *Concepts of Space* (Cambridge, Mass., 1954), pp. 118–24.

4 I.B. Cohen, *Franklin and Newton: An Inquiry into Speculative Newtonian Experimental Science and Franklin's Work in Electricity as an Example Thereof* (Philadelphia, 1956), pp. 93–4.

5 Charles Darwin, *On the Origin of Species* . . . (authorized edition from 6th English ed.; New York, 1889), II, 295–6.

6 Max Planck, *Scientific Autobiography and Other Papers*, trans. F. Gaynor (New York, 1949), pp. 33–4.

53   Paul Feyerabend
From *Against Method*

Introduction

Ordnung ist heutzutage meistens dort,
wo nichts ist.
Es ist eine Mangelerscheinung.

Brecht

Science is an essentially anarchistic enterprise: theoretical anarchism is more humanitarian and more likely to encourage progress than its law-and-order alternatives.

The following essay is written in the conviction that *anarchism*, while perhaps not the most attractive *political* philosophy, is certainly excellent medicine for *epistemology*, and for the *philosophy of science*.

The reason is not difficult to find.

'History generally, and the history of revolutions in particular, is always richer in content, more varied, more many-sided, more lively and subtle than even' the best historian and the best methodologist can imagine.[1] History is full of 'accidents and conjunctures and curious juxtapositions of events'[2] and it demonstrates to us the 'complexity of human change and the unpredictable character of the ultimate consequences of any given act or decision of men'.[3] Are we really to believe that the naive and simple-minded rules which methodologists take as their guide are capable of accounting for such a 'maze of interactions'?[4] And is it not clear that successful *participation* in a process of this kind is possible only for a ruthless opportunist who is not tied to any particular philosophy and who adopts whatever procedure seems to fit the occasion?

This is indeed the conclusion that has been drawn by intelligent and thoughtful observers. 'Two very important practical conclusions follow from this [character of the historical process],' writes Lenin,[5] continuing the passage from which I have just quoted. 'First, that in order to fulfil its task, the revolutionary class [i.e. the class of those who want to change either a part of society such as science, or society as whole] must be able to master *all* forms or aspects of social activity without exception [it must be able to understand, and to apply, not only one particular methodology, but any methodology, and any variation thereof it can imagine] . . . ; second, [it]

From Paul Feyerabend, *Against Method*, Verso, 1978, pp. 17–22.

must be ready to pass from one to another in the quickest and most unexpected manner.' 'The external conditions,' writes Einstein,[6] 'which are set for [the scientist] by the facts of experience do not permit him to let himself be too much restricted, in the construction of his conceptual world, by the adherence to an epistemological system. He therefore must appear to the systematic epistemologist as a type of unscrupulous opportunist. . . .' A complex medium containing surprising and unforeseen developments demands complex procedures and defies analysis on the basis of rules which have been set up in advance and without regard to the ever-changing conditions of history.

Now it is, of course, possible to simplify the medium in which a scientist works by simplifying its main actors. The history of science, after all, does not just consist of facts and conclusions drawn from facts. It also contains ideas, interpretations of facts, problems created by conflicting interpretations, mistakes, and so on. On closer analysis we even find that science knows no 'bare facts' at all but that the 'facts' that enter our knowledge are already viewed in a certain way and are, therefore, essentially ideational. This being the case, the history of science will be as complex, chaotic, full of mistakes, and entertaining as the ideas it contains, and these ideas in turn will be as complex, chaotic, full of mistakes, and entertaining as are the minds of those who invented them. Conversely, a little brainwashing will go a long way in making the history of science duller, simpler, more uniform, more 'objective' and more easily accessible to treatment by strict and unchangeable rules.

Scientific education as we know it today has precisely this aim. It simplifies 'science' by simplifying its participants: first, a domain of research is defined. The domain is separated from the rest of history (physics, for example, is separated from metaphysics and from theology) and given a 'logic' of its own. A thorough training in such a 'logic' then conditions those working in the domain; it makes *their actions* more uniform and it freezes large parts of the *historical process* as well. Stable 'facts' arise and persevere despite the vicissitudes of history. An essential part of the training that makes such facts appear consists in the attempt to inhibit intuitions that might lead to a blurring of boundaries. A person's religion, for example, or his metaphysics, or his sense of humour (his *natural* sense of humour and not the inbred and always rather nasty kind of jocularity one finds in specialized professions) must not have the slightest connection with his scientific activity. His imagination is restrained, and even his language ceases to be his own.[7] This is again reflected in the nature of scientific 'facts' which are experienced as being independent of opinion, belief, and cultural background.

It is thus *possible* to create a tradition that is held together by strict rules, and that is also successful to some extent. But is it *desirable* to support such a tradition to the exclusion of everything else? Should we transfer to it the sole rights for dealing in knowledge, so that any result that has been obtained by other methods is at once ruled out of court? This is the question I intend to ask in the present essay. And to this question my answer will be a firm and resounding NO.

There are two reasons why such an answer seems to be appropriate. The first reason is that the world which we want to explore is a largely unknown entity. We must, therefore, keep our options open and we must not restrict ourselves in advance. Epistemological prescriptions may look splendid when compared with other epistemological prescriptions, or with general principles – but who can guarantee that they are the best way to discover, not just a few isolated 'facts', but also some deep-lying secrets of nature? The second reason is that a scientific education as described above (and as practised in our schools) cannot be reconciled with a humanitarian attitude. It is in conflict 'with the cultivation of individuality which alone produces, or can produce, well-developed human beings';[8] it 'maims by compression, like a Chinese lady's foot, every part of human nature which stands out prominently, and tends to make a person markedly different in outline'[9] from the ideals of rationality that happen to be fashionable in science, or in the philosophy of science. The attempt to increase liberty, to lead a full and rewarding life, and the corresponding attempt to discover the secrets of nature and of man entails, therefore, the rejection of all universal standards and of all rigid traditions. (Naturally, it also entails the rejection of a large part of contemporary science.)

It is surprising to see how rarely the stultifying effect of 'the Laws of Reason' or of scientific practice is examined by professional anarchists. Professional anarchists oppose any kind of restriction and they demand that the individual be permitted to develop freely, unhampered by laws, duties or obligations. And yet they swallow without protest all the severe standards which scientists and logicians impose upon research and upon any kind of knowledge-creating and knowledge-changing activity. Occasionally, the laws of scientific method, or what are thought to be the laws of scientific method by a particular writer, are even integrated into anarchism itself. 'Anarchism is a world concept based upon a mechanical explanation of all phenomena,' writes Kropotkin.[10] 'Its method of investigation is that of the exact natural sciences . . . the method of induction and deduction.' 'It is not so clear,' writes a modern 'radical' professor at Columbia,[11] 'that scientific research demands an absolute freedom of speech and debate. Rather the evidence suggests that certain kinds of unfreedom place no obstacle in the way of science. . . .'

There are certainly some people to whom this is 'not so clear'. Let us, therefore, start with our outline of an anarchistic methodology and a corresponding anarchistic science.[12] There is no need to fear that the diminished concern for law and order in science and society that characterizes an anarchism of this kind will lead to chaos. The human nervous system is too well organized for that.[13] There may, of course, come a time when it will be necessary to give reason a temporary advantage and when it will be wise to defend its rules to the exclusion of everything else. I do not think that we are living in such a time today.

Notes

1 'History as a whole, and the history of revolutions in particular, is always richer in content, more varied, more multiform, more lively and ingenious than is imagined by even the best parties, the most conscious vanguards of the most advanced classes' (V.I. Lenin, 'Left-Wing Communism – An Infantile Disorder', *Selected Works*, Vol. 3, London, 1967, p. 401). Lenin is addressing parties and revolutionary vanguards rather than scientists and methodologists; the lesson, however, is the same. Cf. footnote 5.

2 Herbert Butterfield, *The Whig Interpretation of History*, New York, 1965, p. 66.

3 ibid., p. 21.

4 ibid., p. 25, cf. Hegel, *Philosophie der Geschichte, Werke*, Vol. 9, ed. Edward Gans, Berlin, 1837, p. 9: 'But what experience and history teach us is this, that nations and governments have never learned anything from history, or acted according to rules that might have derived from it. Every period has such peculiar circumstances, is in such an individual state, that decisions will have to be made, and decisions *can* only be made, in it and out of it.' – 'Very clever'; 'shrewd and very clever'; 'NB' writes Lenin in his marginal notes to this passage. (*Collected Works*, Vol. 38, London, 1961, p. 307.)

5 ibid. We see here very clearly how a few substitutions can turn a political lesson into a lesson for *methodology*. This is not at all surprising. Methodology and politics are both means for moving from one historical stage to another. The only difference is that the standard methodologies disregard the fact that history constantly produces new features. We also see how an individual, such as Lenin, who is not intimidated by traditional boundaries and whose thought is not tied to the ideology of a profession, can give useful advice to everyone, philosophers of science included.

6 Albert Einstein, *Albert Einstein: Philosopher Scientist*, ed. P.A. Schilpp, New York, 1951, pp. 683f.

7 For the deterioration of language that follows any increase of professionalism cf. my essay 'Experts in a Free Society', *The Critic*, November/December 1970.

8 John Stuart Mill, 'On Liberty', *The Philosophy of John Stuart Mill*, ed. Marshall Cohen, New York, 1961, p. 258.

9 ibid., p. 265.

10 Peter Alexeivich Kropotkin, 'Modern Science and Anarchism', *Kropotkin's Revolutionary Pamphlets*, ed. R.W. Baldwin, New York, 1970, pp. 150–2. 'It is one of Ibsen's great distinctions that nothing was valid for him but science.' B. Shaw, *Back to Methuselah*, New York, 1921, xcvii. Commenting on these and similar phenomena Strindberg writes (*Antibarbarus*): 'A generation that had the courage to get rid of God, to crush the state and church, and to overthrow society and morality, still bowed before Science. And in Science, where freedom ought to reign, the order of the day was "believe in the authorities or off with your head".'

11 R.P. Wolff, *The Poverty of Liberalism*, Boston, 1968, p. 15. For a more detailed

criticism of Wolff *see* footnote 52 of my essay 'Against Method' in *Minnesota Studies in the Philosophy of Science*, Vol. 4, Minneapolis, 1970.

12 When choosing the term 'anarchism' for my enterprise I simply followed general usage. However anarchism, as it has been practised in the past and as it is being practised today by an ever increasing number of people, has features I am not prepared to support. It cares little for human lives and human happiness (except for the lives and the happiness of those who belong to some special group); and it contains precisely the kind of Puritanical dedication and seriousness which I detest. (There are some exquisite exceptions such as Cohn-Bendit, but they are in the minority.) It is for these reasons that I now prefer to use the term *Dadaism*. A Dadaist would not hurt a fly – let alone a human being. A Dadaist is utterly unimpressed by any serious enterprise and he smells a rat whenever people stop smiling and assume that attitude and those facial expressions which indicate that something important is about to be said. A Dadaist is convinced that a worthwhile life will arise only when we start taking things *lightly* and when we remove from our speech the profound but already putrid meanings it has accumulated over the centuries ('search for truth'; 'defence of justice'; 'passionate concern'; etc., etc.) A Dadaist is prepared to initiate joyful experiments even in those domains where change and experimentation seem to be out of the question (example: the basic functions of language). I hope that having read the pamphlet the reader will remember me as a flippant Dadaist and *not* as a serious anarchist.

13 Even in undetermined and ambiguous situations, uniformity of action is soon achieved and adhered to tenaciously. *See* Muzafer Sherif, *The Psychology of Social Norms*, New York, 1964.

TIME AND SPACE

54   Wyndham Lewis
'Art and Literature'

I regard *Ulysses* as a *time-book*; and by that I mean that it lays its emphasis upon, for choice manipulates, and in a doctrinaire manner, the self-conscious time-sense that has now been erected into a universal philosophy. This it does beneath the spell of a similar creative impulse to that by which Proust worked. The classical unities of time and place are buried beneath its scale, however, and in this All-life-in-a-day scheme there is small place for them. Yet at the outset they are solemnly insisted on as a guiding principle to be fanatically observed. And certainly some barbarous version of the classical formula is at work throughout, like a conserted *daimon* attending the author, to keep him obsessionally faithful to the time-place, or space-time, programme.

The genteel-demotic, native subject-matter of Mr Joyce assists him to a great deal of intense, sad, insipid, local colour. An early life-experience that had removed him from the small middle-class milieu would also have removed him from his local colour, and to a less extent from his time-factor. To this he adds the legendary clatter and bustle of Donnybrook Fair. Beyond that he is not above stealing a few fairies from Mr Yeats, and then sending them in the company of Dr Freud to ride a broomstick on the Brocken. Adventures of that order, in the middle of the book, take us still further from the ideal of the Unities, and both Space and Time temporarily evaporate. But on the whole the reader is conscious that he is beneath the intensive dictatorship of Space-time – the god of Professor Alexander and such a great number of people, in fact, that we can almost be said to be treading on holy ground when we compose ourselves to read a work dedicated to that deity, either in philosophy or fiction.

That Joyce and Proust are both dedicated to Time is generally appreciated, of course; Joyce is often compared to Proust on that score. Both Proust and Joyce exhibit, it is said, the exasperated time-sense of the contemporary man of the industrial age; which is undeniable, if the outward form of their respective work is alone considered. The ardent recapitulation of a dead thing – though so recently dead, and not on its own merits a very significant one – and as much the 'local colour' as what may be called the

From Julian Symons (ed.), *The Essential Wyndham Lewis*, Vintage Press, 1991, pp. 195–8, 200–5.

local time, ally them. But having got so far, I should put in a qualification which would, I think, unexpectedly discriminate these two methods.

*

I will interject at this point a note on the subject of the temporal equivalent of 'local colour,' since I have had occasion to refer to it once or twice. I will not enter into the confusing discussion of which is space and which time in any given complex. I will suppose that there is some partly discrete quality which can come under the separate head of 'time,' and so for certain purposes be something else than the 'local colour.'

This psychological time, or duration, this mood that is as fixed as the matter accompanying it, is as romantic and picturesque as is 'local colour,' and usually as shallow a thing as that. Some realization of this is essential. *We can posit a time-district, as it were, just as much as we can a place with its individual physical properties.* And neither the local colour, nor the local time of the *time-district*, is what is recorded *sub specie aeternitatis*, it is unnecessary to say.

Both may, however, become obsessions, and are so, I believe, to-day. But that is merely – that is my argument – because people are in process of being locked into both places *and* times. (This can be illustrated, where place is concerned, in the way that Signor Mussolini is locking the Italians into Italy, and refusing them passports for abroad.)

We are now sufficiently prepared and can educe the heart of this obscure organism that so overshadows contemporary thought, by showing its analogies. That the time-fanaticism is in some way connected with the nationalisms and the regionalisms which are politically so much in evidence, and so intensively cultivated, seems certain – since 'time' is also to some extent a region, or it can be regarded in that light. We have spoken of a *time-district*, and that is exact. Professor Whitehead uses the significant phrase 'mental climate.' This is by no means a fanciful affiliation; for *time* and *place* are the closest neighbours, and what happens to one is likely to be shared by the other. And if that is so, the *time-mind* would be much the same as the geographic one, fanatically circumscribing this or that territorial unit with a superstitious exclusiveness, an aggressive nationalist romance. Has not time-romance, or a fierce partisanship on behalf of a *time*, a family likeness, at least, with similar partisanship on behalf of a *place*?

And then, too, the so much mocked and detested non-nationalist, universal mind (whose politics would be goethean, we can say, to place them, and whose highest tolerance would approximate to that best seen in the classical chinese intelligence) would have to be reckoned with – once the *time-mind* had been isolated by a thorough analysis, and its essential antagonisms exposed. These two types of mind would be found confronted, eternally hostile to each other, or at least eternally different – for the hostility would be more noticeable on the side of the partisan, the 'time,' mind, the mind of fashion, than on the side of the other. This is all that I shall say on this very interesting point, for the moment.

The philosophy of the space-timeist is identical with the old, and as many people had hoped, exploded, bergsonian philosophy of *psychological time* (or *durée*, as he called it). It is essential to grasp this continuity between the earlier flux of Bergson, with its Time-god, and the einsteinian flux, with its god, Space-time. Alexander, and his pupil Whitehead, are the best-known exponents, of philosophers writing in English, of these doctrines. It will not require a very close scrutiny of *Space Time and Deity*, for instance, and then of some characteristic book of Bergson's, to assure yourself that you are dealing with minds of the same stamp.

Temperamentally – emotionally, that is, and emotion is as important in philosophy as in other things – the earlier bergsonian, such as Péguy, for instance, and the relativist or space-timeist, are identical. The best testimony of this is the enthusiastic reception given by Bergson, the old time-philosopher, to Einstein, the later space-timeist. He recognized his god, Duration, cast into the imposing material of a physical theory, improved and amalgamated with Space, in a more insidious unity than he had been able to give to his paramount philosophic principle. Similarly the attitude of Whitehead, Alexander and so forth, where Bergson is concerned, is noticeably one of a considered respect, very different from the atmosphere of disrepute into which Bergson had fallen prior to the triumph of Relativity Theory. The so-called 'Emergent' principle of Lloyd Morgan, adopted by Alexander and the rest, is our old friend 'Creative Evolution,' under another name, and with a few additional attributes. 'Emergent Evolution' can for all practical purposes be regarded as synonymous with 'Creative Evolution.'

So from, say, the birth of Bergson to the present day, one vast orthodoxy has been in process of maturing in the world of science and philosophy. The material had already collected into a considerable patrimony by the time Bergson was ready to give it a philosophic form. The Darwinian Theory and all the background of nineteenth-century materialistic thought was already behind it. Under the characteristic headings Duration and Relativity the nineteenth-century mechanistic belief has now assumed a final form. It is there for any one to study at his leisure, and to take or leave. It will assume, from time to time, many new shapes, but it will certainly not change its essential nature again till its doomsday; for I believe that in it we have reached one of the poles of the human intelligence, the negative, as it were. So it is deeply rooted, very ancient, and quite defined.

Bergson and his time-philosophy exactly corresponds to Proust, the abstract for the other's concrete. There is so far no outstanding exponent in literature or art of einsteinian physics, for necessarily there is a certain interval, as things are, between the idea and the representation. But such a figure will no doubt occur; and further theorists of this great school will be accompanied by yet further artists, applying its philosophy to life. Or perhaps, since now the general outline of the cult is settled, and the changes within it will be incidental, largely, they may crop up simultaneously. Indeed, Proust and Joyce are examples to hand of how already it does not matter very much to what phase of the one great movement the interpreter belongs.

Without all the uniform pervasive growth of the time-philosophy starting from the little seed planted by Bergson, discredited, and now spreading more vigorously than ever, there would be no *Ulysses,* or there would be no *A La Recherche du Temps Perdu.* There would be no 'time-composition' of Miss Stein; no fugues in words. In short, Mr Joyce is very strictly of the school of Bergson-Einstein, Stein-Proust. He is of the great time-school they represent. His book is a *time-book,* as I have said, in that sense. He has embraced the time-doctrine very completely. And it is as the critic of that doctrine and of that school that I have approached the analysis of his writings up to date. (I insert this last time-clause because there is no reason at all to suppose that he may not be influenced in turn by my criticism; and, indeed, I hope it may be so, for he would be a very valuable adherent.)

Yet that the time-sense is really exasperated in Joyce in the fashion that it is in Proust, Dada, Pound or Miss Stein, may be doubted. He has a very keen preoccupation with the Past, it is certain; he does lay things down side by side, carefully dated; and added to that, he has some rather loosely and romantically held notion of periodicity. But I believe that all these things amount to with him is this: as a careful, even meticulous, craftsman, with a long training of doctrinaire naturalism, the detail – the time-detail as much as anything else – assumes an exaggerated importance for him. And I am sure that he would be put to his trumps to say how he came by much of the time-machinery that he possesses. Until he was told, I dare say that he did not know he had it, even; for he is 'an instinctive,' like Pound, in that respect; there is not very much reflection going on at any time inside the head of Mr James Joyce. That is indeed the characteristic condition of *the craftsman,* pure and simple.

The method that underlies *Ulysses* is known as the 'telling from the inside.' As that description denotes, it is psychological. Carried out in the particular manner used in *Ulysses,* it lands the reader inside an Aladdin's cave of incredible bric-à-brac in which a dense mass of dead stuff is collected, from 1901 toothpaste, a bar or two of Sweet Rosie O'Grady, to pre-nordic architecture. An immense *nature-morte* is the result. This ensues from the method of confining the reader in a circumscribed psychological space into which several encyclopaedias have been emptied. It results from the constipation induced in the movement of the narrative.

The amount of *stuff* – unorganized brute material – that the more active principle of drama has to wade through, under the circumstances, slows it down to the pace at which, inevitably, the sluggish tide of the author's bric-à-brac passes the observer, at the saluting post, or in this case, the reader. It is a suffocating, moeotic expanse of objects, all of them lifeless, the sewage of a Past twenty years old, all neatly arranged in a meticulous sequence. The newspaper in which Mr Bloom's bloater is wrapped up, say, must press on to the cold body of the fish, reversed, the account of the bicycle accident that was reported on the fated day chosen for this Odyssey; or that at least is the idea.

At the end of a long reading of *Ulysses* you feel that it is the very nightmare of the naturalistic method that you have been experiencing. Much as you may cherish the merely physical enthusiasm that expresses itself in this stupendous outpouring of *matter*, or *stuff*, you wish, on the spot, to be transported to some more abstract region for a time, where the dates of the various toothpastes, the brewery and laundry receipts, the growing pile of punched 'bus-tickets, the growing holes in the baby's socks and the darn that repairs them, assume less importance. It is your impulse perhaps quickly to get your mind where there is nothing but air and rock, however inhospitable and featureless, and a little timeless, too. You will have had a glut, for the moment (if you have really persevered), of *matter*, procured you by the turning on of all this river of what now is rubbish, but which was not *then*, by the obsessional application of the naturalistic method associated with the exacerbated time-sense. And the fact that you were not in the open air, but closed up inside somebody else's head, will not make things any better. It will have been your catharsis of the objective accumulations that obstinately collect in even the most active mind.

Now in the graphic and plastic arts that stage of fanatic naturalism long ago has been passed. All the machinery appropriate to its production has long since been discarded, luckily for the pure creative impulse of the artist. The nineteenth-century naturalism of that obsessional, fanatical order is what you find on the one hand in *Ulysses*. On the other, you have a great variety of recent influences enabling Mr Joyce to use it in the way that he did.

To create new beauty, and to supply a new material, is the obvious affair of art of any kind to-day. But that is a statement that by itself would convey very little. Without stopping to unfold that now, I will summarize what I understand by its opposite. Its opposite is that that thrives upon the *time-philosophy* that it has invented for itself, or which has been imposed upon it or provided for it.

The inner meaning of the *time-philosophy*, from whatever standpoint you approach it, and however much you paste it over with confusing advertisements of 'life,' of 'organism,' is the doctrine of a mechanistic universe; periodic; timeless, or nothing but 'time,' whichever you prefer; and, above all, essentially *dead*. A certain *deadness*, a lack of nervous power, an aversion to anything suggesting animal vigour, characterizes all the art, as has already been pointed out, issuing from this philosophy. Or in the exact mixing in the space-timeist scheme of all the 'matter' and all the 'organism' together, you get to a sort of vegetable or vermiform *average*. It is very mechanical; and according to our human, aristocratic standards of highly-organized life, it is very dead.

The theoretic truth that the time-philosophy affirms is a mechanistic one. It is the conception of an aged intelligence, grown mechanical and living upon routine and memory, essentially; its tendency, in its characteristic working, is infallibly to transform the living into the machine, with a small, unascertained, but uninteresting margin of freedom. It is the fruit, of course, of the puritan mind, born in the nineteenth century upon the desolate principles promoted by the too-rapidly mechanized life of the European.

---

55 F.H. Bradley
From *Appearance and Reality*

It is mere superstition to suppose that an appeal to experience can prove reality. That I find something in existence in the world or in my self, shows that this something exists, and it cannot show more. Any deliverance of consciousness – whether original or acquired – is but a deliverance of consciousness. It is in no case an oracle and a revelation which we have to accept. It is a fact, like other facts, to be dealt with; and there is no presumption anywhere that any fact is better than appearance. The 'given' of course is given; it must be recognized, and it cannot be ignored. But between recognizing a datum and receiving blindly its content as reality is a very wide interval. We may put it thus once for all – there is nothing given which is sacred. Metaphysics can respect no element of experience except on compulsion. It can reverence nothing but what by criticism and denial the more unmistakably asserts itself.

Time is so far from enduring the test of criticism, that at a touch it falls apart and proclaims itself illusory. . . . What I must attempt here first is to show how by its inconsistency time directs us beyond itself. It points to something higher in which it is included and transcended.

In the first place change, as we saw, must be relative to a permanent.

From F.H. Bradley, *Appearance and Reality*, Clarendon, Oxford, 1930, pp. 182–5, 189–90.

Doubtless here was a contradiction which we found was not soluble. But, for all that, the fact remains that change demands some permanence within which succession happens. I do not say that this demand is consistent, and, on the contrary, I wish to emphasize the point that it is not so. It is inconsistent, and yet it is none the less essential. And I urge that therefore change desires to pass beyond simple change. It seeks to become a change which is somehow consistent with permanence. Thus, in asserting itself, time tries to commit suicide as itself, to transcend its own character and to be taken up in what is higher.

And we may draw this same conclusion from another inconsistency. The relation of the present to the future and to the past shows once more time's attempt to transcend its own nature. Any lapse, that for any purpose you take as one period, becomes forthwith a present. And then this lapse is treated as if it existed all at once. For how otherwise could it be spoken of as one thing at all? Unless it *is*, I do not see how we have a right to regard it as possessing a character. And unless it is present, I am quite unable to understand with what meaning we can assert that it *is*. And, I think, the common behaviour of science might have been enough by itself to provoke reflection on this head. We may say that science, recognizing on the one side, on the other side quite ignores the existence of time. For it habitually treats past and future as one thing with the present. The character of an existence is determined by what it has been and by what it is (potentially) about to be. But if these attributes, on the other hand, are not present, how can they be real? Again in establishing a Law, itself without special relation to time, science treats facts from various dates as all possessing the same value. Yet how, if we seriously mean to take time as real, can the past be reality? It would, I trust, be idle to expand here these obvious considerations. They should suffice to point out that for science reality at least *tries* to be timeless, and that succession, as such, can be treated as something without rights and as mere appearance.

This same tendency becomes visible in another application. The whole movement of our mind implies disregard of time. Not only does intellect accept what is true once for true always, and thus fearlessly take its stand on the Identity of Indiscernibles – not only is this so, but the whole mass of what is called 'Association' implies the same principle. For such a connexion does not hold except between universals.[1] The associated elements are divorced from their temporal context; they are set free in union, and ready to form fresh unions without regard for time's reality. This is in effect to degrade time to the level of appearance. But our entire mental life, on the other hand, has its movement through this law. Our whole being practically implies it, and to suppose that we can rebel would be mere self-deception. Here again we have found the irresistible tendency to transcend time. We are forced once more to see in it the false appearance of a timeless reality.

It will be objected perhaps that in this manner we do not get rid of time. In those eternal connexions which rule in darkness our lowest psychical nature, or are used consciously by science, succession may remain. A law is not always a law of what merely coexists, but it often gives the relation of antecedent and sequent. The remark is true, but certainly it could not show that time is self-consistent. And it is the inconsistency, and hence the self-transcendence of time which here we are urging. This temporal succession, which persists still in the causal relation, does but secure to the end the old discrepancy. It resists, but it cannot remove, time's inherent tendency to pass beyond itself. Time is an appearance which contradicts itself, and endeavours vainly to appear as an attribute of the timeless.

. . . The Absolute is timeless, but it possesses time as an isolated aspect, an aspect which, in ceasing to be isolated, loses its special character. It is there, but blended into a whole which we cannot realize. But that we cannot realize it, and do not know how in particular it can exist, does not show it to be impossible. It is possible, and, as before, its possibility is enough. For that which can be, and upon a general ground must be – that surely is real.

I will pass now to another point, the *direction* of time. Just as we tend to assume that all phenomena form one series, so we ascribe to every series one single direction. But this assumption too is baseless. It is natural to set up a point in the future towards which all events run, or from which they arrive, or which may seem to serve in some other way to give direction to the stream. But examination soon shows the imperfection of this natural view. For the direction, and the distinction between past and future, entirely depends upon *our* experience.[2] That side, on which fresh sensations come in, is what we mean by the future. In our perception of change elements go out, and something new comes to us constantly; and we construct the time-series entirely with reference to this experience. Thus, whether we regard events as running forwards from the past, or as emerging from the future, in any case we use one method of taking our bearings. Our fixed direction is given solely by the advent of new arrivals.

But, if this is so, then direction is relative to *our* world. You may object that it is fixed in the very nature of things, and so imparts its own order to our special sphere. Yet how this assumption can be justified I do not understand. Of course there is something not ourselves which makes this difference exist in our beings, something too which compels us to arrange other lives and all our facts in one order. But must this something, therefore, in reality and in itself, be direction? I can find no reason for thinking so. No doubt we naturally regard the whole world of phenomena as a single time-series; we assume that the successive contents of every other finite being are arranged in this construction, and we take for granted that their streams all flow in one direction. But our assumption clearly is not defensible. For let us suppose, first, that there are beings who can come in contact in no way with that world which we experience. Is this supposition self-contradictory, or anything but possible? And let us suppose, next, that in the Absolute the direction of these lives runs opposite to our own. I ask again, is such an idea either meaningless or untenable? Of course, *if* in any way *I* could experience *their* world, I should fail to understand it. Death would come before birth, the blow would follow the wound, and all must seem to be irrational. It would seem to me so, but its inconsistency would not exist except for my partial experience. If I did not experience their order, to me it would be nothing. Or, if I could see it from a point of view beyond the limits of my life, I might find a reality which itself had, as such, no direction. And I might there perceive characters, which for the several finite beings give direction to their lives, which, as such, do not fall within finite experience, and which, if apprehended, show *both* directions harmoniously combined in a consistent whole.

To transcend experience and to reach a world of Things-in-themselves, I agree, is impossible. But does it follow that the whole universe in every sense is a possible object of *my* experience? Is the collection of things and persons, which makes *my* world, the sum total of existence? I know no ground for an affirmative answer to this question. That many material systems should exist, without a material central-point, and with no relation in space – where is the self-contradiction? That various worlds of experience should be distinct, and, for themselves, fail to enter one into the other – where is the impossibility? That arises only when we endorse, and take our stand upon, a prejudice. That the unity in the Absolute is merely our kind of unity, that spaces there must have a spatial centre, and times a temporal point of meeting – these assumptions are based on nothing.

Notes

1 On these points *see* my *Principles of Logic*.
2 *See* on this point *Mind*, xii, pp. 579–82. We think forwards, one may say, on the same principle on which fish feed with their heads pointing up the stream.

We are reflecting on the essence of modern science in order that we may apprehend in it its metaphysical ground. What understanding of what is and what concept of truth provide the basis for the fact that science is being transformed into research?

Knowing, as research, calls whatever is to account with regard to the way in which and the extent to which it lets itself be put at the disposal of representation. Research has disposal over anything that is when it can either calculate it in its future course in advance or verify a calculation about it as past. Nature, in being calculated in advance, and history, in being historiographically verified as past, become, as it were, 'set in place' [*gestellt*].[1] Nature and history become the objects of a representing that explains. Such representing counts on nature and takes account of history. Only that which becomes object in this way *is* – is considered to be in being. We first arrive at science as research when the Being of whatever is, is sought in such objectiveness.

This objectifying of whatever is, is accomplished in a setting-before, a representing, that aims at bringing each particular being before it in such a way that man who calculates can be sure, and that means be certain, of that being. We first arrive at science as research when and only when truth has been transformed into the certainty of representation. What it is to be is for the first time defined as the objectiveness of representing, and truth is first defined as the certainty of representing, in the metaphysics of Descartes. The title of Descartes's principal work reads: *Meditationes de prima philosophia* (Meditations on First Philosophy). *Prōtē philosophia* is the designation coined by Aristotle for what is later called metaphysics. The whole of modern metaphysics taken together, Nietzsche included, maintains itself within the interpretation of what it is to be and of truth that was prepared by Descartes.

Now if science as research is an essential phenomenon of the modern age, it must be that that which constitutes the metaphysical ground of research determines first and long beforehand the essence of that age generally. The essence of the modern age can be seen in the fact that man frees himself from the bonds of the Middle Ages in freeing himself to himself. But this correct characterization remains, nevertheless, superficial.

From Martin Heidegger, *The Question Concerning Technology and Other Essays*, Harper and Row, 1977, pp. 126–30.

It leads to those errors that prevent us from comprehending the essential foundation of the modern age and, from there, judging the scope of the age's essence. Certainly the modern age has, as a consequence of the liberation of man, introduced subjectivism and individualism. But it remains just as certain that no age before this one has produced a comparable objectivism and that in no age before this has the non-individual, in the form of the collective, come to acceptance as having worth. Essential here is the necessary interplay between subjectivism and objectivism. It is precisely this reciprocal conditioning of one by the other that points back to events more profound.

What is decisive is not that man frees himself to himself from previous obligations, but that the very essence of man itself changes, in that man becomes subject. We must understand this word *subiectum*, however, as the translation of the Greek *hypokeimenon*. The word names that-which-lies-before, which, as ground, gathers everything onto itself. This metaphysical meaning of the concept of subject has first of all no special relationship to man and none at all to the I.

However, when man becomes the primary and only real *subiectum*, that means: Man becomes that being upon which all that is, is grounded as regards the manner of its Being and its truth. Man becomes the relational center of that which is as such. But this is possible only when the comprehension of what is as a whole changes. In what does this change manifest itself? What, in keeping with it, is the essence of the modern age?

When we reflect on the modern age, we are questioning concerning the modern world picture (*Weltbild*).[2] We characterize the latter by throwing it into relief over against the medieval and the ancient world pictures. But why do we ask concerning a world picture in our interpreting of a historical age? Does every period of history have its world picture, and indeed in such a way as to concern itself from time to time about that world picture? Or is this, after all, only a modern kind of representing, this asking concerning a world picture?

What is a world picture? Obviously a picture of the world. But what does 'world' mean here? What does 'picture' mean? 'World' serves here as a name for what is, in its entirety. The name is not limited to the cosmos, to nature. History also belongs to the world. Yet even nature and history, and both interpenetrating in their underlying and transcending of one another, do not exhaust the world. In this designation the ground of the world is meant also, no matter how its relation to the world is thought.

With the word 'picture' we think first of all of a copy of something. Accordingly, the world picture would be a painting, so to speak, of what is as a whole. But 'world picture' means more than this. We mean by it the world itself, the world as such, what is, in its entirety, just as it is normative and binding for us. 'Picture' here does not mean some imitation, but rather what sounds forth in the colloquial expression, 'We get the picture' (literally, we are in the picture) concerning something. This means the matter stands before us exactly as it stands with it for us. 'To get into the picture' (literally, to put oneself into the picture) with respect to something means to set whatever is, itself, in place before oneself just in the way that it stands with it, and to have it fixedly before oneself as set up in this way. But a decisive determinant in the essence of the picture is still missing. 'We get the picture' concerning something does not mean only that what is, is set before us, is represented to us, in general, but that what is stands before us – in all that belongs to it and all that stands together in it – as a system. 'To get the picture' throbs with being acquainted with something, with being equipped and prepared for it. Where the world becomes picture, what is, in its entirety, is juxtaposed as that for which man is prepared and which, correspondingly, he therefore intends to bring before himself and have before himself, and consequently intends in a decisive sense to set in place before himself. Hence world picture, when understood essentially, does not mean a picture of the world but the world conceived and grasped as picture. What is, in its entirety, is now taken in such a way that it first is in being and only is in being to the extent that it is set up by man, who represents and sets forth.[3] Wherever we have the world picture, an essential decision takes place regarding what is, in its entirety. The Being of whatever is, is sought and found in the representedness of the latter.

However, everywhere that whatever is, is *not* interpreted in this way, the world also cannot enter into a picture; there can be no world picture. The fact that whatever is comes into being in and through representedness transforms the age in which this occurs into a new age in contrast with the preceding one. The expressions 'world picture of the modern age' and 'modern world picture' both mean the same thing and both assume something that never could have been before, namely, a medieval and an ancient world picture. The world picture does not change from an earlier medieval one into a modern one, but rather the fact that the world becomes picture at all is what distinguishes the essence of the modern age (*der Neuzeit*).[4] For the Middle Ages, in contrast, that which is, is the *ens creatum*, that which is created by the personal Creator-God as the highest cause. Here, to be in being means to belong within a specific rank of the order of what has been created – a rank appointed from the beginning – and as thus caused, to correspond to the cause of creation (*analogia entis*) (Appendix 7). But never does the Being of that which is consist here in the fact that it is brought before man as the objective, in the fact that it is placed in the realm of man's knowing and of his having disposal, and that it is in being only in this way.

Notes

1 The verb *stellen*, with the meanings to set in place, to set upon (i.e., to challenge forth), and to supply, is invariably fundamental in Heidegger's understanding of the modern age. *See* in this essay the discussion of the setting in place of the world as picture, pp. 280–1.

2 The conventional translation of *Weltbild* would be 'conception of the world' or 'philosophy of life.' The more literal translation, 'world picture,' is needed for the following of Heidegger's discussion; but it is worth noting that 'conception of the world' bears a close relation to Heidegger's theme of man's representing of the world as picture.

3 *durch den vorstellenden-herstellenden Menschen gestellt ist.*

4 *Die Neuzeit* is more literally 'the new age.' Having repeatedly used this word in this discussion, Heidegger will soon elucidate the meaning of the 'newness' of which it speaks [the discussion is not included in the extract reprinted here].

---

57 David Harvey
From *The Condition of Postmodernity*

Marshall Berman (1982) equates modernity (among other things) with a certain mode of experience of space and time. Daniel Bell (1978, 107–11) argues that the various movements that brought modernism to its apogee had to work out a new logic in the conception of space and motion. He suggests, furthermore, that the organization of space has 'become the primary aesthetic problem of mid-twentieth century culture as the problem of time (in Bergson, Proust, and Joyce) was the primary aesthetic problem of the first decades of this century.' Frederic Jameson (1984b) attributes the postmodern shift to a crisis in our experience of space and time, a crisis in which spatial categories come to dominate those of time, while themselves undergoing such a mutation that we cannot keep pace. 'We do not yet possess the perceptual equipment to match this new kind of hyperspace,' he writes, 'in part because our perceptual habits were formed in that older kind of space I have called the space of high modernism.'

Space and time are basic categories of human existence. Yet we rarely debate their meanings; we tend to take them for granted, and give them common-sense or self-evident attributions. We record the passage of time in seconds, minutes, hours, days, months, years, decades, centuries, and eras, as if everything has its place upon a single objective time scale. Even though time in physics is a difficult and contentious concept, we do not

From David Harvey, *The Condition of Postmodernity*, Blackwell, 1989, pp. 201–2, 205–6.

Table 1 Gurvich's typology of social times

Type	Level	Form	Social formations
Enduring time	ecological	continuous time in which past is projected in the present and future; easily quantifiable	kinships and locality groupings (particularly rural peasant societies and patriarchal structures)
Deceptive time	organized society	long and slowed down duration masking sudden and unexpected crises and ruptures between past and present	large cities and political 'publics'; charismatic and theocratic societies
Erratic time	social roles, collective attitudes (fashion) and technical mixes	time of uncertainty and accentuated contingency in which present prevails over past and future	non-political 'publics' (social movements and fashion-followers); classes in process of formation
Cyclical time	mystical unions	past, present and future projected into each other accentuating continuity within change; diminution of contingency	astrology-followers; archaic societies in which mythological, mystical and magical beliefs prevail
Retarded time	social symbols	future becomes present so late as to be outmoded as soon as it is crystallized	community and its social symbols; guilds, professions etc. feudalism
Alternating time	rules, signals, signs and collective conduct	past and future compete in the present; discontinuity without contingency	dynamic economic groups; transition epochs (inception of capitalism)

Table 1 *cont.*

Type	Level	Form	Social formations
Time in advance of itself (rushing forward)	collective transformative action and innovation	discontinuity, contingency; qualitative change triumphant; the future becomes present	competitive capitalism; speculation
Explosive time	revolutionary ferment and collective creation	present and past dissolved into a transcendent future	revolutions and radical transformations of global structures

Source: Gurvitch (1964)

usually let that interfere with the common-sense of time around which we organize daily routines. We recognize, of course, that our mental processes and perceptions can play tricks, make seconds feel like light years, or pleasurable hours pass by so fast we hardly notice. We may also learn to appreciate how different societies (or even different sub-groups) cultivate quite different senses of time (*see* Table 1).

Consider, for example, one of the more startling schisms in our intellectual heritage concerning conceptions of time and space. Social theories (and I here think of traditions emanating from Marx, Weber, Adam Smith, and Marshall) typically privilege time over space in their formulations. They broadly assume either the existence of some pre-existing spatial order within which temporal processes operate, or that spatial barriers have been so reduced as to render space a contingent rather than fundamental aspect to human action. Aesthetic theory, on the other hand, is deeply concerned with 'the spatialization of time.'

It is a tribute to the compartmentalizations in Western thought that this disjunction has for so long passed largely unremarked. On the surface, the difference is not too hard to understand. Social theory has always focused on processes of social change, modernization, and revolution (technical, social, political). Progress is its theoretical object, and historical time its primary dimension. Indeed, progress entails the conquest of space, the tearing down of all spatial barriers, and the ultimate 'annihilation of space through time.' The reduction of space to a contingent category is implied in the notion of progress itself. Since modernity is about the experience of progress through modernization, writings on that theme have tended to emphasize temporality, the process of *becoming*, rather than *being* in space and place. Even Foucault (1984, 70), obsessed as he confesses himself to be with spatial metaphors, wonders, when pressed, when and why it happened that 'space was treated as the dead, the fixed, the undialectical, the immobile' while 'time, on the contrary, was richness, fecundity, life, dialectic.'

Aesthetic theory, on the other hand, seeks out the rules that allow eternal and immutable truths to be conveyed in the midst of the maelstrom of flux and change. The architect, to take the most obvious case, tries to communicate certain values through the construction of a spatial form. Painters, sculptors, poets, and writers of all sorts do no less. Even the written word abstracts properties from the flux of experience and fixes them in spatial form. 'The invention of printing embedded the word in *space*,' it has been said, and writing – a 'set of tiny marks marching in neat line, like armies of insects, across pages and pages of white paper' – is, therefore, a definite spatialization (quoted in McHale, 1987, 179–81). Any system of representation, in fact, is a spatialization of sorts which automatically freezes the flow of experience and in so doing distorts what it strives to represent. 'Writing,' says Bourdieu (1977, 156), 'tears practice and discourse out of the flow of time.' For this reason, Bergson, the great theorist of becoming, of time as flux, was incensed that it took the spatializations of the clock to tell the time.

REPRESENTATION AND THE IMAGE

58   Clive Bell
'Art'

The starting-point for all systems of aesthetics must be the personal experience of a peculiar emotion. The objects that provoke this emotion we call works of art. All sensitive people agree that there is a peculiar emotion provoked by works of art. I do not mean, of course, that all works provoke the same emotion. On the contrary, every work produces a different emotion. But all these emotions are recognizably the same in kind; so far, at any rate, the best opinion is on my side. That there is a particular kind of emotion provoked by works of visual art, and that this emotion is provoked by every kind of visual art, by pictures, sculptures, buildings, pots, carvings, textiles, etc., etc., is not disputed, I think, by anyone capable of feeling it. This emotion is called the aesthetic emotion; and if we can discover some quality common and peculiar to all the objects that provoke it, we shall have solved what I take to be the central problem of aesthetics. We shall have discovered the essential quality in a work of art, the quality that distinguishes works of art from all other classes of objects.

For either all works of visual art have some common quality, or when we speak of 'works of art' we gibber. Everyone speak of 'art,' making a mental classification by which he distinguishes the class 'works of art' from all other classes. What is the justification of this classification? What is the quality common and peculiar to all members of this class? Whatever it be, no doubt it is often found in company with other qualities; but they are adventitious – it is essential. There must be some one quality without which a work of art cannot exist; possessing which, in the least degree, no work is altogether worthless. What is this quality? What quality is shared by all objects that provoke our aesthetic emotions? What quality is common to Sta. Sophia and the windows at Chartres, Mexican sculpture, a Persian bowl, Chinese carpets, Giotto's frescoes at Padua, and the masterpieces of Poussin, Piero della Francesca, and Cézanne? Only one answer seems possible – significant form. In each, lines and colours combined in a particular way, certain forms and relations of forms, stir our aesthetic emotions. These relations and combinations of lines and colours, these aesthetically moving forms, I call 'Significant Form'; and 'Significant Form' is the one quality common to all works of visual art.

From J.B. Bullen (ed.), *Art*, Oxford University Press, 1987, pp. 6–10, 25–7.

At this point it may be objected that I am making aesthetics a purely subjective business, since my only data are personal experiences of a particular emotion. It will be said that the objects that provoke this emotion vary with each individual, and that therefore a system of aesthetics can have no objective validity. It must be replied that any system of aesthetics which pretends to be based on some objective truth is so palpably ridiculous as not to be worth discussing. We have no other means of recognizing a work of art than our feeling for it. The objects that provoke aesthetic emotion vary with each individual. Aesthetic judgments are, as the saying goes, matters of taste; and about tastes, as everyone is proud to admit, there is no disputing. A good critic may be able to make me see in a picture that had left me cold things that I had overlooked, till at last, receiving the aesthetic emotion, I recognize it as a work of art. To be continually pointing out those parts, the sum, or rather the combination, of which unite to produce significant form, is the function of criticism. But it is useless for a critic to tell me that something is a work of art; he must make me feel it for myself. This he can do only by making me see; he must get at my emotions through my eyes. Unless he can make me see something that moves me, he cannot force my emotions. I have no right to consider anything a work of art to which I cannot react emotionally; and I have no right to look for the essential quality in anything that I have not *felt* to be a work of art. The critic can affect my aesthetic theories only by affecting my aesthetic experience. All systems of aesthetics must be based on personal experience – that is to say, they must be subjective.

Let no one imagine that representation is bad in itself; a realistic form may be as significant, in its place as part of the design, as an abstract. But if a representative form has value, it is as form, not as representation. The representative element in a work of art may or may not be harmful; always it is irrelevant. For, to appreciate a work of art we need bring with us nothing from life, no knowledge of its ideas and affairs, no familiarity with its emotions. Art transports us from the world of man's activity to a world of aesthetic exaltation. For a moment we are shut off from human interests; our anticipations and memories are arrested; we are lifted above the stream of life. The pure mathematician rapt in his studies knows a state of mind which I take to be similar, if not identical. He feels an emotion for his speculations which arises from no perceived relation between them and the lives of men, but springs, inhuman or super-human, from the heart of an abstract science. I wonder, sometimes, whether the appreciators of art and of mathematical solutions are not even more closely allied. Before we feel an aesthetic emotion for a combination of forms, do we not perceive intellectually the rightness and necessity of the combination? If we do, it would explain the fact that passing rapidly through a room we recognize a picture to be good, although we cannot say that it has provoked much emotion. We seem to have recognized intellectually the rightness of its forms without staying to fix our attention, and collect, as it were, their emotional significance. If this were so, it would be permissible to inquire whether it was the forms themselves or our perception of their rightness and necessity that caused aesthetic emotion. But I do not think I need linger to discuss the matter here. I have been inquiring why certain combinations of forms move us; I should not have travelled by other roads had I enquired, instead, why certain combinations are perceived to be right and necessary, and why our perception of their rightness and necessity is moving. What I have to say is this: the rapt philosopher, and he who contemplates a work of art, inhabit a world with an intense and peculiar significance of its own; that significance is unrelated to the significance of life. In this world the emotions of life find no place. It is a world with emotions of its own.

---

59 Susanne K. Langer
From *Philosophy in a New Key*

Any miscarriage of the symbolic process is an abrogation of our human freedom: the constraint imposed by a foreign language, or a lapse of one's own linguistic ability such as Sir Henry Head has described as loss of abstract concepts,[1] or pathological repression that causes all sorts of distorted personal symbols to encroach on literal thought and empirical judgment, or lack of logical power, knowledge, food for thought, or imagination to envisage our problems clearly and negotiably. All such obstacles may block the free functioning of mind. But the most disastrous hindrance is disorientation, the failure or destruction of life-symbols and loss or repression of votive acts. A life that does not incorporate some degree of ritual, of gesture and attitude, has no mental anchorage. It is prosaic to the point of total indifference, purely casual, devoid of that structure of intellect and feeling which we call 'personality.'

Therefore interference with acts that have ritual value (conscious or unconscious) is always felt as the most intolerable injury one man, or group of men, can do to another. Freedom of conscience is the basis of all personal freedom. To constrain a man against his principles – make a pacifist bear arms, a patriot insult his flag, a pagan receive baptism – is to endanger his attitude toward the world, his personal strength and single-mindedness.

From Susanne K. Langer, *Philosophy in a New Key*, Harvard University Press, pp. 290–4.

No matter how fantastic may be the dogmas he holds sacred, how much his living rites conflict with the will or convenience of society, it is never a light matter to demand their violation. Men fight passionately against being forced to do lip-service, because the enactment of a rite is always, in some measure, assent to its meaning; so that the very expression of an alien mythology, incompatible with one's own vision of 'fact' or 'truth,' works to the corruption of that vision. It is a breach of personality. To be obliged to confess, teach, or acclaim falsehood is always felt as an insult exceeding even ridicule and abuse. Common insult is a blow at one's ego; but constraint of conscience strikes at one's ego and super-ego, one's whole world, humanity, and purpose. It takes a strong mind to keep its orientation without overt symbols, acts, assertions, and social corroborations; to maintain it in the face of the confounding pattern of enacted heresy is more than average mentality can do.

We have to adapt our peculiarly human mental functions – our symbolic functions – to given limitations, exactly as we must adapt all our biological activities. The mind, like all other organs, can draw its sustenance only from the surrounding world; our metaphysical symbols must spring from reality. Such adaptation always requires time, habit, tradition, and intimate knowledge of a way of life. If, now, the field of our unconscious symbolic orientation is suddenly plowed up by tremendous changes in the external world and in the social order, we lose our hold, our convictions, and therewith our effectual purposes. In modern civilization there are two great threats to mental security: the new mode of living, which has made the old nature-symbols alien to our minds, and the new mode of working, which makes personal activity meaningless, inacceptable to the hungry imagination. Most men never see the goods they produce, but stand by a traveling belt and turn a million identical passing screws or close a million identical passing wrappers in a succession of hours, days, years. This sort of activity is too poor, too empty, for even the most ingenious mind to invest it with symbolic content. Work is no longer a sphere of ritual; and so the nearest and surest source of mental satisfaction has dried up. At the same time, the displacement of the permanent homestead by the modern rented tenement – now here, now there – has cut another anchor-line of the human mind. Most people have no home that is a symbol of their childhood, not even a definite memory of one place to serve that purpose. Many no longer know the language that was once their mother-tongue. All old symbols are gone, and thousands of average lives offer no new materials to a creative imagination. This, rather than physical want, is the starvation that threatens the modern worker, the tyranny of the machine. The withdrawal of all natural means for expressing the unity of personal life is a major cause of the distraction, irreligion, and unrest that mark the proletariat of all countries. Technical progress is putting man's freedom of mind in jeopardy.

In such a time people are excited about any general convictions or ideals they may have. Numberless hybrid religions spring up, mysteries, causes, ideologies, all passionately embraced and badly argued. A vague longing for the old tribal unity makes nationalism look like salvation, and arouses the most fantastic bursts of chauvinism and self-righteousness; the wildest anthropological and historical legends; the deprecation and distortion of learning; and in place of orthodox sermons, that systematic purveying of loose, half-baked ideas which our generation knows as 'propaganda.' There are committees and ministries of propaganda in our world, as there were evangelical missions and watch-and-ward societies in the world of our fathers. No wonder that philosophers looking at this pandemonium of self-assertion, self-justification, and social and political fantasy view it as a reaction against the Age of Reason. After centuries of science and progress, they conclude, the pendulum swings the other way: the irrational forces of our animal nature must hold their Witches' Sabbath.

A philosophy that knows only deductive or inductive logic as reason, and classes all other human functions as 'emotive,' irrational, and animalian, can see only regression to a prelogical state in the present passionate and unscientific ideologies. All it can show us as the approach to Parnassus is the way of factual data, hypothesis, trial, judgment, and generalization. All other things our minds do are dismissed as irrelevant to intellectual progress; they are residues, emotional disturbances, or throwbacks to animal estate.

But a theory of mind whose keynote is the symbolific function, whose problem is the morphology of significance, is not obliged to draw that bifurcating line between science and folly. It can see these ructions and upheavals of the modern mind not as lapses of rational interest, caused by animal impulse, but as the exact contrary – as a new phase of savagedom, indeed, but inspired by the rational need of envisagement and understanding. The springs of European thought have run dry – those deep springs of imagination that furnish the basic concepts for a whole intellectual order, the first discernments, the generative ideas of our *Weltanschauung*. New conceptual forms are crowding them out, but are themselves in the mythical phase, the 'implicit' stage of symbolic formulation. We cannot analyze the contents of those vast symbols – Race, Unity, Manifest Destiny, Humanity – over which we fight so ruthlessly; if we could, it would mean that they were already furnishing discursive terms, clear issues, and we would all be busy philosophizing instead of waging holy wars. We would have the new world that humanity is dreaming of, and would be eagerly building the edifice of knowledge out of new insights. It is the sane, efficient, work-a-day business of free minds – discursive reasoning about well-conceived problems – that is disturbed or actually suspended in this apparent age of unreason; but the force which governs that age is still the force of *mind*, the impulse toward symbolic formulation, expression, and understanding of experience.

The continual pursuit of meanings – wider, clearer, more negotiable, more articulate meanings – is philosophy. It permeates all mental life:

sometimes in the conscious form of metaphysical thought, sometimes in the free, confident manipulation of established ideas to derive their more precise, detailed implications, and sometimes – in the greatest creative periods – in the form of passionate mythical, ritual, and devotional expression. In primitive society such expression meets with little or no obstacle; for the first dawn of mentality has nothing to regret. Only as one culture supersedes another, every new insight is bought with the life of an older certainty. The confusion of form and content which characterizes our worship of life-symbols works to the frustration of well-ordered discursive reason, men act inappropriately, blindly, and viciously; but what they are thus wildly and mistakenly trying to do is human, intellectual, and necessary. Standards of science and ethics must condemn it, for its overt form is rife with error; traditional philosophy must despair of it because it cannot meet any epistemological criterion; but in a wider philosophy of symbolism it finds a measure of understanding. If there is any virtue in the theory of what I have called 'symbolic transformation,' then this theory should elucidate not only the achievements of that function, but also its miscarriages, its limitations, and its by-products of illusion and error. Freedom of thought cannot be reborn without throes; language, art, morality, and science have all given us pain as well as power. For, as Professor Whitehead has frankly and humbly declared: 'Error is the price we pay for progress.'

Note

1 *See* 'Disorders of Symbolic Thinking and Expression,' *British Journal of Psychology*, XI (1920–21), part II, 179–93.

60 Alain Robbe-Grillet
From *Snapshots and Toward a New Novel*

To reject our alleged 'nature' and the vocabulary that perpetuates its myth, to treat objects as purely external and superficial, is not – as people have claimed – to deny man, but to refuse to accept the 'pan-anthropic' content of traditional, and probably every other, humanism. In the final analysis it is merely to carry my claim to personal liberty to its logical conclusion.

From Alain Robbe-Grillet, *Snapshots and Toward a New Novel*, tr. Barbara Wright, Calder and Boyars, pp. 81–5.

And so nothing must be overlooked in this cleansing operation. Looking at it more closely we see that it is not only anthropocentric analogies (mental or visceral ones) that must be called into question. *All* analogies are equally dangerous. Perhaps the most dangerous are the most insidious, the ones that don't even mention man.

Let us give a few random examples. . . . To see the shape of a horse in the sky may still be nothing but simple description, and of no consequence. But to speak of a cloud 'galloping', or of its 'tousled mane', is already less innocent. For if a cloud (or a wave, or a hill) possesses a mane; if, further on, a stallion's mane starts 'shooting arrows'; if the arrow . . . etc., such imagery will take the reader out of the universe of forms and plunge him into a universe of meanings. He will be invited to conceive of a profound connection between the wave and the horse: passion, pride, power, violence. . . . The idea of a nature inevitably leads to that of a nature common to all things, which means *superior*. The idea of interiorness always leads to that of transcendence.

And the poison gradually spreads: from the bow to the horse, from the horse to the wave – and from the sea to love. A common nature, once again, can only be the eternal answer to the *only question* put by our Greco-Christian civilization: the Sphinx is there in front of me, she questions me, I don't even have to try to understand the terms of the riddle she asks me, for there is only one possible answer, one single answer to everything – man.

Well, this is not so.

There is more than one question, and more than one answer. Man is no more, from his own point of view, than the only witness.

Man looks at the world, but the world doesn't look back at him. Man sees things and he notices, now, that he can escape the metaphysical pact that other men made for him in days gone by, and that by the same token he can escape slavery and fear. That he can . . . that he *will be able to*, at least, one day.

But this doesn't mean that he refuses all contact with the world. On the contrary, he agrees to use it for material ends; a utensil, as such, never has depth, a utensil is entirely matter and form – and destination.

Man gets hold of his hammer (or a stone he has chosen) and hits a post he wants to drive into the ground. While he is using it to this end, the hammer (or the stone) is no more than form and matter – its weight, its striking surface, and its opposite extremity by which it can be held. Afterwards, man puts down the tool. If he has no further need of it the hammer is now no more than one thing among other things; it has no meaning apart from its use.

And the man of today (or of tomorrow . . .) feels no sense of deprivation or affliction at this absence of meaning. He no longer feels lost at the idea of such a vacuum. His heart no longer needs to take refuge in an abyss.

For if he rejects communion, he also rejects tragedy.

Tragedy may here be defined as an attempt to reclaim the distance that exists between man and things, and give it a new kind of value, so that in effect it becomes an ordeal where victory consists in being vanquished. Tragedy, then, figures as the ultimate invention of humanism in its attempt to allow nothing to escape it. Since the harmony between man and things has finally been denounced, the humanist saves his empire by immediately setting up a new form of solidarity, the divorce in itself becoming a major road to redemption.

It is still almost a communion, but it is *painful*, always just about to be dealt with, but always postponed, and its efficacy is in proportion to the inaccessibility of its character. It is a *reversal*, it is a trap – and it is a falsification.

It is easy to see, in fact, just how far this sort of union is perverted: instead of trying to discover something good, in this case it is concerned with hallowing something evil. Unhappiness, failure, solitude, guilt, madness, these are the hazards of our existence that they want us to welcome as the surest tokens of our salvation. To welcome, not to accept: we are supposed to nourish them at our expense, at the same time as we go on struggling against them. For tragedy contains neither true acceptance nor real refusal. It is the sublimation of a disparity.

Let us, as an example, recapitulate the functioning of 'solitude'. I call. No one answers me. Instead of concluding that there is no one there – which could be an observation, pure and simple, dated and placed, in space and time – I decide to act as if someone were in fact there, and as if, for one reason or another, he were refusing to answer. From then on the silence that follows my appeal is no longer a *real* silence, it has become pregnant with content, with depth, with a soul – which immediately plunges me back into my own soul. The distance between my cry, as I hear it, and the mute (perhaps deaf) interlocutor to whom it is addressed, becomes a sort of anguish, my hope and my despair, a sense to my life. Henceforth nothing will count for me save this false vacuum and the problems it causes me. Should I go on calling? Should I call more loudly? Should I use other words? I try again. . . . I very soon realize that no one is going to answer, but the invisible presence that I continue to create by my cry forces me to go on, for all eternity, sending out my unhappy cry into the silence. Its echo soon starts to deafen me.

As if spellbound, I call again . . . and again. My sick conscience finally considers my exacerbated solitude as a superior necessity, my assurance of redemption. And for this to be accomplished I am obliged, until the day I die, to go on crying in the wilderness.

What usually happens then is that my solitude ceases to be an accidental and temporary fact of my existence and becomes part of me, of the whole world, of all men; once again, it becomes our nature. It is a solitude for all time.

Wherever there is distance, separation, dichotomy, division, there is the possibility of feeling them as suffering, and then of elevating this suffering into a sublime necessity. This pseudo-necessity leads to a metaphysical beyond, but at the same time closes the door to any realistic future. Tragedy may console us today, but it prevents us making more worthwhile conquests tomorrow. Apparently in perpetual motion, its actual effect is to paralyze the universe in a kind of agitated malediction. When tragedy tries to make us love our misery, we forget all about trying to find a remedy for it.

We are here faced with an oblique attack on the part of contemporary humanism which may well take unfair advantage of us. As the attempted reclamation is no longer aimed at things themselves, we might at first sight think that the rupture between them and man has in any case been consummated. But we soon discover that this is not the case at all; that, whether we sign an agreement with things or with their absence, it's all one in the end; the 'spiritual bridge' between them and ourselves remains, and even comes out of the operation somewhat strengthened.

That is why tragic thought never aims at suppressing distances, but, on the contrary, wantonly multiplies them. The distance between man and other men, the distance between man and himself, between man and the world, between the world and itself – nothing is left intact. Everything is torn, fissured, split, displaced. A sort of secret distance appears within the most homogeneous objects and the least ambiguous situations. But it is precisely an *inner distance*, a false distance, which is in reality an open road, which is, in other words, already a reconciliation.

Everything is contaminated. And yet it seems that the novel is tragedy's chosen field. From girls in love who become nuns, to policemen-gangsters, by way of all the tormented criminals, pure-souled prostitutes, just and upright men compelled by their consciences to act unjustly, loving sadists, and logical lunatics, a proper 'character' in a novel must above all be *double*. The more *ambiguous* the plot, the more 'human' it will be. Finally, the more contradictions the book as a whole contains, the more true to life it will be.

It is easy to make fun of this. It is less easy to free ourselves from the way our mental civilization conditions us to accept tragedy. We can even say that the refusal of the ideas of 'nature' and predestination leads us *first of all* to tragedy. There is no significant work of contemporary literature that does not contain both an affirmation of our freedom and the 'tragic' seed of its abandonment.

INDEX